Weddings For Dummies Cheat Sheet

Nuptial Numbers

How Many Servers?

Type of Service	Recommended Number of Servers
Formal, multi-course meal	one to two waiters per ten to 12 guests.
Simple menu or buffet	one waiter per 25 guests.
Pre-dinner cocktails	one bartender per 50 to 75 guests, combined with wine passed by waiters.

Note: *The ratio of servers to guests varies according to region and formality.*

How Much Space?

Space	Recommended Square Feet Per Person
Ceremony	8
Cocktails (pre-meal)	8
Cocktails with dance floor	10
Cocktails with hors d'oeuvres stations	12-13
Seated and served meal with dance floor	13-15
Dance floor	3 (for a dancing crowd)

How Much Liquor? Standard Full-Bar Amounts for Cocktails

Liquor	Amount per 100 Guests	Minimum for Fewer Than 100 Guests
Beer	2 cases	2 cases
Blended whiskey	1-2 liters	1 liter
Bourbon	1-2 liters	1 liter
Campari (optional)	1 liter	1 liter
Champagne	1 1/2 cases	1 liter
Dry vermouth*	2	1
Gin	2 liters	2 liters
Light rum	2 liters	1 liter
Red wine	8 bottles	4 bottles
Scotch	3 liters	2 liters
Sweet vermouth*	2	1
Tequila (optional)	1 liter	1 liter
Vodka	6 liters	2 liters
White wine	1 1/2 cases	8 bottles

** 750 ml bottles*

Note: *Amounts do not include specialty drinks.*

What Size Tablecloth?

Table Diameter	Floor-Length Cloth
60 inches	120 inches
54 inches	114 inches
48 inches	108 inches
36 inches	96 inches

...For Dummies: Bestselling Book Series for Beginners

Weddings For Dummies®

Ten Survival Strategies

- **Choose your attendants** based on mutual affection, not on their modeling prowess.
- **Save time** in a crunch by having your envelopes delivered to you while the invitations are being printed so you can have them addressed, stamped, and ready for stuffing ahead of time.
- **Avoid traffic jams and gruesome lines** by serving a seated first course at buffet receptions.
- **Write out a wedding-day schedule** as detailed as the itinerary for a state visit. Send it to everyone involved in the ceremony. (See Chapter 18.)
- **Play a vigorous round of "Simon says"** in your wedding dress at the final fitting to make sure you can move freely — unless you intend to spend the reception fanning yourself on your *chaise longue*.
- **Check out your septic system's capacity** before deciding to have an at-home wedding.
- **Plan your wedding as a team.** This process is a rehearsal for your married life.
- **Compile not only a Play List** for the band, but also — and perhaps more important — a Don't Play List.
- **Ask your caterer to pack up a full sampling** of the wedding meal for you to take to your honeymoon suite because you may be too busy to eat at your reception.
- **Scratch calla lilies from your list of flowers** for the bouquet you are going to toss. These flowers have the aerodynamics of javelins.

Ways to Save Money: Pound Wise . . .

- Trim the guest list. For every person you provide with food, beverage, transportation, and flowers, costs rise exponentially.
- If you're having a band at your reception, contract with them for a few of the members to play for your wedding ceremony. Their fee for pulling double duty is usually considerably less than the cost of hiring additional musicians solely for the ceremony.
- Book the rehearsal dinner or next-day breakfast with the same caterer and negotiate price considerations for both.
- Instruct the person in charge of the waiters that you want wine glasses gently topped off rather than indiscriminately filled to the brim. Champagne for a toast should be offered to each guest rather than poured by rote. Also ask that the waiters not bus half-full glasses.
- Consider hosting a brunch or lavish cocktail reception in lieu of a more traditional meal.
- Count the *couples* on your guest list and order invitations per couple rather than per guest.

. . . And Pound Foolish

- Having a cash bar. We would much rather see you find another way to cut costs.
- Cutting the service staff. Could make the difference between a gracious event and a "survival of the pushiest" competition for guests to get served.
- Using a tent without a back-up space large enough for all your guests in case of bad weather.
- Thinking a "simple at-home wedding" will save you money.
- Forgoing meals for the band or photographer.

Cheat Sheet $2.95 value. Item 5055-1.
For more information about IDG Books, call 1-800-762-2974.

...For Dummies: Bestselling Book Series for Beginners

Praise For Weddings For Dummies

"Nobody knows wedding planning like Marcy Blum. From invitations, dresses, attendants, and rings to bands, food, flowers, and honeymoons, *Weddings For Dummies* is the ultimate guide to creating — and enjoying — your big day."

— Ed Koch, Former Mayor of New York City

"In *Weddings For Dummies,* Marcy Blum and Laura Fisher Kaiser have revolutionized the wedding-planning process. Their book is worth buying for the budget tips alone. Their research into wedding logistics is equally impressive; who knew that each wedding guest requires exactly three square feet of space on the dance floor?"

— Nancy Marx Better, Senior Contributing Editor, *SmartMoney Magazine,* New York

"A book that's really in touch with what engaged couples want for *their* specific wedding. Brides-to-be benefit from Marcy Blum's experience with every kind of wedding planning challenge. That, combined with both authors' sense of humor, paves the way to a happy day!"

— Cele G. Lalli, Vice President / Editor-in-chief, *Modern Bride*

"Do you really want to enjoy your wedding celebration and then hear rave reviews afterward? Then give Marcy Blum all the work behind the scenes — you can't afford not to."

— Monica Hickey, Director - Custom/Couture Bridal Designs, Saks Fifth Avenue, NY

"*Weddings For Dummies* will help you say 'I do' with confidence and a smile. Marcy offers straight talk that makes sense and all the information any couple needs to plan a great wedding."

— Maria McBride-Mellinger, Author of *The Perfect Wedding, The Wedding Dress, and Bridal Flowers*

"Brides- and grooms-to-be can rest easy! *Weddings For Dummies* is filled with lots of smart ideas — and all presented with wit, humor, and great common sense. Marcy Blum's expertise and savvy professionalism render this an incredibly detailed and fun-to-read wedding planning bible. She and Laura Fisher Kaiser outline everything you need to know to make planning your wedding a breeze. Getting married has never been easier!"

— Diane Forden, Editor in Chief, *Bridal Guide Magazine*

"Marcy Blum has created magical weddings for hundreds of engaged couples. Every bride-to-be who dreams of a beautiful, memorable wedding celebration will benefit from her boundless creativity, and the tricks of the trade she shares here."

— Millie Martini Bratten, Editor-in-Chief, *Bride's Magazine*

"*Weddings For Dummies* is chock-full of endless ideas and useful resources for brides and grooms alike. Whether you are getting married for the first (or second, or third . . .) time, this witty and insightful book provides all the information you need. From finding the dress to booking the hall to selecting the wedding party to communicating with vendors, Blum and Fisher Kaiser leave no stone unturned in the realm of weddings. A fun, useful, and informative read from a veteran in the wedding industry."

— Adam Sandow, President of *Honeymoon* magazine

"Sassy! Before you say, 'I Do,' you must read this book. An easy-to-use guide with practical tips and advice. Blum and Kaiser pull no punches to guide the betrothed through the minefield that is planning a wedding in the late 1990s.

— Alan and Denise Fields, Authors, *Bridal Bargains* and *The Bridal Gown Guide*

"Anyone planning a wedding should read this book. The game rules, tip, and caution icons highlight practical advice that everyone can understand and follow."

— Adrienne Vittadini, Fashion Designer

"For those entering the wilderness of wedding planning, there is no better guide than Marcy Blum. She is funny, she is smart, she is cool, she's seen it all. No one knows more about flowers, centerpieces, diamond rings, wedding gowns, and life in general. From bridesmaid dresses to avoiding tacky trends, take her advice!"

— Lois Smith Brady, Wedding Columnist, *New York Times*

by Marcy Blum
and Laura Fisher Kaiser

IDG Books Worldwide, Inc.
An International Data Group Company

Foster City, CA ♦ Chicago, IL ♦ Indianapolis, IN ♦ New York, NY

Weddings For Dummies®

Published by
IDG Books Worldwide, Inc.
An International Data Group Company
919 E. Hillsdale Blvd.
Suite 400
Foster City, CA 94404
www.idgbooks.com (IDG Books Worldwide Web site)
www.dummies.com (Dummies Press Web site)

Library of Congress Catalog Card No.: 97-80697

ISBN: 0-7645-5055-1

Printed in the United States of America

10 9 8 7 6 5 4 3

1E/RY/RR/ZY/IN

Distributed in the United States by IDG Books Worldwide, Inc.

Distributed by Macmillan Canada for Canada; by Transworld Publishers Limited in the United Kingdom; by IDG Norge Books for Norway; by IDG Sweden Books for Sweden; by Woodslane Pty. Ltd. for Australia; by Woodslane (NZ) Ltd. for New Zealand; by Addison Wesley Longman Singapore Pte Ltd. for Singapore, Malaysia, Thailand, and Indonesia; by Norma Comunicaciones S.A. for Colombia; by Intersoft for South Africa; by International Thomson Publishing for Germany, Austria and Switzerland; by Distribuidora Cuspide for Argentina; by Livraria Cultura for Brazil; by Ediciencia S.A. for Ecuador; by Ediciones ZETA S.C.R. Ltda. for Peru; by WS Computer Publishing Corporation, Inc., for the Philippines; by Contemporanea de Ediciones for Venezuela; by Express Computer Distributors for the Caribbean and West Indies; by Micronesia Media Distributor, Inc. for Micronesia; by Grupo Editorial Norma S.A. for Guatemala; by Chips Computadoras S.A. de C.V. for Mexico; by Editorial Norma de Panama S.A. for Panama; by Wouters Import for Belgium; by American Bookshops for Finland. Authorized Sales Agent: Anthony Rudkin Associates for the Middle East and North Africa.

For general information on IDG Books Worldwide's books in the U.S., please call our Consumer Customer Service department at 800-762-2974. For reseller information, including discounts and premium sales, please call our Reseller Customer Service department at 800-434-3422.

For information on where to purchase IDG Books Worldwide's books outside the U.S., please contact our International Sales department at 317-596-5530 or fax 317-596-5692.

For information on foreign language translations, please contact our Foreign & Subsidiary Rights department at 650-655-3021 or fax 650-655-3281.

For sales inquiries and special prices for bulk quantities, please contact our Sales department at 650-655-3200 or write to the address above.

For information on using IDG Books Worldwide's books in the classroom or for ordering examination copies, please contact our Educational Sales department at 800-434-2086 or fax 317-596-5499.

For press review copies, author interviews, or other publicity information, please contact our Public Relations department at 650-655-3000 or fax 650-655-3299.

For authorization to photocopy items for corporate, personal, or educational use, please contact Copyright Clearance Center, 222 Rosewood Drive, Danvers, MA 01923, or fax 978-750-4470.

About the Authors

Marcy Blum (Manhattan, NY), a graduate of the Culinary Institute of America, has been planning weddings, parties, and events of all kinds for more than 18 years. She has been quoted in numerous publications from *The New York Times* to *The Wall Street Journal* and *People Magazine* and has appeared on *Good Morning America, The Ricki Lake Show,* and *Hard Copy,* among others. Marcy has also spoken on weddings and events across the country and consults on myriad projects for various wedding-related businesses. Her company, Marcy Blum Associates, Inc., was started in 1985.

Laura Fisher Kaiser (Manhattan, NY) is a senior editor at *This Old House* magazine. Having done bridesmaid duty twice, she planned her own wedding to Michael Kaiser from beginning to end during the writing of this book. The former editor in chief of *Avenue* magazine and a former reporter at *Manhattan, inc.*, she has written extensively about the fashion world and cultural trends in American society. Her work has also appeared in *Town & Country, The New York Times,* the *Los Angeles Times, New York Woman,* and *Texas Monthly*.

ABOUT IDG BOOKS WORLDWIDE

Welcome to the world of IDG Books Worldwide.

IDG Books Worldwide, Inc., is a subsidiary of International Data Group, the world's largest publisher of computer-related information and the leading global provider of information services on information technology. IDG was founded more than 30 years ago by Patrick J. McGovern and now employs more than 9,000 people worldwide. IDG publishes more than 290 computer publications in over 75 countries. More than 90 million people read one or more IDG publications each month.

Launched in 1990, IDG Books Worldwide is today the #1 publisher of best-selling computer books in the United States. We are proud to have received eight awards from the Computer Press Association in recognition of editorial excellence and three from Computer Currents' First Annual Readers' Choice Awards. Our best-selling *...For Dummies®* series has more than 50 million copies in print with translations in 31 languages. IDG Books Worldwide, through a joint venture with IDG's Hi-Tech Beijing, became the first U.S. publisher to publish a computer book in the People's Republic of China. In record time, IDG Books Worldwide has become the first choice for millions of readers around the world who want to learn how to better manage their businesses.

Our mission is simple: Every one of our books is designed to bring extra value and skill-building instructions to the reader. Our books are written by experts who understand and care about our readers. The knowledge base of our editorial staff comes from years of experience in publishing, education, and journalism — experience we use to produce books to carry us into the new millennium. In short, we care about books, so we attract the best people. We devote special attention to details such as audience, interior design, use of icons, and illustrations. And because we use an efficient process of authoring, editing, and desktop publishing our books electronically, we can spend more time ensuring superior content and less time on the technicalities of making books.

You can count on our commitment to deliver high-quality books at competitive prices on topics you want to read about. At IDG Books Worldwide, we continue in the IDG tradition of delivering quality for more than 30 years. You'll find no better book on a subject than one from IDG Books Worldwide.

John Kilcullen
Chairman and CEO
IDG Books Worldwide, Inc.

Steven Berkowitz
President and Publisher
IDG Books Worldwide, Inc.

Eighth Annual Computer Press Awards 1992

Ninth Annual Computer Press Awards 1993

Tenth Annual Computer Press Awards 1994

Eleventh Annual Computer Press Awards 1995

IDG is the world's leading IT media, research and exposition company. Founded, in 1964, IDG had 1997 revenues of $2.05 billion and has more than 9,000 employees worldwide. IDG offers the widest range of media options that reach IT buyers in 75 countries representing 95% of worldwide IT spending. IDG's diverse product and services portfolio spans six key areas including print publishing, online publishing, expositions and conferences, market research, education and training, and global marketing services. More than 90 million people read one or more of IDG's 290 magazines and newspapers, including IDG's leading global brands — Computerworld, PC World, Network World, Macworld and the Channel World family of publications. IDG Books Worldwide is one of the fastest-growing computer book publishers in the world, with more than 700 titles in 36 languages. The "...For Dummies®" series alone has more than 50 million copies in print. IDG offers online users the largest network of technology-specific Web sites around the world through IDG.net (http://www.idg.net), which comprises more than 225 targeted Web sites in 55 countries worldwide. International Data Corporation (IDC) is the world's largest provider of information technology data, analysis and consulting, with research centers in over 41 countries and more than 400 research analysts worldwide. IDG World Expo is a leading producer of more than 168 globally branded conferences and expositions in 35 countries including E3 (Electronic Entertainment Expo), Macworld Expo, ComNet, Windows World Expo, ICE (Internet Commerce Expo), Agenda, DEMO, and Spotlight. IDG's training subsidiary, ExecuTrain, is the world's largest computer training company, with more than 230 locations worldwide and 785 training courses. IDG Marketing Services helps industry-leading IT companies build international brand recognition by developing global integrated marketing programs via IDG's print, online and exposition products worldwide. Further information about the company can be found at www.idg.com.

10/8/98

Dedication

From Marcy Blum: For my mother and best friend, Gertrude Blum, who taught me to love learning, and for my father, Harold Blum, who taught me to love people.

From Laura Fisher Kaiser: For Michael, who decided that I should have first-hand experience to write this book, and for my parents, Loretta and George Fisher, who have always demonstrated the rewards of getting married.

Authors' Acknowledgments

As in producing a wedding, this book required the input, expertise, patience, and nurturing of many friends and professionals.

Thank you to our agents, Mark Reiter and Carolyn Krupp, who had the intuition to fix us up on a "blind date." And thank you to Nancy Marx Better and Maria McBride Mellinger, who initially referred both of us to IMG.

We are most grateful for the talents of our illustrator, Liz Kurtzman, and our cartoonist, Rich Tennant. We thank the team at IDG, including Tammy Castleman, Nickole Harris, and Catherine Schmitz. We especially thank Sarah Kennedy for her hand-holding, and our project editor, Jennifer Ehrlich, whose patience and conscientiousness got us through the rough spots.

Thanks also to the experts who pored over the manuscript to make sure that any couple reading this book could really pull off a wedding: Tony Arzt of Supreme Video; Michael Eigen of Michael Eigen Jewelry; Terry deRoy Gruber of Gruber Photographers; David Hechler of Harold Hechler Associates; Gail Kittenplan of Gail Kittenplan Associates; Joann Rahill of Disney Fairy Tale Weddings; Rita Bloom Smith of Creative Parties Ltd.; Jen Stone of StoneKelly; Nate Weil of HQ Productions; Paul Weinberg of Mambo Music; and Sylvia Weinstock of Sylvia Weinstock Cakes.

The following companies, experts, and associations provided us with invaluable insights and information: Nancy Aucone of the Bridal Boutique of Manhasset; Glorie Austern of the Calligraphy Company, Inc; Dave Bunting at Executive Restroom Trailers; Club Med; Andre P.V. de La Barre of Event Planning Design Consultants, Inc.; Fairy Tale Weddings at Walt Disney World; Denise and Alan Fields; Marc Friedland of Creative Intelligence; Annie Thurow, *Modern Bride;* Jane Frost and Steve Frost of Stamford Tent Company; Liese Gardner of *Special Events*; Rozanne Gold; Diana Harris of Glorious Events; Monica Hickey of The Wedding Dress at Saks Fifth Avenue; Charles Kaiser; Elizabeth Kasha at Cartier; Tereza Kuljis; Michel and Mary Ann Zelnik of Kleinfeld; Brian Leahy and Robin Strauss of Frost Lighting; Larry Lustberg of Stortz Lighting; Liz Newmark and Carl Sacks of Great Performances; Janet MacEachen at Abigail Kirsch Culinary Productions Ltd.; Jack Orr of OrrHouse Music; Gary Page of G. Page Wholesale Flowers; Steve

Paster and Laura Leigh Moorefield of Alpine Creative Group; Chris Robbins of Robbins Wolfe Catering; Gordon Sherman; Liz Trasmundi of Party Rental, Ltd; Jensen/Boga and John Lynch of Sandals Resorts International.

For generously sharing with us their keen insight of fashion, style, and beauty, we thank Betty Lou Aluisio, Laura Geller, Laurie Krauz, Rachel Leonard, Tia Mazza, and Maria Verel.

We are honored to feature menus created by Barry Colman of More Than A Mouthful; Mary Micucci of Along Came Mary; Andy and Meryl Snow of Feastivities; Myra Gotoff of Calihan Gotoff; and Waldy Malouf of the Rainbow Room. In fact, we thank all the consummate professionals at Rainbow, particularly Dorothy Burdumi, Dale Degroff, and Tony Zazula.

For the inspiring decor in the photos in this book, we are indebted to: Atlas Floral; Preston Bailey; Anthony Ferraz; Valorie Hart; Robert Isabell; Brian Leahy and Robin Strauss of Frost Lighting; Renny Reynolds; and StoneKelly. For taking the art of wedding cakes to new heights and allowing us to show off their baking prowess we thank Ana Paz Specialty Cakes; Jan Kish of la petite fleur; Cheryl Lew of Montclair Baking; Rosemary Cheris Littman of Rosemary's Cakes, Inc.; Colette Peters of Colette Peters Cakes; Melanie Wynne of It Figures; John and Mike's Amazing Cakes; and, again, the inimitable Sylvia Weinstock.

We greatly appreciate the generosity and excellence of photographers Maureen Edwards DeFries; David Hechler; Lambert Photographs; Alex Kirkbride; Laurie Klein Gallery; Andy Marcus; and Sarah Merians. We especially want to thank Terry deRoy Gruber for his wonderful work.

Thank you to the home team at Marcy Blum Associates who researched, surfed the 'Net, and made countless phone calls. We are especially grateful to Rodney Gray and Felicia Branescu for picking up the slack and providing their nurturing and support, and to Meg Bowles and Cynthia Reeder as well. Thanks to Jack Orr for "building" our office. A big kiss also to Gordon Grody and Paul Weinberg, who graciously put up with our turning their living room into Wedding Central all summer.

On a more personal note from Marcy: heartfelt thanks to Peter Aschkenasy for his 23 years of unshakable faith in me; to my brother, Howard, his wife, Jenny, and their children Anna, Dani, and Tony for making all the difference; Millie Bratten, Cele Lalli, and Barbara Tober, for their advice, support, and friendship; and to all my "graduates" — the brides and grooms, who over the years have allowed me to be a part of their most special day.

And from Laura: thanks to Marcia Sherrill and Tamara Rubin for being the attendants of my dreams; and to *This Old House* editor in chief Steve Petranek for allowing me to take the time to write this book.

Publisher's Acknowledgments

We're proud of this book; please register your comments through our IDG Books Worldwide Online Registration Form located at `http://my2cents.dummies.com`.

Some of the people who helped bring this book to market include the following:

Acquisitions, Development, and Editorial

Project Editor: Jennifer Ehrlich

Acquisitions Editor: Sarah Kennedy

Senior Copy Editor: Tamara Castleman

Technical Editors: Tony Arzt, Michael Eigen, Terry deRoy Gruber, David Hechler, Gail Kittenplan, Joann Rahill, Rita Bloom Smith, Jen Stone, Nate Weil, Paul Weinberg, Sylvia Weinstock

Editorial Manager: Leah P. Cameron

Editorial Assistants: Donna Love, Paul E. Kuzmic, Darren Meiss

Production

Project Coordinator: Regina Snyder

Layout and Graphics: Steve Arany, Lou Boudreau, Linda M. Boyer, Angela F. Hunckler, Jane E. Martin, Drew R. Moore, Anna Rohrer, Brent Savage, Kate Snell

Special Art: Elizabeth Kurtzman

Proofreaders: Nancy L. Reinhardt, Christine Berman, Kelli Botta, Michelle Croninger, Joel K. Draper, Rachel Garvey, Nancy Price, Rebecca Senninger, Janet M. Withers

Indexer: Sharon Hilgenberg

Special Help: Constance Carlisle, Copy Editor; Stephanie Koutek, Proof Editor; Elizabeth Netedu Kuball, Copy Editor

General and Administrative

IDG Books Worldwide, Inc.: John Kilcullen, CEO; Steven Berkowitz, President and Publisher

IDG Books Technology Publishing: Brenda McLaughlin, Senior Vice President and Group Publisher

Dummies Technology Press and Dummies Editorial: Diane Graves Steele, Vice President and Associate Publisher; Mary Bednarek, Director of Acquisitions and Product Development; Kristin A. Cocks, Editorial Director

Dummies Trade Press: Kathleen A. Welton, Vice President and Publisher; Kevin Thornton, Acquisitions Manager

IDG Books Production for Dummies Press: Michael R. Britton, Vice President of Production and Creative Services; Cindy L. Phipps, Manager of Project Coordination, Production Proofreading, and Indexing; Kathie S. Schutte, Supervisor of Page Layout; Shelley Lea, Supervisor of Graphics and Design; Debbie J. Gates, Production Systems Specialist; Robert Springer, Supervisor of Proofreading; Debbie Stailey, Special Projects Coordinator; Tony Augsburger, Supervisor of Reprints and Bluelines

Dummies Packaging and Book Design: Robin Seaman, Creative Director; Kavish + Kavish, Cover Design

♦

The publisher would like to give special thanks to Patrick J. McGovern, without whom this book would not have been possible.

♦

Contents at a Glance

Cartoons at a Glance
By Rich Tennant
The 5th Wave
By Rich Tennant
"It was the only tent they could get on such short notice. Just watch your step around the trapeze rigging."
page 341
The 5th Wave
By Rich Tennant
FROM THAT FIRST, CHANCE ENCOUNTER, JOHN AND MARSHA KNEW THEY WERE DESTINED TO BE TOGETHER.
DOO DA DOO DA
page 5
The 5th Wave
By Rich Tennant
"I told you we should have registered."
page 231
The 5th Wave
By Rich Tennant
"Just play something light and airy until the other musicians show up."
page 69
The 5th Wave
By Rich Tennant
JUST MARRIED
"After all that planning and preparation it seems inappropriate to have a sign that says 'JUST' married."
page 295
The 5th Wave
By Rich Tennant
"...and here's yet another photo of Marsha and me ruining a perfectly good shot of the back of Uncle Leo's head."
page 119
Fax: 978-546-7747 • E-mail: the5wave@tiac.net

Table of Contents

Introduction

A wedding, whether it's a quiet civil ceremony in a judge's chamber or a pull-out-all-the-stops spectacle, requires equal parts planning, diplomacy, and nerve. We admit the whole thing can seem overwhelming at times. After all, of the three most profound rites of passage — being born, getting married, and dying — getting married is the only one a person might have any say in or be able to remember once it's over. But we are here to tell you: *Do not freak out.*

Our mission is to demystify the scary stuff and provide an antidote to briditis, that odd affliction that turns perfectly capable, rational women headed for the altar into delirious hellhags. However, this book is not just for brides. Because weddings (not to mention marriages) are joint ventures, we recommend that the bride and groom participate equally in its creation. If you've done zero planning, we'll get you up and running. No matter what stage you're in, however, we won't make you go back and start over because you've done something "wrong." There is, generally speaking, no single right way. What makes you and your intended happy is the right way for you.

How to Use This Book

We did not write *Weddings For Dummies* as another book filled with strict rules of "weddiquette" or ways of having the perfect wedding (on your 200-acre estate with a dining room that seats 300). *Weddings For Dummies* is both a reference book and a users' manual guaranteed to be dog-eared by the time you walk down the aisle. This book can be picked up at any stage of your wedding plans. Look up a specific facet or read the book cover to cover if you are just embarking on your planning journey.

How This Book Is Organized

Rather than lay out a strict protocol or chronology, we've organized this book according to what makes sense. We've included professional tips to suit every budget. And we've culled the best innovations from Marcy's arsenal without neglecting the sensibilities of sticklers for tradition. And while some wedding experts love to dictate timelines about when to do what, we find that contrived deadlines produce more anxiety than efficiency. A wedding can be two years or two months in the making. Either way, success depends on thinking through every detail before slapping down one red penny. Let *your* priorities determine the timing for everything from setting the date to ducking out for the honeymoon.

Part I: The Glass Slipper Fits — Now What?

Answer: get rolling before you either have time to panic, take tranquilizers, or hyperventilate. These first chapters hit some of the biggest concerns up front.

Chapter 1 explains what happens from the moment someone proposes, providing a logical step-by-step process to making your dream wedding fit your reality. Chapter 2 moves on to where and when to have your wedding. Chapter 3 guides you through purchasing the bridal ensemble that's right for you.

Part II: "I Now Pronounce You . . ."

The pivotal moment of all weddings is the ceremony, and in this part we detail how to make that as special as possible.

In Chapter 4 we help you select the wedding party and explain what you can and cannot expect of them. In Chapter 5 we get to the emotional center of a wedding — the ceremony — with clear explanations of various customs and rites. In Chapter 6, we take a look at some unusual wedding styles.

Part III: Eat, Drink, and Be Very Merry

This part focuses on the reception, including helping you decide what to serve, what to wash it down with, how to decorate, whom to hire, and what to listen to throughout.

Chapter 7 is devoted to the element that sets the tone perhaps more than anything else: the music. Chapter 8 helps you determine the style and scope of the nuptial feast. The wedding cake, though, requires a chapter unto itself, hence Chapter 9. Then we order up a round of advice in Chapter 10 on what to serve in the beverage department.

Chapter 11 focuses on the big picture — decor, lighting, and tables. Once you've knocked yourself out with the decor, you want to capture it on film for posterity, so in Chapter 12 we help you hire the right photo and video professionals.

Part IV: Marital Minutiae

In this section we examine several key aspects of getting married — before, during, and after the wedding.

Chapter 13 deals with the printed word, from invitations to newspaper announcements to thank-you notes. You'll need the last for Chapter 14, which covers gifts and registries, reminding us how nice it is to receive.

Chapter 15 explains the ring thing, while Chapter 16 is a catch-all for all those legal and financial technicalities, from blood tests to prenuptial agreements.

Part V: 3-2-1, Blast Off!

This section helps launch you into matrimonial orbit and offers a few strategies for a gentle landing.

Chapter 17 provides a smorgasboard of parties surrounding the wedding. Chapter 18 alone is worth the price of this book for its comprehensive schedule of a typical wedding day. That hard-earned frolic in the sun (or wherever) requires planning, too, and in Chapter 19 we arrange the particulars of a blissful getaway.

Part VI: The Part of Tens

A favorite among *...For Dummies* fans, this section rounds up a lot of information for quick reference, including common pitfalls and innovative solutions regarding guests lists, hospitality, and other matrimonial matters.

Chapter 20 provides ten painless ways to save money. Chapter 21 analyzes several technological advances to help you stay sane during the planning. In Chapter 22 we try to save you from falling into some tacky wedding traps, and in Chapter 23 we explain some sweet ways you can make your wedding special. Finally, in Chapter 24, we share with you some tips for life after the wedding from couples who have been married a long, long time.

Throughout this book, we mention many organizations, publications, and companies that may be helpful to you in your planning. You can find more details about them in the Appendix.

Icons Used in This Book

No matter the budget, anyone planning a wedding wants to get the most bang for the buck. This symbol means we are about to impart vital information regarding a practical money matter. While many times we tell you how to save money, we just as often explain why pinching pennies in a particular area may not be wise.

Although we do not advocate being a slave to calendars and endless To-Do Lists, every now and then a timely reminder or heads up is in order. When you see this symbol, adjust your *personal* wedding timetable accordingly.

Weddings, like life, can be unpredictable, but certain mistakes, pitfalls, and tacky traps are easily avoided. Defuse these little bombs before they explode.

This quizzical fellow is a familiar face to *...For Dummies* aficionados, and when it comes to weddings, his favorite part is figuring out those pesky details such as tablecloth dimensions and diamond classifications. You may not need to know this stuff, but if you do, he's there to tell you.

Some aspects of creating a successful wedding are so important — and so easily overlooked — they bear emphasizing (and sometimes) repeating. We'll mark these aspects with this symbol.

DO IT TOGETHER

Contrary to what some Neanderthals may think, the bride *and* groom should be responsible for pulling the wedding together. Of course, a natural delineation of duties may occur, but some things require input from both parties. When you see these entwined wedding rings, it signals a decision or matter that you should consult each other on.

Yes, we realize that your Aunt Myrtle graduated with honors from the TJTWID (That's Just The Way It's Done) Etiquette Academy, but we're here to tell you that times have changed and so have certain ironclad rules of decorum. When you see this icon, expect either an alternative way for handling a sticky wedding situation or simply a heads-up on making everyone feel comfortable.

TIP

Take it from us — you're about to read some information you can really use.

Although people in every culture get married, the way they do it can vary greatly around the world. Next to this icon, we highlight many fascinating customs and traditions from various cultures, ethnic groups, and religions.

We interrupt this book to bring you a word from our bride—that's me, Laura. In the course of writing this book, Marcy, as you may expect, planned several weddings for various clients while I coincidentally planned my own (aided by Marcy's expertise). We decided to make me the Dummies guinea pig, testing out ideas and theories, particularly since mine was a long-distance wedding, which can be tricky at best. In sidebars thoughout this book, I offer personal observations and tips based on my own experience.

All This for One Day?

Yes, but what a day! Just remember to do three things: be flexible, have fun, and *breathe.*

Part I
The Glass Slipper Fits — Now What?

In this part . . .

The two of you have decided to move into the world of marital bliss and we couldn't be happier for you! Now, before the initial glow wears off and panic ensues, we're here to give you that first nudge toward planning the wedding that's right for you. The chapters in this part of the book discuss some of the important, up-front work that you should begin right away. Look fear in the face and *read on.*

Chapter 1
The IZE Have It

In This Chapter

- Figuring out what's important to you
- Setting a realistic budget
- Exposing the when-to-do-what fallacy
- Hiring a wedding consultant

You came home once to find that his black cat had redecorated your white living room — and you thought it was hilarious. He found it endearing the night you became violently ill on margaritas at your firm's Christmas party. This is it — true love. And you're ready for the big step.

In spite of what you've heard, the time between your engagement and your marriage need not go down in the annals of your relationship as the Dark Ages. What follows is a series of "exercIZEs" to kick off your wedding planning and set you on the right track to pulling off the wedding of your dreams. As you familarIZE, fantasIZE, prioritIZE, and so on, the goal is to figure out what is important to both of you and to achieve your vision with as little acrimony and heartburn as possible.

Familiarize: Start Spreading the News

Some etiquette books still advise that a man ask a woman's parents for her hand. However, some brides may be offended by the connotation of ownership. Nonetheless, once someone has proposed, we recommend that you exercise respect and courtesy by telling your parents first. This is not the time, however, to ask them to foot the bill. Give them oxygen. Let them bask in the glow a bit. (If there's no glow in sight, proceed directly to Chapter 19 and consider having a honeymoon-wedding, also known as an elopement.) This is a natural time for the first communiqué between the bride's and groom's parents if they don't already know each other.

We recommend you rely on your own sense of whose parents should initiate contact. If it's a toss-up, you can fall back on tradition and suggest that the groom's parents call the bride's.

If either of you has children, tell the kids before you tell other people (or other people tell them). Life is not like *The Brady Bunch;* the merging of families can be highly charged, even if everyone seems to get along famously.

We realize that you are overjoyed with your decision to marry, but don't let your enthusiasm lead you to draft 82 people for your wedding party as you spread the news among your friends and relatives. If you've known since you were two who your best man or maid of honor is to be, then by all means that person should be among the first few people to know. Otherwise, hold off broadcasting even tentative plans until you know how many of your 2,000 closest friends you can actually invite.

Fantasize: Dream On (This May Be Your Only Chance)

All too often, people begin planning their wedding by setting a strict budget and then trying to shoehorn in all the things they think they *should* have in their wedding. This process not only doesn't work, but it can also leave you feeling like you can't afford to have your dream wedding in any way, shape, or form. We suggest you work backward. Before you rein in your dreams, imagine that no budgetary or logistical constraints exist. Start thinking about all the elements that would go into your fantasy wedding. Be as specific as you can, using all your senses. Are there aspects you've dreamed of since you were a child? How big is it? What color are the bridesmaid's dresses? What does the band sound like? Who's there? Where are you? What does it smell like? What are you eating? What are you drinking? What time of day is it?

Write down these thoughts on a piece of paper and exchange them with your spouse-to-be. You may feel more comfortable brainstorming out loud together, but the point is that you should both be honest and open-minded. Take each other's fantasies seriously. Refrain from making dismissive snorting sounds. This type of open exchange is neither a mind game nor an exercise in futility, but rather a very helpful step in discovering what both of you really want.

Prioritize: What's Important Here?

Now, take all of your fantasy elements and put them in some order of importance. Are towering bouquets of white lilies more important than drinking fine Champagne? Are you flexible on the time of year? The time of day? Must you have a couture gown or would you be willing to go with something less lavish and spend more money on a seven-piece orchestra so you can use those ballroom dancing lessons? Does it have to be the country club or would Aunt Myrtle's parlor serve the same purpose?

Compare your priority list with your intended's. Maybe you both agree that having a sit-down dinner is not so important. Perhaps you've always pictured getting married barefoot on the beach but your better half thinks only a black-tie hotel wedding will impress everyone back home. What compromises are you both willing to make? (This is good practice for the rest of your lives.)

Visualize: Reality Checklist

The next step is to take these priorities and paint the picture of where you're going to park your money. Start by estimating the cost of each of the most important elements. This provides you with a rough budget, a way to set some parameters; you'll flesh it out later.

Remember that none of this is etched in stone, so you can afford to be flexible. Assuming you can't afford the world's most exotic flowers or rarest Champagne, assess which parts of your prioritized fantasy lineup might really work. While you both may have in mind a caviar and blini bar, you may also see a band that sets you on fire. Because having both will blow your whole budget, one has to go. To facilitate that decision, think back on what sticks in your memory about great weddings you've been to. Was it the food? The setting? The music?

Weddings are not planned in a vacuum. Nor do they end when the cake is cut. You may encounter both familial and interpersonal ramifications that last far longer than this one day. A good idea, therefore, is to find out at the very beginning what these issues may be. When in doubt, compromise. For example, adhere to a dietary code or add one more bridesmaid to appease in-law relations. Doing so makes for a happier day and in later years you'll thank us.

Guest-imating your costs

It's never too early to make a preliminary guest list *in writing.* Thinking about whom to invite and who will actually show up has a tremendous impact on the way your wedding planning evolves. The number in your head may not correspond to the number in reality, and seeing the names on paper helps check your natural propensity to invite anyone who's anywhere near you. While certain costs such as space rental, officiant fees, music, and the wedding dress are usually fixed (once you've decided on them, that is), items such as centerpieces, food, and beverages change in proportion to the number of guests attending. The difference between 100 and 125 guests may mean three more tables and everything that entails at the reception. Only you can decide whether those people make the day more special or simply blow your budget.

To make sure you include everybody who matters, ask your prospective in-laws to submit a list of names and/or an estimate of the number of people they would like to see there. That doesn't mean that the two of you will decide to invite them all, but you need some idea so you can budget appropriately. Collecting names early can save you time later because, for example, you'll be able to skip investigating venues that are too big or too small.

Organize: Breaking Down the Details without Breaking Down

If the word *organize* strikes fear in your gut, then you really need to read this. And even if you're certifiably obsessive-compulsive, you may benefit from reading the following tips on getting organized and setting a budget. (Come to think of it, ever notice that control freaks read books like *How to Alphabetize Your Wardrobe* more than those who really need them?)

Getting it together

Approach your wedding as any other big project in your life: "Chunk" it into manageable pieces. Group several little steps into segments and plot them along a timeline or calendar, setting deadlines that jibe with everything else going on in your life:

- **Jot tasks and deadlines down on your calendar.** Use a pencil in case things change. In fact, they will change. Count on it.
- **Organize your time so that you are as gentle on yourself as possible.** If you are starting medical school, changing jobs, or moving, this is probably not the time to plan a complex wedding with a cast of

thousands. Although weddings are happy occasions, they are nonetheless stressful. Ask yourselves, "How much are we willing to give up?" Answer honestly.

- **Carry a notebook with you at all times so you can make a note of ideas as they pop into your head.** Those light bulbs often switch on at the most unlikely moments, and even though you think you could never possibly forget such an excellent idea, somehow it gets lost amid all that other important stuff crammed into your brain (especially while you are engaged). Having a notebook and a writing instrument within easy grabbing distance allows you to capture those inspirations — "re: embroidered silk, not taffeta!" or "call baker re: apricot frosting"— as they blip across your brainwaves. Another option: pocket voice recorders (see Chapter 21).
- **Start keeping track of your guests as early as possible.** Use either a computerized spreadsheet or a stack of 3 x 5 index cards in a box. Each entry contains data on everyone to whom you send an invitation — the correct spelling, address, RSVP, gift, spouse or significant other, and who invited them. Such a compilation proves invaluable when planning your seating chart.

TIP

An accordion file is handy for keeping track of all the ephemera that multiplies as you plan your big day: contracts, menus, wine labels, brochures, guest lists, fabric swatches, stationery samples, photos, plane tickets, receipts, magazine articles, and so on.

CAUTION

Just as you collect ideas and pictures of things you want for your wedding, it's equally important to note things you *don't* want. That way you have a better chance of remembering, for example, to tell the caterer that Aunt Myrtle is fatally allergic to clams or to tell the band that under no circumstances are they to play *Joy to the World.*

The M word (and we don't mean marriage)

Before you start liquidating your IRA, we can't stress enough what a wedding should *not* be: a cause of grief and anxiety. Perhaps in the back of your mind you're worried that guests will dissect every aspect of the reception, playing that tacky guessing game "How Much Do You Think This Cost?" Stop. Such thoughts can drive you crazy and make you skew your budget based on someone else's priorities. Besides, if you have friends who really think such things, why are you inviting them to your wedding?

Take a deep breath

A wedding without a doubt ranks as one of life's big expenditures:

- The average cost of a new car: $18,360.
- The average cost of a four-year college education including tuition, room, and board at a public institution: $7,118. At a private institution: $25,302.
- The average cost of a formal wedding with approximately 174 guests: $17,634.

Because weddings tend to cost more than may seem reasonable or possible, here are some more tips that can help you get a grip on your budget:

- If you are paying for the entire wedding or a large portion of it, we recommend a session with an accountant or financial planner, who can help you figure out what you can really afford and how to pay for it.
- The simplest way to manage your wedding budget is to open a dedicated wedding account so you know exactly how much money goes in and how much comes out.
- If someone else is contributing toward your wedding, try to get the money in a lump sum if at all possible.
- When it comes to paying for big-ticket items such as the dress or the space-rental fee, charge them to a credit card that gives you something in return (like frequent-flier miles). We assume that you're clever, so we don't need to remind you to pay the balance before interest accrues.

Consider putting the budget on a computerized spreadsheet, as shown in Figure 1-1, using a program such as Excel. Unless you plan special events for a living, it's difficult if not impossible to know what you may have to spend for catering, space rental, and the like. At the most, you may have a vague idea of the total amount you are able — or want — to spend. Input that bottom-line dollar amount first.

Based on your estimated bottom line, start filling in guesstimates for various items. As you research vendors and bids, make adjustments in the actual cost column. You may have wildly overestimated the cost of renting linens or been dreaming when you thought silk flowers where cheaper than the real thing. Typically, you may find vendors' estimates much higher than your guesses. Don't panic — yet. This spreadsheet is simply to help you understand the big picture and what your choices are going to cost. Seeing the numbers laid out keeps you from indulging in magical thinking — that somehow all the numbers will just fall into place.

Microsoft Excel - Wedpre~1

	A	B	C	D
1	**Kerfuffle-Blandsky Wedding**			
2	*Preliminary Budget*			
3		**Estimated**		
4	**Expense**	**Cost**	**High Bid**	**Low Bid**
5	Flowers	**$700**	$2,000	$600
6	Gown	**$2,000**	$2,500	$800
7	Invitations	**$400**	$680	$500
8	Catering	**$4,000**	$9,500	$4,800
30	**Total**	**$22,000**	$31,000	$28,500

Sheet1 / Sheet2 / Sheet3 / Sheet4 / Sheet5 / Sheet6

Figure 1-1: A spreadsheet like this one can help you to be realistic about your wedding planning.

Once you've narrowed down the field, make a second spreadsheet based on your final choices and your revised bottom-line budget (unless you've won the Ripley's Bridal Believe It or Not and your bottom line hasn't changed). The spreadsheet in Figure 1-2 shows you how to record expenditures, deposits paid, and outstanding balances. Used religiously, it prevents you from going over budget as your mounting anxiety tempts you to spend ever more money.

Include a column in your budget for a 10 percent cushion on all expenses and for the bottom line. Unless you are a psychic, you are bound to underestimate some costs and overestimate others. This 10 percent represents the highest amount you are willing to spend if need be. Just knowing that you're prepared with this contingency can save you from having a premature budgetary meltdown.

Microsoft Excel - ch1spdsht

File Edit View Insert Format Tools Data Window Help

	A	B	C	D	E	F	G	H	I
1	**Kerfuffle-Blandsky Wedding June 5**								
2	*Adjusted Budget as of 4/1*								
3			**Deposit**	**Balance**	**Due**	**Total**			
4	**Item**	**Cost**	**Paid**	**Due**	**Date**	**Paid**			
5	Flowers	$800	$300	$500	5-Jun				
6	Gown	$2,000	$1,000	$1,000	10-Apr				
7	Invitations	$680	$680	0	9-Mar	$680			
8	Catering	$5,000	$2,500	$2,500	5-Jun				
29									
30	**Total**	**$25,000**	**$9,050**	**$15,950**		**$680**			
31									
32									
33									
34									
35									
36									
37									
38									
39									
40									

Sheet1 / Sheet2 / Sheet3 / Sheet4 / Sheet5 / Sheet6

Figure 1-2: Use a revised spreadsheet to keep you on track and out of the poorhouse.

Synchronize: The Timetable Myth

With the exception of invitations, which can take up to eight weeks to print and mail, almost every aspect of a wedding can be accomplished in less than two months. Not that we suggest waiting until the last minute, but you do not have to be a slave to someone else's timetable. Okay, now here's the big shocker: *Weddings For Dummies* does not have the ubiquitous wedding timeline that tells you, for example, "Two days before: polish your left toenail." We believe this etched-in-stone manifesto strikes terror in the hearts of even the most courageous couple. In devising your customized timetable, allow your priorities, budget, personal schedules, and reality constraints to come into play. (See Chapter 18 for a sample schedule.) Having said that, keep in mind that you do need to do some things in advance:

- **Party site and band:** Two things that you should book ASAP are the venue and the musical entertainment, especially if you think you want to get married in high season at a highly desirable spot. Then again, if you're a gourmet, booking the caterer might take precedence.

  It pays to be flexible. Booking a venue for Sunday afternoon is usually less expensive than Saturday night. What's more, if you're intent on having the wedding at the most popular place in town, that spot may be booked every Saturday night for the next two years.

- **Invitations:** Invitations are traditionally mailed six weeks before the wedding, but we suggest eight weeks. Exceptions do exist, specifically if you have international guests, who should receive invitations ten weeks ahead of time. Almost all out-of-towners will need to take off extra time from work or make special arrangements to attend, so a good idea is to either send them invitations early or send a card alerting them to "save the date" six months in advance if possible. (See stationery samples in Chapter 13.)

  If you're pressed for time, consider asking guests to RSVP by phone (see Chapter 21) or e-mail rather than by mail.

- **Pick the date:** In picking the date it helps to do some reconnaissance. Maybe your maid of honor goes on a spa retreat at the same time every year. Or your future mother-in-law already has tickets for a three-month Arctic cruise next summer. People may put in requests, but you can't please everyone. Other factors can affect the best time to have your wedding. Perhaps you want the photographs to have a black and white photojournalistic look, but the one person within 500 miles who does that is booked. Either you go with a more traditional photographer or you shift the date.

  In the end, you must decide what's best for you and the majority of guests. Once you've set the date, stick to it. Your guests will have to deal with it. And you will find that most of them will deal very well.

Peak versus off-peak

Some couples are sentimental about dates — they want to get married on New Year's eve to symbolize their new start together or on one of their birthdays or on the anniversary of their first kiss. While this may seem sweet, watch out in case your special spot on the calendar falls on another holiday, an inconvenient day of the week, or at the *peak* (read "more costly") time of year. January, February, and March are typically slow months in most parts of the United States. The most popular time to get married is May through October.

Piggybacking a holiday

It's often tempting to have a wedding coincide with another major holiday. This can work if your family usually gets together anyway at this time, or if people coming from out of town need a few extra days' cushion and the holiday provides some extra time off work.

And another thing . . .

In your exhaustive wedding research, you may have come across various formulas that suggest you can make budgeting a breeze by allocating "standard" percentages for each component of your wedding. Sad to say, it ain't so. Every wedding is different. For example, the majority of dollars for an at-home tent wedding go toward the tent and rentals. For a hotel wedding, food and beverage are most likely the largest allocation.

Here, fully disclosed perhaps for the first time in print, is a definitive list of the items you may need to include in your budget. Look fear in the face and read:

Ceremony

- Ceremony flowers
  - Altar flowers
  - Chuppah
  - Personal
    - Bouquets
    - Boutonnieres
  - Pew bows or flowers
  - Tossing bouquet
- Church fee
- Flower baskets
- Officiant fee
- Organist
- Programs
- Mass books
- Ring pillows
- Yarmulkes

Clothing

- Alterations
- Attendants' attire
  - Dresses
  - Hats
  - Flower girl's ensemble
  - Gloves
  - Ring bearers' garb
  - Shoes
  - Tuxedoes/suits
  - Waistcoats
- Bride's ensemble
  - Dress or suit
  - Gloves
  - Hair
  - Headpiece and veil
  - Jewelry
  - Makeup
  - Nails
  - Shoes
  - Undergarments
- Groom's garb
  - Cufflinks and studs
  - Cummerbund
  - Manicure
  - Shoes
  - Tuxedo/suit
  - Tie
  - Waistcoat

Gifts

- Attendants
- Bride and groom (to each other)
- Parents
- Party favors
- Welcome baskets

Miscellaneous

- Additional psychotherapy sessions
- Babysitter
- Gratuities
- Massages
- Relaxation tapes
- Sales tax
- Ten percent cushion

Music

- Band(s)
- Ceremony musicians
- Cartage fees
- Cocktail music
- Costuming
- Disc jockey
- Microphone for toasts
- Overtime
- Piano rental
- Sound system

Other events

- Cocktail party
- Next-day brunch
- Rehearsal dinner

Photography

- Album fees
- Negatives
- Photographer's fee (possibly including):
  - Albums
  - Assistant(s)
  - Film
  - Labor
  - Processing
- Pre-wedding portrait
- Reprints
- Videography

Reception

- Beverage
  - Bar "setups"
    - Fruit
    - Ice
    - Juices
  - Bartenders

- Cake
  - Cutting fee
  - Groom's
  - Wedding (or bride's)
- Centerpieces
- Food
  - Additional meals:
    - Band
    - Other non-catering staff
    - Photographer
    - Videographer
- Rentals
  - Appropriate chairs
  - Band platform
  - Candles
  - China
  - Coat check
  - Dance floor
  - Glass
  - Linens
  - Portable restrooms
  - Restroom attendants
  - Restroom toiletries
  - Serving staff
  - Silverware
  - Tables
  - Tent
    - Air conditioning/heat
    - Floor
    - Lighting
- Room treatments
- Space rental
- Special lighting
- Table numbers

Rings

- Engagement
- Wedding

Stationery

- At-home cards
- Calligraphy
- Escort cards
- Guest book
- Informals (thank-you notes)
- Invitations
  - Inner and outer envelopes
  - Reception/ceremony cards
- Map and direction cards
- Place cards
- Postage
- Reply cards

Transportation and lodging

- Bride and groom
- Guests
- Parents
- Wedding party

Wedding consultant

- Additional staff
- Expenses
- Fee

On the other hand, sometimes people resent having their precious vacation time eaten up with a social obligation — especially if the date falls during a frequent flier blackout period. If they must sacrifice, however, they may expect the gracious host to make sure there is plenty to keep them entertained. In cases like these, you could find yourself playing social director for several days before and after the wedding. This can be both time consuming and exhausting.

Another drawback to piggybacking your wedding with a holiday is cost. Think how much you would charge to work on a holiday. The service staff feels the same way.

In cities with a large Jewish population, such as New York or Los Angeles, if you're willing to get married on a Friday night as opposed to Saturday after sunset, you stand a better chance of getting a good deal. Also, there are many Jewish holidays on which a Jewish couple cannot get married, but a gentile couple could. However, this should not be taken to the extreme — a gentile couple getting married on Yom Kippur or a Jewish couple getting married on Christmas Eve may find that many of their guests can't or won't show up.

Deputize: Who You Gonna Call?

We presume you've purchased this book because you have some vested interest in producing your own wedding. However, like it or not, even if everyone you know has been in psychotherapy for 40 years, in our society, money means power. Consequently, if your parents or in-laws are paying for a portion of the wedding, they do get a vote. This situation may prove to be one of the trickiest you face, requiring utmost diplomacy in the course of planning. Other people often have specific fantasies regarding *your* wedding, which may be diametrically opposite yours.

Measure the importance of financial contributions against your resolve for certain aspects of your wedding. This is something only you can determine. If you are accepting a great proportion of money from others, be prepared to take a great proportion of their advice. Decide which is more important to you: more financial help or total control.

Should people become overbearing, try to turn the situation around. Listen to every word of their input, thank them with all the grace and charm for which you are undoubtedly known, and then quietly make decisions with your fiancé(e) and announce them sweetly but firmly.

Delegating details — who's doing the work

Before meddlers become too meddlesome, put them to work on a simple project, such as researching places for out-of-towners to stay or tracking down Aunt Myrtle's mother's famous punch recipe. We strongly advocate the gentle exploitation of family and friends, but keep in mind that involving someone in your wedding means inviting them. Ask favors only from close friends, or from people who have nothing to lose or gain from helping you. The best way to solicit help is to ask for recommendations from family or friends who have been through this. That way they feel they've done something to help you and are absolved from the responsibility of interfering further.

Think over all offers of help before accepting them. Just because your best friend says she can calligraph does not mean she's very good at it. Deputize sensibly. The idea is to save you time, not make more work, cost you more money, or cause hurt feelings.

Before the going gets tough, the tough call the pros

Professional wedding planners used to be considered an extravagance or relegated to the role of social secretary. In the past decade, however, more couples have begun to rely on their expertise and you see them frequently at weddings these days. They are not hard to spot; just look for the hyperventilating commando frantically waving a clipboard.

The best time to hire a wedding planner (also known as a *coordinator, producer,* or *consultant*) is at the beginning of the process. Some planners, however, can be brought in at any point to handle just a few aspects or serve as the director of events on the actual wedding day. If you've enjoyed a wedding and it seemed well-organized, ask the couple who was responsible. The yellow pages are also a possible source, but be aware that any clever bridal entrepreneur from photographers to caterers may list themselves as planners. Before you make an appointment, find out whether they plan weddings first and foremost or whether weddings are a mere sideline. A tried and true way to find a reputable one is to ask other suppliers such as caterers, florists, and photographers. Trade associations are another good place to start, but bear in mind that these are listings, not recommendations.

Expect to pay between 10 and 15 percent of your total wedding budget for a planner to coordinate the entire wedding. Most often, planners charge in three ways: a flat fee, hourly, or as a percentage. As with everything else in life, nothing is free. In the case of planners who do not charge anything to you, the client — explaining that they make their money solely on commissions from vendors — either their commissions are hefty or they won't be in business very long.

A good wedding planner should be someone who:

- Negotiates and/or translates contracts
- Advises on locations, bands, and photographers, yet is willing to work with your selections
- Points out logistical aspects of your preliminary plan that may need refining
- Offers insights based on experience
- Is detail-oriented
- Has taste, style, and creativity
- Is a liaison between you and your vendors
- Gets you more bang for the buck

- Organizes and keeps planning on track
- Allows you to engage in good cop/bad cop scenarios with your intended, mother, and mother-in-law (you, of course, being the good cop)
- Is objective (a big advantage in charged situations)
- Has a working knowledge of all aspects of a wedding
- Provides current references and other evidence of a good track record
- Is particularly helpful in planning a long-distance or destination wedding
- Demonstrates a good sense of humor
- You have a great rapport with

On the other hand, a good wedding consultant is *not*:

- A member of the etiquette police
- Available 24 hours a day
- Just a general contractor
- Just a personal shopper
- A representative for one particular vendor, such as the hotel banquet manager or florist
- Your sister
- Your Aunt Myrtle
- Your mother

Chapter 2
Space: The First Frontier

In This Chapter

- Narrowing down the wedding site
- Collapsing the great tent myth
- Finding a house of worship
- Scouting spaces by phone
- Interviewing banquet managers and caterers

Quick quiz: Have you and your intended agreed — or at least compromised — on the wedding you want? Do you have a preliminary head count? Have you set a realistic budget? Has at least one of you broken down in tears? If not, consider going to Chapter 1 and practicing your exercIZEs.

Where you get married reflects your style, taste, and priorities. Whether you choose a religious ceremony in a local house of worship followed by an old-fashioned reception at home, or invent new traditions some place far away, finding a tie-the-knot spot is one of the first things to cross off your list because the hot spaces (or *venues*) are often booked a year in advance. In popular resort areas, hotels and other lodgings fill up quickly as well. And, of course, until you know where you're getting married, moving on to other decisions, such as ordering invitations and finalizing the menu, is impossible.

A World of Possibilities

Start with the big picture, narrowing down the location by region, state, city, and finally venue. As we mentioned before, money is power, so you need to take into account who's covering the cost and where *they* want to have the wedding. Consider also who may actually come (which is not always the same as whom you *want* to come) and how far they have to travel. Where do most of your friends live? Your relatives?

Tradition favors having the wedding in the bride's hometown over the groom's. But that's not always feasible or desirable.

If neither of you have roots in your present community, you may opt for neutral territory or a favorite vacation spot. However, are you prepared to pay guests' travel costs or are your guests well-heeled enough to cover the expense? How often are the local airports shut down due to weather? And if you're looking at a resort town, are peak-season costs exorbitant? Often, two cities that appear equal in every other way vary greatly in cost of living. (See Chapter 19 on planning destination and long-distance weddings.)

TIP

For planning an out-of-town wedding, a phone book from the local area is indispensable. You can order consumer yellow pages for any city from US West (one of the seven Baby Bells) for $7 to $40. Call 800-422-8793. (You can also peruse Yellow Pages online or on CD-ROM. See Chapter 21 for details.)

CAUTION

If you're planning a religious ceremony, hold off on booking anything until you clear the dates, location, and timing with the priest, rabbi, or minister you want to have officiate. A clergyperson may deem your ceremony plans inappropriate for reasons you never dreamed of such as secular music, contemporary readings, or your "edited" version of the traditional vows.

Should you come upon a church or synagogue within reasonable proximity of your reception, don't expect to be able to just walk in and book it as if it were a catering hall. Many sensitive issues are involved. If you have a relationship with a clergyperson or other official religious authority through your family or as a couple, enlist his or her help in communicating with the powers that be at the house of worship you're interested in.

Elementary, my dear Watson — researching like a pro

Before you set out on a wild goose chase, spend some time amassing as much material on various locations as possible. As your vision becomes clearer, all these tidbits of information should naturally gravitate to one of two piles: gold mine or utterly irrelevant piffle.

You can find information about wedding sites in a wide range of places, including:

- **Books:** *Places: A Directory of Public Places for Private Events & Private Places for Public Functions* by Hannelore Hahn covers spaces from ballrooms to breweries in major cities. *Far & Away Weddings* by wedding watchdogs Denise and Alan Fields is a must-have for planning destination weddings without losing your shirt.
- **Bridal shows:** Location vendors display at these exhibitions, which range from huge bridal fairs to invitation-only events at department stores.

- **Caterers:** Because off-premise locations are their stock in trade, caterers are tuned into what is available. To find a unique space, you might interview caterers for their suggestions.
- **Chambers of commerce:** Especially useful as a first stop for planning an out-of-town wedding, chambers of commerce can recommend venues, caterers, vendors, and even officiants, though they generally refer only to member establishments. Many send brochures and other information upon request.
- **Consumer magazines:** Besides the requisite *Bride's, Modern Bride,* and *Bridal Guide, Martha Stewart Living* and *Town & Country* put out special bridal issues. Look for regional magazines such as *Planning Your New York Wedding, Virginia Bride, Mariage Québec,* and the like. *Honeymoon* provides ideas for destination weddings as well as romantic getaways afterward, and *Condé Nast Traveler* can broaden your horizons. The Canadian magazine *WeddingBells* and the British magazines *Dolce Vita* and *You and Your Wedding* are also worth checking out.
- **Internet:** Using an Internet search engine, type in the words *wedding* and *planning* to access numerous sites (although some are more helpful than others). You can also locate chambers of commerce and tourist bureaus. (See Chapter 21 for addresses to look for.)
- **Newspapers:** Peruse the wedding announcements in your local newspaper or that of the city where you want to be married. Besides telling where the ceremony is held, they also sometimes mention the reception site.
- **Subscription newsletters:** *Romantic Places, Easy Escapes,* and *Andrew Harper's Hideaway Report* are a few of the specialized publications that reveal little-known and unusual destinations.
- **Travel brochures and catalogs:** The Independent Innkeepers' Association publishes *The Innkeeper's Register,* a guide to more than 300 country inns in North America. The Innovanna Corporation publishes *Romantic Wedding Destinations,* a compendium of companies that provide wedding packages and services in the United States, Bermuda, and the Caribbean. Ask your travel agent for brochures and videos.
- **Trade magazines:** *Locations* and *Special Events* are geared toward the events-planning industry and full of articles, professional tips, and advertisements for venues, vendors, caterers, and other services. *Agenda* publishes editions for Boston, Chicago, Dallas, New York, Philadelphia, San Francisco, South Florida, Southern California, and Washington, D.C.

Becoming an investigative reporter

Your own attitude plays a key role in your search for an original, magical place to get married. Think of yourself as the Woodward and Bernstein of the wedding set, meaning:

- **Be gutsy:** Get personal suggestions from people whom you consider arbiters of taste and style.
- **Be curious:** Perhaps you or someone you know attended a wedding that was stunning, but for some reason — cost, location, size — the venue is not quite right for you. Find out what other spots the couple passed up. Their reject list may contain your dream site.
- **Be creative:** Inquire about unconventional spaces to rent such as private homes, lofts, museums, galleries, boats, and private gardens. Owners who have never thought of renting out their property may consider it for a wedding.

Setting Your Sites

If you're not going to be married in a house of worship, you need a place to have a ceremony, a cocktail hour (if you have one), and a reception. Your first choice should be a site that can handle all three.

The turning of the room

Finding versatile spaces is not easy. Consequently, you may need to *turn a room.* This banquet term refers to resetting a room for another function. A space that must double for ceremony and cocktail area requires that chairs be moved and bars unveiled while guests are in the room. If the ceremony and reception are in the same room, guests are ushered to a separate cocktail area while the ceremony room is turned.

An elaborate decor may involve extra labor costs to be expedited or may be impossible to carry off in the time between ceremony and reception. Your decor concept should not dictate the length of the cocktail hour. Sculpting miniature English gardens on each table, for example, may take an inordinately long time. By the time they're seated, some guests may be too sloshed to notice or care whether they have a rose tree or a redwood towering above them.

Ceremony here, reception there

Consequently, even if getting married in a house of worship is not a priority, you may opt to have the ceremony and reception at different locations to avoid any room-turn awkwardness. Doing so, however, means extra expense:

- **Fees:** A donation or rental fee for the ceremony site.
- **Flowers:** Some people recommend having the chuppah or altar flowers do double duty by whisking them from the ceremony to the reception. Separate venues, however, can make this practice unwieldy. Compare the cost of additional flowers with the moving expense (if you're not painstakingly moving them yourself as your first act as husband and wife). If the savings are truly significant, make sure that the recycled flowers are rearranged artfully at the reception so guests don't think the florist delivered the ceremony flowers to the wrong place.
- **Transportation:** Don't automatically think that shuttling guests from ceremony to reception is not your responsibility. Unless your guests are all driving, think what happens when 200 people pour out of a church in a rainstorm with not a cab in sight. Not pretty.

What's more, the timing between the two sites must jibe. If the ceremony ends at 5:30 and the reception space, which is 35 minutes away, will be ready at 6:45 (need a calculator?), don't think you can fudge it. Invariably, your guests will arrive 20 minutes before the space is set — in time to see the band lugging their amplifiers across the dining room floor. (Horrors!) (For a sample wedding-day schedule, see Chapter 18.)

Sorting out your spaces

Two catering concepts worth knowing are *on premise* and *off premise.* In hotels, restaurants, private clubs, and banquet establishments, the catering services are in-house or "on prem." For lofts, private homes, museums, galleries, and so on, you need to hire an off-premise caterer. Some of these spaces have lists of caterers they either allow or recommend. Whether you've fallen in love with a particular off-premise space or have designs on a brilliant caterer, be certain they can work together. By the same token, keep in mind that sometimes great food and a gorgeous on-premise space are mutually exclusive. If you feel the food is equally or more important than the space, start by finding a caterer, who in turn may lead you to the space. (See Chapter 8 for finding a great caterer.)

If you have your eye on a *private club,* you need to be sponsored by a member or a member of a club that has a reciprocal agreement. This can be a catch-22 because often the club won't let you peruse the site without first having a sponsor — and how are you to find a sponsor without finding out who the members are? In addition to having an in-house caterer, clubs may have stringent or seemingly peculiar rules.

Scouting by phone . . .

The phone interview lets you preview the service you may receive. Do they return calls promptly? Do they seem flexible or are they more "take it or leave it" in attitude? Do you get a sense they would be happy (not desperate, just pleased) to host your wedding? Are they too busy to talk to you? Condescending? Rude? Evasive?

In the initial phone call:

- Get the name and title of the person on the other end of the phone. (You'd be amazed at how often busboys quote prices and availability.)
- Ask what room(s) are available for your wedding date and time. If another event may be booked in the space earlier in the day, how much set-up time do they allot between events?
- Ask for food and beverage price estimates. (For a breakdown of what those may be, see Chapters 8 and 10.)

Up close and personal

Once you've done your preliminary nosing around, investigate spaces with your fiancé(e), or a close friend whose opinion you trust. Don't take your parents or future in-laws on this qualifying round. You want to have intelligent, researched responses to the possible downsides before they spot them and panic.

Two ways to pay

Catering halls, restaurants, hotels, and banquet facilities often offer space-food-liquor packages, so asking about one without considering the others is almost impossible. The terms to know are:

- **All-inclusive:** Always relates to food, beverage, tax, and tip, but may not include such extras as bartenders, bathroom attendants, cake, carvers, coat room, and valet parking.
- **Plus-plus:** Relates to having tax and gratuity added on to your food and beverage price. This figure may skew your whole budget, so don't ignore it. For example, if your meal and bar price is "$75 per person plus-plus," your tax is 8.25%, and the gratuity is 20%, that comes to an additional $21.18 per person, making your actual cost $96.18 per person. Oh well, you didn't need to have any flowers, right?

When you go to see a space, take copious notes. Ask for brochures and to see photos of other events that have taken place there. If none are available, snap a few photos — but ask permission first because some places consider their layout and decor proprietary information. Do this because by the time you've seen the 12th place on your first free weekend (ha!) you will not remember which hotel had the deep green walls you hated or the fluorescent lights reminiscent of a New York subway station.

Remember, you're still in the preliminary stages; listen to your gut feelings. This is not the time to start thinking about how you could transform a space you basically don't like. If the place depresses you, move on. This reconnaissance mission is exhausting enough without getting into minutia or taking the entire two-hour tour with the banquet manager out of politeness.

Keep a grip on your demeanor. Yes, we encourage you to be an educated consumer, but this is no time to launch into your Ralph Nader impersonation. Behave rationally and professionally, not suspiciously. Try not to display infectious briditis or groomitis. Food and beverage personnel are people, too. And if you wind up holding your wedding there, they will remember you, for better or worse.

Spacing out

In determining whether a space is large enough for various parts of your wedding, take the venue's numbers with a grain of salt. Not that banquet managers would lie, but their job is, after all, to fill spaces with warm bodies. Ask for floor plans and diagrams of table configurations. Whipping out a tape measure doesn't hurt either. Here are some general rules, which also apply to tents:

- **Ceremony:** You need 8 square feet per person, including the aisle and actual ceremony spot. For example, for 150 guests, including the wedding party, you need a 1,200-square foot space.
- **Cocktails:** For pre-meal cocktails, figure on 8 square feet per person plus, which includes seating for one-third of the people and sufficient space for bars. If you want a dance floor in the cocktail area, you need 10 square feet per person. In addition, hors d'oeuvres stations generally require 12 to 13 square feet per person.
- **Reception:** A fully seated buffet with dance floor requires 16 to 20 square feet per person. A seated and served dinner with dance floor calls for 13 to 15 square feet per person.
- **Dance floor:** 2.5 square feet per person allows for approximately half of the guests dancing at once. If you think yours is a "dancing" crowd, have 3 square feet per person. To accomodate a band, allow 20 to 25 square feet per instrument.

Ask very specifically about what parts of the space are available. You may have in your mind's eye that the inn's exquisite rose garden would be the perfect place to take pictures, only to find out, the day of the rehearsal, that it's actually off-limits.

Time to play 20,000 questions

You're serious about the space? Time for more questions — lots of questions! Some apply to hotels and the like; others are useful for a rental space.

- How many people can you seat (with dancing) for A) buffet stations or B) a sit-down dinner? Ask to see floor plans, diagrams, and photos, including photos of events other than weddings to give you decorating ideas.
- What is the square footage?
- How does the space "work"? Where do guests enter? If the venue is in a building via an elevator, is there a doorman downstairs and/or an elevator operator? How are guests directed after they arrive on the floor? Where is the coatroom? Where should the escort card table go?
- Where would you hold the ceremony (if you haven't already decided)?
- Where would you serve cocktails?
- How long does it take to turn the room (if needed)?
- If another event is taking place concurrently, how does the manager keep them from running into each other? (Nothing is worse than bridal crossing.)
- What is the space rental fee? How many hours does it cover? Is there a maximum number of hours? When does overtime kick in?
- Must you pay fees for additional rooms?
- Do they offer price considerations for certain times or days?
- Is dancing allowed? Is there a dance floor? Is it built in, a roll-out, or in parquet squares? What is the maximum number of dancers the floor will hold?
- Is there a piano on the premises? Upright or baby grand?
- Is there a sound system in place? Is there a rental fee for it or for additional microphones?
- Might the establishment book other weddings or events before, at the same time, or after?
- What are the acoustics like? Does sound *bleed* (meaning music and laughter travel from one room to another)?

- If there are glaring problems such as chipped paint, scaffolding, or broken mirrors, will they assure you in writing that they will be fixed by your wedding?
- Are the chandeliers clean and all the bulbs working?
- How does the lighting look best? Do the lights have dimmers?
- What is the heat and air situation?
- What are the smoking rules?
- How many bathrooms are there and what do they look like? (Very important.)
- Where can the bride get dressed? The groom?
- Where can you take photographs?
- What are the parking facilities?
- What are the rules about using their vendors — the hotel's designated florist or band, for example?
- What are the *hidden* labor costs — security guards, bathroom attendants, coat check, or union electricians?
- Will the person showing you the space work with you throughout the entire process? If not, who will?
- How far in advance can or must a reservation be confirmed?
- What kind of security deposit is required? By when? What is the refund policy? How long will they hold the space for you without a deposit and will they give you a right of first refusal?
- What uniforms does the wait staff wear? Does the staff comprise both males and females?
- What is the method of service — French, Russian, or á la carte? (See Chapter 8 for a lesson in service styles.)
- Does the caterer feel that the kitchen space is adequate?
- Has the caterer worked in the space before?
- What is included in the price (china, glass, linens, silverware, tables, and so on)? What is the estimate for rentals?
- Can the caterer provide references?
- How much and what kind of insurance is required? Does the caterer have insurance and will it cover you?
- Are permits, such as a certificate of occupancy or parking, necessary?
- Is the wedding cake included?
- How many captains will there be? How many servers per table?

- Will they feed your "staff" (photographer, band, and so on) and at what cost?
- Is it possible to have a choice of dishes? If so, is there a surcharge? What's the number of alternate menu items they usually prepare? What about meals for diabetic, kosher, or vegetarian guests?

Many places refuse to hold *tastings* of their menus for "shoppers" and we do empathize. Producing a meal for two (or four) is both costly and labor intensive, especially for off-premise caterers. We feel, however, that once you have booked the facility or caterer, you are entitled to a tasting and you should negotiate this up front before signing the contract. If the food is not up to par, you are entitled to tastings until it is (but beware of this warning sign).

As you question a prospective caterer or banquet manager, get a clear idea of the rules regarding drinks, as that affects overall cost and logistics. (For a complete run-down of your bar needs, see Chapter 10.)

There's No Place Like Home

While your sunny little hamlet may seem perfect for a wedding, the only time to really assess its appropriateness is during a monsoon. That said, consider these questions:

- Should a weather disaster strike and you're having the wedding outside, is the house big enough to use as a back-up?
- What is the bathroom and/or septic capacity?
- Where will guests park?
- Assuming that you're lucky enough to have a beautiful day and you will be outdoors, what is the fly and/or mosquito population? Do you need to fog the property?
- How up-to-date and powerful is the electricity? Plugging in a single 100-cup coffee urn can cause an entire house to go dark. Do you have a generator?
- Does your kitchen have sufficient space for a caterer?
- Who is available to receive deliveries of rentals, flowers, food, and so on?
- How much time for *set-up* and *break-down* (assembling and dismantling the tent and so on) is required and can you live in your house during it? Who is responsible for putting your house back in order? If you are, do you have time to work miracles before you leave for the honeymoon?

Tents and more tense

Although at-home and estate weddings can be utterly picturesque, that they are simple or inexpensive is a myth. The reason: You usually have to rent a tent. Because most houses lack a ballroom or indoor tennis court that can accommodate row upon row of chairs — unless you limit the guest list to a handful of deserving souls — at least part of the wedding must take place outdoors. Putting up a canopy is neither costly nor complicated, but a flimsy awning does absolutely no good if it's raining, freezing cold, or stifling hot. The only way to be absolutely secure is to have a full-fledged tent.

Proper placement

Make sure your property has an appropriate spot to put the tent. If your backyard resembles the Badlands, erecting a tent without flooring is risky. Floors can be prohibitively expensive because of the labor, but here's the conundrum: Not having a floor leaves you vulnerable to potential fiascoes — off-balance tables and chairs, an uneven dance floor, and, most ruinous, water seepage. A downpour on your wedding day isn't the only weather report you have to worry about. If it has rained recently, water seeps up from the ground, even if the tent is on a hill. Add a hundred pairs of high heels poking divots in the lawn and so much for the verdant expanse that made you decide your home was the perfect spot for the most important day of your life. (Anyone for a little white-water rafting?)

Catering cover

You need an additional tent for the caterer. And where you have more than one tent you need canopies and walkways between them.

Decor delimma

Consider how you will light and decorate the tent. Even if you plan something simple, you're looking at a great white expanse punctuated by glaring industrial tent poles. Disguising all of this can be heart-stoppingly expensive. (See Chapter 11 for tent-decorating ideas.)

Tents generally come in one of three designs, as shown in Figure 2-1:

- **Century:** Has one or several peaks and can be either a pole tent or frame tent.
- **Frame:** Supported by a frame with no poles down the center. Also called a *clear-span frame tent.*
- **Pole:** Has quarter poles — that go around the perimeter — as well as center poles down the middle of the tent. Pole tents must be staked to the ground, which means that they don't work very well in rock gardens or on asphalt.

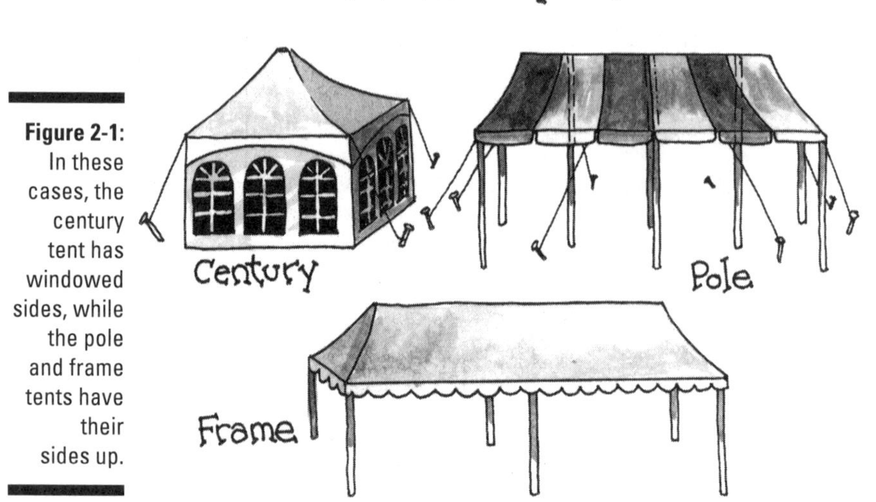

Figure 2-1: In these cases, the century tent has windowed sides, while the pole and frame tents have their sides up.

Comfort zone

Heating, albeit primitive, is affordable, but air conditioning is very expensive and energy-scarfing. Anybody who has been to a tent party where the power conked out will urge you to spring for a back-up generator. Just be sure to place it far enough away so guests don't have to shout over the incessant hum. If you are imagining the drama of a starlit sky though a clear tent ceiling, keep in mind that without air conditioning tents tend to fog up and under a sunny sky can turn into hot, miserable terrariums.

Tent contracts are particularly tricky. Suppliers usually erect tents several days before a wedding, so even if you (bravely) believe the weather forecast is so unfailingly positive that you do not want to have the tents erected at all, you must still pay 50 percent or more of the estimated bill to cover labor, on the assumption that the tent supplier turned away other jobs for your wedding. You usually have a 48- to 72-hour window for a final decision (as specified in your contract) regarding whether to connect tents and canopies. For these you usually pay only 25 percent of the deposit if you decide not to have them erected.

The flushing bride

In the category of little-facts-you-never-dreamed-you-would-need-to-know-but-aren't-you-glad-we're-printing-them-here, the toilet situation requires utmost attention. Just like parking, coat room organization, and guest transportation, bathrooms should not be an afterthought. People are often loath to spend money on such an unglamorous detail of their wedding, but adequate and "commodious" toilet facilities are a crucial aspect of hospitality.

When renting portable toilets, keep in mind that each one is good for a maximum of 125 uses. As a general rule, an average person uses the toilet once in three hours. If you have 500 guests for three hours, you need four toilets (500÷125 = 4). If they are staying for six hours, you need eight toilets.

Designate one set of toilets for men and another for women. Even if the guest ratio of men to women is one to one, have more toilets for women because they, as everybody knows, take longer. At all costs, you want to spare your guests mistaking a long snaking bathroom line for the conga line.

Portable toilets range from rustic construction-site designs to trailers fully outfitted with toilet stalls, mirrors, sinks, and faux marble vanities. Whichever you choose, having tented walkways and a separate lighted tent for portable toilets (especially for evening weddings) makes sense.

Even if you have enough toilets in your house, be sure to double check the septic situation. You often have to drain septic tanks beforehand so that your restrooms can accommodate the number of guests.

Anticipating special needs

If you have guests who are elderly, handicapped, or ill, make them as comfortable as possible. That means providing transportation and making sure the ceremony and reception — including portable toilets — are wheelchair accessible when necessary. Because people who can't see or move well can often get left out of the fun, be especially gracious by seating them in places of honor, devoting quality visiting time with them, and appointing someone to keep on top of special hospitality needs.

Chapter 3

And the Bride Wore . . . Whatever She Pleased

In This Chapter

- Finessing optical delusions and other dress details
- Dressing from the neck up
- Figuring out which white is right
- Getting the goods
- Deciding what to wear underneath it all

"Know, first, who you are; and then adorn yourself accordingly."

— Epictetus, *Discourses,* 3:1

Princess, queen, siren, lass, vixen/virgin, movie star, fashion plate, Venus flytrap — fashion designers are immensely creative in imagining what role women want to play. As frivolous as some designer visions seem, buying into a fantasy is easy because the sartorial side of nuptials can throw even the most confident women for a loop. The single garment known simply as a *wedding gown,* after all, is loaded with meaning: It symbolizes the start of a new life, is perhaps the costliest piece of clothing you will ever buy, must endure several of the most nerve-wracking hours of your life, will be inspected by umpteen pairs of eyes, and will be photographed relentlessly. Thinking about it, shopping for it, and purchasing it causes many women anxiety bordering on sheer panic. Hopefully, we can mitigate the situation.

For starters, bear in mind that the dress that ultimately makes you happiest is the one that reflects your inner self — the woman with whom you are most content. Secondly, realize that your dress is just one part of your entire ensemble, which includes your headpiece, veil, shoes, makeup, hair, stockings, and jewelry. You may stave off a heart attack or two by considering one element at a time.

The Long and Short of It

If you bought this book in the hope that we would tell you exactly what is appropriate dress for the precise time and degree of formality of your wedding, we're sorry to disappoint you. If pedants want to debate the proper glove length for "formal daytime" as opposed to "semi-formal evening," that's their business. We just don't feel comfortable doing so. If your invitation specifies "black tie" and you're hosting several hundred guests to a six-course, seated meal with a 20-piece orchestra serenading them, somehow we know you're not going to show up in a pin-stripe suit.

What you *do* need to decide before dress-hunting are three salient particulars, which rely heavily on common sense and personal style:

- **When:** As in the season and time of day. Although we do not believe in being a slave to arcane (and ridiculous) rules, we do believe that certain social conventions have merit. Heavy fabrics such as brocades, damasks, and satins are most comfortable in late fall and winter. A spaghetti-strap crepe dress works better in hot weather. Most people don't feel comfortable wearing black tie to a luncheon, or sport jackets to a ball room. Remember that you are the central character in the show being cast and all the players' costuming revolves around your ensemble.
- **Where:** Will you be getting married in a church or synagogue where bare shoulders are disrespectful (or prohibited)? Or are you having both your ceremony and reception in a space that permits you to let your own sense of taste and style dictate the dress?
- **Price:** How much are you willing to spend? And how likely are you to change your mind? Be realistic and up front with salespeople about your dress budget. You can save a lot of time if everyone isn't playing cat and mouse.

The shape of you to come

As with other aspects of your wedding planning, to make order out of seeming chaos, take in the big picture before fixating on the details. As you try on each dress, do the *squint test*: Stand back, squint your eyes, and look at the *silhouette,* or overall shape, of the dress. After several rounds of this you may realize that certain silhouettes look better on you than do others.

Figures 3-1 and 3-2 and the following list define the classic silhouettes:

- **A-line:** Flared from the waist to the hem, usually with a fitted waist, though no horizontal waistline. Also called a *princess line.* A flattering silhouette for most body types.

Before you shop

In preparing to shop, get a handle on wedding dress lingo. Knowing that *charmeuse* is not a hot new French singer and *flyaway* does not refer to a bad hair day will keep you from feeling intimidated or exasperated when dealing with salespeople. Take a trip to a fabric store and gather some swatches that appeal to you. Clip pictures from both bridal and general-interest magazines that convey the style or mood you want for your wedding. If you find yourself gravitating toward images that are very different from one another, don't fret. At this point, "knowing what you want is actually less important than knowing what you *don't* want," says Nancy Aucone, co-owner of the Bridal Boutique in Manhasset, Long Island. At the same time, be open-minded. Sometimes the only way to know what won't work is by trying on a lot of dresses.

If you're like most women, you're not used to wearing anything remotely similar to a wedding gown. This can make figuring out the best style for you a daunting task. It helps to understand and be comfortable with your body. New York-based image consultant Laurie Krauz advises clients to stand alone in front of a full-length mirror in a well-lit area, strip naked, and take a good but uncritical look at themselves. "Bodies are artwork — there is no good and bad, just what is," she says. "Shopping for the wedding dress to fix what's 'bad' will only make you miserable." Your dress should play up your best features so that's what people notice when you walk in the room.

The first time you venture out to try on dresses, leave the credit cards at home and bring only one trusted friend with you. In a perfect world you could take a snapshot, but most salons prohibit this until you make a purchase. Make notes. Pay attention to first impressions. If you are really lucky you may have the ultimate bridal shopping epiphany: "You'll know it's the perfect gown for you," says Rachel Leonard, fashion director of *Bride's* magazine, "when someone looks at you in the dress and their eyes well up with tears."

- **Ball gown:** A very full skirt that brushes the floor. The waistline falls at your natural waist. The classic fairy tale wedding gown silhouette. Particularly suited to bodies that are tall and curvy.
- **Empire:** The bodice is cropped and the waist seam ends just below the bust line to create a flattering elongated effect. Looks best on straight bodies, though not necessarily with low or large breasts.
- **Mermaid:** Narrow, body-hugging bodice that flares dramatically at or below the knee. Also known as a *trumpet skirt.* Usually cut on the bias. Good for showing off your curves, especially if you're tall. Some women find the cut constricting, others like the shimmy effect. Think Ginger on *Gilligan's Island.*
- **Sheath:** A narrow, close-fitting gown that goes to the floor in an unbroken line. Less snug and therefore more forgiving than the mermaid, making it a favorite among women of different figure types. Not for kneeling.

- **Slip:** Like a long tank top, but especially sexy cut on the bias. The simplest and, on the right figure, the most elegant.

Figure 3-1: These traditional silhouettes are synonymous with wedding gowns.

Muddling through the middle

The waistline plays a large role in determining the gown's silhouette. Again, the trick is to pick a style that works *with* your body rather than attempting to compensate for a "flaw." Look through your wardrobe; probably many of your favorite things have comfortable, flattering waistlines.

Now consider which of these waistlines is right for you (refer to Figures 3-1 and 3-2 for a visual):

- **Basque:** Forms an elongated triangle beneath your natural waistline. The lower point can be raised or lowered to make the silhouette more flattering, but always should lie flat. Always diminishes the width of the dress at the waistline, making it good for women who are bigger on the bottom than on top. Virtually non-existent in general fashion and becoming passé in bridal styles, where it was once quite prevalent.
- **Drop waist:** The waistline falls several inches below the natural waist. Can make your waist appear longer and slimmer, but may also make your legs look shorter.

Figure 3-2: Thanks in part to John F. Kennedy Jr.'s wife, Carolyn Bessette, sleek minimalist styles are gaining popularity.

- **Empire:** The waist seam ends just below the bust line. The waistline appears to begin above the natural waist.
- **Natural:** Comes in at your natural waist, which is (ideally) the narrowest point of your torso.

Up to your neck in style

The neckline is next in the style triumvirate (along with the waistline and sleeves) that determines the bodice of your dress. Figure 3-3 shows you a few neckline variations and the following list gives you a broad range of possibilities:

Getting into the gown

Getting dressed on your wedding day is a two-person job. (If it's in your budget, you might hire the shop's alterations specialist to help you.) Unzip the dress all the way down. If you have a petticoat, put it into the dress, making sure the waists match up. Have your designated "lady in waiting" hold up the dress for you with the bodice falling forward. Put your hands on your waist, arms akimbo. Without losing your balance, step into your dress rather than pulling it over your head. If you must do the latter, cover your head with a zippered head netting (available at drugstores) or a scarf so your makeup doesn't ruin your dress or vice versa. To pull the loops over a parade of covered buttons marching from neck to hip, a crochet hook may seem like the eighth wonder of the world as you try to get dressed in less than three hours. Once the gown is on, put on your headpiece. Sit on a backless stool with the dress fluffed out around, not under, you.

- **Bateau neck:** Follows the line of the collarbone straight across, is high in front and back, and usually skims both shoulder blades.
- **Décolletage:** Plunging and cleavage-revealing.
- **Halter:** A strap that attaches to either side of the bust and wraps around the neck. Bare and revealing and needs to be worn with a cover-up for a religious ceremony.
- **Jewel:** A simple curve at the base of the neck.
- **Keyhole:** A keyhole- or tear-shaped opening either at the neckline or in the back of the dress.
- **Portrait:** A fold of fabric creates a shawl-like collar, framing the face. Usually worn off the shoulder. Can be flattering on angular bodies, but matronly if not cut low enough.
- **Sabrina:** A nearly horizontal line from shoulder blade to shoulder blade. Like a bateau neck, but it starts two inches in from each shoulder, so the neck opening is more narrow.
- **Scoop:** Rounded but lower than a jewel neck, perhaps even revealing a hint of cleavage.
- **Sweetheart:** Open, somewhat decolleté, sweeping down, dipping to a point in the middle of the bust and forming a heart shape. High in back. Works well on a curvy figure.
- **V-neck:** Forms a point, making the neck look longer and slimmer.

Figure 3-3: Choose a neckline that flatters your figure and your face.

- **Wedding-band collar:** A band that is high on the neck usually in a contrasting fabric to the rest of the bodice; often lace is the material used. Emphasizes a long, slender neck.

Arm negotiations

In bridal and other fashion, you can no longer ascertain the season by the length of the sleeves. After countless hours at the gym, many buff brides are going sleeveless no matter how chilly, and women who either don't love their arms or never feel completely dressed in anything but full-length sleeves are wearing sheer sleeves to their wrists even during the dog days of summer. As illustrated in Figure 3-4, wedding dress sleeve styles still run the gamut from romantic to modern:

- **Balloon:** Wide, elbow-length sleeves.
- **Dolman:** Wide armholes extending out from the waist of the dress, and tightening at the wrist. Also called bat wings. A bit of Morticia from *The Addams Family,* but heavy drama with the right dress — one that is tight and slinky.
- **Fitted point:** Long, fitted sleeves that come to a V-shaped point at the top of the hand. Dainty and old world.
- **Juliet:** Short puff at the shoulder. Fitted on lower part of arm. A period look á la the Shakespearean heroine.

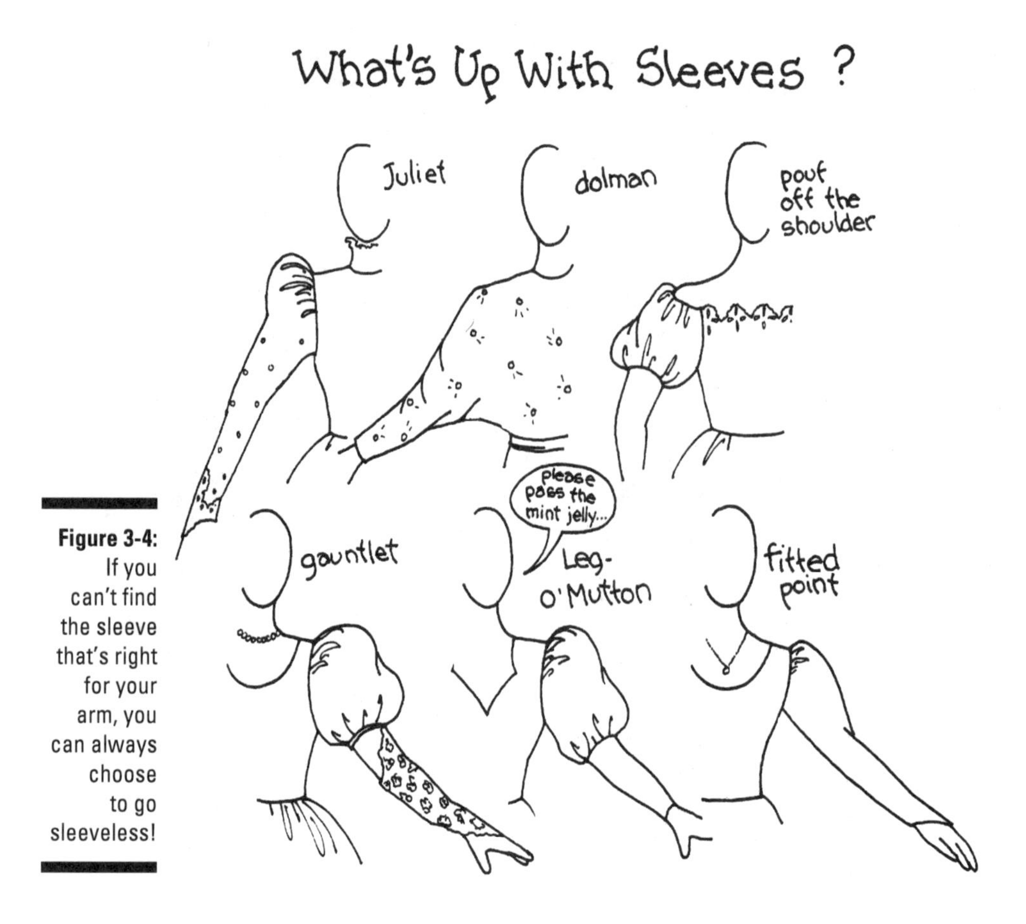

Figure 3-4: If you can't find the sleeve that's right for your arm, you can always choose to go sleeveless!

- **T-shirt:** As the name implies, sleeve closely fitted to the shoulder. Halfway between cap and short sleeve.
- **Three-quarters:** Ends just below the elbow and is finished with a small cuff or band. Very '50s.

Looking back

Take into account that guests will be gazing at you from behind during the entire ceremony, so the back of your dress should have some detailing. Some dresses are virtually plain in the front with all the ornamentation on the rear. If you have a lovely back, consider the possibilities: scooped backs edged with silk flowers or composed of illusion, a halter neckline, or strapless gown that is completely backless. Conversely, women who are larger on the bottom than the top might think twice before plastering a dramatic butterfly bow at their tailbone or sporting a dress with a train that, when bustled, resembles an ice cream truck attached to their derriere.

To what lengths will you go?

Yes, we live in a strange world. A bride may wear a very ornate knee-length dress to a black-tie wedding or waltz into a wedding luncheon in a bejeweled full-lenth ball gown.

Typically, wedding dresses come in various lengths:

- **Ballerina skirt:** Full from the waist, just gracing the tops of your ankles. Works well with a tulle skirt.
- **Full-length or floor-length:** The toes of your shoes should show. The back hem should be short enough to dance in without you or your partner stepping on your dress and tripping you.
- **High-low:** The skirt is cut shorter in front, usually to mid-calf, and goes to floor-length in back.
- **Knee-length:** The hemline covers the knees. Coco Chanel believed that the most flattering length for any woman was one-finger-length below the knee.

Happy trains to you

Perhaps more than any other aspect of your dress, the bridal train has transformational powers. It forces you to walk a little differently; it swishes around luxuriously; it makes you feel positively regal. The longer the train, the more you may want to decorate it with bands, bows, pearls, sequins, crystals, or other embellishments that add glamour and ballast to the dress.

Various lengths include:

- **Sweep:** The shortest train, just brushing the floor or the tops of your shoes. Also called *brush.*
- **Chapel:** Extends four feet from the waist.
- **Cathedral:** Extends nine feet from the waist (roughly five or six feet behind the bride). If it is very long, such as Princess Diana's 25-foot number, it's called *royal* or *monarch.* Managing such a huge amount of fabric often requires *pages,* young boys who hold up the train as you walk down the aisle. (See Chapter 4 for a full explanation of page duties.)

The shape of your train is determined as much by its length as the way the fabric is attached to your dress. Your train may simply be a factor of how your dress is cut, but if it is a separate piece of fabric, you may choose one of these styles:

- **Court:** Attached at the shoulders and falls to the floor.
- **Detachable:** Attached with hooks and loops. Can be wrapped around like a long skirt over a short dress or designed like a train over a long dress.
- **Watteau:** Attached at the neckline and forms box pleats and falls loosely to the hem, sweeping into a train.

Both Chinese-American and Japenese-American brides may change attire several times during the wedding day. The higher the family's status, the more changes.

Which white is right?

By the late 1800s, when white had become the standard in bridal gowns, *Ladies Home Journal* advised readers: "Thought must be given to the becomingness of the shade, for after all, there are as many tints in white as in other colors; the one that may suit the pale blond is absolutely unbecoming to the rosy brunette. Dead white, which has the glint of blue about it, is seldom becoming to anyone. It brings out the imperfections of the complexion, tends to deaden the gloss of the hair, and dulls the brightness of the eyes. The white that touches on the cream or coffee shade is undoubtedly the most artistic."

We certainly couldn't have said it better. Indeed, white is never just white. What the bridal shops call *diamond white* is soft white, usually found only in expensive silk. *Blue-white* is generally polyester and unflattering to most blondes. *White-white* is more expensive than blue-white and called *Italian satin,* even though it is polyester.

Ah, but you've probably already realized that things in Bride Land are never that simple. Thanks to designers such as Vera Wang, Ulla Maia, and Holly Harp, bridal gowns are taking increasingly more cues from mainstream fashion, which means that white is just the beginning. Consider trimming your dress in brilliant yellow satin or opt for the surprise of a dainty row of black velvet ribbons running down the back of a full skirt. A peach or blue chiffon imparts a subtle aura. European designers are having a heyday with their "coffee and cream" collections — bodices and skirts in shades of deep beige and taupe. Or skip white altogether and walk down the aisle wearing a gold brocade ball gown, or a sheath in re-embroidered lace over blue silk.

Hustle and bustle

Unless you've chosen a sweep train or a detachable train, or you plan to stand in one place all night, you need to bustle your train at some point after the ceremony. Take your appointed train bustler (such as your wedding consultant or maid of honor) with you to your last fitting so she can learn the correct method. Once your dress is bustled, usually securely at the waist, the entire hem should be even. The fabric should drape gracefully and not too fully so you can sit comfortably.

Some brides wait until after the first dance to bustle. Until then, somebody has to be in charge of your train, folding you into the car, holding the train when you get out, and letting it unfurl as you walk down the aisle. Another option is to attach a loop to your train that you slip over your wrist, allowing you to "carry" your own train all night. This works only with lightweight fabric, and even then requires a certain agility. Do not, for example, plan to do any overhead clapping.

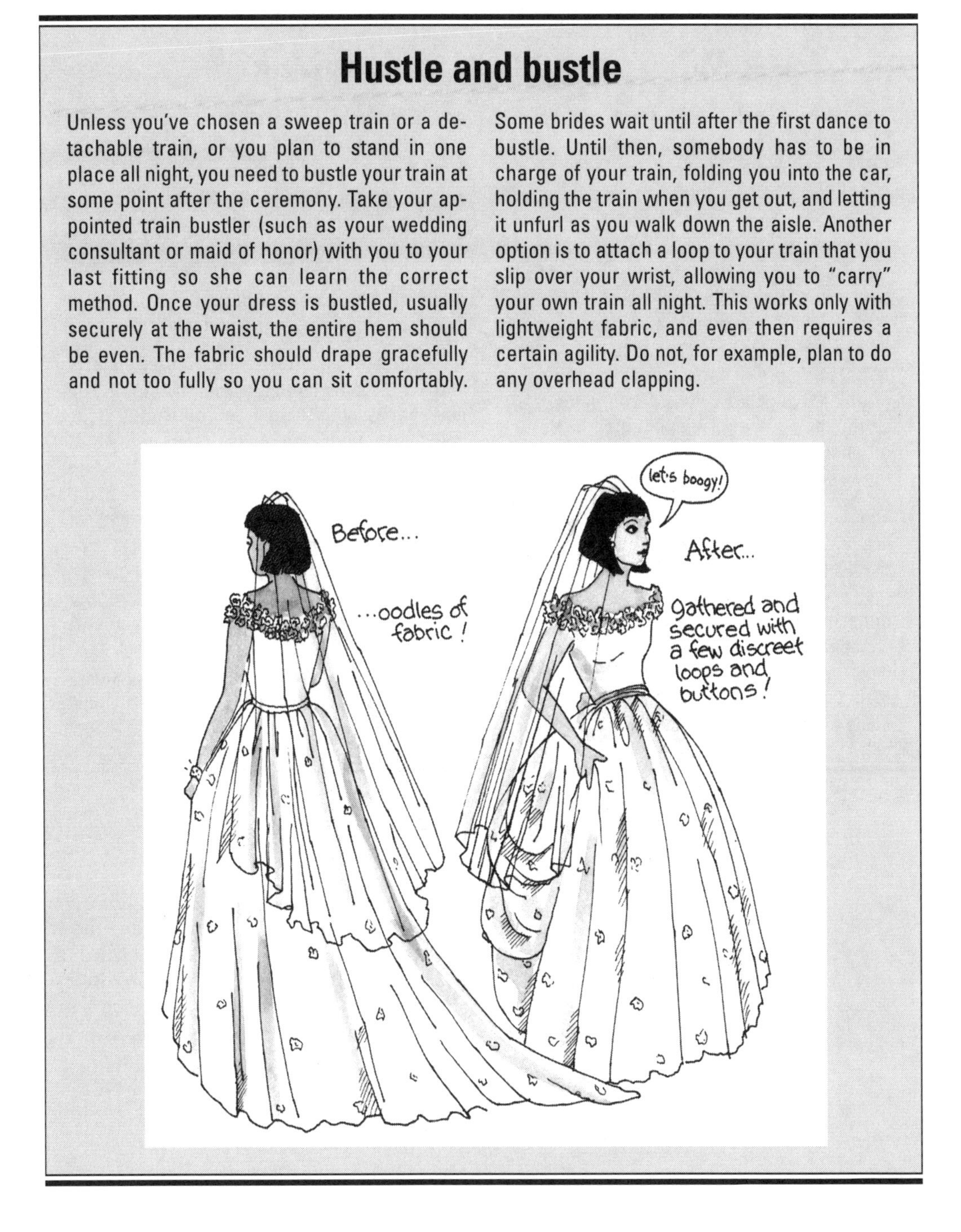

What's white got to do with it?

The white wedding gown has waxed and waned through the ages. In ancient Egypt, brides wore layers of pleated white linen, and in Greece and Rome white was the color of celebration. The first bride recorded in modern times to wear white from the top of her head to the tip of her toes was Anne of Brittany at her 1498 wedding to Louis XII of France. She did not, however, set a lasting trend. Brides for many generations to come wore any color of their choosing with the exception of green, which was considered unlucky and worn only by the fairies (although in Norway green is in fact a joyous color and often worn for weddings).

The wedding dress as once-in-a-lifetime garb is a fairly new concept as well. As recently as the 1920s the majority of brides dressed for their weddings as they did for any celebratory occasion, in their best outfit. Upper-class women had their dresses custom made, but wore them at parties for at least a year after their wedding. Wedding gowns were often made of silk (because it dyes well) and styled so they could be converted into evening gowns when covered in tulle. Couturiers removed any silk orange blossoms because they were solely for bridal wear. In Edith Wharton's *The Age Of Innocence,* newlywed May Archer asks her husband what to wear to a party. When he suggests her wedding gown, she replies: "If only I had it here. But it's gone to Paris to be made over for next winter."

A wedding dress did wonders for the homely and less than fashionable Queen Victoria. The newspapers heralded her grace and style, calling her wedding day her "hour of beauty" thanks to her impeccable choice of wedding attire: a rich white satin gown devoid of all the embellishments popular among the wealthy of the time and cut low (but, of course, appropriately so) with a train she carried over her arm. Her accessories consisted of a simple wreath of orange blossoms in her hair, diamond earrings, and a diamond necklace. This 1840 vision of transformation made white wedding dresses the rage and their popularity remains unabated.

The case for lace

Delicate-looking yet strong, lace is the perfect metaphor for brides. Before the industrial revolution, European lace-makers toiled in damp basements to keep fine flax fibers from drying out, painstakingly producing only a third of an inch a week. Today, although machine-made and no longer the province solely of aristocrats, fine lace can still be pricey. But even a small piece artfully incorporated into the design of a dress looks regal.

Lace comes in hundreds of patterns, weaves, and shades. Knowing the names is helpful, but in the end, go with the look and feel. See Table 3-1 and Figure 3-5 for a primer on some of the various types of lace.

Table 3-1 Popular Lace Patterns for Bridal Wear

Lace	*Description*
Alençon	Needle point. Typically in floral pattern outlined with heavy threads on a net background. *Re-embroidered Alençon* means it has been stitched over with pearls, sequins, or other trim.
Chantilly	Delicate hexagonal mesh with a scrolled and floral pattern. Scalloped edges.
Guipere	Heavy or large directional patterns. No mesh background. Often shiny and heavy. Holds its shape and form.
Point d'esprit	Fine net with oval or square dots woven in grid-like pattern.
Schiffli	Lightweight, old fashioned-looking patterns embroidered on English net, which is stronger than the net usually used for lace.
Venise	Heavy needlepoint without a net background. Usually cotton. Higher relief than Alençon, but more delicate than guipere, with which it is often confused.

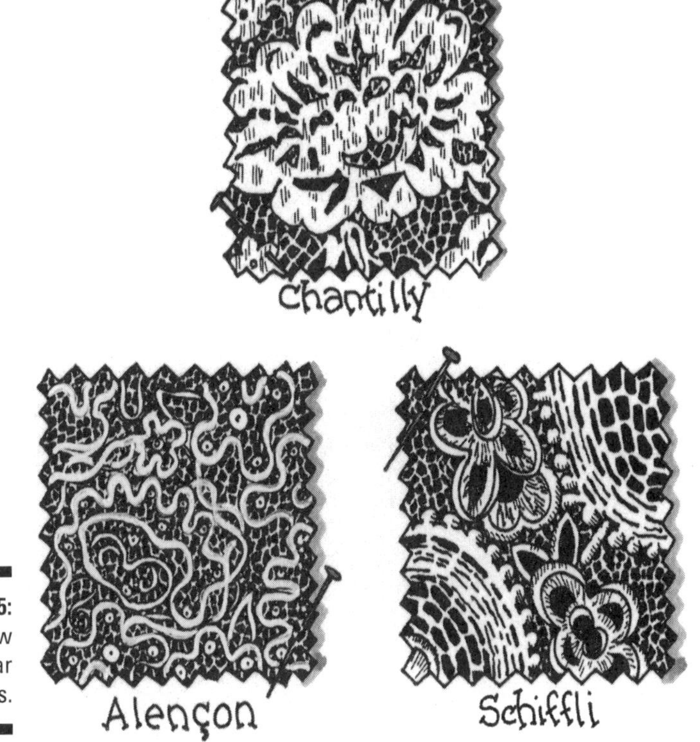

Figure 3-5: A few popular lace styles.

A piece of lace with one scalloped edge is called a *flounce.* A *galloon* is a strip of lace or embroidery with both edges scalloped or indented.

The icing on the dress

A dress gets much of its sparkle and individuality from "finishers," trims and ornaments that usually work best when applied with masterful restraint as opposed to with a shovel. These elements may include one or more of the following:

- **Appliqués:** Additions re-embroidered or sewn onto the fabric of the gown.
- **Border trims:** Braid, ribbon, ruffled, or scalloped edges.
- **Bugle beads:** Small cylindrical glass or plastic beads used for ornamentation. Beads are hand-sewn on expensive gowns, hand-glued on less expensive ones.
- **Edging:** Lace, cord, embroidered band, or silk satin that outlines a section of fabric. For example, a bodice with alternating bands of lace and satin.
- **Embroidery:** Can be sewn over illusion or other bridal fabrics in either the same or contrasting colors.
- **Fringe:** Used as an embellishment or all-over for a flapper look. Some designers bead the fringe.
- **Jewels:** One of the newest looks features an illusion back peppered with faux jewels.
- **Ribbons and bows:** Used in various sizes and lengths, from one giant butterfly bow in back to many tiny bows sprinkled over a tulle skirt, and from silk ribbon closures on a corseted gown to floor-length streamers.
- **Seed pearls:** Very small and often irregular pearls used to adorn garments, head pieces, and shoes.
- **Sequins and paillettes:** Flat, disc-shaped, plastic beads sewn on to give dresses a twinkly, modern look. Unlike sequins, paillettes jiggle.
- **Silk flowers:** Either the same color as the dress or in contrasting colors. Used to highlight a specific area such as the back or neckline, or as an all-over embellishment.

Getting the Goods

When it comes to buying a wedding dress, the lay of the land goes something like this: You try on samples at a salon. Once you find one you like, the salon takes your measurements and any other custom-order information ("substitute jewel neckline for sweetheart"), and sends the order to the manufacturer. Depending on the designer and manufacturer, your dress is both custom cut and finished to your specifications, or simply ordered in the closest size on the manufacturer's sizing chart and altered by the salon to fit. For the majority of brides this "customized" dress is the only piece of clothing they will ever own that's created solely for them.

The perfect dress for you is out there, even if it has yet to be designed and sewn. Here's where you may find it:

- **Bridal salons:** Most brides purchase their gowns at these establishments, which range from Kleinfeld to mom-and-pop bridal stores and designer-owned boutiques. Many bridal boutiques offer everything for the bridal ensemble including headpieces, shoes, and accessories. Think twice about dropping by without an appointment. In fact, you can save tons of time and undue fist clenching by scheduling your appointment during off-peak hours. The larger the store, generally the better the prices because of the store's buying power. Some couture bridal designers allow you to order your gown with myriad changes, from the neckline to the entire bodice, others allow only specific changes. In any case, the expertise of the salon's in-house alterations crew is an important factor to weigh.
- **Consignment:** If you hit the right shop on the right day, you may walk out with the dress of your dreams. Selection of sizes is obviously limited, and of course with rare exceptions, the dresses have been previously altered. On the upside: you can be pretty sure that the dress has been worn only once, if that.
- **Designer:** Some well-known private designers work with brides personally to create one-of-a kind dresses. Starting with the bride's vision, they work together to choose fabrics, create the style, and decide the detailing. The designer oversees each fitting as well as the hand-sewing and finishing. Many bridal salons may refer you to capable designers willing to create a dress from scratch. These one-of-a kind dresses vary greatly in price depending on the designer, the fabrics, and the embellishments. Aside from the obvious advantages, these dresses generally take less time to make than those from manufacturers, which produce in much greater volume per season.
- **Off-the-rack discounters or warehouses:** Designs are either samples from seasons past, overstocks by manufacturers, or knock-offs made in overseas factories. A large variety of dresses in all sizes. Prices can range from marginally less expensive to an outright steal, though the atmosphere is definitely for those on a mission to shop, not to be pampered.

See yourself as others see you

Kleinfeld, the world's largest bridal retailer, has honed wedding-gown shopping to such a science that they've invented stock characters to describe their typical customers. Who might they think you are as you walk through the door?

- **Ivana:** Fashion first, she needs to impress. She is often "ethnic royalty." Typical examples include the bride who had 820 guests and the bride who bought 10 $10,000 gowns for her bridesmaids.
- **Cinderella:** Wide-eyed, younger, pliable, princess-to-be — usually very impressionable. Has dreamed of being a princess all her life.
- **Annie Hall:** Low-key individualist. Wants something unusual.
- **Ms:** Professional, determined, in-charge, realist. Determined to be as successful as her groom. Sets aside 90 minutes to find a wedding gown, and demands an efficient and productive experience. Often conflicted between a tailored look and a romantic one.
- **Muffy:** Seeks classic elegance and tradition. Belongs to a conservative social strata that rejects change and the very latest styles. Has been bred to appreciate fine materials and quality workmanship.
- **Sis:** Seeks simplicity and shudders at ostentation. Thinks of herself as an uncomplicated gal who wants to have children right away and decorate her home with lovely little homemade touches. Impressionable and hopelessly romantic.

— Courtesy of Kleinfeld

- **Rentals:** The idea of renting a dress you wear only once may sound good, but it requires extensive research because rental stores are few and far between. The rental companies claim that bridal magazines discriminate against them, refusing to cover them or let them advertise for fear of alienating the retail trade. The magazines contend that people simply don't want to rent wedding dresses. In any case, consider what a psychic friend of ours says on the subject: "The confluence of vibes from who-knows-how-many previous wearers could send you over the edge on your wedding day."
- **Sample sales:** These sales usually consist of sample dresses from previous seasons and feature a limited range of sizes. As wedding dresses increasingly follow the fashion cycle, a dress from even six months ago may look dated, so go for a classic style. Also, because samples tend to get shopworn even in spots not readily visible, check carefully before pouncing on a bargain. You may regret buying a dress on impulse that requires extensive (and expensive) alterations.

- **Sew your own:** Making your own dress is definitely not for novices. The fabrics are dear, so if you are not a skilled seamstress, consider carefully before undertaking a project so fraught with emotion. For a preview of what you'd be getting into, we recommend the book *Bridal Couture* by Susan Khalje.
- **Tailors:** A talented tailor or seamstress may be a frustrated designer or at least skilled enough to create a pattern from a magazine photo. They make a muslin pattern, then cut the actual fabric precisely to your measurements. Creating a bridal gown is a specialty — you do not want to be the bridal guinea pig. Get references, look at photos of other dresses they have done, and be very specific about what you want.
- **Trunk shows:** Often held at bridal salons and occasionally at hotels, these shows enable you to see a designer's dresses on live models. If you purchase a dress at that time, the designers may advise and fit you personally.
- **Vintage:** If you can fit into your mother's or grandmother's dress you may want to accessorize it with period accoutrements. If the moths have turned the dress into a large lace hankie, however, you may want to find a designer who can incorporate remnants into a contemporary design. Some antiques dealers specialize in vintage dresses and accessories. Finding an antique dress can be tricky. Depending on the era, you may need a girdle or corset. Alterations are virtually impossible depending on the fabric's fragility.

Quality control

For most of us, deciphering whether a dress is *mass-produced* — cut en masse by laser and sewn with machines — or individually cut and sewn is virtually impossible. But don't get hung up on that point. Before purchasing, inspect carefully, checking the quality of the workmanship. Don't expect the quality of the dress to be much better than that of the sample. If the sample doesn't have, say, covered buttons, neither will the one you order.

Your inspection checklist should cover:

- **Fabrication:** Do naps on separate fabric panels run the same way? (You don't want one panel to look shiny and another matte.) Is the lace free of snags? Is the fabric in good shape (as opposed to being pilled or worn)? Does the dress have a lining? Can you tell exactly what the fabric is? Does the style take advantage of patterns in the lace?
- **Stains:** If the dress is off the rack, rented, or on consignment, are there any perspiration, food, or lipstick stains? Can they be removed? Is it free of glue marks?

- **Sewing:** Are seams sewn straight and smooth? Is the fabric free of tiny tell-tale holes from ripped-out stitches? Are lace patterns matched up or laid out evenly? Are the lace seams invisible? Are skirt layers sewn individually? Are the hems of heavy fabrics stitched with horsehair to make them stand out? Are seams finished with surge stitching so the inside edges won't fray? Is the seam allowance generous? Do illusion panels lie flat? Are all layers sewn separately? (If sewn all together, they may pucker.)
- **Aesthetics:** If a long row of buttons goes down the back, do they have a zipper underneath? Are cloth-covered buttons the same fabric as the dress? Is the interfacing fused to the outer layer? (It shouldn't be!) Check for loose threads on beading — one tug may undo an entire row.
- **Security:** Are beads, loops, and appliqués secure? Does the dress have extra hooks and eyes at crucial stress points? Does the zipper extend to the widest point of your hips to prevent tears? If the gown is strapless, does the bodice have boning for support?

Getting the right fit

You try on a wedding dress in your regular size and you can't get it zipped. Mismarked, you think. But several more dresses in the same size are equally snug. "Have I gained that much water weight?" you wonder. You try the next size up. Not much better. Then the next size. What's going on here? When it comes to sizing, bridal dresses follow a peculiar logic all their own. They generally run small, so don't get obsessed with the size. (It's just a number, after all). Put your ego aside and order a size larger if that's what it takes. Don't buy a smaller dress thinking you're going to lose weight before the wedding. If you've been known to go up and down when under stress (due to nerves, many brides gain or shed up to 10 or 15 pounds before a wedding) go with a larger size and have your final fitting close to your wedding day. Making tucks and darts generally works better than letting out seams, especially if the seam allowance is minimal.

Pregnant and post-partum brides are hardly novelties these days, but the bridal industry does not cater to them. Fortunately, a growing number of maternity stores carry elegant evening wear that may sometimes be adapted for weddings. Custom-made dresses are the other option. Just be sure to put off the final fitting until as close to your wedding as possible.

Plan on between two and four fittings. From your second fitting on, bring the right undergarments and shoes (see the upcoming section for more information). Your gown may need minor or major alterations. A gown that doesn't feel right as a sample most likely can never be made to feel right. The bodice should lie flat. Sleeves that have buttons or detail trim on the wrist should be shortened from the shoulder not simply turned under at the wrist. Likewise, a hem with a special finish such as detail scalloping should be shortened from the waist not the bottom.

Alterations mean just that: to alter the dress, not change it completely. If you decide sometime during this process that you hate the dress and want to change it completely, the salon may or may not be able (or willing) to work miracles.

A garment that fits correctly should not have to be tugged and yanked into place every five minutes. Bustiers can be particularly problematic, even on chesty gals.

Play "Simon Says" to find out whether you can move. Sit. Kneel. Do the Twist. Can you rotate your arms like a windmill? Does the fabric pull across your hips or bust? One small tear can lead to a major *rrrriip* and soon you'll look like a big white maypole.

When buying your gown and setting up your fitting schedule, find out ahead of time the shop's policies. Specifically, you want to know about:

- Additional charges for plus sizes, rush orders, special colors, or phone orders.
- The cancellation policy and how much of the deposit is non-refundable. Typically, you forfeit the deposit if the dress has been cut.
- Bustling charges.
- Fitting charges.
- Charges for adding extra beading or ornamentation to the headpiece.
- Whether design specs, exact color, and wedding date are all on the sales slip.

Underneath It All

Many wedding dresses require elaborate foundations to enhance the silhouette. Long-line bra-girdles with boning and underwires, push-up bras, and new high-tech girdle-slips can all play a major role in the fit of your dress.

Buy the bra and other undergarments you plan to wear under your dress before the dress's final fitting. Your everyday bra, for example, may not lift your bust in quite the same way, which can throw off the entire line and fit.

Here's what may be going on underneath your dress:

- **Brassiere:** Some designers build bras into not only strapless and low-backed dresses, but also into other designs to create a clean line. If you wear a bustier, wear a low-backed strapless bra.

No matter how much you like your body, you may find that your fantasy wedding dress needs some filling out. Some foundations provide a little cushion in the rear or in the bust. If you need to give Mother Nature an even bigger boost short of surgery, invest in a pair of gel "breasts" that slip into your bra. These breasts look so natural that on your wedding night your hubby may be disappointed (or relieved) to discover that marriage hasn't changed you *that* much.

If your dress is low-cut, sew a snap on the front and back of your bra that attaches to the dress. On a sleeveless dress, sew little catches with snaps in the straps through which you thread your bra straps. These tricks keep your bra from playing peek-a-boo.

- **Crinoline:** A stiff underskirt made of horsehair or cotton to give ball gowns fullness. Originated by the famed 19th-century fashion designer Charles Frederick Worth, who also introduced the hoop skirt and bustle.
- **Garter:** While you may feel personally titillated by wearing a garter belt and thigh-high stockings, they won't give you the smoothest line in a sheath dress and even under a ball gown they can come unsnapped during a strenuous session of "Hot, Hot, Hot!"
- **Petticoats:** Many gowns have built-in petticoats, or you can buy them separately in the same silhouettes as bridal gowns. Experiment with the number of crinolines. Even if two look perfect, add one more just to be sure. Big gowns need fuller and stiffer petticoats. Wear them for all your fittings.
- **Slip:** For a long sheath, you probably want to wear a delicious slip. New body-hugging slips act as gentle, long-line girdles, extending from waist to mid-calf. Just make sure yours doesn't ride up when you walk.
- **Stockings:** *Always* wear stockings under a wedding dress. Bare legs don't look finished somehow (unless you're getting married on a beach, but that's another story). Avoid patterned stockings. If you're wearing a sheer or close-fitted dress, the sexy garter-belt-and-thigh-high-stocking look may produce some unsightly puckers and bulges, not to mention being rather uncomfortable. Your mother may want you to wear stockings with reinforced toes, but that's a no-no with open-toed shoes. To avoid panty lines, buy either butt-friendly undies or stockings with built-in underwear. When in doubt, wear pantyhose without underwear.

No Mean Feet

Don't think that because your dress is long your shoes are invisible. They aren't. Your feet are actually seen again and again: getting in and out of the car, walking down the aisle, during the first dance. Cheap shoes cheapen your whole look. Many petite women are obsessed with high heels and being petite ourselves, we understand this. But if you must wear heels, rather than

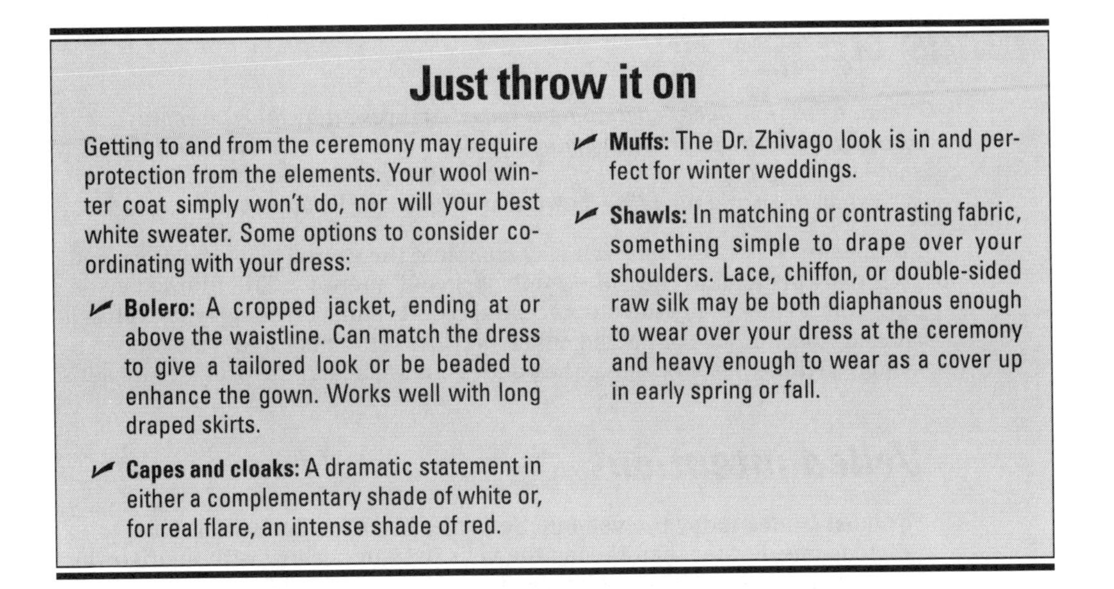

Just throw it on

Getting to and from the ceremony may require protection from the elements. Your wool winter coat simply won't do, nor will your best white sweater. Some options to consider coordinating with your dress:

- **Bolero:** A cropped jacket, ending at or above the waistline. Can match the dress to give a tailored look or be beaded to enhance the gown. Works well with long draped skirts.
- **Capes and cloaks:** A dramatic statement in either a complementary shade of white or, for real flare, an intense shade of red.
- **Muffs:** The Dr. Zhivago look is in and perfect for winter weddings.
- **Shawls:** In matching or contrasting fabric, something simple to drape over your shoulders. Lace, chiffon, or double-sided raw silk may be both diaphanous enough to wear over your dress at the ceremony and heavy enough to wear as a cover up in early spring or fall.

the usually advised pump, buy a good pair (meaning expensive) and bring ballet slippers to change into. While you may be ebullient enough to think you'll look adorable dancing barefoot, you may not like the way it looks in photos. If you're concerned about getting good use from your shoe investment, go for satin or peau de soie, which can be dyed to match your dress and redyed after the wedding.

A plain skirt calls for a pair of beautifully detailed shoes trimmed with bows, beading, or jeweled clip-ons. Ornate shoes with an ornate dress may be overkill, however. A subtle embellishment on the heel, toe, or throat (the opening in the vamp of a shoe at the instep) may be enough. The fabric on a shoe does not have to match that of the dress, and in fact mixing textures often looks better.

Only Little Bo Peep and certain Victorian-style dresses look good with lace-up granny boots. Trendy styles with exaggerated toes or heels look best with contemporary dresses. Shoes with back straps must fit perfectly — neither too tight nor a smidgen too loose. Maneuvering in your dress may be tricky enough.

Gently roughen up the soles of your shoes with sandpaper and, if necessary, a sharp kitchen knife. Also, practice walking and dancing in your wedding shoes (on a clean floor, of course) until you feel completely comfortable in them.

Heads Up

"Dear, dear! How queer everything is today! And yesterday things went on just as usual. I wonder if I've been changed in the night? Let me think: was I the same when I got up this morning? . . . But if I'm not the same, the next question is, Who in the world am I?" — Lewis Carrol, *Alice in Wonderland*

Putting on a headpiece and veil may complete the weird transformation, from your daily persona to (hear the cymbals?) your alter-ego: THE BRIDE! Perhaps this feeling is due to your ancestral blood running through your veins. In ancient Rome, brides appeared enveloped in a saffron-colored haze that symbolized the flame of Vesta, the goddess of home and the provider of life.

Veiled intentions

For most brides today the veil functions more as a fashion icon than a religious one. Rather than buying the veils designers show with their gowns, many brides order customized veils. Length (shown in Figure 3-6), number of layers, trim, fabric, and shade are all dictated by the style and mood of your dress and should be in proportion to your entire silhouette. Among the options:

- **Angel:** Long, straight veil cut wide at the sides like angel wings.
- **Ballerina:** Ends just above the floor. Also called *waltz.*
- **Birdcage:** Falls to just below the chin, covering the face. Often worn attached to a small hat.
- **Blusher:** A short veil that covers the bride's face as she enters the ceremony.

  Strict etiquette mavens consider veils, particularly blushers, inappropriate for second-time or pregnant brides. On the other hand, some people object to a veil's other connotation: the handing over of the woman to a man. Gender politics aside, a blusher can serve a practical purpose, protecting you from inquisitive stares as you walk, trembling, down the aisle.

- **Butterfly:** Oval-shaped and folded in half. Ribbon edging follows a crescent shape rather than a straight line.
- **Cascade:** Two or more layers of various lengths. Some layers can be removed. Can do double duty as a blusher. Bottom layer(s) can act as "petticoat(s)", fluffing out top veil. Too many layers can look opaque, effectively turning the bride into the invisible woman. This veil is old-fashioned looking compared to a blunt cut.
- **Cathedral:** Falls $3^1/_2$ yards from the headpiece.
- **Chapel:** A yard shorter than a cathedral veil. Often worn with a sweep train to give the illusion of a longer train.

- **Elbow:** A blusher that goes to your elbows.
- **Fingertip:** Extends to your knee — only kidding. The veil touches the tips of your fingers, a length that often works with ball gowns and is therefore one of the most popular.
- **Flyaway:** Touches or just covers shoulders. Sometimes called a Madonna veil.
- **Mantilla:** A long, Spanish-style, circular piece of lace that frames the face. Can be attached to a high metal armature and is usually secured with a comb. The fabric is either lace or lace-edged tulle. Sew clear plastic snaps on both your mantilla and the shoulders of your dress to keep the fabric draped gracefully.
- **Snood:** Netting that holds hair at the nape of the neck.

If your dress is ornate, wear a plain veil. A simple dress, however, can take either a plain or ornate veil. Any ornamentation on the veil, such as flowers or crystals, should start below where your dress ornamentation ends. Decoration on a cathedral veil, for example, should cover only the bottom third. Crystals reflect light and usually photograph better than rhinestones, which can look like black dots. Ribbon trim may look better than unfinished tulle, but depending on the length of your veil, a ribbon could create a horizontal line across your middle, effectively stopping the eye and making you look shorter.

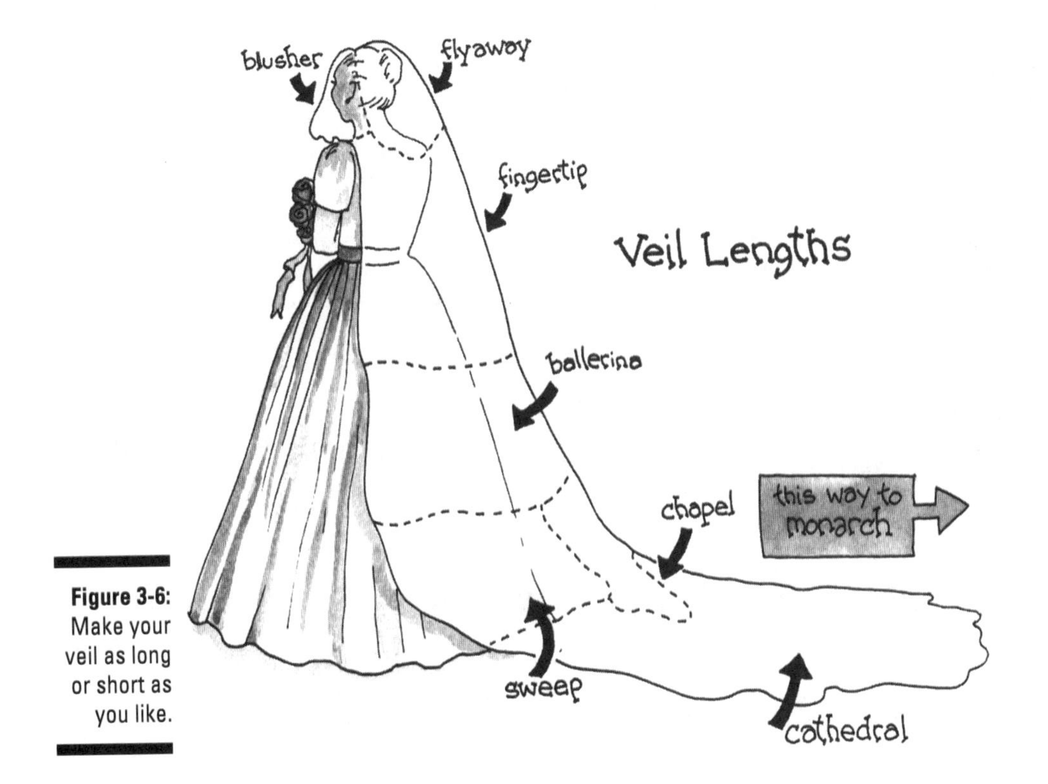

Figure 3-6: Make your veil as long or short as you like.

Lifting the veil on the past

By the fourth century, as the Anglo-Saxons grew more civilized, grooms changed their *modus operandi* from capturing brides to actually purchasing them by paying a "wedd." Weddings, were then conducted behind a "care cloth" reminiscent of the Jewish chuppah. This action was intended to protect the bride from the envious leers of those who had not yet purchased a bride of their very own, as well as from the evil spirits, who as usual, were thought to be after the bride. Because ceremonies consisted of rowdy secular parties, lifting this cloth symbolized the bride's completing the journey from her father's house and taking on the role of a married woman. This custom is thought to be the genesis of the blusher both acting as a shield as the bride approaches the altar and being lifted for good after the ceremony.

A poufy veil or headpiece does not necessarily make you look taller. In fact, if you're short, a super poufy veil can make you look like a mushroom. Many women are opting for narrow-cut veils, which create a vertical line. Remember, your head is not flat. (At least we hope not.) Examine a veil from all angles, preferably while you're trying on your dress. One that suits you from the back may not flatter your face or vice versa.

If you're lucky enough to have lace from your mother and/or grandmother's wedding dress, you can use it to create a new veil. Avoid making the mistake of trying to dye an antique veil. Its appeal lies in its uniqueness and should not match the dress exactly. Likewise, on a new veil, the seed pearls, sequins, or other adornments don't need to match those on your dress. All the elements should merely complement each other.

Japanese brides wear a white cloth called a *wataboushi* to cover their faces and another white cloth called a *tsunokakushi* to cover the "jealous horns" on their head. Both "veils" are removed during the traditional Shinto ceremony.

Chinese brides wear an ornate headdress of gilded silver inlaid with kingfisher feathers and pearls called a *phoenix crown* (golden phoenixes are the symbol of brides). Their faces are covered with layers upon layers of red silk during the ceremony to protect them as they are thought to be at their most vulnerable during this time when they are in transition between their parents' house and the groom's family home.

Hats, headpieces, crowns, and doodads

A *headpiece*, another of those great wed-speak terms, is what a bride wears on her head. Worn either alone or as an anchor for the veil(s), it is an integral part of the ensemble and can be the finishing touch that makes for perfection.

Whether your headpiece is off-the-rack or custom-made, consider its color, design, and ornamentation in relation to your entire wedding ensemble. Bring along a swatch and photo of your dress, accessories you intend to wear, and even photos of the bouquet you have in mind to help figure out the right kind of headpiece. The trend has been toward smaller headpieces, which complement the narrow veils. In fact, Tia Mazza, a milliner for Saks Fifth Avenue and Kleinfeld, tells us that the most popular headpieces of late are extremely subtle half-headbands.

The key to finding what's best for you is to try on as many variations of the basic styles:

- **Cloche:** A small helmet-like cap, usually with a deep rounded crown and narrow brim. Netting can be attached to create a pouf, a cloud, or an eye veil.
- **Hat:** These can be in any variety of styles and sizes — large-brimmed hats trimmed with lace, flowers, and/or pearls; pillboxes; or wispy little cocktail concoctions.

  Many African-American brides reflect their heritage through their headwear, from Nefertiti-style hats to caps covered in Kwanza fabric. Goddess Queen N'zinga braids, wound around the top of the head, are sometimes worn in lieu of a headpiece.
- **Headbands:** Various widths that follow the shape of the skull and are decorated with fabric, seed pearls, and flowers. They can serve as the base for saucer-styled tulle in lieu of a veil.
- **Juliet cap:** Often made of elaborately decorated mesh. A larger version is called a *skullcap.*
- **Profile:** A comb decorated with sprays, pearls, or sequins and worn asymmetrically on one side or at the nape of the neck.

Caveat emptor

An Orthodox Jewish tradition that has been adopted by many secular Jews is the *badeken,* a Yiddish term for *covering up,* which, historically is attributed to one of two events. The first is the story of Jacob, who, expecting to find Rachel when he unveiled his bride, discovered he had been duped into marrying her older sister, Leah. In the second tale, Rebekah was of such extraordinary modesty that she covered herself with her veil when she first saw Isaac, her husband to be. During the *badeken,* the bride is surrounded by female friends and relatives and sits in a throne-like chair decorated with flowers. The groom, attended by his male friends and relatives, "inspects" the bride to make sure he has the right one before lowering the veil. As the groom lowers the veil, he (or the Rabbi) recites a Biblical blessing, welcoming her as a bride who will be like the matriarchs: Sarah, Rebecca, Rachel, and Leah.

The turning point

Soon after my dress was finished, I visited New York milliner Susan van der Linde. Because my dress was so simple — a sleeveless Empire silhouette made of Chantilly lace and several layers of delicious silk chiffon — I wasn't sure I wanted to wear anything on my head, and certainly nothing as paternalistic as a veil. Little did I realize that like so many things in planning my wedding, I was about to throw these preconceptions out the window. Susan took one look at my dress and plucked a darling little cocktail hat from her display. There was hardly anything to the hat: It looked like two inverted commas perched asymmetrically on my head. She draped some tulle netting around my face like a cumulus cloud. Peering in the mirror, I almost didn't recognize myself. Suddenly I could see who I was: a bride who would be walking — or floating — toward her future husband. I felt transformed.

Susan made me a version of the cocktail hat using leftover scraps from my dress, which my designer, Terence Teng, had thoughtfully saved. She actually made two veils, a blusher that formed an architectural frame around my head, and a ballerina-length veil that billowed out behind me. I wore them throughout my reception, and took them off only with great reluctance before I went to bed, sad that I would never have another opportunity to wear these special veils.

- **Tiara:** The key accessory for playing Queen for a Day. Extremely popular of late.

  In Orthodox Eastern and Byzantine Catholic ceremonies, the most solemn moment is the "crowning" of the bride and groom when metal crowns or floral wreaths are held over their heads. This part of the ceremony symbolizes that they are king and queen of a heavenly kingdom on earth.

- **Wreaths, garlands, and circlets:** Composed of flowers, twigs, and/or ribbon. The maker needs your exact cranium measurement. A romantic, organic look with a couple of drawbacks: By the end of the day, a flower wreath can feel like the world's heaviest doughnut on your head, and in photographs twig wreaths can make you look like you've sprouted antennae.

How to secure a headpiece

Whereas multiple veils that are removed at various times during the wedding are often attached with Velcro to the headpiece, the blusher is usually not attached to the headpiece but rather pinned to your hair. Attaching the actual headpiece to your head is somewhat more complicated. Inside some headpieces are rows of fabric or horsehair braid loops through which you thread bobby pins. Or you can attach an elastic string to the headpiece behind your ears and under your hair.

Use white bobby pins even if you have dark hair so they blend in with the headpiece or veil.

As you can see in Figure 3-7, when attaching a headpiece with combs, you need to give the teeth something to "bite" into, especially if you have fine hair.

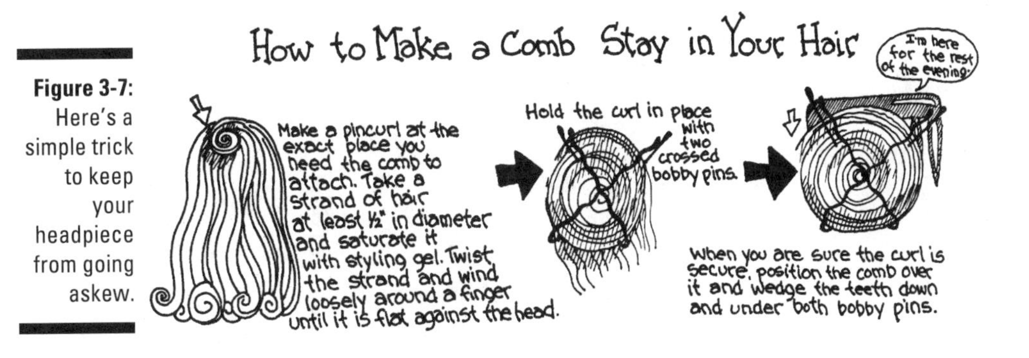

Figure 3-7: Here's a simple trick to keep your headpiece from going askew.

From Hair to Eternity

Brides wilt, even in sub-zero weather. Start the day with your hair a little higher, wider, and more done than you're accustomed to. By the time you get to the reception, you will be lucky if it looks teased at all. But remember that people are less interested in seeing your new cutting-edge hairdo than your face.

Imagine a picture frame extending from the neckline of your gown to several inches above your head. A big elaborate headpiece on top of a big elaborate hairdo may look like you're modeling the wedding cake.

If you do want to do something special with your hair, once you've chosen your dress and headpiece, take a trip to your hairdresser to experiment. Give yourself enough lead time in case you decide to add highlights or let your bangs grow out for the wedding. Also think about whether you're removing any or all of your headpiece and veil(s) after the ceremony, letting down your hair, or changing clothes entirely. Some people opt to have a hairdresser on site to do touch-ups after the ceremony.

Insist on smelling and feeling anything that's put in your hair. You don't want products that clash with your perfume or stick to anyone's face while you're dancing.

TIP

Spills, splits, and other sartorial snafus

Although the term *bridal emergency* may seem redundant, you will breathe easier knowing you are prepared to face any fiasco that may befall you or your dress. If you are getting dressed at your ceremony/reception space such as a hotel or loft, or even if you are having a cozy home wedding, gather the following items together in one place. Use a gym bag or other large tote, preferably one with compartments that you can mark using masking tape and a pen. You will be frenzied enough without having to dump everything out in a big pile. Here's what goes in all those compartments:

- A sewing kit, including quality thread in white and ecru or whatever other colors are relevant (such as the color of the bridesmaids dresses and the men's attire)
- Smelling salts
- White chalk (a savior for lipstick on a wedding dress or shirt collar)
- Studs, cufflinks, and one or two bow ties (don't ask)
- Bobby pins, safety pins, straight pins, hair pins, extra boutonniere pins (you just can't have too many pins!)
- Make-up for touch-ups
- Ballet slippers for dancing
- Not one but two extra pairs of stockings
- Brush, hairspray, comb
- Blow dryer (less for hair-dos than anything else that gets soaked)
- Toothbrush, toothpaste, mouthwash, and dental floss
- Clear nail polish, nail glue, and emory board
- Tweezers and crochet hook (to get at button hooks and other teeny places)
- Aspirin
- Sedatives
- Straws — for a quick drink without messing up lipstick
- Tampons and sanitary napkins
- Earring backs
- Masking tape for ripped hems
- Extra copies of schedule and directions to the reception (see Chapter 18)
- Antacid

If you have fine hair and plan on wearing your hair in a chignon, you may want to wash your hair the day before, rather than the day of, the wedding to give it more oomph. Otherwise your sleek knot may slip out.

Hair today . . .

Your classic pageboy cut is fine for business, but your wedding vision features you with flowing tresses that rival Rapunzel's. If you don't have time (or patience) to grow your locks, fake it. Many salons specialize in hair extensions and falls, often made with real hair, that look and feel natural.

. . . Gone tomorrow

If your dress is sleeveless and you have dark hair on your arms, you may consider waxing, which many women find more satisfactory than depilatories or shaving. While the process doesn't tickle, it's not torture either. Many salons offer European-style cold waxing, which is less painful. Other areas that may benefit from a treatment are your underarms, legs, bikini line, upper lip, and eyebrows.

Although the effects of waxing last longer than those of shaving, schedule it a few days before your wedding so you're as smooth as a seal. Make sure your little hairs are at least a quarter-inch long so the wax can grab onto them.

Making Your Face Wedding-Proof

Although you want to look special on your wedding, deviating too much from your routine is asking for trouble. We would hate to see your groom shaking his head in panicked confusion as a white-clad someone who looks only vaguely familiar marches toward him down the aisle. If you want a slightly different look, rehearse your makeup as you would the ceremony, but do so well in advance, not the day before. Your wedding day is not the time to try out anything new such as contact lenses, acrylic nail tips, or perfumes. Because of the healing time required, schedule acid peels at least two months before your wedding, and facials, sunless tanners, and vigorous loofah scrubs at least a week before. Unless you want to look in your photos like you had just stepped out of Mme. Toussaud's, avoid trendy makeup techniques such as heavy black eyeliner or white lipstick. Stick with timeless, neutral colors, but be careful about using colors that are too subtle because you may looked washed out. New York makeup artist Maria Verel always reminds clients that as the day progresses they can add more makeup, but trying to take off only a little is not easy. Go for a softer approach in daylight and touch it up for night.

We asked several of New York's best makeup artists for their tips in putting your best wedding-day face forward. Their advice:

- **Blemishes:** If you get a blemish right before the wedding, try to find an all-night dermatologist. If one is not available, paint the area with camouflage cream using a thin eyeliner brush before applying foundation. Attempting to pick or squeeze the problem away only makes it worse.
- **Cheeks:** For the blushing bride look, use rosy hues and blend well.

- **Eyes:** To make the whites of your eyes crystal clear, use white or blue pencil on the inside of the lower lid. (If your eyes are sensitive, however, they may try to flush out the liner, making for unsightly globs in your tear ducts.) Grays, taupes, and smoky colors as well as charcoal liners on the eyelids usually photograph well. Laura Geller, a New York makeup artist who specializes in brides and their attendants, advises that before you apply mascara, use a colorless lash thickener rather than a mascara that contains fibers.
- **Foundation:** Blend well for a minimum makeup look. Use feather strokes toward the bottom of the face to avoid a demarcation line.
- **Lips:** Use a lip liner and lip sealer so color doesn't bleed, cake, or peel. Red lipstick works best for dark skin and olive complexions. Otherwise, unless it's your signature look, use soft pastels. Matte lipsticks last longer. Either use a silicone-based lipstick or apply your normal lipstick, blot it thoroughly, and color over your lips with a pencil. Lip gloss is a magnet for hair, veils, gnats, and other people. Save it for after the ceremony and before photographs.
- **Skin tone:** To get an even skin tone all over your body, avoid tanning beds, sunless tanning lotions (which can turn your skin, eyebrows, and hair orange), and body makeup. For problem spots — scars, brown spots, discolorations — inquire at a good makeup counter about waterproof camouflage creams such as Dermablend. If you tend to get blotchy or break out in hives, use a benadryl cream on the affected area.

Finishing Touches

After devoting so much time and energy to getting your dress and head gear under control, accessories may seem like an afterthought, but they shouldn't look like it. Try different combinations of jewelry and gloves until you get the right balance.

Hand-some gloves

If you feel perplexed when you look in the mirror, like something is missing, the right pair of gloves may do the trick. Generally, you wear short gloves with long sleeves and long gloves with short-sleeved or sleeveless dresses. The style, fabric, and texture should complement the dress. Kid leather is considered the dressiest, but satin spandex, crushed velvet, and sheer organza can look ultra elegant. The fabric should be matte; shiny looks chintzy and will bring undue attention to your hands and arms.

A make-up rehearsal

Wanting to look ravishing but recognizable on my wedding day, I called New York makeup artist Maria Verel. As an editor, I had worked with Maria on magazine photo shoots and was familiar with her work in helping people such as Diane Sawyer, Emmylou Harris, and Anna Deavere Smith look their most gorgeous. There was just one catch: My wedding was out of state and Maria's day rate was out of this world. I decided to do the next best thing — schedule a dry run with her, and have my matron of honor, Marcia, learn how to recreate Maria's method — or paint my face by numbers, so to speak.

A month before my wedding, Maria spread her tubes and brushes over my dining table and sat me under a halogen lamp. (Daylight is actually the best light for applying makeup without garish results; the halogen was simply the brightest light we could muster in my apartment.) I had already neglected to follow Maria's first piece of advice and collect a bunch of magazine pictures of what I wanted (or didn't want) to look like. Luckily, she is stylistically clairvoyant. After I showed her my dress, headpiece, and veil, she had a precise idea of the direction to go in.

Finally we got down to business. The first step was to pick a foundation and concealer to match my skin tone. Actually, she said, the color should match my *neck* so there's no demarcation line. Over this she put a light dusting of loose translucent powder. "Makeup can harbor bacteria, so you might spring for some new things," Maria said tactfully, eyeing my pathetic collection of half-empty tubes and jars. "While you're at it, treat yourself to a good set of brushes. They're worth it because they will last a lifetime." Using one of her own silky large brushes, she applied a soft pinkish blush, blending carefully to create a glow with no visible lines. Next came eyebrow pencil, using light feathery strokes to give me a more defined arch. A matching brow powder applied finished the effect perfectly.

My eyes themselves were a production. In lieu of eyelid foundation, which can crease, she brushed them with shell-pink powder as a base, followed by an espresso powder shadow for definition. She outlined the lashes with a dark taupe pencil on top and a light taupe on the bottom.

Then the piéce de resistance: false eyelashes, or at least little clusters of lashes, which can be bought at any drugstore. First I curled my lashes myself with an eyelash curler. Then Maria put a dollop of Duo, a liquid surgical adhesive, on the back of her hand. When the adhesive was slightly tacky, she grabbed a cluster with tweezers, dabbed it in the adhesive, and stuck it right at the hairline of my natural lashes, toward the outer corner of my eye. Marcia, a truly courageous friend, tried applying one. The first attempt went missing in action until several hours later when Michael, my fiancé, spotted it on my back and tried to end its life with a rolled-up newspaper. Attempt number two was only slightly better, but by three she was golden. Maria applied waterproof mascara, blended my eye shadow, and added a frosted bronze powder highlighter on my brow bone with a medium brush. As with many of the techniques, Marcia, being a proper Southern belle, was already quite adept at liquid brown eyeliner, the finishing touch for my to-die-for eyes.

(continued)

(continued)

For my lips Maria mixed two inexpensive lipsticks in tawny and nude shades, that together became a magical color for me, and outlined my lips in an equally neutral shade so that I looked eminently kissable.

Finally, Maria had one more piece of advice: I should wear my makeup in situations where I'm stressed, sweating, and even crying. She suggested I wear it to the gym, all the while imagining everything that can go wrong at the wedding, then complete the evening by renting a tear-jerker movie. If I didn't end up looking like a Picasso, this alter ego would survive the wedding.

Glove lengths are expressed by the number of buttons they have (or would have). A one-button glove is wrist length. Two-, four-, six-, and eight- button gloves all end between the wrist and elbow. The longest is a 16-button glove, which ends above the elbow. In addition to knowing the glove length, you must know your glove size, which generally corresponds to your dress size. Stretchy gloves come in small-medium-large sizes.

Gloves can have jeweled cuffs or iridescent sequins, tiny pearls, or beads down the length of the arm. Do the squint test with the gloves on and let your arms hang down to make sure that the ends don't form a horizontal line that cuts you or the gown in an unflattering place. To soften a hard edge, sew a lace flounce, small silk flowers, or bows at the hem.

Somehow your ring finger needs to be exposed during the ceremony. You can go with fingerless gloves or make a slit along the seam of the ring finger. In the latter, you slide your finger out and tuck the loose glove finger inside the palm so it's not left dangling. Or you may remove the gloves altogether. This procedure should look like neither a strip tease nor a tug o' war. Practice removing your gloves before the ceremony by gently tugging on each finger of the left hand and sliding off the glove right side out. (You may remove only one glove, but you'll want to put it back on before the recessional unless you're Michael Jackson.) Hand the gloves, along with your bouquet, to your maid of honor. After you exchange vows, your attendant hands back your gloves and you carry them as you leave. And when you eat, daintily remove your gloves. You don't want to turn them into five-fingered napkins.

A *mousquetaire* is a long elbow-length or over-the-elbow glove with a buttoned opening at the inside of the wrist. When you are exchanging rings during the ceremony, you unbutton the left glove, slip your hand through the opening, and tuck the hand portion of the glove inside the rest of the glove. Later you can do the same thing with both hands for eating, shaking hands, or simply cooling off during the reception. Victorian women invented this neat trick (of course) since they spent half their lives in gloves.

Gloves or no gloves, get your nails in tip-top shape. Get regular manicures (and pedicures) for several weeks before the wedding. On your wedding day, consider springing for a manicurist to make a housecall. Painting your nails the night before can result in sheet prints and gives you all the more time to mar the lacquer.

All that glitters

Opinions about jewelry are as varied as wedding dresses themselves. An off-the-shoulder gown might look best with no embellishment. Pearls are the bridal favorite, and it may be touching to wear your mother's, but unless they're the perfect length for the neckline of your dress, they may take away from, not add to, the effect.

Many brides are now choosing to wear funkier jewelry than in the past. Beautiful faux jewel earrings or a chunky necklace may set off a gown beautifully, particularly in white gold or silver. Proportion is the key. Bracelets are overkill with gloves and may detract from your hands, which play such an important role in the ceremony.

As you decide what's right for you, consider the opinion of Monica Hickey, director of The Wedding Dress at Saks: "Brides shouldn't wear necklaces — they should show off their young, beautiful necks. And they should never *ever* wear a watch to their wedding. Time should fly when you are having fun."

After Chinese-American brides make their final costume change — usually into a Western-style outfit — during the reception, they are also expected to show off their "dowry" by piling on all the jewelry they own. This custom may explain why some families now hire security guards for weddings.

Hindu brides wear saris threaded with gold and silver and drape themselves in an abundance of jewelry belonging to her family or given by the groom. If the bride is still not sufficiently ornamented, the family rents more jewelry.

Bagging it

When it comes to bags, the best advice is to get a good night's sleep — oops, wrong page! Seriously, even if you normally need a tractor trailer to transport your daily necessities, the exquisite hand bag that accompanies your raiment can accommodate only a minimum of survival tools — lipstick, powder, breath mints, mascara, handkerchief. Stow bigger, bulkier items (hairbrushes, hairspray, hair dryers) in the bathroom or your dressing room.

This miniature purse does not make the trip with you down the aisle. In fact, you don't wear it at all. Arrange for someone to hang on to it during the ceremony and leave it on your seat at the reception.

After the Party

While you're away on your honeymoon, have someone take your gown to the cleaners and point out all the spots, such as sugar stains, needing special treatment. Some people suggest waiting a week because stains such as champagne don't show up for a few days. Some cleaners specialize in cleaning wedding dresses and you should use one of these. The best use clean fluid and do each dress individually.

Specify how you want the dress packed and inspect it when you get it back. The dress should be wrapped in acid-free tissue and stored in an acid-free box that is not airtight because natural fibers need to breathe. If the box has a window, it should be acetate (which is acid-free) not plastic. Store the headpiece separately; metal parts can rust or turn a dress brown. You may store both the dress and veil without a box in a clean white or muslin sheet in a dry, dark place. Caution: A basement may be too damp and an attic too hot. Wherever you store the dress, check it every year in case stains such as mildew start to develop.

Part II

"I Now Pronounce You . . ."

"Just play something light and airy until the other musicians show up."

In this part . . .

The day of your wedding should be as perfect as possible — after all, you've been planning for (what seems like) an eternity. The chapters in this part help you to choose your wedding party and understand the ins and outs of the ceremony. We even include a chapter that looks into some alternative ways to approach The Big Day.

Chapter 4
A Circle of Friends

In This Chapter

- Choosing supporting players
- Conducting yourselves becomingly
- Finding sartorial strategies for the wedding party

The wedding starts in one hour. As the bride struggles into her petticoat, she puts the heel of her shoe through the lace and topples over. Laying there helplessly in a heap, she gazes up to see two sour-faced women with their arms crossed glaring at each other. "When is someone coming to do my hair?" one of them wails. "Well," the other fumes, "if Muffy would get out of the bathroom I could at least pluck my eyebrows." The bride looks about for her maid of honor to act as referee. She's glued to the mirror in a fit of self loathing. "I want to *burn* this dress," she snarls.

Across town in his apartment, the groom and his best man pace, looking at their watches. The doorbell rings; one of the ushers has arrived. "Sorry about the tux, man," he mutters as he sees the groom's eyes cross. "It fit perfectly at the prom." As the other gentlemen arrive, one later than the next, a somewhat pathetic display of men's formal fashion parades across the living room. The best man is bewildered — he had, after all, painstakingly outlined the group uniform. The groom, meanwhile, is knocking down his third scotch, wondering how such a great group of guys — his buddies! — could be so utterly clueless. Is this a case of subliminal sabotage or mere apathy?

They may be your siblings or cousins or best friends. But that does not make them suited for wedding duty. To prevent major wigouts, screen your attendants with care, and once they're anointed, brief them clearly but lovingly of your expectations. Whatever you do, don't let your evil pre-wedding persona give them just cause to gang up on you.

Choosing Your Entourage

As you decide how many and what kind of attendants to have in your wedding party, think through what you expect them to do. (To figure out where they all go in the processional, see Chapter 5.) Ideally, attendants perform duties to get the wedding off the ground and keep *you* grounded:

- **Maid (or matron, if married) of honor:** Head cheerleader, sounding board, therapist, saint, gofer (on occasion), and actress, pretending to care about the marital minutiae as much as the bride does. May serve as a fashion consultant for bride and attendants' garb, and as the schoolmarm, keeping other attendants in line. Responsible for throwing a bridal shower and for subtly and gracefully getting the word out as to where the couple is registered. Sees to it that the bride is properly corseted, zipped, buttoned, powdered, and primped on her wedding day. May throw a wedding shower and/or dream up a special group gift for the bride (in addition to her own gift to the couple). Holds the groom's ring (if it's a double-ring ceremony) and bride's bouquet and/or gloves during the ceremony. Signs the marriage license as an official witness. Offers a toast to the couple at the reception. She is also responsible at the ceremony for making sure all the female attendants look dazzling, receive the appropriate flowers, stand gracefully, and don't torment the bride.

  It used to be that if you had both a maid and a matron of honor, the maid took precedence, standing closer to you at the altar and handling more responsibilities. Now, however, if you have both, they may split up the job. For example, one may hold your bouquet, the other the ring.

  Remember that not every married woman loves the connotations of the word *matron.* Many brides have redubbed their honor attendants "best woman" or "best person." Which brings us to another point: The person who stands up for you does not have to be the same sex as you. If you're a bride whose best friend is a guy, make him your best person. Likewise, if you're a groom whose best pal is a woman, appoint her to the job.

- **Best man:** A master at strong yet subtle emotional support because most men are not skilled at asking for it. Telepathy is a good quality. So is punctuality: If the groom arrives late with a crooked tie, the best man takes the heat. Arranges the bachelor party. Selects a gift for the groom from all the ushers. (Also buys his own gift for the couple.) Oversees the ushers if there's no head usher, making sure they are appropriately dressed as well as gentlemanly. Holds the bride's ring at the ceremony. Quietly slips the fee into the clergyman's hand after the ceremony. Signs marriage license as a witness. Makes a stirring toast at the reception.

- **Bridesmaid:** Is the epitome of charm at wedding and prewedding events. May collaborate with maid of honor and other bridesmaids in planning a shower. Should make all complaints about the dress and its cost before purchase. May not apply lipstick at the altar. In theory, is on call for anything the bride needs, particularly in the realm of emotional support. In reality, may be too far out of the loop to be effective.

- **Groomsman or usher:** In most parts of the U.S. the terms are interchangable. Acts jovial and comedic but not raunchy at the bachelor party. Takes ushering duties seriously enough to refrain from downing scotches until after the photographs. Possesses a photographic memory, able to match names, or at least ceremony seat assignments, with faces he's met only once before. A human compass, escorting guests to their seats and directing them to parking lots, bathrooms, dining rooms, and so on. A good ratio is one usher per 50 guests. Two ushers unfurl the runner down the aisle right before the ceremony begins.

In many areas, ushers and groomsmen have distinctly different roles. Ushers arrive 45 minutes before the ceremony, assist in seating guests, and then sit down before the ceremony begins. Groomsmen stay with the groom, much as the bridesmaids traditionally stay with the bride, and make their entrance as they walk down the aisle and take their places at the front of the ceremony.

- **Head usher:** Rounds up the other ushers and gets them to the ceremony on time, dressed appropriately and looking dapper. May escort one or both mothers to their seats during the ceremony.
- **Flower girl:** Looks adorable. Old enough to make it to the end of the aisle without Mommy or Daddy on their knees pleading in a stage whisper for her to keep moving. Chosen because the couple is inordinately fond of her and/or her parents, not because she looks like a Laura Ashley model. Scatters petals or carries a basket, tussy mussy, or wreath (see Chapter 11 for floral details). Smiles sweetly all the way.
- **Ring bearer:** Like the flower girl, must look precious but be mature enough to complete his journey down the aisle without bursting into tears or taking a detour in mid-procession. Carries a pillow with the ring(s) tied on. Looks adorable in short pants with white socks and shoes, but can also wear long pants that coordinate with (but not look like a doll-sized version of) the groomsmen's attire.
- **Pages and/or train bearers:** Usually work in pairs. Are an absurd pretension unless the bride is wearing a train long enough to warrant help. Keeps cathedral trains from dragging on the ground or going awry. Should be old enough to look poised and in control of a heavy train, not as if the processional is a white-knuckle wedding ride at Disney World.

- **Junior bridesmaids and ushers:** The default category for youngsters (meaning anywhere between 7 and 15) who are no longer cute enough to serve as flower girls and ring boys but not yet grown up enough to be full-fledged attendants. Like their adult counterparts, they walk down the aisle and act charming. However, girls wear dresses that are similar to but less sophisticated than those of older bridesmaids, and boys wear tuxedos or suits.

Making the cut

The average wedding in the United States has two to six bridesmaids and ushers in addition to a maid of honor and best man. Unless you're choreographing your wedding to look like a halftime show (which is certainly your prerogative), you don't need a cast of thousands fanning out from the altar. Many people have trouble narrowing down the field, feeling that if they ask one friend or sibling, they must ask another, and so on. Don't feel that because you were an usher or a bridesmaid at someone's wedding ten years ago, you need to reciprocate the honor. People understand that relationships change. In a seemingly impossible dilemma, some possible solutions: Ask your mother or father to be your best person, have your wedding party comprised only of children (as done in England and France), or appoint only siblings.

When it comes to assigning other roles to make people feel a special part of your wedding, asking someone to deliver a poem, sing a song, or be one of the chuppah pole bearers is truly an honor. But asking someone to hold the guest book, hand out escort cards, double-check the seating chart, or some other "plum" assignment may seem like you're attempting to come up with something to keep them from feeling left out.

Prenuptial agreements with your friends

Just as the attendants exist to make your life easier, you must behave with all the grace and magnanimity toward them that you can muster during this anxious time. In the same way you and your intended wisely chose each other for your wondrous points and in spite of the downsides, don't choose your attendants thinking you can change them. Remember that they are not indentured servants or workers for hire who can be dismissed because they fail to love (or look stunning in) the mauve leg-o'-mutton-sleeved frock or lemon yellow Nehru dinner jacket you've picked out for them. Compromising on the attendant's costume is just one example of gracious pre-wedding deportment.

Next Stop: Wardrobe

The wedding clone concept dates back to fifth-century Britain, when bridesmaids and groomsmen, exhibiting amazing loyalty, dressed identically to the bride and groom to fool evil spirits that might harass the happy couple on their way to be joined. (Evil spirits being rather near-sighted, apparently.) Somehow, over seventeen centuries, the original concept has become a little mixed up. Female attendants now dress to look like each other (yet not enough like the bride to fool even the dimmest evil spirit), and the male attendants dress to approximate the groom. (For details regarding the dress at military weddings, see Chapter 16.)

Where did all these people come from?

Bridesmaids and bridegroomsmen (now usually called groomsmen or ushers) have been around as long as there have been brides and grooms. In ancient Greece, a group of women, composed of those who were both happily married and experienced in the wonders of motherhood, accompanied brides to their weddings. Their good fortune was supposed to rub off on the bride and the group was intended to shield her from evil between the house of her father and that of her husband. The entire procession was preceded by children — predecessors to modern-day flower girls — who tossed out grains and old herbs in reverence to the gods who would, hopefully, in return ensure the bride's fertility.

In Anglo-Saxon times, the forerunners of groomsmen helped their friends carry off maidens for marriage, occasionally managing to ensnare an extra one for themselves. Consequently, the maidens banded together when traveling, to avoid capture. Eventually, groomsmen evolved into the escort the groom sent for his new bride; these sterling young men were known as *brides-knights.*

In Elizabethan times, the bride's attendants — unmarried maidens without the responsibilities of husbands and families — spent months weaving garlands and fashioning favors for their friend's up-coming nuptials. During the three-day wedding feast, they attended to the bride. By the Victorian era, bridal attendants were occupied for months with shopping and sewing for the trousseau. The bride thanked these attendants by outfitting them in gowns as extravagant as her own wedding dress. In fact, women vied for the honor of attending a bride, hoping that being seen in public looking ravishing and loyal would impress a young man enough to consider her for his bride.

As the bride and groom, dictating any aspect of each other's wedding garb is not the best strategy for pre-marital harmony. You should be in sync, however, for the big picture. Your attendants and parents then take their cue from your outfits.

Hell's freezing and pigs are flying: bridesmaids' dresses are getting stylish

One approach for bridesmaids' dresses is to choose something that has more style than workmanship and is very cheap — something that at a distance could even pass for a far more expensive outfit. No tears, therefore, are shed when it disintegrates by the end of the reception. Your second choice — one that is increasingly easy to do — is to outfit your bridesmaids in dresses that can enter the witness protection program after the wedding so no one ever suspects their nuptial past. Several designers such as Cynthia Rowley, Heidi Weisel, and Nicole Miller have embarked on a mission to rid the world of bridesmaid dresses that can double as tablecloths for a prom; and companies such as Dessy Creations and Watters & Watters, which have manufactured bridesmaid dresses for eons, have changed their style direction as well.

"I thought you were paying for this"

When you ask people to be in your wedding, they're often flattered and honored — until they find out what it's costing them. Admittedly, some tours of duty are more expensive than others, so either be sensitive about asking those who can't afford to be an attendant or be prepared to defray (or pick up entirely) the cost for them. Whatever you decide, the time to explain the expenses and who is responsible for them is when you do the asking. The items that most often produce misunderstandings are:

- **Appropriate clothing:** Traditionally, attendants are responsible for buying or renting their clothes, but sometimes you may buy a particular item as a gift, such as designer shoes for the bridesmaids or waistcoats for the ushers. If your taste in attendants garb runs to the extravagant, you must chip in (at the least) for anything that is above moderate pricing.
- **Bridesmaids' hair and makeup:** Clarify whether attendants are responsible for getting and/or paying for their own hair and makeup. If you do pay for any of it, set parameters so you don't end up paying for falls, applying false eyelashes, or other extra-charge items.
- **Long-distance transportation:** Out-of-town weddings may require a serious financial investment by guests, but at least they have the option of simply not attending. If your wedding party, however, is expected to pay for plane fare on top of all their other expenses, make sure that your relationship and their wallets can take it.
- **Local transportation:** You should provide transportation for attendants to the ceremony (and reception, if it's not in the same venue). If, as is common, bridesmaids have gotten dressed in what will later be the honeymoon suite, they need to take their things with them when they leave for the reception. As for ushers, they usually don't get dressed all in the same place, so they get themselves to the ceremony site. If you want them to be at a certain place, for photographs either before or after the ceremony, consider transporting them en masse. After the reception, transporting attendants to where they are staying is not necessarily your responsibility, as often they neither leave at the same time nor are bound for the same destination.

Such a vast array of smart suits, slip dresses, and stylish gowns are available to choose from that the only excuse for choosing monstrosities in colors cooked up by the mad bridal scientists is pure mean-spiritedness.

Of course, finding a dress that looks good on several different women is another issue. Even if you manage to pull this one off, you can be sure that not all the women will be convinced they look terrific. The effort you devote to this search depends on how desperately you want your attendants to look like a bridal "party." Consider, more importantly, who these women are. If your friends are your friends because they are individualists, don't try to turn them into a matched set of septuplets. They'll only feel uncomfortable and look it as well.

You might consider several styles in complementary colors and silhouettes from the same designer. If you want to liberate your bridesmaids (and you really trust their judgment), give them a few parameters — color, length, fabric — and tell them to come up with something they like. Similar dresses can be accessorized differently to let each wearer's identity shine through: one with a coordinating stole, another cinched with an obi sash, and another wearing a boa of flowers in lieu of a bouquet. Different jewelry and hairstyles also help the women feel that they haven't disappeared completely into the amorphous mass of The Bridal Party.

Guy garb

The groom and his attendants are as much a part of this set piece as the bride and hers. Ushers should look and feel the epitome of debonair. A heavy wool tuxedo at a mid-afternoon garden wedding in August does not make you feel as crisp and confident as a navy jacket with off-white trousers might. This is common sense, but it's easy to get flummoxed in figuring out what *is* appropriate. However, rather than monopolizing valuable brain cells with trying to decode the difference between, say, informal daytime and semiformal afternoon, we suggest you choose something that makes you and your ushers feel comfortable, dashing, sexy, and in command — not like a band of woeful penguins stranded on an iceberg.

The following list and Figure 4-1 show you some of the elements of style at your disposal, which range from the traditional to the trendy.

- **Ascot:** A neck scarf, usually secured with a stick pin. Looks pretentious in almost any other situation except at a formal morning wedding, where it is quite glamorous. They usually complement the gray and white stripe of the pants with a cutaway jacket but may be of another pattern.
- **Bow tie:** Worn with tuxedos and dinner jackets. May be the ubiquitous black, but consider wedding-like silver, or an elegant black on black damask; should coordinate with cummerbund or waistcoat. Hand-tied looks spiffiest, either bat wing or butterfly style (see Figure 4-2 for instructions on tying the bat wing), but if you want a novelty color or pattern, you may have to go for pretied. Shiny materials and garish colors should be reserved for magicians.
- **Cummerbund:** A satin sash with pleats that face up. (See Figure 4-4.) Worn in lieu of suspenders or vest. Should coordinate with the bow tie, although not necessarily with the bridesmaids' dresses.
- **Cutaway or morning coat:** In its traditional design, this coat is for the most formal morning weddings. A novel experience in dressing up for men used to wearing jeans and T-shirts. Coats are black or gray with a single button at waist and one broad tail at back. Worn with a winged-collared dress shirt, ascot, and striped trousers. If you're going all out, add gloves, spats, and top hat, and even a walking stick. Can be made a bit less formal with a patterned tie in lieu of the ascot.

Figure 4-1: To go all out with a cutaway coat, don top hat, gloves, spats, and cane (top left). In white or ivory, the double-breasted dinner jacket is a classic (top right). A dinner jacket is great for a casual wedding or a rehearsal dinner (bottom left). Here's a look if you want to pull out all the stops (bottom right).

- **Dinner jacket:** In classic white or ivory or a subtle pattern of the same, with peaked lapels or shawl collar. Works well in summer months or in warm climes, in the afternoon or evening, and is considered an appropriate substitute for a standard tuxedo. Looks particularly swell with formal black trousers with side satin stripe. Think Humphrey Bogart in *Casablanca*. Can be purchased or rented from a formal wear shop (with some vigilance you may unearth one in an antique clothing boutique). You may wear a white dinner jacket even if your ushers are in black tuxedo jackets. Some designers are showing white on white suits replete with vests.
- **Four-in-hand tie:** Clever term meant to confuse you. It is very similar to an ordinary tie, just in a more formal fabric. To ensure its characteristic fullness, tie it so you create a dimple or crease in the center of the tie below the knot (see Figure 4-3). Silver dresses up a navy suit; a whimsical pattern makes it more casual.
- **French cuffs:** Roll-back shirt cuffs fastened with cuff links. Spend some time shopping for interesting cuff links for both you and your ushers. Attention to this detail attests to your impeccable taste.
- **Mandarin collar:** Flash back to the Nehru jacket of the sixties. High-necked band collar that has become fashionable for both shirts and jackets. A Mandarin collar looks good with high-neck vests. (See Figure 4-5.)

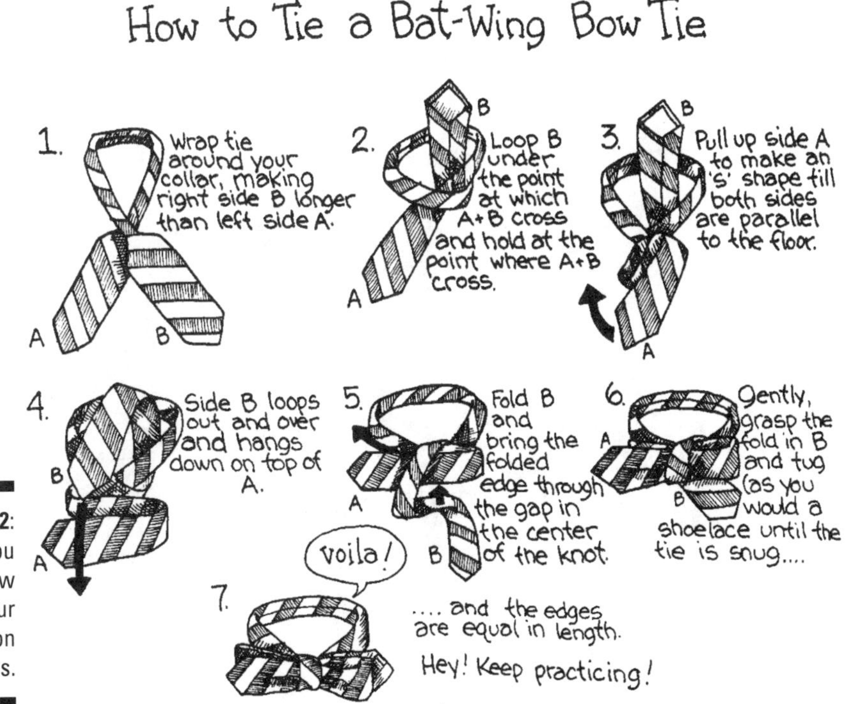

Figure 4-2: Now you can throw out all your clip-on bow ties.

- **Notch lapel:** This jacket lapel boasts V-shaped cuts pointing inward where the collar and lapel meet the jacket (as in Figure 4-4).
- **Peaked lapel:** A jacket lapel that includes two points of fabric on either side that project upward, with narrow spacing between the lapel and collar.
- **Shawl collar:** A rounded jacket lapel (as in Figure 4-4) that rolls back in a continuous tapering line. Double-shawl collars, which are in vogue, roll to reveal satin lining. Looks very elegant trimmed with satin stripe or contrasting piping.
- **Shoes:** Patent pumps (low-cut slip-on shoes with a ribbed ribbon bow in front) go with very formal attire and patent leather or polished calf dress shoes go with other outfits. White bucks or saddle shoes beautifully offset a navy or seersucker blazer with white pants. In any case, shoes must be in excellent condition.
- **Spread collar:** Dressy shirt collar with a high band that sits slightly up on the neck. Also called the English spread, as it was invented by the Duke of Kent and is still favored by Prince Charles.
- **Stroller coat:** Variation of morning coat, usually hip length. Looks good with fancy waistcoats. Designers such as Kenzo and Christian Dior Paris have in recent years shown versions with a touch of whimsy.
- **Suspenders or braces:** Wear to avoid the homeboy groom look. Wearing a belt *and* suspenders together, however, makes you look insecure.

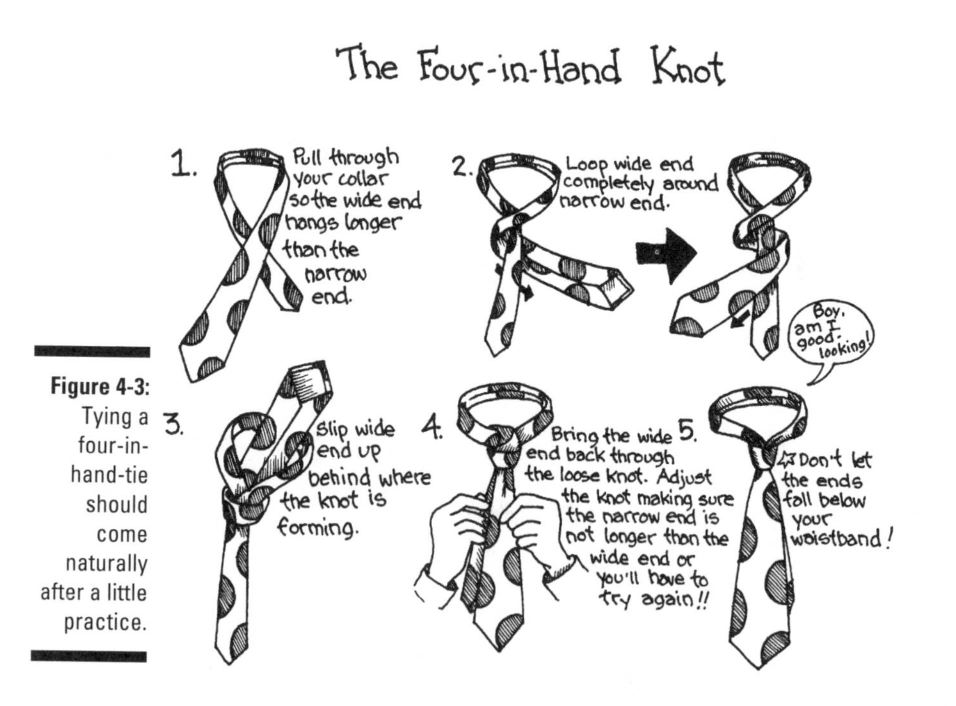

Figure 4-3: Tying a four-in-hand-tie should come naturally after a little practice.

- **Tails:** A jacket that is short in front with two longer "tails" hanging in back. Worn with a white pique shirt, vest, and bow tie (as in "white tie and tails"). Very formal.
- **Turndown collar:** The collar literally turns down, as on a regular business shirt, making it slightly less dressy but more comfortable than the winged. These shirts often feature soft pleated fronts and French cuffs.
- **Tuxedo or black tie:** Usually worn after 6 p.m., but can appear at a formal day wedding anytime after noon. A black or gray jacket. Single or double breasted. Shawl, peak, or notched lapels (two of which are featured in Figure 4-4). Worn with matching trousers, bow tie, and vest or cummerbund.

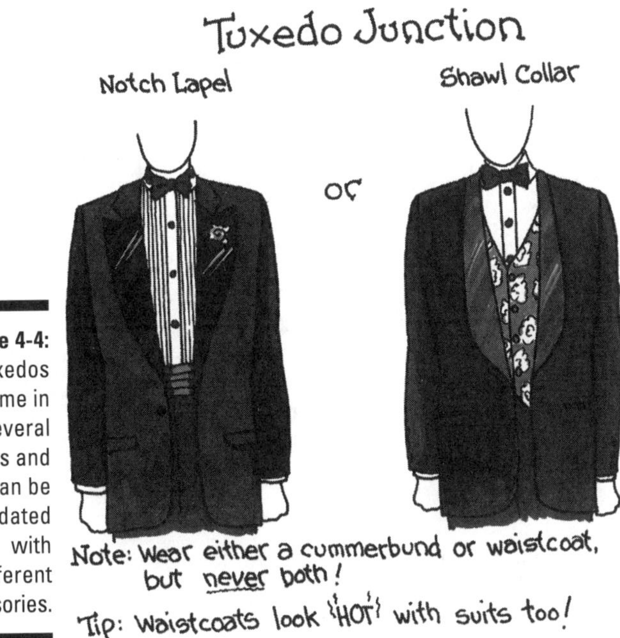

Figure 4-4: Tuxedos come in several styles and can be updated with different accessories.

- **Waistcoat or vest:** A vest that covers the trouser waistband (see Figures 4-1 and 4-4). May match or contrast with the fabric of the jacket. Has become the major fashion statement for men's formal wear. Designers such as Terence Teng are turning out custom and off-the-rack vests that are as beautiful as tapestries. In rich colorful satin, white pique, luxurious brocade, or woven grosgrain ribbon, these creations are perfect gifts for ushers.
- **Winged collar**: Very dressy. Collar band stands up, but the tips fold down. Front panels of a shirt with a winged collar may be pleated. (See Figure 4-5.) Looks best on men with long, slender necks.

Ushers should be either nattily dressed to match each other or purposely diverse. You especially don't want three ushers who have, say, winged collars and plaid bow ties, and one who has a lay-down collar and a black bow tie. The poor guy will look like central casting made a dreadful mistake. Asking groomsmen to wear their best dark suit usually produces more cohesive results than a line-up of tuxedos from different eras.

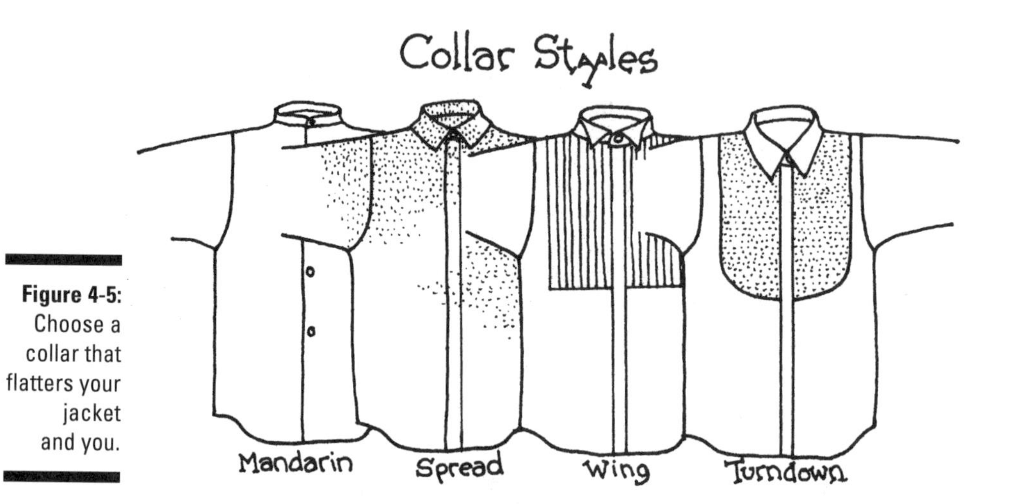

Figure 4-5: Choose a collar that flatters your jacket and you.

Buying a tuxedo or a good suit is always a better investment than renting a cheap tuxedo. Rented tuxedos unfortunately often look like rented tuxedos, as ill-fitting and uncomfortable as bad toupèes. They are also not cheap, running between 25 and 50 percent of the purchase price of an average tuxedo. Chances are you'll get more wear out of a tuxedo you own than you may think. Remember, also, that you will be looking at these photos for the rest of your life.

Finding the right suit, tuxedo, and accessories can take as much time as locating the perfect wedding gown. If you're getting married in a popular wedding month, and are planning on renting for yourself and/or the ushers, reserve the tuxedos as soon as possible so you don't wind up with the dregs. Because you'll be on your honeymoon, have the best man return rented outfits the first working day after the wedding.

If you do rent, you can usually pick up the suit two or three days in advance. Check to make sure that all the buttons are on and secure and that the tux has no stains, cigarette burns, or other attractive "extras."

The fit is key. Place your arms at your sides, fingers extended. The hem of the jacket should be no longer than your middle finger. The sleeve should grace the top of your hand, and your shirt cuff should peek out from the jacket sleeve no more than half an inch. Your trousers should skim the heel of your shoe in back and break slightly over the tops of your shoes in front.

A final word about the groom's grooming: Get a haircut a week or two before the wedding, and a manicure the day before. Even if you've never had a manicure before, on this day everyone will be checking out your hands, so pamper yourself. In fact, why stop there? The bride isn't the only one who deserves a full regimen of facials, massages, and seaweed body wraps. Weddings offer plenty of stress to go around, so take care of yourself.

Who wants to look like a mother of the bride?

If you intend to have your mother stand with your bridesmaids for the ceremony, suggest she shop for something that complements their ensembles. Otherwise, she may wear whatever color or style she feels best in as long as it is in the same realm of formality as the rest of the wedding party. Mothers of the bride and groom should confer on this aspect, but they needn't shop for the same color or style — the idea is ludicrous and sure to backfire. Similarly, if your mother is a tailored, sporty dresser, don't insist on draping her in sequins; if she is a drama queen, let her go for it. Arguing because you have some strict vision of your day that allows for no variations is more trouble than it's worth. Remember, your mother may very well have been obsessing about this day far longer than you have.

Dandy daddies

As in life, somebody has to get the short straw. In most weddings, unfortunately, it's the fathers. Long the brunt of cinematic jokes from Spencer Tracy to Steve Martin, fathers of the bride supposedly suffer in near-apoplectic silence as they write check after check and are largely ignored in nuptial fashion discussions. Fathers of the groom fare even worse — they don't even rate as a joke. To mitigate this situation, costume your father similarly to the ushers. Consider his personal style in the same way you would that of your attendants and mothers. Similarly, the groom's father looks best and feels most comfortable if he, too, is dressed in the same manner as the ushers.

Giving Back

So, enough about you. What are you going to do for all those selfless souls (attendants, officiant, parents, planner) who have stood by you during the creation of your masterpiece and are now prepared to deliver a flawless performance at the wedding? You need to give them something that is both a memento of the wedding and personally meaningful to them.

The rehearsal dinner is an ideal time to present these gifts (although some people choose to do it at the bridal tea or luncheon or the bachelor's dinner). As you give each token of your appreciation, make a toast to the recipient.

Just because you're on a budget doesn't mean that you're stuck giving tie clips and fake pearls. Nor do you have to give each person the same thing. Here are some creative ways to say thank you:

- A pair of champagne flutes etched with the attendants' monogram. You help the waiter at dinner present a filled glass to the correct recipients, and when it is whisked away after a toast, have it boxed with a second matching glass and given to the attendants when they leave.
- If you're getting married in a dramatic setting, a professional photo of the location in a silver frame with an inscribed thank you on it.
- Antique glass, watches, or silver serving pieces wrapped with a handwritten card describing the item's provenance and vintage.
- Jeweled shoe clips for women to wear at the wedding and to future festive occasions.
- A charm bracelet with a starter charm chosen for each bridesmaid.
- A gift and a professional service: a unique indoor potted tree and a year's visits from a plant service; a basket of massage oils and aromatherapy candles and three visits from a massage therapist; or a wok and a course in Szechuan cooking.

For your beloved

Among ancient Danish and Germanic tribes, husbands traditionally presented their new wives with a special piece of jewelry the morning after the wedding night as a symbol of their love. Today many couples set aside a time either just before or right after their wedding to give each other an especially meaningful and personal token of their affection. These gifts need not be extravagant – in fact, they may be as simple as a handsomely bound edition of love sonnets inscribed with a heartfelt message, a small keepsake box, or a watch, perhaps engraved with your wedding date.

Chapter 5

The Main Event: The Ceremony

In This Chapter

- Working with your officiant
- Personalizing your vows
- Going over the ceremonial play-by-play
- Cueing all the players

Although the ceremony — the exchange of vows — is the most important part of your whole wedding, as you bury yourself in prenuptial minutia, the ceremony, believe it or not, is one aspect that may fall through the cracks. If you and your intended are the same faith and you belong to a house of worship, the tendency is to assume that everything will fall into place without much thought from you. In fact, once most ceremonies start, they chug along with a life of their own. But before you get to that point you must invest a good deal of time in thought — deep thought — and soul-searching. The ceremony is about not only your love for each other, but also your relationship to your family and the community. What do your vows mean? How do you feel about religion? For many couples, the answers to these questions shape the destiny of their marriage. We are, after all, talking about *forever* here. (Suddenly, don't all those decisions about which kind of hors d'oeuvres to serve seem trivial?)

Understanding how you feel about Life's Big Questions prepares you for planning a ceremony that is meaningful to you and those around you. Even if your faith has a fairly set script, you may still need to consider the music, pre-wedding counseling with your officiant, and personalizing your actual vows. If you are of different faiths, you may want an interfaith ceremony. If neither of you subscribe to any religion in particular, you may create a nonsectarian ceremony, melding together parts of different religious and cultural traditions that reflect who you are and the commitment you want to make to each other.

We cover several topics related to the ceremony in other chapters. See Chapter 2 for finding a site or house of worship; Chapter 11 for tips on decor and candlelight ceremonies; Chapter 16 for the marriage license; and Chapter 18 for transportation issues and a typical wedding-day schedule.

What to Ask a Prospective Officiant

You may be getting married by your family clergyperson. If, however, you are "hiring" an officiant you don't know, make sure that you understand exactly under what auspices your marriage will be. Ask to see the officiant's credentials for performing ceremonies in particular faiths, and call the organization with which the officiant is affiliated to ask for references. Just because someone is licensed by the state to perform a ceremony does not mean that he or she is ordained by a religious body.

If you are having a secular, inter-faith, or nondenominational ceremony, you may feel strongly about how the officiant alludes to God, spirituality, or specific religions. Be respectful, but go over these points very clearly, so you are not married in a ceremony with religious aspects you are not comfortable with.

One of the best ways to see if an officiant suits you is to see him or her in action. If feasible, attend a wedding ceremony, mass, or other service presided over by this person.

You want to meet with your officiant before the wedding and go over the ceremony. During the interview, ask the following questions:

- What is the timing of the ceremony? What is the last thing that happens in the ceremony so musicians will know when to start the recessional?
- What are the rules and recommendations regarding music for the ceremony? (See "Music to Your Ears" in this chapter.)
- Would the officiant perform the ceremony in a venue other than a house of worship, if that is your preference?
- What is the officiant's fee and when do you pay it? Do you pay the officiant directly or make a donation to the house of worship?
- What is the basic ceremony script and at what points may you include your own vows (if that's even allowed)?
- What premarital preparation programs are required, such as pre-Cana or counseling?
- May you sign the marriage license *before* the ceremony for convenience?
- Are video cameras and/or flash photography allowed in the house of worship? If so, what are the specific rules?
- Will the officiant be present at the rehearsal?

In any ceremony where two people officiate, only one may be the official signatory on the legal documents. Be clear about which one that will be.

TIP

Special situations call for special officiants

Perhaps trying to resolve religious differences has become too complicated or perhaps neither of you is religious. In either case, a civil ceremony may be appropriate. Check with your town clerk to find out who in your area is licensed by the state to perform civil ceremonies — judges, mayors, registered clergy, and so on. (Notary publics can perform legal marriages in only three states at this writing: Florida, Maine, and South Carolina.) Although these ceremonies are essentially secular, some officiants allow you to incorporate some religious symbols.

You may want to have someone who is not officially licensed perform the ceremony. In the U.S., the state will recognize the marriage only if you have someone else who is licensed by the state fill out the legal documents.

If you want an interfaith ceremony or simply a ceremony that is secular yet spiritual, you may contact the following organizations:

- American Humanist Association
- Ethical Culture Society (a humanist group that includes no references to God in its ceremonies)
- Religious Society of Friends (see "Quaker" ceremonies in this chapter)
- Unitarian Society (see "Unitarian/Universalist" ceremonies in this chapter)

Religious Rites and Rules

Even if you've been a devout member of your faith all your life, you may still not be familiar with the wedding rituals, which in some cases can be quite involved. Delineating all the particulars of every religious and ethnic wedding tradition is beyond the scope of this book. But we do offer a cursory look at the major religious wedding customs, whether you are focusing on one religion, contemplating an interfaith wedding, or curious about various customs, that you may select à la carte to create a meaningful script of your own.

Buddhist

Founded in southern Nepal in the sixth and fifth centuries B.C.E., Buddhism is the predominant religion of Eastern and Central Asia, with 307 million followers. They study the teachings of its founder, Siddhartha Gautama — known as Buddha, or Enlightened One — who achieved enlightenment (nirvana) through meditation and by practicing good and moral behavior. To reach nirvana, however, you are subjected to repeated lifetimes that are good or bad depending on your actions (karma).

Although people in Japan favor Shinto-style weddings, many Japanese-Americans choose to marry in Buddhist temples, which in the United States are more numerous than Shinto shrines (which actually number only ten, all on the West Coast). In both countries, however, Western Christian-style weddings are also popular — and "style" is the operative word because the ceremony may be concerned more with style than religious convictions.

Because Buddhism holds that humans are flawed, individuals do not marry other individuals but rather make a pledge to the greater Truth, which is perfect and eternal. Ceremonies are simple, usually designed by the couple and based on Buddhist scriptures. Typically, the couple walks down the aisle carrying a string of 21 beads called *o juju*. The beads, which are like a rosary but shorter, represent the couple, their families, and Buddha. The couple uses *o juju* to offer prayers and incense to Buddha. A Buddhist monk blesses the nuptial union and the couple says their vows. The couple then may share sake (considered by many to be a secular tradition) and, after a few more words from the monk, turn to thank their parents, offering hugs and flowers, thus completing the circle.

Hindu

Hinduism describes a vast array of sects that comprise 648 million followers. Emanating from indigenous religions of India and Aryan religions, Hinduism was brought to India in 1500 B.C.E., and codified in the Veda and Upanishads, the sacred scriptures of Hinduism. All Hindu weddings are performed by a priest and considered a sacred trust, yet they vary greatly from region to region. Depending on geographic location, family customs, caste, and personal taste, weddings may be a few hours (often the case in North America) to several days long. Hindus believe that many paths lead to the same summit, as it were, so intermarriage is much less of a threat on religious grounds than a potential loss of cultural identity. The wedding rites are prescribed in the Holy Scripture known as the *Veda,* but ceremonies do not have to be performed in a holy temple. The family and priest usually consult astrological charts for an auspicious date.

GAME RULES

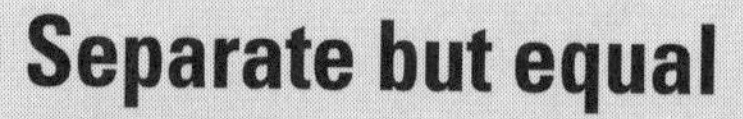

Separate but equal

Sometimes as a compromise or out of respect to the parents or grandparents, couples of different faiths have two separate services (as opposed to having two different clergy members at the same service). A two-ceremony wedding may be a small religious ceremony one day and a larger civil one the next, or perhaps two religious ceremonies within moments of each other at the same venue.

A typical ceremony may start with an *Ahvnanam* or greeting of the guests with flowers and perhaps a red powder called *kumkuma*. After invoking all the elements of nature and divine energies to witness and aid the proceedings, the priest sprinkles holy water and chants Sanskrit mantras to purify the bride and groom. The bride wears a traditional red and gold sari and lots of jewelry. The parents of the bride may wash the groom's feet while he sits in a chair behind a cloth curtain, and offer him gifts of bananas, coconuts, and so on — all the while earnestly asking him to accept their daughter in marriage. The "Auspicious Moment" occurs when the bride and groom affix a paste of cumin seeds and *jaggery* (an unrefined brown sugar made from palm sap) with their right palms to each other's heads to symbolize their inseparableness. The groom accepts the bride as his wife by tying strings, a pendant, or a gold necklace around her neck. The couple place garlands on each other to show their adoration and shower rice on each other's head to symbolize prosperity.

The bride and groom then take seven steps (called *Saptapadi*) around a sacrificial fire to signify their vows. With each step they pray for different blessings such as wealth, happiness, devotion, and so on. At some point during the ceremony, the bride may stand on a stone to symbolize loyalty and faithfulness.

Jewish

Four main divisions of Judaism exist: Orthodox and Conservative, which are very religious, and Reform and Reconstructionist, which can be far less stringent. The officiant at a Jewish wedding is the one who "orders" the wedding because Jews believe they are not married by someone, but rather marry each other. The person who presides over the wedding may be a cantor, rabbi, community leader, or scholar. Consequently, a ceremony may be recognized by the state but not the religion, or vice versa.

Finding a practicing rabbi to officiate at the marriage of a Jew and a non-Jew can be difficult. Orthodox and Conservatives will not; Reform and Reconstructionists often will, depending on the individual circumstances. However, rabbis and cantors who are unaffiliated may preside for a large fee — perhaps even without meeting the couple beforehand. (Finding a Christian or Catholic clergy to co-officiate is easier, in part because they see their religion as descending from Judaism.)

Weddings may not be held on the Sabbath — from Friday sundown to Saturday sundown. On the Sabbath, work and travel are forbidden, and you may not have two celebrations (the Sabbath being one) at once. If you are planning a religious ceremony, check the dates carefully with your rabbi. Jewish weddings are forbidden on major holidays such as Rosh Hashanah, Yom Kippur, Passover, Shavuot, and Sukkot. Three weeks in July and August, and the seven weeks between Passover and Shavuot (usually April and May)

are also off limits. When you set your date, check an almanac to find out the exact time the sun sets. Then find out whether your officiant will begin to travel only after that and at what time he or she will perform a ceremony. Some rabbis insist on one and a half hours after sundown to be absolutely sure not to violate a tenet.

A Jewish ceremony may take place anywhere — and outdoor spots are very popular — but they must take place under a *chuppah* (huppah), or Jewish wedding canopy. The chuppah carries many symbols of ancestral Judaism. Because the Jews were nomads, their weddings historically took place outside under the stars to make the point that the couple should bear as many children as there are stars in the sky. Eventually ceremonies took place under a tent to protect the couple's spirituality and today the chuppah is imbued with a variety of meanings: the groom's home into which he brings the bride, a home filled with hospitality (open on all sides), and as a metaphor for the groom covering or taking the bride.

In a traditional, religious, Jewish ceremony, the groom entertains friends and relatives in a private room before the wedding (some Sephardic or Spanish Jews do not believe in any of these ceremonial rituals). Dating back to the second or third century B.C.E., it was necessary to have two Jewish adult males, unrelated to each other or to the bride and groom, witness and sign a plain document — the *ketubah.* Modern ketubahs are often written in English as well as in Hebrew, are beautifully calligraphed with gold-illuminated drawings, and are witnessed by both men and women friends. The groom later presents the ketubah to the bride under the chuppah. The witnesses then must be positioned to see and hear the wedding ceremony.

Often, the groom and his companions then go to the bride's room for the *bedeken* (see the veils section of Chapter 3). Even some very religious women, however, have rejected this ritual because they find it reminiscent of the Middle Eastern *Purdah,* or heavy veiling, of women.

Although the Jewish wedding processional has no official rules, they usually follow a traditional format as shown in Figure 5-1. The rabbi and cantor (if you have one) lead the processional, followed by the bride's grandparents and the groom's grandparents, who take their seats in the first row. The right side is the bride's; the left is the groom's.

The cantor sings and guests may sing as well. The music should be upbeat but stately. The wedding party follows in this order: ushers; best man; groom with his parents, who take their places on the left side of the chuppah; bridesmaids, either coupled or single file; maid of honor; and finally the bride and her parents, who take their places on the right. (For tips on pacing the group, see "Practice Makes Perfect" later in this chapter.)

Including parents in the ceremony symbolizes that marriage is a joining of two families, not just individuals. If one or both sets of parents are divorced amicably, they should join their child walking down the aisle. But if the separation is not friendly, they may either forego standing under the chuppah or have another child or relative escort each of them to the chuppah. In that situation, the bride may have another escort or walk alone. Some couples actually prefer the latter scenario — or to walk down the aisle together — because they find being "given away" offensive.

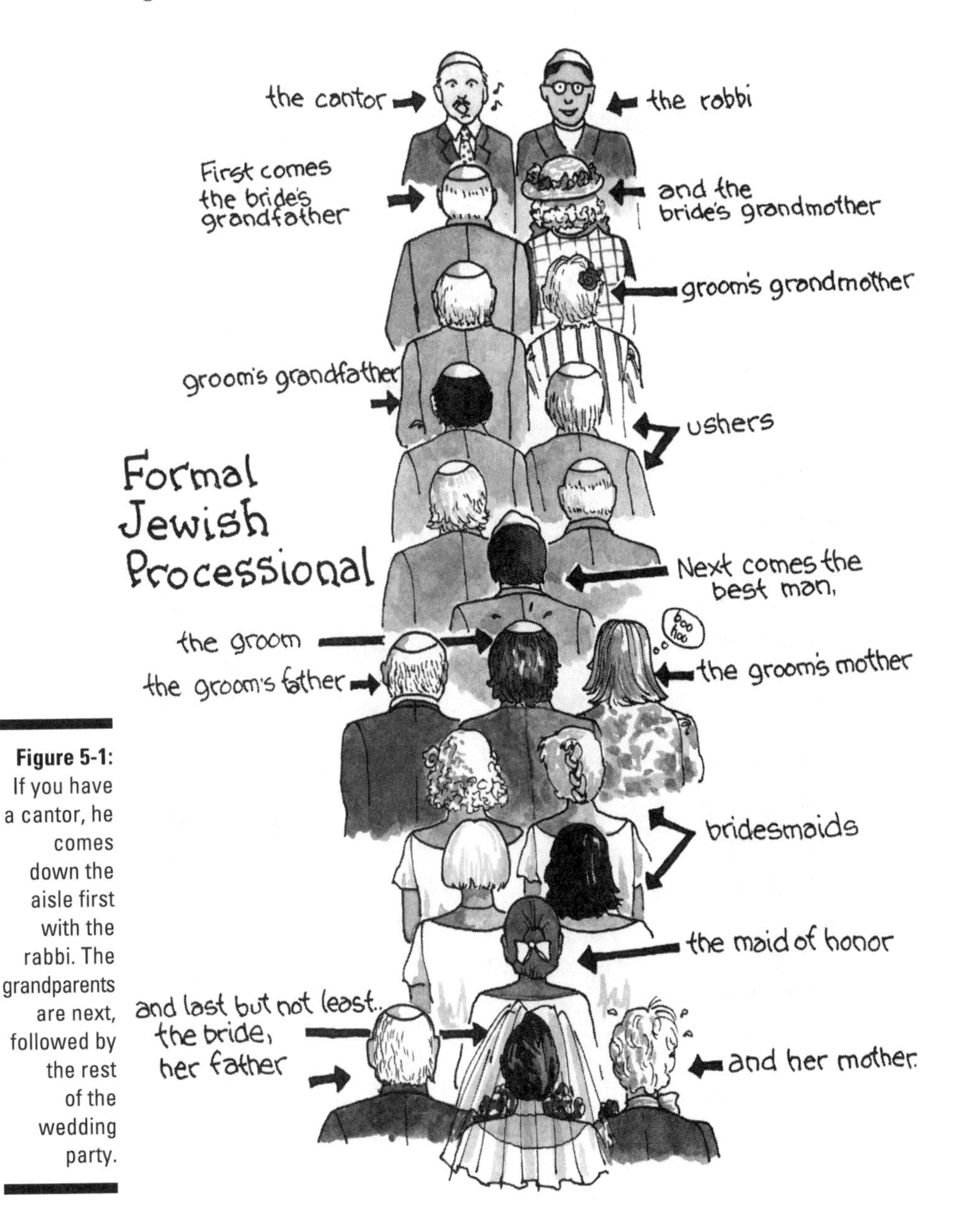

Figure 5-1: If you have a cantor, he comes down the aisle first with the rabbi. The grandparents are next, followed by the rest of the wedding party.

The groom usually approaches the bride before she reaches the chuppah and escorts her to the chuppah, symbolizing his bringing her into his house. Figure 5-2 depicts the basic formation of a Jewish wedding under the chuppah.

Depending on your adherence to Jewish law, you may decide to incorporate some or all of the religious aspects of the ceremony.

Figure 5-2: A Jewish wedding under a chuppah consists of the groom's parents on the left, the bride's on the right, the bride and groom, and honor attendants.

A ritual that is currently almost exclusively enacted by Orthodox Jews may seem intrinsically mystical or unbearably sexist depending on your beliefs. The bride circles around the groom seven times, as if she is enveloping him in the train of her gown. Then she takes her place at his right.

After everyone is under the chuppah, the rabbi welcomes the guests, including the bride and groom and asks for God's blessings. The ceremony begins with the blessing over the wine, from which the bride and groom take sips. Either the bride's mother or a friend has the honor of taking up her veil. The centerpiece of the ceremony is the giving of the ring. The groom places the ring — which should be solid with no stones so the bride is not deceived about its value — on the bride's right index finger. (She later moves it to whichever finger she wants.) The rabbi reads the *ketubah* aloud and the groom presents it to the bride (as it is her property), who hands it to an attendant or her parents for safekeeping. The rabbi makes a short speech about the couple, who then may add poems, prayers, or personal words.

The next part begins with another wine blessing and the couple drink either from a second cup or from the first. (Some couples now bring two kiddush cups, one to symbolize the past and relatives who have died and the other to symbolize the future.) The *sheva b'rachot,* or seven blessings comes next. The officiant then pronounces the bride and groom legally married and often adds a benediction to conclude the service.

The most familiar part of the Jewish ceremony, the breaking of the glass, is next. The groom historically stomps on the glass, but some couples now break it together. This ritual has been interpreted many ways — a reminder of the destruction of the temple, the fragility of marriage, and the intensity of the sexual union.

Wrap the glass well in several heavy cloth napkins to avoid mishaps. If both the bride and groom are smashing the glass, they should go for something quite fragile, such as a champagne flute, because the soles of the bride's shoes are usually thin. (Some people use light bulbs, but we think the symbolism is lacking.) If the ceremony is on grass, place a piece of wood under the glass. If the bride's shoes are really quite delicate, she may want to place her foot gently on top of her husband's as he stomps down.

With that, the recessional music begins and the bride and groom turn to walk up the aisle. The father and mother of the bride follow directly behind, and the groom's parents behind them. The best man and maid of honor come next, followed by the ushers and bridesmaids in pairs.

At a religious wedding the couple then goes to *Yichud*. Originally when the couple consummated the marriage, the *Yichud* is now a time-out, giving the couple ten or fifteen minutes of private time after the emotion of the ceremony. This custom is so appealing that couples from many different beliefs are adopting it.

Finding an officiant for a Jewish wedding

If both the bride and groom are Jewish and are affiliated with a synagogue (or their parents are), getting married in that synagogue is no problem. Most rabbis are amenable to co-officiating with another rabbi — the other family's rabbi, for example. If, however, you are not connected to any synagogue or religious organization, start your search for a rabbi by asking people you know for recommendations.

For Reform rabbis, you can also try the local office of the Union of American Congregations; for Conservative rabbis, the United Synagogue of America. For rabbis and cantors who perform interfaith ceremonies, look in the back of local wedding magazines and in the Yellow Pages under *Religion.*

Israelis who live on a kibbutz are often accompanied by every family from the kibbutz and may arrive at their ceremony on tractors or other work vehicles. Sephardic Jews usually have both mothers accompany the bride and both fathers accompany the groom down the aisle.

To remarry in a Jewish ceremony, one must have a *get,* or religious divorce.

Mormon

Mormons (members of the Church of Jesus Christ of Latter Day Saints) have two kinds of ceremonies. The *temple ceremony,* which takes place in one of 44 Mormon temples around the world, is reserved for active, worthy Church members. The couple, dressed in white, kneels before the altar and is "sealed" together for eternity. The ceremony is considered so sacred that members are not allowed to divulge many details about it to outsiders.

The other ceremony, the *chapel ceremony,* is far less restricted, but couples are considered married only until death, as opposed to eternity. Many couples have this ceremony first and then the temple version later — but only if they are both Mormon. A Mormon may marry a non-Mormon only in a civil ceremony.

Muslim

In Islam, the woman makes the offer of marriage, usually through her father or another male relative. This arrangement is supposed to guarantee that both partners come to the marriage of their own free will. After accepting the proposal, the groom gives the bride a *mahr,* or gift, such as property, jewelry, or even education. (Muslim women must marry Muslim men; however, Muslim men may marry non-Muslim women as long as their children are raised Muslim.)

Although marriage is one of the most desirable states for Muslims, the ceremony is simple and takes only about five minutes. The bride and groom are typically in separate rooms, usually in an office as opposed to a mosque, while the *wali,* the bride's representative, answers questions posed by a religious sheik (an Islamic magistrate). The groom answers for himself and three male witnesses stand by. Once the sheik is satisfied that the groom has provided a suitable *mahr,* they sign the papers and the couple is pronounced man and wife. A week or two later, the couple has a public celebration with a series of parties and rituals, which the groom and his family pay for.

Orthodox Eastern

The Orthodox Eastern Church split with the Roman Catholic Church in 1054 and is today the second largest Christian community in the world with 158 million followers. Members adhere to a strict dogma, but belong to many different denominations that reflect their ethnic identity — the Church of Greece, the Church of Cyprus, and the Russian Orthodox Church, to name a few. Orthodox Eastern are allowed but not encouraged to marry non-Orthodox baptized Christians.

Because the Church considers marriage a sacrament, the service must take place inside a church. The ceremony begins with the Betrothal outside the church doors, where the rings are blessed and exchanged. (The rings go on the right hand, not the left.) The priest leads the couple into the church and onto a white cloth in front of the wedding platform. Someone in the processional carries a wedding icon and the couple holds lighted candles throughout the service.

Whereas rings symbolize betrothal, crowns — made of metal or floral wreaths — symbolize the actual marriage. The Crowning is the central moment of the service, both signifying the formation of a new family unit and recalling the sacrifice of the martyrs, who (whether or not they had to wear a crown of thorns) gave their lives for God just as the couple must be willing to give their lives for each other. In lieu of Communion, the couple drinks from the "common cup of joys and sorrows." The couple does not say their vows aloud. While wearing the crowns, the couple walks around a table or platform containing such Holy Things as the gospel book. As with other rituals, they perform this act three times to signify the Holy Trinity of the Father, Son, and Holy Spirit. When the couple has completed their circumambulations, the priest removes the crowns and gives the final blessing: "Be thou magnified, O bridegroom."

Protestant

The original Protestant church is the Church of England (also called the Anglican Church), which was formed in 1534 when King Henry VIII broke with the Roman Catholic Church "in protest" of Rome's refusal to annul his marriage so he could marry Anne Boleyn. The Anglican Orthodox Church in the United States has 6,000 members, but the Episcopal Church is the more successful U.S. offshoot, with 2.7 million members. Protestantism also has several other major denominations as well as hundreds of small independent denominations in local communities.

Episcopal

Marriage is a sacrament and must take place in a chapel unless the local bishop has granted a special dispensation. *The Book of Common Prayer* (first ratified in 1789) prescribes the marriage ceremony, which may or may not include Communion.

The ceremony is fairly traditional; the bride's father walks her down the aisle (see Figure 5-3). As the procession enters, a hymn, psalm, or anthem is sung or played. The celebrant (who may be a priest, bishop, or, in some communities, a deacon) makes some introductory remarks, beginning with the familiar, "Dearly beloved: We have come together. . . ." A declaration of consent follows, which means that the celebrant asks the bride and groom whether they will have each other in marriage. They reply "I will," and the celebrant asks the congregation whether they will "uphold these two persons in their marriage." Assuming they all say "We will," a song follows. Next is the "Ministry of the Word" — a reading from the Holy Scripture. If there is to be a Communion, a passage from the Gospel concludes the Readings. A homily or other response to the Readings may follow.

The couple exchanges vows and the celebrant blesses the rings. After one or more prayers, the celebrant blesses the marriage as the husband and wife kneel.

"The Peace" follows, with the celebrant saying, "The peace of the Lord be always with you." The congregation says, "And also with you," the cue for the newlyweds to greet each other and for greetings to be exchanged throughout the congregation. If Communion is to follow, the couple may present the offerings of bread and wine and receive Communion first, after the ministers. When both a bishop and priest are present and officiating, the bishop should pronounce the blessing and preside at the Eucharist.

Mainstream denominations

Baptist, Lutheran, Methodist, and Presbyterian denominations consider marriage a holy and desirable union, but not a sacrament. Congregations vary in the degree to which they allow you to personalize the ceremony, although almost all allow you to get married outside of a house of worship. Their ceremonies all use Biblical passages, involve an exchange of vows and rings, and a blessing by the celebrant.

Thanks to television and the movies, most people are familiar with the Protestant ceremony. Indeed, all Protestant weddings include a traditional processional, as depicted in Figure 5-3, and a recessional. ***Note:*** These illustrations are not to scale — pace the processional, as we mention in "Practice Makes Perfect" later in this chapter.

Although Figure 5-1 and Figure 5-3 show ushers paired with ushers and bridesmaids paired with bridesmaids, you may want to pair them as male-female couples for the processional and/or recessional, or at the altar.

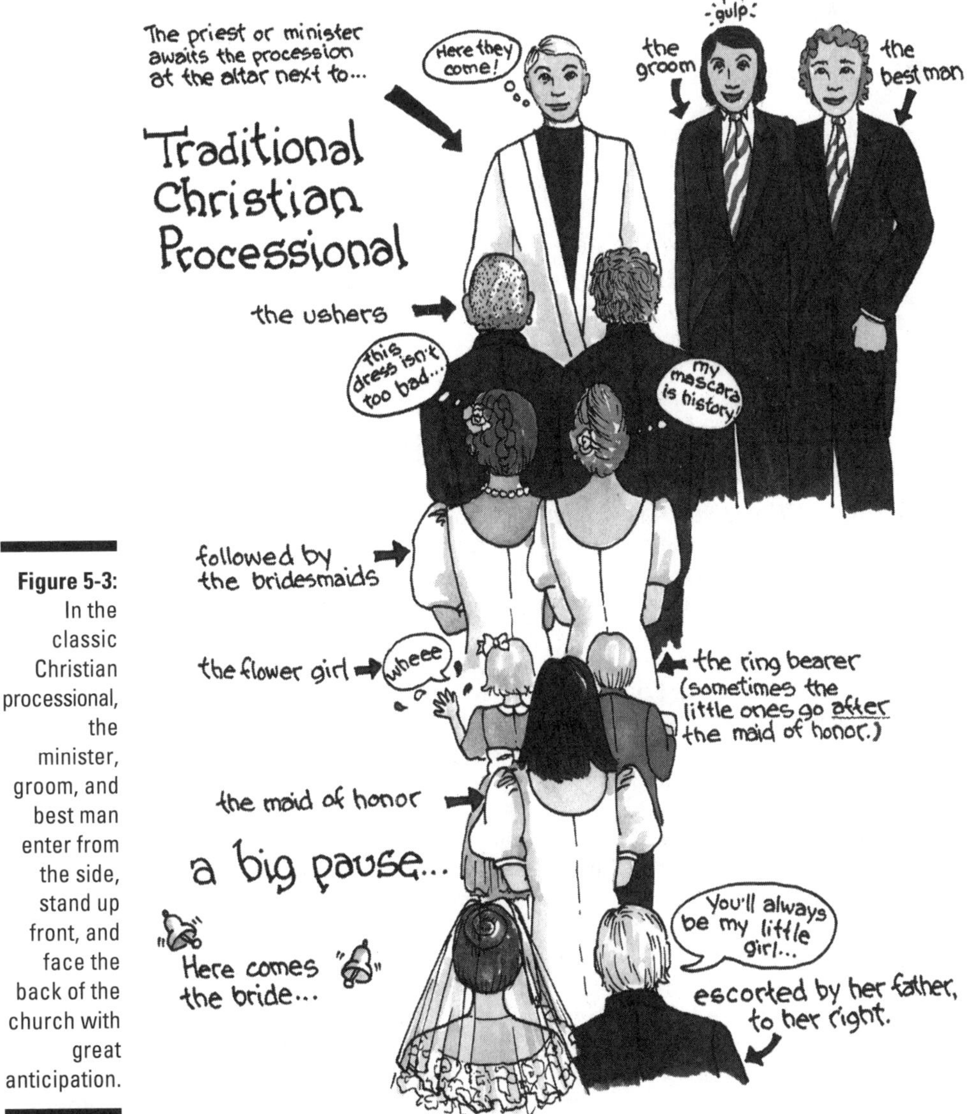

Figure 5-3: In the classic Christian processional, the minister, groom, and best man enter from the side, stand up front, and face the back of the church with great anticipation.

Before the processional begins, the bride's mother is the last person to be seated. Usually she is given the first seat nearest the aisle, in the first row and a seat is left empty next to her for the bride's father. If the parents are divorced, the father (and his new significant other if he has one) sits in the row behind the bride's mother, who sits with her new significant other if she has one.

After the rest of the wedding party is standing in place at the altar, they should all turn to face the bride, who starts her walk after a sufficiently dramatic pause.

Before walking down the aisle, the bride should transfer her engagement ring to her right hand, because most people find wearing a wedding ring outside an engagement ring awkward.

When the bride appears at the back of the church, the congregation may or may not stand, depending on the tradition. If they do, they wait for a cue from the minister to sit down again.

As the bride nears the altar, her father lifts the veil, kisses her, and puts the veil back down. The celebrant asks something like, "Who gives this woman to be married?" to which the father (or whoever is "giving away" the bride) replies, "I do." (Sometimes both the mother and father say, "We do.") The father may hug or shake hands with the groom before sitting down. The groom offers his left arm and the bride adjusts her bouquet to accept his arm.

Many couples who believe that the presentation of the bride is patronizing are omitting it from their ceremonies. The celebrant, in that case, never asks, "Who gives this woman to be married?" Therefore, the father sits down after replacing the bride's veil (and greeting the groom). Another variation is to have the bride walk alone or borrow from the Jewish tradition of having both parents escort her down the aisle.

The bridesmaids and ushers, who fan out from the altar at an angle (see Figure 5-4), should pivot slightly, so they face the bride but do not turn their backs completely to the audience. If you choose to have a flower girl and ring bearer and they are bound to squirm through the ceremony, you may have them sit in the front row.

Mainstream Protestant ceremonies may last only a few minutes, depending on the number of readings and songs. They are in many ways similar to Episcopal ceremonies, with prayers, hymns, and readings. Communion, however, is rarely held.

As soon as the ceremony ends, the recessional music starts up. The bride and groom are the first to go down the aisle, followed by the maid of honor and best man. (In some cases, the flower girl and ringer bearer follow the bride and groom, but it depends on whether they are old enough to recognize their cue to get back in formation.) The bridesmaids and ushers follow. Next come the bride's parents, and then the groom's.

Figure 5-4: The bride and groom are the only ones who may have their backs to the audience. The rest of the wedding party turns slightly, facing toward the front, but not so much that their backs are to the audience.

Quaker

Given their disdain for sacraments and ritual, Quakers (members of the Religious Society of Friends), marry in perhaps the simplest fashion. To be married in a "meeting house," the couple must apply to the Committee for Ministry and Council, which generally meets once a month and in turn appoints a "clearance committee" that interviews the couple to determine the clarity of their intention. This process can take a couple of months. The church has no clergy per se; after the committee approves the intended union, "overseers" are appointed to make the wedding arrangements and, for the most part, the bride and groom act as their own ministers.

As with a typical Friends meeting, a wedding is characterized by quiet meditation. At some point, when the couple is ready, they stand and make their vows to each other. They then exchange rings and sign a Quaker wedding license. A close friend or relative may read the certificate aloud before the group settles back into silent worship. During this time, guests may rise and speak if moved to do so. Inevitably, many warm and heartfelt "messages" come pouring forth.

Many non-Quaker couples choose to get a Quaker wedding license, which states in effect that the two people are marrying themselves. You can get the license regardless of whether you have an actual Quaker wedding. You need only to have two witnesses sign the document to make your marriage legal.

Roman Catholic

Marriage is one of the seven sacraments, so if two Catholics are getting married, the wedding must take place in a Catholic Church for the marriage to be sanctified. Permission to wed outside a chapel can be granted only by the vicar general's office in any diocese.

You must provide several documents to prove that you are free to marry in the Church:

- **Baptismal certificate**
- **Letter of freedom** stating that you have never contracted marriage either civilly or in a church service
- **Letter of permission** from your parents if you are under 21 years old
- **Premarital "investigation"** — actually, just a data sheet, filled out during an informal interview with your priest
- **Publication of *banns*** (the publication or public announcement of the engaged couple's intention to marry), usually read at mass on three consecutive Sundays before the wedding

Ordinarily, the marriage should take place in the bride's parish, so the groom must get a letter of notification from his parish that his banns will be announced three times. If you are not a member of a particular parish, speak to the pastor regarding the canonical rule and a dispensation.

When it comes to interfaith marriages, a Catholic can get a dispensation to marry a baptized non-Catholic or an unbaptized partner. A Catholic can also get a "dispensation from form" to marry in a non-Catholic ceremony. Your partner's minister or rabbi may assist at the wedding by reading a Scripture passage, praying a prayer, saying a few words, or giving a blessing. Only a priest or deacon, however, may perform the actual ceremony if you are getting married in a Catholic church. Most parishes do not publish the banns for an interfaith marriage unless you request it.

The marriage date must be set at least six months and in some parishes as much as a year in advance. In the intervening months, you must undergo pre-Cana preparation. Many parishes offer pre-Cana programs through intensive weekend workshops, which cover such topics as self-awareness, human sexuality, communicating, decision making, "Natural Family Planning," sacrament, and so on.

Byzantine Catholic

More than one million of the world's 900 million Catholics are Byzantine (or Eastern Rite) Catholic. Like Roman (or Western Rite) Catholics, Byzantine Catholics adhere to Catholic Canon Law and are under the jurisdiction of the Holy See in Rome, which means that marriage is a sacrament and weddings must take place inside a church. But like members of the Orthodox Eastern Church, with whom they share cultural roots, Byzantine Catholics also keep alive the customs and traditions of their ethnic heritage, which include prescribed, ornate pageantry (similar to that of Orthodox Eastern weddings) as part of the wedding ritual. (The church comprises Ukrainian, Maronite, Melkite, Romanian, Slovakian, Armenian, Chaldean, and Assyrian Catholics.)

The liturgical celebration is fairly set, although the couple may — with their priest's approval — amend the vows set forth by the Church, choose to light a wedding candle (read more about candlelight ceremonies in Chapter 11), and offer their own prayer or petition of thanks. Before the recessional, the bride may also place a bouquet on the Blessed Virgin Mary's shrine or statue.

The couple may have a ceremony without a Mass or ceremony incorporated into a Mass (and called a Nuptial Mass). The couple may enter the ceremony with a traditional processional — the priest waits with the groom at the altar as the bride, preceded by her attendants, walks down the aisle with her father. (See Figure 5-3.) Or the priest and his assistants may welcome the bride and groom and their families at the door of the church, before they all proceed to the sanctuary. During the ceremony, the bride and groom remain in front of the altar. Throughout the ceremony, they may have to kneel, stand, or sit.

The priest recites an opening prayer (usually of the couple's choosing), followed by readings, including a Gospel passage. The couple exchanges vows and rings, which the priest blesses. If the ceremony takes place outside a Mass, the ceremony concludes with the priest saying another prayer and the Nuptial blessing.

In the case of a Nuptial Mass, the service continues with the priest calling for the "Sign of Peace" in which everyone turns and shakes hands with their neighbor, saying, "Peace be with you" or something similar. A member of the couple's family may then present a "gift" of bread and wine for Communion to commemorate Christ's Last Supper. The bread and wine are consecrated and taken as the body and blood of Christ. After Communion, the priest says the concluding prayer and Nuptial blessing.

Shinto

Founded in the sixth century B.C.E. to distinguish Japanese beliefs from those of Buddhism, this ancient religion stresses reverence for ancestors as well as belief in many spiritual beings and gods, known as *kami*. The Japanese pay tribute to *kami* at shrines and festivals, but otherwise adhere to no overall dogma. Therefore, Buddhism and the social customs and spiritual practices of Shinto are not mutually exclusive. In fact, many wedding ceremonies incorporate traditions from both. For example, the *sansankudo* (see Chapter 10), where the bride and groom share sips of *sake* (rice wine), is a Shinto rite that is a part of many Japanese-American Buddhist ceremonies. (See Buddhist ceremonies in this chapter.)

A traditional Shinto-style ceremony is small and rather private, comprising the immediate families, the *nakoudo* (the matchmakers who arranged for the couple to meet), and the priest. The bride wears a white kimono with a fancy headpiece and the groom wears a black kimono with a striped *hakama* (shirt-like pants) and a black jacket. Before the couple enters, the priest cleanses and blesses the four corners of the room. The couple sits or kneels on rice paper, which covers the floor, as the priest recites Shinto prayers. If the ceremony takes place in a Shinto shrine, Imperial Japanese music may play.

Sikhism

The day before a Sikh wedding, the bride's legs and hands are painted with henna designs. The next morning, her female relatives adorn her with jewels and makeup and she dons an elaborate traditional sari in red, pink, or white. Whether or not the ceremony is held in a Sikh temple, called a *guardwara,* it takes place in the morning, which is considered the happy time of day.

Before the ceremony begins, the bride's parents welcome the groom and his parents, garlanding them with flowers. The bride enters and garlands the groom with more flowers and he returns the gesture by garlanding her. Professional singers called *raagis* perform as guests enter and sit around a central platform, upon which the holy book, *Guru Granth Sahib Ji,* is displayed.

The couple sits before the man (a *granthi* or *pathi*) who reads the holy book. Depending on the family's tradition, either the mother or father hands one end of a pink sash to the groom (sometimes placing it on his shoulder) and the other end to the bride. Verses recited from the *Granth* explain the couple's duties in married life. One of the parents, priest, or groom may tie the sash to the bride's headpiece — literally tying the knot and symbolizing the bond that joins the couple.

The couple exchanges vows and then walks around the holy book four times *(lavaans),* the husband leading, to signify their journey together. After each circle, the bride and groom kneel and bow toward the *Granth*. The pathi may address the parents and grandparents regarding their roles in supporting the couple. The *raagis* usually sing a concluding song as the bride and groom exchange a sweet food called a *karah parshad*.

This whole ceremony takes about an hour and a half. When it's over, guests greet the couple, placing a hand on their head, garlanding them with flowers, throwing petals, and often putting a token amount of money into the pink cloth, which the bride and groom still hold.

Unitarian-Universalist Society

By definition, Unitarian-Universalists are "non-creedal" and each congregation determines its own affairs and operates within local custom. Though its roots are Judeo-Christian, the religion is not Christian but rather pluralistic. Marriage is viewed as a holy union but not a sacrament — couples create their own ceremony out of religious and humanistic traditions that are meaningful to them. Consequently, the society has been a haven for interfaith marriages since its founding in 1961.

Our hodgepodge ceremony

Because Michael is a non-religious Jew and I'm a WASP-Catholic-Buddhist-whatever, we couldn't see ourselves having a religious or interfaith ceremony, but we did end up infusing our ceremony with several Jewish elements.

First, because I love the symbolism of it, I wanted a chuppah (which we constructed according to the directions in Chapter 11 and it turned out beautifully). Then we decided to have the two blessings over wine so we could use the kiddush cup that belonged to Michael's late father. To decide which side we would each stand on, we tossed a coin and ended up coincidentally following the Jewish tradition of having the bride to the right of the groom. And we couldn't resist the breaking of the glass — an exclamation point to the most breathless few moments of our lives.

We both chose something to express our feelings and honor the other. One of my closest friends read my choice, *The Chuppah* by Marge Piercy. Michael, harking back to his hippie days, chose Bob Dylan's *Wedding Song*, which never sounded better than when my brother, an accomplished musician, sang it that day, his acoustic guitar resonating throughout the garden. (We edited out two of the eight verses, which weren't appropriate to our situation.) For the rest of the ceremony, we massaged several tidbits from various ceremonies into one Judeo-Christian-Zen-Buddhist-Humanist script, to which our officiant added some moving words of his own. Our officiant, incidentally, was the only one who had the foresight to bring a handkerchief with him — something everyone needed desperately by the time it was all over.

Express Yourself

Besides having an officiant declare you legally married, the other key moment of your ceremony is the taking of vows. Although the eloquent phrasings found in religious ceremonies for this solemn promise have certainly stood the test of time, you may feel that they fall short in expressing what is truly in your heart. And yet, when you try to articulate the numbing joy you feel about your beloved and the great unknowable before you, the words seem banal, lifeless, trite. What can you say that hasn't been said before? After all, haven't poets been writing about love for eons? Yes, but that doesn't mean you can't give it a whirl. Even if the words are already out there, they haven't been said by *you*.

Whether you are creating your own vows or simply looking for ways to personalize your ceremony, consider these ideas:

- Start by making a list of all the words that describe your spouse to be, why you fell in love with this person, and what your hopes are for the future.
- Keep a notebook or journal for jotting down bits of poetry, song lyrics, or movie scenes that strike a chord in you or that have been floating around in your subconscious for ages.
- As obvious as it may seem, look up such topics as love, passion, and marriage in encyclopedias, books of quotations, dictionaries, and on the Internet. Seeing these ideas distilled down to their basic concepts may spark your creativity.
- Dig for unusual sonnets, poems, songs, and the like. Really listen to the words. Might a particular piece or a few lines work in your ceremony?
- Think about the people around you. You may want to briefly acknowledge family and friends, thanking God (or whomever) for the dearly departed who were important to you or saying prayers for the good health of elderly relatives and so on.
- Include your children if you have any, or nieces and nephews. This may be the grandest day of their lives too (at least for a while). And they will be around longer than anyone else to keep your wedding day memories alive.
- Incorporate a ritual or poem from your ethnic heritage or from one you admire.
- As you start putting together your thoughts, keep your vows upbeat and positive. Avoid anything maudlin.
- Remember that you want to create a dialog, not two monologues.

Personalized vows for a ceremony in a house of worship usually have to be approved by your officiant to make sure that you aren't inadvertently saying anything offensive or disrespectful.

Among the rights that the West Africans were denied when they were brought to America as slaves was the right to marry. They had always been prepared to have a family life, so they invented traditions to secretly signify marriage rituals. Following a wedding in Africa, it was customary for brides to sweep their in-laws' residence so slave couples would jump over a broom to the beat of a drum. "Jumping the broom" became well-known thanks in part to Alex Haley's epic *Roots*. As African-Americans increasingly identify with their heritage, many are again jumping the broom as part of their marriage rites (see Figure 5-5).

Figure 5-5: Many African-American couples "jump the broom" as their ancestors did.

Photo by Terry deRoy Gruber

If you've written your own vows and especially if they include a long poem or passage, write them on 3 x 5 cards. Ask someone who will be at the altar or bimah with you and who has a pocket to hang onto them until you need them during the ceremony.

Music to Your Ears

Whether or not your ceremony is religious, music plays a crucial role in setting the tone. From the prelude to the recessional, you can personalize your ceremony through your musicial selections. Instrumentals may convey a feeling of spirituality and transcendence, while the lyrics of certain songs may be an extension of your vows.

If you are planning an outdoor ceremony, classical musicians — particularly harpists — will insist on some covering from the sun. Because these instruments are so expensive, even the threat of a drizzle in another state may keep the harpist from performing unless he or she is in a building or a tent.

If you are marrying in a religious venue, the musical selections must be approved. For many Christians, the *Wedding March* (commonly known as "Here Comes the Bride") from the Wagner opera *Lohengrin* as the processional, and Mendelssohn's *Wedding March* from *A Midsummer Night's Dream* as the recessional are as integral to their ceremony as the vows. Conversely, most synagogues do not allow either selection to be played because Mendelssohn converted to Christianity and Wagner was a notorious anti-Semite.

Dozens of classical music pieces, although beautiful, have been heard so often at wedding ceremonies that they have lost the ability to inspire. If those pieces aren't your cup of tea, begin your search by listening to tapes or CDs of classical wedding music collections. If you don't have any luck with that, expand your musical horizons and listen to other classical selections. Consider, for example, such baroque composers as Handel, Marcello, and Quantz.

Before you get your heart set on a particular piece of music, check to see if it can be played by a solo organist or if it works for the number of musicians in the group you have contracted. Some of the pieces you consider may be either for entire orchestras and cannot be scored for a small group or may call for specific instruments that are not in your ensemble. For ways to find musicians for hire, see Chapter 7.

The prelude music, if there are no restrictions, may comprise any number of possibilities — an a cappella trio, an operatic soloist, or a quartet that specializes in classical renditions of Beatles songs. Some couples, tired of the usual variety of classical wedding music, opt for taped music for their ceremony. Jazz favorites from Duke Ellington to Ella Fitzgerald and Nat King Cole put guests in a wonderfully romantic mood as soon as they arrive.

Often couples plan their music so that it changes for each portion of the processional. One piece for the ushers, another perhaps for the bridesmaids and maid of honor, followed by a pause before a flourish for the entrance of the bride.

The recessional may be a rousing live chorus of gospel singers doing *When The Saints Go Marching In,* a taped favorite, applicable rock song, or even bagpipers. Anything may work as long as it is joyous and celebratory and sends people out the door humming.

Guests must be able to hear both the music and the words at a ceremony. Make sure that you, your officiant, anyone who is delivering a reading, and the musicians can be heard. Depending on the location of your ceremony, this means you must either use a stand-up microphone or mike the site or the participants.

Practice Makes Perfect

Rehearsals not only make the wedding run smoothly, but also tremendously reduce the angst level. If you have children in the ceremony, the rehearsal helps them get a sensory hold on what they will be doing. (Come to think of it, that's why adults need rehearsals, too.)

Attendants may be quite blasé when handed a wedding-day schedule (see Chapter 18) at the rehearsal, and may even make hilarious jokes about the "mindless minutiae" and the "control freak" who penned it. These are usually the same folks who ask for a new copy an hour before the ceremony and clutch it as if it were a life-support system.

If you're getting married in a private home or other space where there is a phone, silence the ringer or disconnect the line for the duration of the ceremony.

A quick run-through

You usually hold the rehearsal the night before the wedding, ideally where the ceremony is to be. The time should be late enough in the afternoon to accommodate those coming from work, but early enough so you can greet other guests arriving for the rehearsal dinner. Now is not the time to start choreographing your rehearsal. With a delineated schedule, a rehearsal shouldn't take more than 45 minutes, even for an elaborate ceremony. If you have people coming to the rehearsal who haven't seen each other in a long time, allot extra time to get hugs, kisses, and gossip out of the way.

Rehearsals in a church or synagogue usually involve the officiant as well as the person responsible for the chapel who puts everyone through their paces. If your officiant participates in your rehearsal, you should invite him or her (and spouse) to the rehearsal dinner. An officiant who is your family clergyperson or a friend should also be invited (with spouse) to the reception. You may ask the clergyperson to say grace or the rabbi to offer the traditional prayer over the challah bread. However, note that Orthodox and Conservative rabbis will most likely not attend a non-kosher reception, even if you provide a special meal for them. Clarify this point before inviting them to avoid any embarrassment.

If your ceremony is in a space that is always booked for other events, request as early as possible in your planning to reserve the space for your rehearsal. The manager, if given enough time, may hold the space for you or schedule other events around you to accommodate a short rehearsal.

If you are getting married at a hotel or banquet hall that does numerous weddings, the captain or maitre d' will most likely coordinate the rehearsal for you. Your wedding coordinator may also be in charge of the line-up. If you can't rehearse where your ceremony is going to be, improvise in another space, perhaps where the dinner is being held, timing it so you finish before the other guests get there. Set up the first row of chairs with an aisle in the middle — the point is to give participants an idea of where to stand as well as whom they are walking with and in what order.

Unless you have hired the church organist to play for your ceremony, getting the musicians you've hired to play at the rehearsal as well is usually cost-prohibitive. Fortunately, music is not really necessary for a walk through. If, however, you'll sleep better having the "total experience," bring a tape of your music and a portable cassette recorder and have someone cue it at the right moments for the processional and recessional.

You need to give the participants a visual cue so they know when to go next down the aisle. You may tell them to wait until the person(s) ahead of them has reached a certain row. If you don't have a wedding consultant, you need to appoint someone director who can cue the musicians and the wedding party.

Many brides are superstitious about participating in their wedding rehearsal and often have a friend stand in for them.

When setting up chairs for a ceremony in an off-premise location, be sure that you overestimate the width of the aisle. Test it and retest it and insist that the caterer go over it with you. Your ceremony will be completely thrown off if you appear in a trained dress with both parents on either side, and you cannot negotiate the space between the chairs without resorting to single file.

Get with the program

Programs are a meaningful addition to your ceremony. They serve as mementos, honor the participants, and guide guests who may not know the particulars of a religious ceremony.

You may lay out your ceremony program with desktop publishing software before taking it to a printer, or have your program calligraphed, the cover offset on a heavy card stock and the inside copied onto plain paper. As a finishing touch, thread a satin ribbon through the cover or have the cover embossed.

Programs vary as much as ceremonies do. The front generally says the name of the couple, the date, and the place or perhaps something like "The Marriage Ceremony of Charlotte and Charles." You may also adorn the cover with a hand-painted flower or a pen and ink sketch of the locale, if it is unique.

The inside front cover, if you have several pages, is often where you thank family and friends for their support. The next page may list everyone involved in the ceremony — the officiant(s), the bride and groom, their parents, and the wedding party. When listing the music, include the prelude, the processional, any music or songs during the ceremony (including hymn numbers), and the recessional. Also include readings.

If you have many guests who may be unfamiliar with the ceremony traditions — for example, when to respond at particular points during Nuptial Mass — you may include a detailed ceremony. Otherwise, don't tell guests more than they need to know about your wedding day schedule (see Chapter 18).

On the back cover, you may put a personally meaningful poem, bit of prose, or blessing. This is also a good spot to gently explain that use of flash or video cameras is prohibited or goes against your wishes.

Don't forget . . .

One round of both the processional and the recessional should be sufficient. Just make sure that whoever is running the non-religious part of the rehearsal issues these reminders:

- Schedule the prelude music to begin when guests start arriving, 15 minutes to a half hour before the ceremony. After the ceremony, the music should continue until the last person leaves the ceremony area, or as soon as the reception music starts, if the reception is adjacent.
- Ushers should be welcoming and friendly to the guests, not stand in a clump. They should have extra directions to the reception.
- If children are in the ceremony, escort them to the bathroom before the processional.

- Reserved seating, aside from the first two or three rows for close friends or relatives, is rare these days. Because most couples are joining their family and friends together, having the ushers ask, "Bride's side or groom's side" is not necessary.
- When the bride arrives at the altar or bimah, she should hand her bouquet to her maid of honor so that her hands are free. If she is wearing gloves, she should remove these before the ring portion of the ceremony and hand them to an attendant. The attendant should remember to give these items back to the bride before the recessional.

- Keep your knees relaxed. If they lock at the altar for a prolonged period of time, the flow of blood is constricted and you may faint.
- For a Christian ceremony, the bride's mother is the last to be seated. If her husband seats her, he then returns for the bride.
- If you have an aisle runner, two ushers have the job of unfurling it after the bride's mother is seated and before the ceremony begins. They should grab it firmly in both hands and pull it down as straight as possible to the doorway, smoothing out all lumps and wrinkles. Some runners may have to be taped down at the end; ask your florist for a suitable tape.
- Ushers and bridesmaids should look happy and relaxed when walking down the aisle.
- Many churches and synagogues have heavy doors at the entranceway. Make sure that someone (usually a sexton or person in charge of the facility) is posted to open the doors and prop them open when the recessional music begins. We hate to see a just-married couple have to stop and wrench the doors open, and then wait for someone to hold them.
- If you do not have a wedding coordinator and you have several cars or limos going to the reception, you need someone to act as ground control. Appoint an usher-and-bridesmaid-traffic-team to handle the job.
- If you have travel time between your ceremony and reception, other musicians should be playing at your reception. The most important time for music is when the first guests enter an empty room.

Chapter 6
Other Aisle Styles

In This Chapter

- Thinking about themes
- Legitimizing same-sex unions
- Saluting military weddings
- Getting married again (and again)

In this chapter, we cover special situations that call for unique weddings. If one or both of you is in the military, if you want a wedding that is a little far out (but not absurd), or if you are both the same sex, you can have a wedding that is at once traditional and modern — and that is a true reflection of you as a couple. We also cover vow renewals and re-marriages. All told, the following is a reality check on the weddings of today.

Theme Me Up, Scotty

Even couples who love the idea of a theme wedding most often do not go for a full-scale effect. A circus theme, for example, where you eat in different rings, have caged tigers at the hors d'oeuvres reception, and garnish the dessert with animal crackers seems more suited to a sweet sixteen party than a wedding. Theme weddings can be complicated, costly, and a little confusing for guests, but if you have your heart set on recreating *The Phantom of The Opera,* for example, go for it — hey, it's your wedding. Just remember that sometimes theme weddings require a light touch; having your father clank across the dance floor in his Galahad armor for a medieval theme is asking a lot. In fact, a little theme can go a long way. If you sprinkle a few thematic touches throughout your wedding, guests get the point without being distracted from the real reason they are there.

You may choose a simple theme — autumn, for example — where the centerpieces are composed of leaves and vines and the room decor evokes a feeling of harvest bounty. But that doesn't mean you stick a thresher in the middle of the dance floor. However, if you are planning something elaborate, consider some interactive entertainment to get guests into the swing.

You can build a theme around almost anything that reflects your personalities, hobbies, and lifestyle. Even if you want a more classic wedding, you may consider incorporating a few thematic elements in other wedding-related fetes. In the following list, we offer a few ideas for decor, props, foods, and entertainment to get your creative juices flowing:

- **Country and western:** Serve down-home barbecue ribs, chicken, beef brisket, cole slaw, beans, and corn on the cob. After dinner, have a band come in for a set accompanied by dancers who teach the Texas Two-Step and line dancing. Consider changing into "western wedding garb" for this part of your reception — a fringed gown for the bride and large-buckle belt for the groom. Perhaps take your leave in a hay wagon wearing ten-gallon hats! One couple created this theme "whole hog" and got married in a barn. A country and western theme also works well for a rehearsal dinner.

  TIP

  For campy "cacti" to decorate tables or buffets, set watermelons on end (cut off the bottoms) in terra-cotta planters and poke wooden skewers into them to simulate the plant's needles.

- **Golf:** Cut AstroTurf into rounds to turn each table into a different hole from your favorite golf courses — and make the long head table a fairway. Turn waiters' service wagons into golf carts by using foam-board and dress the staff in plaid caps to resemble caddies. In a separate room, have golf-driving cages or create a goofy miniature golf course. Create a wedding cake (or groom's cake) that looks like a complete course with all the details from a sand trap to a pond. A miniature bride and groom top the cake in their golfing attire. This theme works for a rehearsal lunch or dinner or a bachelor/bachelorette party as well.

- **Holiday:** Valentine's Day, the Fourth of July, and Christmas all make for spectacular theme weddings. The possibilities for creative decor are numerous and because the day is already imbued with a festive atmosphere, getting your guests into a partying mood is easy. Two caveats, however: As we mention in Chapter 1, many people reserve certain holidays for close family gatherings, and paying holiday rates (usually time and a half or double time) for staff wages may be exorbitant. On the bright side, some spaces may already be decorated for the holiday so you'll need only minor additions.

- **Lounge acts:** If you are having a cocktail reception before a seated dinner, this theme is very "in." Rent sofas or buy cheap ones from a thrift store and cover them with throws of wild fabrics — leopard prints, gaudy purples, gold lames, and so on. Rent high-top tables and cover those with these fabrics as well. Serve a range of martinis (see Chapter 10) before dinner, and at dessert time send cigar smokers to this area and serve liqueurs. Taped lounge music works as background, although a piano player, if the budget allows, is perfect.

- **New Age:** Start with an invitation in multiple, translucent layers and dreamy wording — *Join with us as we join with each other. . . .* Set up tarot card readers, astrologers, and palm and face readers in booths draped in silk for guests to visit at their leisure. Pipe in tapes of lyrical new-age music at the hors d'oeuvres reception (a whole party of this music drives most guests to the doors screaming), lots and lots of candles, and navy blue tablecloths with a stars-and-planet pattern. Hand out velvet bags filled with small crystals and include a fortune phrase from such books as *I Ching* or *A Course In Miracles*.
- **Renaissance:** Get out your gimmal rings and pointy headpieces, known as hennins. Use cotton cloths as underlays on the tables to save money and drape velvet remnants in lush colors on top. Use cornucopias of oranges, apples, lemons, grapes, and nuts as centerpieces. Paint old books, terra cotta planters, and wicker baskets gold. Have dulcimers, harpsichords, lutes, and mandolins playing in the background and hire someone to teach the proper dances. For more ideas, call the Society for Creative Anachronism, which stages medieval and Renaissance festivals around the country.
- **Victorian:** This theme could be a bridal tea that starts with a croquet game, or an entire wedding where the invitation specifies period dress. Pendragon, Ink is a company that calligraphs invitations with delicate, hand-painted flowers; Victorian Papers makes old-timey stationery, stickers, and gift cards. A truly done-up Victorian-style wedding calls for tails or a morning suit for the groom replete with top hat, gloves, and walking stick. The bride may have her dress made for her (*Vintage Fashion Magazine* carries patterns) or rent an antique or reproduction from a store such as Bird-n-Hand Antiques.

As the Victorians were wild about flowers and adored the "Language of Flowers," name each table for the attributes of a flower or herb that is prominent in the centerpiece. The Fidelity table, for example, would have a centerpiece of mostly ivy; the Love table would feature roses; and the Remembrance table rosemary. Provide a mini flower dictionary as favors at each place so guests can ascertain the meaning of their centerpiece.

Choose carefully — some flowers may send the wrong message for a wedding. For example, larkspur means infidelity; marigold, grief; lavender, distrust; and yarrow, war.

Happy and Gay and Getting Married

In some ways, gay and lesbian weddings are not different from heterosexual weddings. Two people vow to honor and cherish, love and respect each other until death. They exchange rings, kiss, and walk up the aisle as everyone cries. The main difference is that despite society's growing acceptance of "unmarried domestic partners," no country fully recognizes marriages between two people of the same sex.

In the United States, a circuit court judge in Hawaii ruled in 1996 that the state failed to show a compelling reason for discriminating against same-sex marriages and ordered the state to start issuing marriage licenses to same-sex couples, which means that at this writing, pending an appeal to the state supreme court, Hawaii may become the first state to legalize same-sex marriages.

Many churches are unapologetically intolerant: the Evangelical Lutheran, Southern Baptist, and United Methodist churches, for example, forbid same-sex marriages to be conducted by their ministers or in their churches; Duke and Emory universities have explicitly banned all gay and lesbian ceremonies in their chapels, much to the outrage of campus protesters.

However, a handful of progressive denominations, such as the United Fellowship of Metropolitan Churches (which was formed more than 25 years ago to address the needs of Christian gays and lesbians), the Reform and Reconstructionist movements of Judaism, the Unitarian Universalist Church (see Chapter 5), and some churches within the United Church of Christ, do permit "commitment," "blessing," or "holy union" ceremonies for homosexual couples. Other tolerant religious groups include Buddhists, Pagans, and Quakers. Harvard University and Stanford University now permit same-sex marriages in their non-denominational chapels (both called Memorial Church, coincidentally), but only for employees, alumni, and students. Some religious leaders also perform same-sex weddings outside of church. The Episcopal Church is debating whether to create a gay and lesbian commitment ceremony. Curiously, the Catholic and Orthodox churches used to have liturgies for same-sex unions — in the Middle Ages — but have abandoned the practice in modern times.

Today's same-sex ceremonies outside a church often weave together a variety of religious and humanist philosophies. In keeping with their idea of an "Open Society," Humanists, in fact, have a ceremony specifically for gays and lesbians. Like many heterosexual couples, most lesbian couples choose to omit the "giving away" part of the Christian ceremony.

Many couples write their own vows, the main point being to make a public declaration of their love and commitment and have their friends and relatives validate their partnership. (See Chapter 5 for other tips on writing vows.) The decor may also reflect your sensibility. One gay couple we know made a chuppah using a wedding dress that belonged to one of their mothers.

If you are planning a same-sex wedding, be prepared to encounter even more annoyingly naïve queries than usual along the lines of "Who's the bride and who's the groom?" Your wedding attire may do little to clear up hetero-confusion — especially if you both wear tuxedos or both wear wedding gowns. Who cares as long as you both are comfortable?

Although many wedding registries are geared toward male-female couples, companies exist that cater to same-sex weddings. Do a search of the World Wide Web using the key words *gay and lesbian and weddings* to find these companies and first-person accounts of such ceremonies.

Operation: Wedding

Although military weddings of the past were an occasion for commissioned male military officers to wear full dress uniform and enlist their fellow military personnel in creating the arch of swords, given today's equal-opportunity military, brides who are commissioned officers are entitled to wear full dress uniform if they wish and female attendants who are in the military may participate in the arch of swords.

That said, military weddings are extremely traditional affairs, usually held in a base chapel or house of worship. The service is no different from that of a civilian wedding except at the end when the bride and groom make a dramatic exit under an arch of swords (Navy) or sabers (Army). As soon as the ceremony is over, the attendants line up on either side of the aisle. The head usher commands, "Draw swords/sabers!" and four to six attendants hold their weapons (blades up) up to form an arch. After the couple passes through, the head usher commands, "Return swords/sabers!" and the attendants return them to their sheaths. Any civilians in the wedding party also line up but merely stand at attention. The sword/saber bearers then turn and continue in the processional. Many couples prefer the arch to be formed on the church steps as they leave, which requires the attendants to make a quick exit by a side door so they can be in place as the bride and groom come out the front.

At the reception, the couple cuts the cake with a sword or saber. Besides flowers or what have you, the decorations often include the American flag and the standard of the military unit. (See Chapter 13 for use of military titles on invitations.)

Surprise!

Virtually unheard of until recently, surprise weddings are gaining popularity among couples who have been married before and/or can handle planning a party but not a full-scale wedding. In this situation, the couple sends out invitations for some sort of celebratory occasion — perhaps a graduation or birthday. Once their lucky guests are assembled, the couple announces that the guests are about to watch them get married. We know of one couple who threw a Halloween party and dressed as a bride and groom. Halfway through the evening, the couple asked for everyone's attention and announced that earlier in the day they had gotten hitched at city hall and wanted to thank everyone for coming to their wedding reception.

The other kind of surprise wedding is risky to say the least, and you better be absolutely sure of yourself before attempting it. In this scenario, multitudes of friends witness the bride or groom springing a proposal on the other and then (hopefully) the wedding that follows.

Private Ceremony, Public Party

If you have a destination or honeymoon-wedding (see Chapter 19), or for other reasons have only a few guests at your ceremony, you may want to throw a bash sometime after the fact. Whether the two of you or your parents host, this party should be an all-out celebration. Display large photos of yourselves getting married — guests love to see them. Mount a montage of photos on foamboard and prop it on an easel or on the escort card table. In a pithy toast to your parents and/or the guests, diplomatically explain why you chose to have your wedding this way. ("We felt we wanted our vows to be private, and they were exactly as we hoped they would be. And now, to have the best of both worlds and be able to celebrate with our loved ones makes everything perfect.") The goal is to tie the two events together so everyone can share your happiness.

One More Time

When it comes to second, third, fourth (and so on) marriages, the rules are no longer different from those for first weddings. If you are one of those people who speak of your first wedding as if it were a dream directed by your parents, now's your chance to create a ceremony and reception that is truly yours. (Think of Samuel Johnson's definition of remarriage: the triumph of hope over experience.) That may mean you approach the altar in full wedding regalia — lace, tulle, white tie, tails — or skip the traditional wedding hoopla in favor of an understated luncheon with you both in elegant suits. Do what is meaningful to you.

One of the most sensitive issues in remarriage is dealing with children from a previous relationship. As with every aspect of child-raising, don't assume anything. To appoint a child best person, which you see as a great honor, may in fact leave the child feeling enormously guilty about the other parent. But to leave children out of the ceremony altogether and have them attend only as guests may alienate them from the new family unit you are forming. Their role in the ceremony should depend on their age, attitude, and relationship with each of you (old and new spouses alike). If any of the children are teenagers, let them invite some friends to the wedding, too. Such overtures can go a long way toward developing peaceful relations for the future. (For tips on dealing with children in this situation, see Chapters 1 and 4.)

Say It Again: Renewing Your Vows

Some couples choose to reaffirm their vows because they didn't (or couldn't) have a religious ceremony the first time and want to be wed in holy matrimony. Other reasons to have reaffirmations include wanting an elaborate party if the original reception was very simple, or celebrating a spiritual or emotional renewal or a significant family event, such as the birth of a grandchild. Because this is not a legally binding ceremony, the couple may have anyone they want officiate. Having the same officiant and attendants can be touching. Religious vow renewals often take place during the regular services in the couple's house of worship. Otherwise, both the ceremony and reception may be at home or, for a blow-out party, in an event space (see Chapter 2).

If you are planning on inviting guests to a vow renewal, make it clear that gifts are out of the question. People may get the idea if you have a very private ceremony and a big bash, but you may have to convey your wishes by word of mouth. This is especially important if you are renewing your vows less than 15 years after your original ones. Unless you have experienced an extraordinary situation, people may feel strange attending a renewal of vows so soon.

Usually the couple themselves issue the invitations, but sometimes their children or, more rarely, other family or friends host the event. Chapter 13 provides a full-blown look at invitation wording, but here's how a typical renewal invitation may read:

The honour of your presence

[The pleasure of your company]

is requested at the reaffirmation

of the wedding vows of

Mr. and Mrs. Wylie Beauregard Blandsky

[Wylie Beauregard and Ida Kerfuffle Blandsky]...

Or, if you want something less formal:

Join with us as we celebrate

our twenty-five years

of joy together

and renew our promises

for eternity . . .

Part III

Eat, Drink, and Be Very Merry

"...and here's yet another photo of Marsha and me ruining a perfectly good shot of the back of Uncle Leo's head."

In this part . . .

Regardless of how grand or simple you plan for your nuptials to be, you will most likely decide to have some sort of a reception afterward. Whether it's cocktails and soft music in the garden or a full-blown gourmet meal with a 14-piece band at a ritzy hotel, we give you all the information you need to make your reception a smashing success. You *and* your guests will be glad you read these chapters.

Chapter 7

Music, Sweet Music

In This Chapter

- Figuring out what is music to your ears
- Finding the perfect band and/or DJ
- Auditioning the talent
- Working with your band leader

You both are giddy with emotion as you glide arm in arm to the dance floor for your first dance together as husband and wife. For a moment you could swear the bandleader, sounding rather like a game show voiceover, just mispronounced your names in his introduction, but you are too busy readying yourselves for the foxtrot you've spent weeks perfecting. With a flourish, the band begins to play. The melody sounds, well, strangely like Aunt Myrtle gargling in the morning at a furious pace.

Tears (but definitely not of joy) run down your cheeks and you pray that you will wake up in a cold sweat, just as you have several times in the past month.

The point is that music is an extremely important aspect of your ceremony and undoubtedly the element that sets the tone and pace of your reception. People may not remember exactly what they ate, but they will remember whether they danced all night or stuffed the dinner rolls in their ears.

Taking a Band Stand

Talented musicians, like prime locations, go fast. No matter how much time you allot for planning your wedding, finding and booking the band should be one of the first things to get done. Also, if your idea of a slow dance consists of hanging on to each other for dear life, start taking dance lessons sooner rather than later so you can look as relaxed and poised as the couple in Figure 7-1.

Figure 7-1: All eyes are upon you for your first dance, so choreograph your moves ahead of time.

Photo by Terry deRoy Gruber

Before you begin band shopping, put your thoughts in order. Who are your guests? Are they all about the same age or do they cover several generations? Do either of you have strong musical preferences? What do you like to listen to? What can't you bear? What could you compromise on without being miserable? Elicit opinions about music from people important to you — your parents and friends — and find out what kind of music keeps them on the dance floor. Bear in mind, however, that in the end you cannot please everybody. As with other aspects of your wedding, you must determine whose enjoyment is most important and plan accordingly.

When hiring a band, you can opt for eclecticism or virtuosity. A band that offers a full repertoire, from swing to funk to ethnic favorites, is probably not expert at all of it. If you, like many couples these days, are averse to traditional wedding bands, fearing a reprise of Bill Murray's lounge lizard act on *Saturday Night Live,* you may wish to hire a very unwedding-like band. Just be sure they are professional enough to remain upright throughout their performance.

Music-union rules sometimes specify the minimum number of musicians that are allowed to play in certain on-premise spaces. For most dancing crowds of 100 or more, you probably want to hire six pieces minimum. If you want specific tunes that require certain instruments, discuss with the bands you interview what makes sense and what is overkill for both the number of guests and the size of the space. Ask the catering or banquet director's opinion as well. More is not always better.

Breakfast and lunch receptions are generally lower key and may not require a band. Although many of the points for evaluating and hiring musicians for the reception also apply to that for the ceremony, for a complete discussion of ceremony music, see Chapter 5.

Where the Bands Are

Looking for the perfect band can bring on audio overload. From time to time you may need a little "band-aid" in the form of a few days off to keep you from hiring the next group you see because you can no longer distinguish one from another.

To find the perfect band, consider the following:

- **Concert promoters:** Call the office and endear yourself to someone up-front. Fabulous bands that open for bigger acts are often available for hire.
- **Friends:** Have they been to any weddings or other parties lately where the band kept the crowd on its feet all night? What kind of music was it? What sort of reception? Can your friends' musical taste be trusted?
- **Hotels:** Call the banquet manager of the nearest large hotel. Better yet, ask the captain or maitre d' because they usually don't have a vested interest in promoting a particular band but care a great deal about one that runs a good party.
- **Music agencies/band representatives:** This is the most common way to find a band of whatever size and style you're interested in.
- **Music colleges:** Call the job-placement office and post "Band Wanted" posters on bulletin boards.
- **Music labels:** Comb the liner notes of albums for studio musicians who may play with other groups and call the American Federation of Musicians for their agents' name. (Don't be disappointed if the back-up band for Sheryl Crow doesn't respond hastily to your query.)
- **Music publications:** Follow the reviews and check the band listings both locally and nationally.
- **Nightclubs:** Call the booker for recommendations and for ways to get in touch with a favorite band's agent.
- **Phone books:** Look under Bands, Music, and Weddings in the Yellow Pages. Some cities also distribute phone books for specific ethnic groups.
- **Vendors**: Photographers, caterers, and other vendors who work on site with bands usually know who is hot.

Auditioning the Band

Wedding tomes delight in advising you to get dolled up and go hear a band in person before signing them. We really have a problem with this because it stands to reason that a bandleader who invites you to witness a band's talents at another wedding would have no qualms about using your reception as a marketing tool as well. The only time you can audition a band at someone else's wedding is if the bandleader assures you that the bride and groom have magnanimously agreed (out of sympathy, no doubt) to have you drop by. When you do, remain inconspicuous.

Audio tapes (or compact discs) and videotapes are often your only way to check out a band. Find out when the recording was made and under what conditions. If recorded at an event, the quality may be uneven. Studio recordings may be technically flawless but bear no semblance to what the band really sounds like. Videotapes can also be technically enhanced and unscrupulous music agents are not above showing photogenic band members dubbed with different, more talented, musicians. Unless you work as a sound technician, this fraud is often hard to spot. You must rely on the reputation and your own instincts.

If you're interested in a band named for a famous bandleader, find out whether she or he is still with the band or the musicians have bought the name. Many bands may be named after this persona. After you determine that the bandleader is indeed the original and the one you want, schedule a meeting with him or her.

Many contemporary bands use *samples* — digital recordings of specific instruments stored on computer disks and played from a keyboard — to augment their sound. You can't tell whether a band uses samples from an audio tape, so be sure to ask. Otherwise, you may feel confounded when you hear a trumpet solo with nary a trumpeter in sight. Ideally, samples are used to enhance instruments being played rather than in lieu of them. If a phantom orchestra doesn't impinge on your sense of reality, or if you like the idea of an invisible chorus of angels serenading your guests, you can save oodles by hiring a one-man-sampler-band.

In general, sampled pianos, basses, organs, and strings are common and sound fine. Sampled guitars, trumpets, saxophones, and other instruments that involve expressive playing techniques tend to sound canned.

In evaluating a band, ask a few questions:

- Does the contract stipulate that the musicians who appear on the video or play on the audio are the ones who perform at your wedding? Always insist on seeing a photograph with audio tapes.
- Is the audio or video tape recorded live or studio produced? Is the sound technically enhanced?

- If you're listening to an audio tape, how many musicians are playing on it? How many vocalists? How many instruments?
- Does the band use techno-tricks on stage such as sampling? (These in themselves are not bad, but you want to know when they are used.)
- When was the tape made? (Their style or players may have changed dramatically.)
- Does the band bring its own sound system? How large a room can it accommodate?
- Who sets up the instruments and when do they arrive?
- Is continuous music in your agreement? Depending on the size of the band, a minimum of one or two musicians should always be on stage while the others are on break.
- What do the band members wear? Does formal dress cost extra?
- Do you need to rent a piano or do they use an electric keyboard?
- Does the bandleader or another band member act as master of ceremonies?
- Is overtime based on the hour or half hour? What leeway do you have? What is the overtime rate?
- Does the band have another gig before or after yours? Is the band prepared to play overtime?
- No matter what their repertoire is, can they play other songs important to you such as a hora or other ethnic classics and favorite pop hits?
- If you have an original or esoteric piece you want played, will they learn it and how much lead time do they need? What do they charge to arrange it?

If you hear a band that you feel certain you are going to book but you need a few days to mull it over, make sure they give you the right of first refusal. In other words, they will call you if someone else is waving a check under their noses for the same date. If they won't, get out your checkbook.

Whether out of laziness or short-term memory loss, many wedding bands trying to get through a set of music that is not their specialty often resort to medleys. We personally find medleys jarring and unsatisfying. If you do too, specify that you want "R-E-S-P-E-C-T" not "R-E-S-P-."

Which reminds us, your Don't Play List is far more important than your Play List. Seemingly benign songs that remind you of a past love, your high school chemistry teacher who hated you, or a band you despise on principle may mar your wedding if your bandleader is not apprised of such. Check the band's own play list as well.

Picking Up the Beat

Once you've written up your wedding-day schedule (see Chapter 18), go over it with the bandleader either by phone or in person. Specifically, you want to clarify:

- **First dance:** The name of the song, when it is to be played, at what tempo, and how you will be introduced.
- **Introductions:** If the bandleader is acting as master of ceremonies and you wish to have family and wedding party members introduced, write down their names phonetically and their relationship to you. Make a special note of people who are divorced, deceased, or not attending to save the bandleader from making a gaffe.
- **Breaks:** When and where, based on a consultation with the maitre d', the band will eat. If you want continuous music, the band must eat in shifts.
- **Gag orders:** Be extremely specific about how and when the bandleader makes announcements. At the same time, be reasonable: Even if you don't want to risk the bandleader running off at the mouth, *somebody* has to tell people when the next course is being served.
- **Etiquette:** Stipulate no eating, drinking, or smoking on stage (unless you don't mind, of course).
- **Stage set:** Ask what their music stands look like and whether they go with your decor or have the name of the band emblazoned on them. The stage should also not look like a dressing room. Provide a secure place for the band to store their personal effects.
- **Who's running the show:** Be certain the maitre d' and bandleaders work together in deciding when guests are dancing and when they are eating.

While this may be your first wedding, it may be the hundred that the band has played this year. A good friend of ours, a talented musician who has graduated from playing weddings, told us that the groups he played with were often so bored that they would fight over the selection of magazines they read surreptitiously on their music stands as they were performing. You can, however, get even jaded musicians to rise to the occasion:

- A well-fed band is a happy band. Musicians work weird hours and have erratic habits. Although you don't have to serve the band what you feed the guests, a leftover sandwich from the cafeteria does not cut it. A full meal served in a decent place plus a drink or beer may in fact make them play better.
- Give the band some leeway. Ask the band what they like to play and include it if possible. Don't dictate the play list down to the millisecond. Trust the pros to get the party moving.

- Early in the reception, you and your betrothed should approach the bandstand and introduce yourselves. Tell the band how happy you are to have them play at your wedding. This gesture alone may shock them into consciousness.
- If the bandleader or manager has specified certain arrangements such as a baby grand piano, a two-level platform, or extra mikes or lighting, make sure these details are attended to. If you can't supply it, tell them well in advance. Arriving at a gig to find specified items missing unnerves musicans.

Parking the band

At sites with an inlaid dance floor, the band's spot is usually obvious. If your reception is in an off-premise site, however, we suggest positioning the band and dance floor so that all the tables are equidistant from the band rather than putting the band at the front of the room so that guests seated at the back must pack a canteen before setting out in search of the dance floor. In principal, having tables between the dance floor and the bandstand cuts off the dynamic between the band and the dancers and can burst the eardrums of guests who happen to be seated in the crossfire. While you may be tempted to place tables *in the round,* you don't want guests gazing at the backs of musicians and their equipment.

Some considerations for the positioning the band:

- Where is the electrical source?
- Does the band need risers?
- What type of chairs does the band need?
- Is special lighting required?

You do not want the band rolling its instruments through the reception on its way to set up. So if you can afford it, pay for early setup. If you are hiring more than one DJ or band, have *all* the equipment set up on stage before the guests arrive. (Picture a double-header concert.)

Sound check

Volume is very subjective. Generation Xers generally like listening to music at a higher decibel level than their parents do. In our opinion, when people are being served or eating, the music (if any at all) should be low enough so people can speak in conversational tones. In any crowd, there is always someone who would find a harp deafening. All you can do is seat them as far away from the speakers as possible.

You must decide before the reception who is in charge of sound level. Nothing gets a bandleader hotter under the collar than getting mixed orders from you and your parents — "Turn it up!" "Turn it down!" "I thought I told you to turn it up!" "Did you see whose signature is on the check? I said turn it *down*!"

Keeping time

You typically hire a band for four hours, not including ceremony, cocktails, or overtime. A common mistake is to cut their starting time extremely close to avoid overtime at the end. Bands, however, are notorious for arriving one minute before show time. If you don't allow a 15-minute cushion in the beginning, you may find yourself hyperventilating as they do their sound check and your guests' stomachs are growling.

A talented bandleader knows how to pace a party. (In any case, give the leader a copy of your wedding schedule per Chapter 18.) Usually, the band plays upbeat — but not uptempo — dance music so that guests can take to the floor upon entering the dining room. The next phase of the party, which may involve toasts, the first course(s), and perhaps the first dance, calls for more sedate music. The band hits its stride after the main course is cleared, and then really kicks in for the latter part of the event. If you have a different concept, spell it out. Some couples want high-energy dance music in between courses from the beginning; others prefer no dancing until after the main course.

Bands sent out by an agency sometimes refuse to play until paid in full, so we advise you to pay your balance the day before. As for overtime, the band will bill you later. Clarify with the bandleader who is in charge of deciding whether the band will play overtime. If you and your spouse are paying for the band, you don't want one of your parents blithely telling the band, "Oh, please just keep playing. We're having such a *fabulous* time!"

Spin Doctors

A disc jockey at a wedding used to be as low-budget a choice as macaroni and cheese for the main course. Today that's not the case but rather a matter of the kind of music you want at your wedding. If your passion is to be a disco queen at your wedding, hire a DJ. If not, you may end up with the saddest of all possibilities: a balding, black-tied crooner singing "I Will Survive."

TIP

When two bands are better than one

If your musical taste differs from that of your fiancé(e) or parents, having two bands can make everyone happy and save you from an evening of mediocrity. After all, an R&B band will never heat up if it has to play at lullaby decibels, and a swing band can be at once pathetic and scary attempting to rock and roll.

Hiring a salsa, Klezmer, Zydeco, or Mariachi band for one set or for the cocktail bar can be a real treat for the guests. Try to find a band that either is very interactive (such as strolling musicans) or can bring dancers with them. The effect can be electric. Even avowed non-dancers may be coaxed onto the dance floor.

Consult with both your main bandleader and the maitre d' about the best time for the second band to come on. See if you can negotiate some leeway on the time, but don't expect the band to shave an hour off its fee.

While for $25 you may be able to hire your multi-pierced neighbor and his boom box, don't risk it. Hire a professional DJ and one adept at weddings rather than one who specializes in bar/bat mitzvahs, confirmations, or sweet sixteens. You may not be pleased to have Day-Glo yo-yos and balloon guitars catapulted at your guests as the DJ urges them to do the "Hokey-Pokey."

A DJ is only as good as the CDs he or she brings. Even though pros have an inventory of zillions, make a list of specific songs you want to ensure that they bring them. If you want your DJ to also act as master of ceremonies, be prepared to pay for two people — a front person and a spinner.

If you can squeeze it into your budget, have a DJ alternate with a live band. Music sounds as it was meant to, the band can play what they're good at, the DJ can offer versatility, and you still get the special energy between live musicians and those on the dance floor that is sometimes missing with a DJ alone.

Aside from the obvious musical questions, interview disc jockeys the same way you would other vendors. As with a band, you may have to go through an agency, which may resist your meeting with a specific one to interview. Your goal is to get past these salespeople and check out the talent. If the company has a reputation for sending out pros, ask to see letters of reference for the individual they plan to send to your reception. Also insist that you get to speak to the DJ by phone before the wedding. Among the things to verify:

- What the DJ will wear
- That the DJ or the agency will check out the electrical requirements and acoustics at your venue, especially if the DJ hasn't worked there before
- What the equipment looks like and whether the DJ needs a draped table for the compact disc player

- The size of the speakers and whether they can be camouflaged (doubtful, as we discuss in Chapter 11)
- Whether the DJ plans on using any theatrical lighting

Starting the Reception on the Right Note

As guests arrive for cocktails, they should be greeted by music. People tend to drift in and, until the crowd reaches critical mass, they need an icebreaker (which background music provides). Musicians should start off fairly loud and decrease the volume as the room fills up so people can hear each other. Decide with the maitre d' where to place the cocktail musicians so they don't interfere with the exits, hors d'oeuvre stations, or bars.

Even if both your ceremony and reception are very traditional, you can add some whimsy to the cocktail hour without unsettling anyone. For example, you may hire a DJ just for cocktails. This is not the place, however, for a performance that demands people's undivided attention.

Depending on your number of guests, you should have two musicians minimum: a solo flute or guitar will not be heard over the clanking of ice in drink glasses, let alone the din of excited post-ceremony chatter. If you have more than 125 guests, seriously consider having three musicians.

Typically you can strike a deal with the musicians in the band for a few of them to play for the ceremony and/or the cocktails at a per-musician price. While this may be a good deal financially, it can be awkward musically and logistically. First of all, unless these musicians are able to play different instruments, your whole evening will sound the same. Secondly, whether your ceremony is in a different location than your reception or in an adjoining room, the musicians have to move to begin playing for cocktails. The musicians will either have to scurry out ahead of the guests leaving the ceremony, or they will be breathlessly setting up as guests arrive for cocktails. Later, when you want the full band set up at least 20 minutes before the guests enter the dining room, the same musicians have to thread through the crowd carrying their instruments unless a second set has been supplied. Even though guests may not notice that the music has stopped, they may find the musicians packing up and leaving odd.

Chapter 8
Booking the Cooking

In This Chapter

- Communicating with your caterer
- Creating memorable menus
- Making simple food fabulous
- Alternatives to the sit-down dinner reception

"He who plays host without giving his personal care to the repast is unworthy of having friends to invite to it."

— Jean Antheime Brillat-Savarin

The ceremony was splendid — neither of you fumbled your vows and there wasn't a dry eye in the house. Now your guests ooh and aah as they promenade into the reception space, which is aglow with candles and as fragrant as the gardens of Giverny. A brigade of tuxedoed staff appears, choreographed as if in a Busby Berkeley musical. In unison, 150 hands reach down and pluck an exotic-looking hors d'oeuvre from a gleaming tray, pop the morsel into their mouths — and begin frantically searching for cocktail napkins in which to spit.

How can you keep this from happening at your reception? Don't expect to wave your magic wedding wand and turn processed cheese slices into brie en croûte — it ain't gonna happen. But creating a meal that is imaginative and tasty does not require magic. All you need is time, tenacity, and trust in your own tastebuds.

Producing Meals That Rise to the Occasion

If you're renting an off-premise space (see Chapter 2), you need to find a caterer. While asking friends for recommendations may seem natural, food taste is really, really subjective.

Consider these alternatives:

- **Restaurant chefs:** Ask the chef at your favorite restaurant whether they cater outside of their premises — or if he or she is particularly impressed with any caterer in the area.
- **Professional associations:** If you're planning a long-distance wedding and have absolutely no clue where to begin, consult a professional association such as the International Special Events Society, 800-688-ISES.
- **Vendors:** The best recommendations often come from other suppliers — bands, florists, party coordinators — who have worked with these caterers and know what really goes on behind the kitchen doors.

Call and ask caterers and banquet managers for a package that includes sample menus. If the packet is stuffed with recommendation letters, as is often the case, the majority should be current. Don't be shy about calling references. Write down your questions before you pick up the phone. Be as specific as possible in relation to the style you have in mind for your reception as well as how much help you can expect with the ceremony and other aspects not directly related to food and service.

Some questions to ask people about their experience with specific caterers:

- Did the caterer deliver what they promised?
- Were expensive items such as shrimp plentiful?
- Was the staff neat and prompt?
- Were there enough bartenders and service people? Did guests ever have to wait for anything?
- Was the food tasty and attractive?
- What were the downsides, if any? (To get an honest answer, qualify this question by saying, "Not that your answer would necessarily keep me from hiring this caterer . . .")

Before making any decisions, meet with caterers in person, preferably at their kitchen/offices. This meeting should give you a fair idea of their manner and workmanship. Are they brusque? Disorganized? Clean? Does their workspace smell yummy? Are they legally licensed? Does their kitchen have posted a certificate of inspection?

Roll up your sleeves

As with other things in life, the greater the interest you take, the better the results and the more you will enjoy it. The best way to start designing your meal is to have some idea of what you would like to serve. Whether you are dealing with an in-house catering operation (such as at a banquet facility, restaurant, club, or hotel) or hiring a caterer for a site you're renting, before you concoct elaborate haute cuisine wish lists, start with their sample menus, which constitute their greatest hits. (If they kept getting complaints about the roast beef, they wouldn't continue putting it on the menu.) Request to meet with the banquet manager and/or catering director and ask them to tell you — for real — the kitchen's strengths and weaknesses. Now is a good time to also ask for sample *function sheets,* which are the staff's list of data as it pertains to an event such as the menu that was actually served, the wines that accompanied it, and other service details. These should give you a realistic idea of how dishes can be mixed and matched.

Perusing dozens of sample menus with tantalizing-sounding dishes can be overwhelming. To focus your search for the perfect meal, take a few preliminary steps:

- **Take a palate poll:** What are your and your intended's favorite restaurants? Favorite meals? What do family and friends like to eat?
- **Adopt a recipe:** Go through cookbooks and food magazines for ideas and concepts. Keep in mind, however, that unless you're holding a wedding for ten people, hand-rolled pasta with carbonara sauce will not translate. Chefs are usually open to using your favorite recipes — as long as they come from reliable sources such as professional cookbooks (available in libraries and bookstores) or other caterers, as opposed to Aunt Myrtle's mah-jongg club.
- **Tap your know-it-all pals:** If you have friends who always know the hot new restaurants or actually work in the food business, ask them for their subjective opinions. ***Caution:*** If they're really helpful, you may have to invite them to your wedding.

Is there a chef in the house?

Find out who is really in charge of cooking your meal — the banquet chef, sous chef, or someone farther down the totem pole. Meeting with a well-known executive chef or the chef for the restaurant kitchen does no good unless one of them is actually involved in the preparation of your event.

If at all possible, meet with the chef to determine what the kitchen staff can produce well for a group of your size. While chefs have a reputation for being intimidating, in our experience they are flattered when someone cares about their opinion and that can have a decided impact on what comes out of the kitchen. If the catering manager and chef, as well as the references you've called, all recommend a very basic menu, listen to them and keep it simple.

Present yourself as someone who feels food is important but also understands what can and cannot be done based on the kitchen, staff, and number of guests. If the chef is against attempting risotto for 200, don't force it. One of the worst mistakes you can make is trying to get a kitchen staff that has barely mastered the art of medium rare to duplicate some fabulous dish you tasted at Spago, especially if the reception is in an off-premise space without kitchen facilities, such as a tent. Professionals are most likely not being stubborn or lazy when they deep-six an idea but rather know what works in a catering oven in the middle of a field. Frequently, it's impossible to cook things from scratch in that scenario, so a caterer has to take into account what can be partially cooked ahead of time and finished on site without affecting the taste. If, however, you sense that the staff is capable of doing more then they've been called upon to do in the past, use your well-honed (by this point) negotiation skills to get them to prepare it as part of the tasting menu.

A matter of tasting

After you book a space or caterer, we feel that you're entitled to a tasting, so make sure that is either spelled out in the contract or in an oral agreement. (For more information on what should be in your contract, see Chapter 16.) Schedule the tasting far enough in advance so that you have time for a second one if needed, though not so far ahead that key ingredients are out of season.

If your wedding is in a banquet space that is part of a restaurant, the meal for your reception may be prepared in a banquet kitchen completely separate from the main restaurant kitchen. Therefore, a meal in the restaurant may bear no resemblance to the food you may have at your wedding.

Taste in tandem. Tastings are one of the most fun aspects of the wedding planning. And considering all the stress and anxiety you two are going through, don't you deserve some fun?

Your caterer will tell you how many people you can bring to the tasting. Besides you and your fiancée, the banquet manager should be there to offer professional comments and suggestions. This also may be a good place to include your parents or in-laws. One couple we know handed out tasting surveys for everyone to fill out. Months later, the questionnaires made a humorous wedding memento.

Ask to taste two or three options for each course. You may be set on filet mignon, but after tasting the chef's specialty lamb, you change your mind completely. The idea for all concerned is to attend only one tasting. However (and this is not going to make us any friends among the catering population), the tasting is not just a rubber stamp. In principle, a kitchen should shine at a meal for four or six. If it doesn't, the meal served to your guests could be even worse.

Ask questions. Is it possible to have this sauce on that dish? What if we served this with coffee ice cream instead of vanilla? Take notes, draw pictures, be ridiculously detailed. Yours is probably not the only event that the chef is working on at the moment and details that are important to you may fall through the cracks unless you furnish notes or a follow-up letter summarizing your desires.

The food's presentation should be exactly as it would be at your wedding. If you decide on poached salmon that is plated, rimmed by a painstakingly drizzled nouvelle sauce, and garnished with flowers at your tasting, a waiter should not dump it from a tray at your reception. If they use the same china, glass, and silver that you've selected for your wedding, all the better. Rental companies are usually delighted to provide you with sample place settings for the tasting.

You are tasting with your eyes as well as your mouth. If to your mind a chicken breast is smooth and looks like a pillow and the chef likes to serve them with grill marks on either side, you want to know that before your wedding.

Because of the cost of labor and ingredients, places often won't let you taste the hors d'oeuvres unless they're booking huge numbers consistently. In such cases, ask if they have an event coming up and if they can make up a "take-out" tray for you to sample at home. (You will, of course, offer to pay for this.) If that's not feasible, can they at least show you photographs and describe ingredients in detail?

Food and wine are meant to be tasted together, so either bring what you would consider serving or ask the caterer to supply some selections in your price range.

Go about the tasting professionally. Don't stuff yourself with every last hors d'oeuvre and lick your plate clean; save room for dessert. Enjoy yourself. This is probably the only time you'll get to savor this meal because chances are you'll not have time to eat at your wedding.

Ask your caterer to pack a picnic basket on your wedding day to assuage the inevitable 3 a.m. munchies. This is also the time to arrange for leftovers to go to a local soup kitchen or "harvesting" charity.

The Beauty of the Feast

The type of meal you choose to serve has as great an effect on your entire wedding as the music. A lunch can be as formal as a dinner provided both are seated and served, but something about an evening event encourages guests to really party. A full meal served via food stations can be as formal or low-key as you wish. Ditto for a cocktail reception where you have only partial seating.

Choose the hors d'oeuvres in conjunction with the rest of the meal, so you don't duplicate foods and perhaps follow up salmon rolls at cocktails with grilled salmon at dinner. Also take into consideration the rehearsal dinner menu. When in doubt, the wedding meal takes precedence.

Post-nuptial nibbles

A cocktail reception usually follows most wedding ceremonies where a complete meal is served. While having a cocktail reception before your meal is not an ironclad law of hospitality, even a single celebratory drink with a few carrot sticks adds to the festivities. Not to mention that wedding ceremonies tend to produce great emotional upwellings, and guests need a release before being herded into the dining room.

Cocktail receptions can be short and sweet. The trend, however, is toward elaborate cocktail periods and less frou-frou main courses. In any case, if cocktails are more than a transition — longer than 20 minutes — you have to serve some food other than chips and nuts.

Serving a variety of hors d'oeuvres can eliminate the need for offering a choice of entrees, for which there can be a surcharge. However, a dozen hors d'oeuvre stations followed by a main course of half a cow does not impress guests with your hospitality or wealth, but instead leaves them immobilized, unable to dance, and most likely sick to their stomachs. The trick is to design a menu that has broad appeal, is appetizing, and leaves guests with energy to party.

In addition to passed hors d'oeuvres, having one or two stations with, say, guacamole and chips and a baked brie not only helps eliminate people jumping the waiters as they come out the kitchen door but also provides a natural gathering spot. We feel hors d'oeuvres should be served with one type per tray rather than mixed together so that guests have a sense of the diversity.

Passed hors d'oeuvres are usually priced per piece or included in the meal package with a choice of hot and cold. For hors d'oeuvre stations such as a raw bar, carving station, or pasta assortment, you are most likely charged per head. You are not out of line to ask how many pieces of each hors d'oeuvre are served within your price level. What seems like a very attractive cocktail reception price could be because they are serving five liverwurst patés per person and one filet en croûte per ten guests. Caterers we queried agree that between eight and ten hors d'oeuvres per person is ample for a one-hour cocktail reception.

When it comes to shrimp, although you can almost never have enough, figure on about three per person; we have never been to a wedding where a single piece was left on a waiter's tray. You are typically charged per piece, even if other hors d'oeuvres are priced as a package. Shrimp are graded according to the number per pound by using the following shorthand terms: 21-25s, 16-20s, U-15s, U-12s, and U-7s. A pound of 16-20s, for example, contains between 16 and 20 shrimp, while a pound of U-15s contains fewer than, or "under," 15. U-7s, therefore, are comparatively huge (and rare).

If you like shrimp, but whole cocktail shrimp are beyond your budget, ask your caterer about more economical alternatives such as mini shrimp toasts or shrimp salad on rye rounds.

Variety shows: Buffet stations

The old-fashioned buffet comprising an endlessly long table with a salad, a main course, a vegetable, and a starch for which you stand in an endlessly long line has been (thankfully) relegated to school cafeterias. Food stations that enable you to serve eclectic and creative meals without traffic jams are very much in vogue. Various types of foods can be had at "stations" around the room. One station may offer carved meats; another, fruits and cheeses; another, stuffed vegetables; and still another, seasonal salad combinations.

Your reception will be much shorter with a buffet than with a served meal because down time between courses disappears. You can add time by serving a seated first course, then inviting a few tables at a time to go to the food stations. This invitation, by the way, should always be delivered discreetly to each table by the headwaiter and *never* announced over the microphone.

Buffet stations are not a bargain option. They are at least as expensive as seated dinners and, depending on what assortment of dishes you choose, they can in fact cost more. Having several stations requires extra plates so that guests can take a fresh one at each station — something to keep in mind if you are renting china. You also need plenty of staff to bus this many plates and man the stations. When guests are allowed to serve themselves, you have no control over portions, and you'd be amazed at how quickly entropy takes over, turning beautifully designed food panoramas into federal disaster areas.

The food, as shown in Figure 8-1, is a large part of the decor. When choosing your menu, pick a variety of colors, textures, and temperatures. A line-up of even the heaviest silver chafing dishes looks fairly institutional. Also, imagine how things will look after they've been sitting in a chafing dish for an hour, although we would hope each dish is replenished before its contents are reduced to a few coagulated lumps. Choose items that can also be served on platters, in beautiful bowls, and from baskets. Ask the caterer: Who decorates the stations? What sort of interesting vessels do they own? Do they have specific props for certain dishes, such as netting for a seafood station? (See Chapter 16 for more about decorating with food.)

Figure 8-1: For an Asian-inspired menu, a food station may incorporate an orchid plant, plates of sushi on galax leaves, and a pagoda-like lantern.

Please be seated

If you are serving a seated lunch or dinner, the first course should be light and simple — cold soup in the spring or summer, a composed salad plate, or vegetables vinaigrette — so the guests are not stuffed to the gills by the time the main course arrives. The number of courses depends both on budget and how you want to time your wedding. Obviously, the more courses, the longer the party.

How do different foods look together? Is everything monochromatic? Might the food look more stately on a larger plate rather than all jostled together? Would it be prettier with the sauce underneath rather than on top? Even if you adore *haricot verts* (your basic green beans), might a stuffed tomato liven up the plate more?

Be clear about how and when things are served. You have spent a great deal of time (and money) on how these tables are going to look when you come into the dining room. One of our personal dislikes: tables that are preset with the first course and/or the accoutrements for coffee service. Although sometimes necessary, preset food makes people question how long it's been there and coffee service on the table looks like the party has to catch a bus.

Food is usually served in one of three ways:

- **French service:** Waiters heat plates and garnish food at a side table or cart called a *guéridon*. If done properly, this technique is very impressive. Although considered for eons the height of elegance, it is rather slow and requires a great deal of space.
- **Russian service:** Waiters serve you from a silver platter. Often erroneously called French service.
- **Plated or à la carte:** Waiters carry the food out on plates. By far the most elegant way to serve plated food is to have waiters carry two plates at a time and, choreographed by the captains, "blanket" the room, completing one table at a time. The main advantage is that the food arrives at each place the way it was meant to look rather than improvised by the waiters. The downside is that service takes longer than French or Russian service.

People who request alternative meals (kosher, vegetarian, and so on) should not be punished by being served their main course when everyone else has gone on to the wedding cake. The best way to keep this from happening is to give the maitre d' a list of guests along with their alternative orders and table numbers as early as possible. (To do this, you need a seating chart; you can find directions in Chapter 11.)

For food to be certified *kosher,* it must meet the requirements of strict Jewish law. Ingredients and the equipment used to produce the food must not contain or come into contact with foodstuffs or materials that are restricted such as pork and shellfish. Contrary to a common misconception, a "rabbi's blessing" is not part of the koshering process. Kosher rules require, among other things, that meat be slaughtered in a certain way and that meat and dairy products not mix.

Skimping on the number of servers can be a penny-wise but pound-foolish decision. Figuring the number of waiters per guests is usually based on ten guests per table. Depending on regional standards the ratio of waiters to guests varies, ranging from two waiters per ten guests (or one table) for an extremely formal meal to one waiter per 25 guests (or two and a half tables) for a simple meal. If you're trying to save money, this is not the place to cut corners. Adding one or two extra servers adds to the overall hospitality of the event more than, say, an extremely expensive wine. Doing so may preclude a scenario where no waiters are on the floor to pour *any* wine because they are all in the kitchen picking up the entree. Getting a waiter's attention should not feel like hailing a cab in a typhoon.

Making Menus Memorable

No matter what kind of wedding feast you have, do not underestimate its powerful symbolism as a grand communion. That does not mean you have to pay a grand tab — but do invest time and creativity in its planning. For inspiration, we asked a few of our favorite catering professionals for some menus from particularly wonderful weddings they've produced. Their specialties and choices vary, yet all are packed with ideas for complementary dishes and stylish serving suggestions that can be adapted to any size wedding or budget.

The Rainbow Room and its banquet rooms are quintessential New York locations. The combination of the extraordinary views from the 64th and 65th floors of Rockefeller Center, Chef Waldy Malouf's exquisite cuisine, and a staff of true pros makes for unforgettable weddings.

Along Came Mary is a Los Angeles-based catering company that is nationally known for their lavish and innovative presentations as well as for their

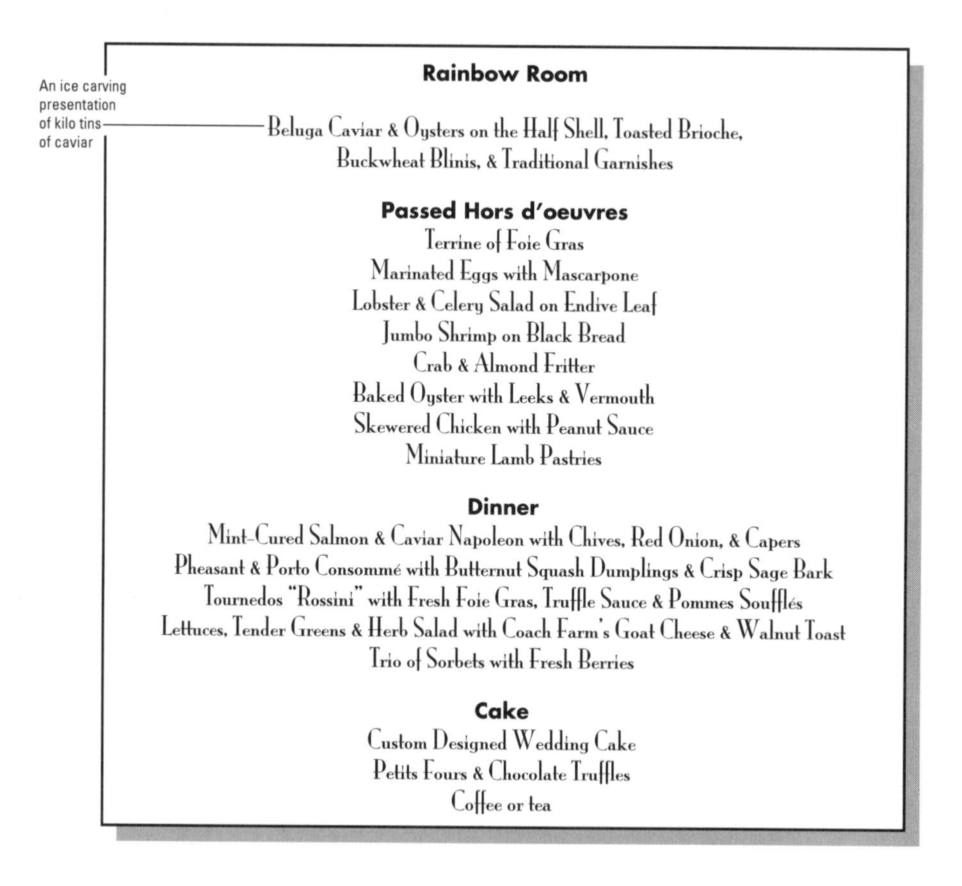

An ice carving presentation of kilo tins of caviar

Rainbow Room

Beluga Caviar & Oysters on the Half Shell, Toasted Brioche,
Buckwheat Blinis, & Traditional Garnishes

Passed Hors d'oeuvres

Terrine of Foie Gras
Marinated Eggs with Mascarpone
Lobster & Celery Salad on Endive Leaf
Jumbo Shrimp on Black Bread
Crab & Almond Fritter
Baked Oyster with Leeks & Vermouth
Skewered Chicken with Peanut Sauce
Miniature Lamb Pastries

Dinner

Mint-Cured Salmon & Caviar Napoleon with Chives, Red Onion, & Capers
Pheasant & Porto Consommé with Butternut Squash Dumplings & Crisp Sage Bark
Tournedos "Rossini" with Fresh Foie Gras, Truffle Sauce & Pommes Soufflés
Lettuces, Tender Greens & Herb Salad with Coach Farm's Goat Cheese & Walnut Toast
Trio of Sorbets with Fresh Berries

Cake

Custom Designed Wedding Cake
Petits Fours & Chocolate Truffles
Coffee or tea

exciting, cutting-edge menus. Their buffet selections showcase "fusion" recipes that draw on many diverse cuisines.

Along Came Mary

Passed Hors d'oeuvres

Potato Rostis sautéed golden brown and topped with crème fraîche and caviar; garnished with fresh dill

Caramelized Onion Pizza topped with sun dried tomatoes, goat cheese, kalamata olives, and fresh thyme

Tequila Cured Salmon sliced paper thin and served on a Corn Chevre Fritter with Grilled Leek Crème Fraîche

Grilled Eggplant & Crispy Risotto Cake with grilled shitake mushrooms, caramelized onions, and fried leeks

Skewered Spring Rolls filled with Florida rock shrimp, ginger, and herbs and served with a sweet chili lime sauce

Mini Shrimp Tostadas of blue corn tortillas topped with homemade guacamole and bay shrimp marinated in lime juice and coriander

First Course

Spring Tomato Compose, a layered salad with grilled, sliced artichoke bottoms, red and yellow vine-ripened tomatoes, grilled asparagus; topped with celery root and garnished with yam chips

Dinner Buffet

Performance Grilled

This term means that foods are cooked on the spot to provide a bit of entertainment

Grilled Santa Barbara Prawns with a warm spicy passion fruit vinaigrette

Grilled Swordfish with a fresh Pineapple Papaya Salsa

Grilled Citrus Olive Chicken marinated in fruity olive oil, roasted garlic, fennel seeds, orange zest, and a splash of wine, then garnished with gaeta olives, an orange demi glace and orange zest curls

Baby Rack of Lamb marinated in red wine, walnut oil, Dijon mustard, and Herbs de Provence and served with choice of Pinot Noir Mint Glace or Tomato Cucumber Mint Salsa

All served with...

Farfalle with Arugula & Sundried Tomatoes scented with white wine, garlic, and freshly grated Parmesan cheese

Roasted Red Potatoes with Olives, Feta, and Mint

Grilled Asparagus drizzled with a flavorful vinaigrette

Roasted Yellow & Red Peppers served with aged Balsamic

Endive & Apple Salad tossed with pecans, crumbled blue cheese, and an apple cider vinaigrette

Bread and Crisps served with sweet butter, tomato concasse, and olive tapenade

Desserts

Wedding Cake

Raspberry, Mango, and Lemon Sorbets

Mary's Hearts (shortbread cookies), Biscotti (almond and filbert flavors dipped in sweet chocolate), and Florentines (delicate lace cookies dipped in dark or white chocolate)

Coffee Service

A highly respected caterer in Chicago, Calihan Gotoff excels in elegant yet unstuffy weddings. They are renowned for delicious food as well as impeccable service.

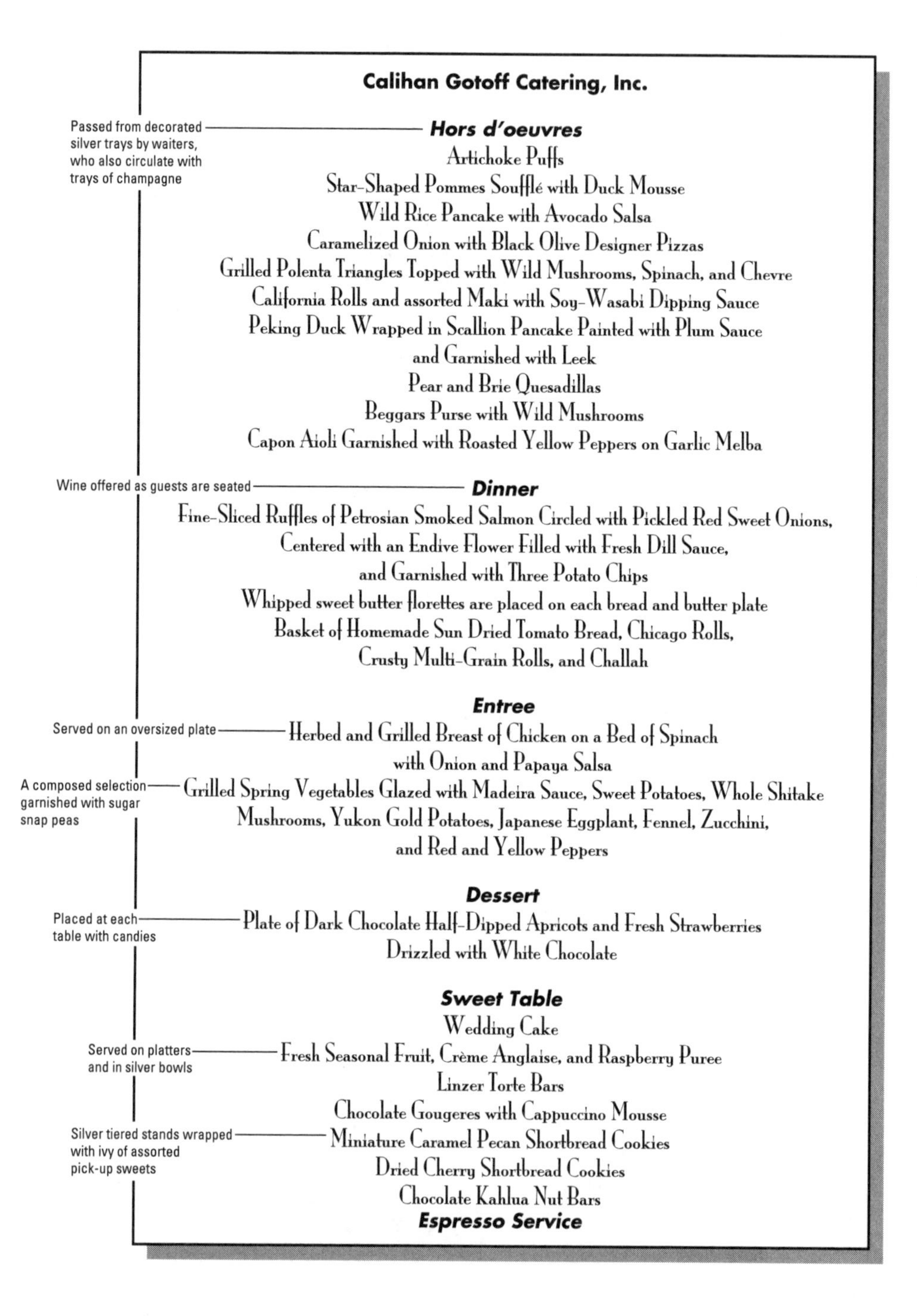
Calihan Gotoff Catering, Inc.

Passed from decorated silver trays by waiters, who also circulate with trays of champagne — **Hors d'oeuvres**

Artichoke Puffs
Star-Shaped Pommes Soufflé with Duck Mousse
Wild Rice Pancake with Avocado Salsa
Caramelized Onion with Black Olive Designer Pizzas
Grilled Polenta Triangles Topped with Wild Mushrooms, Spinach, and Chevre
California Rolls and assorted Maki with Soy-Wasabi Dipping Sauce
Peking Duck Wrapped in Scallion Pancake Painted with Plum Sauce and Garnished with Leek
Pear and Brie Quesadillas
Beggars Purse with Wild Mushrooms
Capon Aioli Garnished with Roasted Yellow Peppers on Garlic Melba

Wine offered as guests are seated — **Dinner**

Fine-Sliced Ruffles of Petrosian Smoked Salmon Circled with Pickled Red Sweet Onions, Centered with an Endive Flower Filled with Fresh Dill Sauce, and Garnished with Three Potato Chips
Whipped sweet butter florettes are placed on each bread and butter plate
Basket of Homemade Sun Dried Tomato Bread, Chicago Rolls, Crusty Multi-Grain Rolls, and Challah

Entree

Served on an oversized plate — Herbed and Grilled Breast of Chicken on a Bed of Spinach with Onion and Papaya Salsa

A composed selection garnished with sugar snap peas — Grilled Spring Vegetables Glazed with Madeira Sauce, Sweet Potatoes, Whole Shitake Mushrooms, Yukon Gold Potatoes, Japanese Eggplant, Fennel, Zucchini, and Red and Yellow Peppers

Dessert

Placed at each table with candies — Plate of Dark Chocolate Half-Dipped Apricots and Fresh Strawberries Drizzled with White Chocolate

Sweet Table

Wedding Cake
Served on platters and in silver bowls — Fresh Seasonal Fruit, Crème Anglaise, and Raspberry Puree
Linzer Torte Bars
Chocolate Gougeres with Cappuccino Mousse
Silver tiered stands wrapped with ivy of assorted pick-up sweets — Miniature Caramel Pecan Shortbread Cookies
Dried Cherry Shortbread Cookies
Chocolate Kahlua Nut Bars

Espresso Service

Based in Berwyn, Pennsylvania, feastivities is a catering company that also coordinates entire events. For weddings, they create the menu, and then work with their own props, china, linens, and other elements which means fewer rentals for — the bride and groom.

Feastivities Catered Events

A beautiful and plentiful display of Italian foods displayed by candlelight in green Italian glass and copper serving pieces amid draped fabrics, whole imported cheeses and meats, and fresh flowers and greens

Antipasto

Tortellini Salad with Pesto, Marinated Artichoke Hearts, Pesto,
Aged Provolone, Genoa Salami, Eggplant with Anchovy Sauce,
Grilled Summer Squash, Grilled Zucchini, Marinated Olives, Tuscan Bean Salad,
Roasted Garlic, Sun Dried Tomatoes, Tomato Salad with Fresh Mozzarella & Basil,
Romano, Pepperoni, Anchovies, Roasted Asparagus
with Pine Nuts, Roasted Peppers, Foccacio & Italian Bread

Butlered Hors d'oeuvres

Chicken Satay, Thai Peanut Dip
Smoked Sea Scallops, Szechwan Sauce
Lemon Grilled Shrimp, Sesame Ginger Sauce
Pepper Charred Tuna Kabobs
Curried Lamb Kabobs, Mango Chutney
Belgian Endive with Smoked Turkey & Dried Apricots

Sautéed to order as guests create their favorite dishes topped with hand-grated Parmesan cheese

Action Stations

Pasta Bar

Egg Fettucini, Penne, Chopped Clams, Crushed Garlic, Olive Oil, Pesto, Creamy Alfredo,
Homemade Marinara, Mushrooms

Hand-carved and served with tarragon or piquant sauces

Poached Salmon Chaud-fraud

Decorated Whole Salmon & Whole Poached Sides with Seasonal Grilled Vegetables
and Confetti Rice with Red & Green Peppers

Presented on copper trays and mirrors

Pastry Display

Linzer Hearts, Coconut Tartlets, Eclairs, Cream Puffs, Fruit Tarts,
Chocolate Dipped Strawberries

Served in antique copper samovars with special condiments. Special touch: chocolate cordial cups for your liqueurs

Coffee Station

Freshly Brewed Coffee, Decaffeinated Coffee, & Gourmet Teas
Whipped Cream, Chocolate Chips, Orange & Lemon Zest, Cocoa,
Raw Sugar, Coconut, Rock Candy Swizzle Sticks,
Cinnamon, Sugar Cubes, Cinnamon Sticks, Lemon Wedges, Chocolate Espresso Beans

More Than A Mouthful's innovative owner, Barry Colman, and his chefs and cooks are graduates of The Culinary Institute of America. Everything from stocks to sauces is made from scratch and, consequently, the results are first-rate. More Than A Mouthful presides over a large banquet space in Los Angeles and is booked year-round for weddings.

More Than A Mouthful

Hors d'oeuvres

Bereks

Puff pastry shells filled with spinach, mushroom, or cheese, baked to a golden brown

Sui Mai

Steamed chicken with vegetables, steamed in a won ton skin, served with a cilantro green onion pesto

Stuffed Mushrooms

Stuffed with spinach filling or duxelles baked with Parmesan cheese

Cut into triangles — *Brie and Apple Quesadillas*

Grilled flour tortillas filled with brie cheese and sliced apples

Grilled Polenta

Wedges of polenta topped with sun dried tomato, pesto, or grilled mushrooms

Eaten with fingers — *Asparagus Spears*

Fresh spears of lightly steamed asparagus with a touch of sweet butter

Buffet Dinner

Mesclun with Vinaigrette

Gourmet baby greens tossed with a balsamic vinaigrette and goat cheese

Served with fried won tons — *Oriental-Style Sea Bass*

Broiled fresh sea bass marinated with soy sauce, garlic, and lemon and garnished with pickled ginger and chives

Carved for each guest — **Mustard & Pepper Crusted Tenderloin**

Roasted filet of beef packed in mustard and peppercorns

Orzo with Chives

Rice-shaped pasta with fresh chives and lemon zest

Spaghetti Squash-Concassé with Tomato & Basil

Squash served with diced fresh tomatoes, garlic, and basil

Artistically arranged on a platter — **Grilled Vegetable Medley**

Grilled baby yellow zucchini, peapods, eggplant, green onions, and carrots

Mashed Potatoes

Caramelized onion & roasted shallot whipped with creamy russet potatoes

Fresh-Baked Rolls

Assorted rolls with dill, rosemary, sourdough, wheat, and pumpernickel

Dessert

Lemon Wedding Cake with Raspberry Filling

Chocolate Truffles

Coffee and Tea

When Dinner Is Not Served

Although seated dinners and lunches are the most popular types of receptions, they're not for everyone. The other options include three-hour cocktail parties, afternoon teas, and wedding breakfasts or brunches. Although these affairs are usually less costly and less fuss, they do require thought and ingenuity.

The reception-as-cocktail-party or can you say, "Just canapés"?

Having just cocktails and hors d'oeuvres — and no meal — for the reception is a fine choice for a variety of circumstances:

- The space you've fallen for can seat only a third or fewer of the guests
- Your reception is a celebratory party that has been postponed for several days or weeks after the ceremony (see Chapters 6 and 19)
- You are an older or previously married couple and don't feel comfortable having a traditional wedding reception
- You have vast numbers of guests you *must* invite but you can't afford a seated meal for all of them
- You simply want an untraditional affair

Open-house cocktail buffets are popular in the South, a holdover perhaps from the days before air conditioning when weddings were held almost universally at night and included a large number of guests.

Two and a half to three hours is the optimum length of a cocktail reception. Anything shorter is too rushed; anything longer feels dragged out. If you go an extra hour, make sure that you have ample food, drink, and cake. In fact, you may consider having a dessert table, as in Figure 8-2, which can also function as a mouth-watering décor element.

The food should include both passed, or butlered, hors d'oeuvres and food stations that are as simple as crudité with dip or as elaborate as carved Peking duck. In any case, nothing should require more than a fork (if that) because seating is limited and you don't want guests wearing the food. Stagger the variety of passed hors d'oeuvres so guests don't get bored. Although you are not serving dinner, you want to provide enough food so that guests are not racing to leave for a real meal. The entire ambiance

Figure 8-2: The wedding cake stars amid an array of desserts.

should be clearly that of a cocktail reception rather than a dinner gone awry. Tables should be no larger than 32 inches in diameter and seat four people, maximum. The room also has to be the appropriate size (see Chapter 2) so it neither echoes when guests speak nor imperils them should the waiter pirouette with a full tray of champagne flutes.

The fact that the reception consists of just cocktails must be specified on the invitation, as in *"Please join us for cocktails and hors d'oeuvres to celebrate our marriage."* This particular wording also makes it clear that guests are not invited to the ceremony.

While a corporate cocktail reception may print both the beginning and ending times ("7 p.m. – 10 p.m."), doing so for a wedding is not gracious. Serving a wedding cake, dessert, and coffee at the beginning of the last hour and toning down the music is usually enough of a hint for guests to wind down the festivities.

Tea for two (hundred)

Having a tea in lieu of a full meal is a popular option for many of the same reasons as the cocktail party reception. Add to those a preference for a day wedding or a desire to include children. The menu may feature many of the stereotypical tea foods — cucumber sandwiches, petits fours, English biscuits — but if you have a sizable crowd, you may consider having the same kind of menu as you would for a cocktail party reception. In fact, you may even include a champagne toast.

A tea may seem like one of the simplest receptions imaginable, but you can personalize it by:

- Offering several unusual flavored teas, available at gourmet shops and specialty stores
- Serving tea from heirloom teapots
- Picking up enough single fine china tea cups and saucers from flea markets and garage sales to give as favors.
- Using only loose tea and sterling silver strainers — no individual tea bags
- Remembering the coffee addicts with a cappuccino and espresso station

Other ways to munch: Breakfast, brunch, or lunch

The wedding breakfast, a mainstay of England, follows a morning ceremony and is actually lunch. To make matters more confusing, a lunch reception is usually more of a light dinner served in the mid-afternoon. For both brunch and lunch, the cocktail reception (if you have one) is often shorter and less elaborate.

Brunch is a thoroughly American compromise and can be one of the least costly meals to produce. Following a late morning or midday ceremony, a typical buffet may consist of bagels, cream cheese spreads, smoked salmon, Danish, mini-quiches, fruit salad, juices, mimosas, and coffee. Stations may offer omelets, waffles, blinis, and fruit pancakes.

Finesse and impress

Some flourishes to further jazz up your meal:

- A variety of good breads to complement each course (for example, cheesy puff pastry sticks with a soup, a crusty sourdough roll with a beef course, and a whole grain walnut toast with cheese and salad)
- Waiters offering freshly grated cheese and ground pepper at the table
- A small dish of herb-infused olive oil in lieu of butter with bread
- Butter molded into florets or other shapes
- Lemon slices served in the ice water
- Sprigs of fresh herbs such as rosemary and tarragon as garnishes
- Multi-colored sugar crystals
- Cappuccino/espresso bar
- Serving hors d'oeuvres in baskets, colorful glass bowls, or chintz hatboxes, or on trays covered with Battenburg lace
- Serving a lush presentation at each table of rich chocolates, fresh fruit, and cookies with dessert and coffee
- Finishing touches on hors d'oeuvre trays (see the following illustration) such as tiny bouquets or offbeat elements such as miniature brides and grooms, balls and chains, or tennis racquets

Chapter 9

A Piece of Cake

In This Chapter

- Concocting your dream cake
- Displaying the cake
- Slicing and pricing

Since ancient times, cakes have been associated with rites of passage from christenings to funerals, and in the wedding cake we see a powerful combination of symbols of fertility, communion, sacrifice, and wishes for *la dolce vita*.

As recently as ten years ago, the wedding cake was still a white cement afterthought, wheeled out to strains of "The Farmer in the Dell" reworked as "The Bride Cuts the Cake," and guests who actually ate a piece put themselves at risk for diabetic shock. Now the wedding cake is a pivotal element of the reception that guests enjoy both admiring and devouring.

Baking Away

Unless your Aunt Myrtle is a world-class pastry chef and has offered to bake her award winning *gâteau de mariage* for your wedding, you need to rev up your tastebuds and go cake shopping. Or, more precisely, bakery shopping. To find a baker who can do the job, you may rely on the same methods for finding a reputable caterer (see Chapter 8), or e-mail the International Cake Exploration Societé (ICES) c/o Earline Moore, a former ICES president at: `Pwd Sugar@aol.com`.

Don't assume that you have to purchase your cake from your banquet hall or caterer; most allow you to supply your own, particularly if they do not specialize in the splendiferous structure you have in mind.

Do, however, double check your caterer's and banquet facility's rules regarding wedding cakes. Even if they allow you to bring in your own cake, they may have to approve the source for insurance reasons.

As when dealing with the caterer, you should assess the bakery's potential and limitations. If you choose the bakery because you've seen and/or tasted its cakes and love them, go through its photo portfolio. Remember that bakeries that don't market themselves as wedding-cake specialists may in fact produce beautiful creations for your special day, so don't rule them out.

When searching for someone suitable to create the *piece de resistance* for your wedding, be thorough. Pastry chefs at restaurants have often been trained in the sugared arts and may jump at the chance to show their stuff.

Focus on the cake early in your planning because popular bakers book up early. If your area is truly lacking in baking talent, don't despair: Consider having your cake shipped from out of town. Many bakers and pastry chefs you read about in magazines send cakes across country with meticulous instructions for keeping and setting them up.

An option that's less costly than having your entire cake shipped is to order a simple tiered cake from a local baker and transform it with custom-made cake tops, sugar flowers, dragées, and other decorative elements that can be mail ordered.

Before meeting with a baker, amass clippings, photos, and books for ideas. Snapshots of your reception venue are helpful as well. To become knowledgeable about flavors, make a point of tasting cakes for dessert when you go out to eat. (We realize that doing so may be a hardship, but try to tough it out.)

Tiers of joy

A plethora of designs are available today as many artists who originally worked in other materials have turned their talents to creating edible art. Cakes no longer have to be round or stacked, no longer have to be white, and no longer have to look like cakes. Many bakers specialize in creating grand *trompe l'oeil* masterpieces that look like precious jewelry boxes, balls and chains, mosaic tile birdbaths, architectural landmarks, oval Shaker boxes, patchwork quilts, wedding dress lace — just about anything meaningful to the couple. (For examples of innovative cakes, turn to the color photo section of this book.)

Tiered cakes can be either *stacked* or *separated.* The layers of stacked cakes are placed one on top of another; separated cakes use decorative elements to physically elevate tiers so they're not touching. Consequently, separated cakes are taller than stacked ones with the same number of tiers and slices. Where plastic "classical" columns were once the only structures used to separate tiers, you can now achieve the same effect with sugar topiaries, cupids, garlanded lucite columns — just about anything that can hold the weight of the top tiers.

Topping the cake is again an occasion for you to brainstorm. As the ubiquitous forever-grimacing plaster bride and groom have gone out of style, cake tops are appearing in a myriad of ingenious guises. Working from photographs, artisans whose sole business is sculpting edible figurines can accurately replicate the couple in a favorite pose such as teeing off, skiing, or driving their convertible. Companies that produce the typical cake ornaments have become somewhat enlightened, producing brides and grooms of all ethnicities and selling them to be easily mixed and matched for either interracial or same-sex couples.

Classic bakers insist that everything on a wedding cake be edible or at least made out of edible ingredients. For that reason, many purists shun fresh flowers on wedding cakes. We personally don't like them, but for other reasons such as insecticides, little buggies, and the awkwardness of having to "deflower" the cake before serving. A crown of fresh flowers that rests solely on the top of the cake, however, can be delicate, pretty, and easy to remove. Other options include preserved flowers such as candied violets and rose petals, and edible flowers such as nasturtiums.

The ethereal look of a wedding cake belies the nuts and bolts needed to make it last throughout a reception. Constructing a tiered cake is an engineering feat that requires reinforcing each layer with small wooden dowels (concealed within the cake) so the layers, which can be quite heavy, don't collapse into each other. Each layer is then separated by corrugated cardboard. Unless your baker specializes in tiered cakes, ordering a multi-tiered confection can get you a wobbly tower in which the top layer falls through and becomes the bottom layer.

Confection selections

The type of cake and fillings are limited only by your imagination and the baker's prowess. We have enjoyed wedding cakes as varied as cream cheese frosted carrot cake, chocolate cheese cake, a hazelnut torte enrobed in dark chocolate, and a truly spectacular classic butter pound cake with a dried cranberry filling iced in cranberry butter cream.

Icing issues and filling facts

In planning the texture, flavor, and look of your cake, a working knowledge of icing and filling options can make communicating with your baker a breeze.

- **Butter cream:** Both an icing and a filling that consists of real butter (not shortening), sugar, and eggs and ranges from ivory to pale yellow in color depending on the number of eggs, the color of the butter, and whether meringue has been mixed in for whitening. Also used to pipe out beautiful and realistic-looking flowers. Mixes well with liqueurs and other flavorings.
- **Dragées:** Gold or silver decorative balls — like BBs — made of candied sugar.
- **Gold and silver leaf:** Used in small amounts as a final touch on iced cakes. Painting with edible real gold and silver is both labor intensive and expensive but quite beautiful for tinted flowers, leaves, and art deco touches.
- **Fondant:** An icing that is either poured in liquid form onto small cakes and petits fours, or rolled out in a sheet, cut, and wrapped around the cake. Its smooth, velvet-like appearance is a perfect surface on which to apply decoration. Refrigerating fondant is not only unnecessary but also unwise because it tends to "weep," forming unappetizing beads of moisture.
- **Marzipan:** Ground almond paste that can be rolled like fondant to cover the cake or used as a base for the fillings between the layers. Can also be hand-molded into such realistic-looking decorations as individual fruits, bunches of grapes, or figures.
- **Modeling chocolate:** Has consistency similar to that of gum paste, though it doesn't get rock hard. White or dark, it can be rolled out like fondant and used to enrobe an entire cake or to embellish a frosted cake with bouquets of chocolate flowers or other whimsical touches.
- **Pastillage, sugar dough, or gum paste:** Used to make hand-shaped fantastical and botanically correct flowers replete with stamens and pistils as well as other cake decorations. Incidentally, though pastillage flowers are exquisite and ostensibly edible, we wouldn't suggest biting into one unless your teeth are made of diamonds.
- **Pulled sugar:** Sugar syrup that is made molten and pulled into such shapes as bows and flowers.
- **Royal icing:** Egg whites beaten with confectioners sugar and lemon juice, then piped with a pastry tube to make intricate decorative elements — piped "lace," trellises, or miniature buds. Very sweet and hardens quickly.
- **Spun sugar:** Strands of caramelized sugar "thrown" to create a magical golden veil over a cake or dessert. Spun sugar cannot be refrigerated and does not hold up for long, making it inappropriate for a cake that you intend to display for several hours.
- **Whipped cream:** The purist's favorite, as either cake filling or icing. Always use pure whipped cream — no other icing stabilizers mixed with it, which increase its longevity but change the taste completely. Whipped cream must be refrigerated.

If you are serving another dessert in addition to the cake, choose complementary flavors. Fresh berries with pastry cream go well with a light butter cake filled with lemon curd, but a chocolate truffle bombe is way too rich for a chocolate mousse cake. The cake itself should also have complementary textures and flavors. For example, a cake wrapped in fondant (which is quite sweet) tastes better with an orange filling than with a thick chocolate ganache.

For variety, sometimes each tier of the wedding cake is a different flavor and/or each tier comprises different flavored layers. Renowned baker Sylvia Weinstock created just such a cake for the wedding of comedian Eddie Murphy and Nicole Mitchell. The five-foot-tall, 400-pound cake featured hundreds of pastel sugar flowers cascading over yellow cake filled with fresh strawberries, fresh banana filling, and whipped cream; chocolate cake with mocha mousse filling; carrot cake with cream cheese filling; and yellow cake filled with lemon mousse and fresh raspberries. And for the top: two hummingbirds made of blown sugar.

Size matters

Depending on the part of the country, the cost per cake slice can range from $1.50 to $10, although custom-designed extravaganzas can run higher. When calculating the size needed, take into account the look of the cake in the room, the number of courses in the meal, and the heaviness of the menu.

If you're having a large wedding reception and you are not interested in displaying a cake of gargantuan proportions, you can save money by having a decorated cake for fewer guests than are in attendance. Feed some guests with simply decorated sheet cakes sliced and served from the kitchen. Request that slices, rather than chunks, are cut from the back-up cake so the ruse is not obvious.

Conversely, if you are having a wedding reception for no more than 50 people, a cake capable of feeding them will not look very large or dramatic. A venue with grand 18-foot ceilings may dwarf a petite cake as well. You may choose a tiered cake with tall separators as opposed to a flatter style. You also may opt to order a cake for 100 or a "cake and a half," if you can afford it, to make a statement.

History in the baking

The earliest record of wedding cakes are found in ancient Greece, where symposium enthusiasts were fond of dipping a *sweet meat* (a honey-laden cake of sesame flour, that is) called *bacchylis* in wine. The ancient Roman wedding ritual included burning a cake of spelt wheat flour called a *confarreatio* over a flame to signify the woman being placed under the jurisdiction of a man and that the marriage was sacred and legal.

Historians believe that nuptial rites later called for the cake to be crumbled over the bride's head to ensure fertility and imbue her with all the bounty of the harvest. Wheat and other grains were seen as life itself, something to be received as a gift and offered up as a blessing. The bride who made her own cake, therefore, risked infertility for her presumptuousness. As the bride received her cake-crumb shower, guests scrambled to catch a lucky bit for themselves to share in her good fortune. This may be the forerunner to the modern-day practice of parceling out the cake to guests and/or of throwing rice, another fertility symbol.

A 17th century French chef is credited with mortaring a stack of buns together with frosting, which led to the modern, tiered wedding cake. The traditional French and Belgian wedding cake, the *croquembouche,* appears to have evolved from the same technique; cream puffs are dipped in hot caramel, which "glues" the pastries together as they are stacked into a tall cone-shape. (*Croquembouche* means literally "to crunch in the mouth.") The pastries are then broken off and served to guests.

American pioneers were also fond of "stack" cakes for weddings — each guest brought one and placed the layers atop each other with a dollop of applesauce in between. As in England, American wedding cakes were traditional dark fruitcakes filled with dried fruits, nuts, and spices. Soaked in liquor, a natural preservative, the top tier was often saved for the couple's first anniversary or the christening of their first child.

Processed sugar transformed European and American wedding cakes in the 18th century, spawning almond marzipan and a smooth, white, ice-like topping that was applied to stacked fruitcakes. Color and decoration came next, followed by "piping" invented by a Bordeaux patissier who figured out how to create designs by feeding icing through a cone with a small hole pierced in the tip. Victorian cakes were confectionery flights of fancy with icing transformed into edible lace, fans, trellised vines, and cascading flowers. Enjoyed primarily by the aristocracy, these were the predecessors of today's ornate wedding cakes.

British royalty figured prominently in setting wedding cake precedents. Queen Victoria's wedding cake in 1840 reportedly weighed 300 pounds, measured 3 yards across and 14 inches high, and was decorated with roses and topped with an ice sculpture of Britannia surrounded by cupids.

In 1947, the cake of Princess Elizabeth and Prince Mountbatten was no less than nine feet tall and 500 pounds. In 1981, a five-tiered hexagonal cake topped with flowers was served at the wedding of Lady Diana Spencer and the Prince of Wales, setting a trend for cakes of that shape for the next decade.

Two Hearts, Two Cakes

Sometimes, you may have two cakes — a bride's cake and a groom's cake. Having never gone out of style in the American South, the groom's cake is increasingly popular in other parts of the U.S. as weddings are being planned by both the bride and groom. As with the main wedding cake, his cake comes in a variety of shapes, sizes, and themes. Richer and denser than the wedding cake, the groom's cake can be served in slivers alongside the wedding cake, wrapped in a beribboned box and sent home with guests, or presented on a dessert buffet.

In the American South, a baker often hides charms attached to ribbons beneath an icing border around the base. Before the cake cutting, each bridesmaid pulls a ribbon. Voilá! Each comes away with a charm: a tiny ring (next to marry), heart (love will come), anchor (hope, adventure), thimble and button (old maid), horseshoe and four-leaf clover (good luck) or *fleur-de-lis* (love will flower). ***Note:*** Not all bakers will make these trinket-laden cakes; some states have laws against baking any foreign object into a cake lest some unwitting guest choke on a good luck charm. Nonetheless, these cakes are also popular at Southern bridal showers, where the bridesmaids frequently collect the charms for a bracelet to give to the bride.

Cake on Display: No Drooling, Please

The cake is usually displayed from the beginning of the reception, so choose a filling and icing that can hold up for the duration. If you are pin-spotting the room (see Chapter 11 for lighting tips), add a spot for the cake table. Otherwise, park it somewhere well lit and in full sight of the guests but off the dance floor or it might wind up on the band leader's head during the first fast dance. Keep in mind the time of year and the length of time the cake will be out, so it doesn't look like a Salvador Dali watch by the time it's cut.

The base of the cake determines the size of the table. A 72-inch round table makes even the most stately cake look minuscule. Make sure that the table is sturdy and is either on wheels or light enough with the cake to be carried by two waiters. Wrap picture wire (as if tying a package) around the table top (see Figure 9-1) Once the tables are covered, you can attach swags, garlands, and sprays with safety pins to the wires in the appropriate places. Layer sheets and/or tulle to give the tablecloth fullness and make it look more stately.

A slice around the world

Practically every culture and country has its own wedding cake recipe.

- **Australia:** Cake tiers are generally rounded and frosted with "plastic icing," a cold mixture that is softer to the bite than cooked fondant or royal icing.
- **Bermuda:** A tiny sapling tops the cake to symbolize a new life of growth and fruition.
- **Denmark:** The wedding cake is called a *kransekage* and composed of 18 layers of almond-meringue rings.
- **France:** Two traditional styles are the giant croquembouche, sometimes arranged as churches, houses, boats, and other novelty objects, or a stacked sponge cake flavored and decorated with confectioner's cream, fruit liqueurs, or icing. A Lorraine tradition demands that the first kiss between a newly married bride and groom be performed over a dish piled with waffles.
- **Greece:** Village women bake sourdough wedding breads and decorate them with beads and blossoms. The bride and groom also traditionally eat a cake made of honey, sesame seed, and quince to symbolize their commitment through good times and bad.
- **Holland:** Cakes are generally iced and decorated with pink or white marzipan roses. In the old days, the groom cut the first slice for the bride, who then cut for her family. Increasingly, however, the couple cuts the cake jointly.
- **Jamaica:** As soon as the engagement is announced, raisins, prunes, dried fruits, and mixed peels are soaked in white rum and wine. This mixture goes into a rich dark cake baked about two weeks before the wedding.
- **Japan:** "Wedding palace" hotels offer couples huge Styrofoam dummy cakes, elaborately decorated and displayed. A real cake is served from the kitchen, often with a small seasonal sweet called a *namagashi*.

Figure 9-1: Make sure your cake table is steady and in proportion to the cake before you decorate it.

Because you have only one cake table, you can splurge on decorating it. Bunch and bundle heirloom laces or festoon a chiffon cloth with ribbons and fresh flowers. The accoutrements are special as well: silver wedding chalices, a beautiful porcelain plate, a keepsake knife or a "heritage" knife inscribed with the couples initials and/or wedding date and those of previous generations from whom it is handed down.

Ask the bakery what kind of serving piece they deliver the cake on. Some provide a flat silver tray. If your baker doesn't have one available, the cake may be delivered on a plain piece of baker's cardboard that you have to decorate. A sweet touch that also amortizes those expensive bridesmaid bouquets after the ceremony is to have the maitre d' or wedding consultant discreetly relieve the bridesmaids of their bouquets, which are then arranged around the cake with a studied casualness. The bridesmaids, incidentally, are usually grateful, being at a loss for how to balance the bouquets with drinks, hors d'oeuvres, and the arm of their significant other.

Arrange to have the cake delivered at least one hour before the reception begins. Cakes are rarely transported fully assembled. Make sure that you know who from the bakery is delivering and setting it up. Apprise your caterer of the delivery time so the cake table can be dressed and ready.

The First Cut Is the Sweetest

In the past, the cake ceremony has been such an anticlimax that brides and grooms used it as an opportunity to act out some thinly disguised aggression by shoving cake in each other's faces. Thankfully, this charming tradition is going by the wayside and the cake cutting has become a moment that is both sentimental and romantic.

Traditionally, the first shared piece symbolizes the couple's first meal together. The cake cutting used to also signal the end of the wedding — because the cake wasn't worth staying to eat. More often now, the cutting is a natural segue after which people who wish to leave may do so, although (we hope) the majority stay and take to the dance floor.

You can gracefully signal that cake cutting is imminent with a reprise of the first-dance music. The bride and/or groom often make their toast at this time. (See Chapter 10 regarding toasts.) After the cutting and toasts are completed, the band plays quietly in the background until the bride and groom finish exchanging the first bites, whereupon the music swells into a full-fledged dance number.

When you schedule your wedding day (see Chapter 18), put in bold type: "Entire band should be ready to play immediately after cake cutting." Many bands seem to think this is the perfect time for a break. If that happens, your party is over.

The cake cutting is also a great photo opportunity. If you were opposed to having many posed formal shots after the ceremony because you didn't want to miss any of the cocktail hour, this is a good time to get them in, so freshen your makeup and straighten your bow ties. You may also invite up both of your families to signify their merging, so allow the photographer and/or videographer to position all of you in the best way.

The head waiter should show you where to make the first cut, particularly if the cake has a dummy layer. To symbolize the couples' shared life together, the groom places his right hand over the bride's, which holds the knife. Together they cut a small piece from the back of the bottom tier. (For cutting procedures at military weddings, see Chapter 19.) Traditionally, the groom feeds the bride first, a small mouthful easily washed down by a sip of champagne. Then the bride feeds the groom. Then, if they're feeling particularly nice, the bride and groom serve a piece to their new in-laws.

We are aware that some couples find this ceremony antiquated and would rather skip it. We have no objections if you feel strongly, although we happen to love this ritual. Besides, guests *expect* to see you cut your cake. They feel cheated if they don't. Some even believe the old superstition that the bride must cut the first piece or risk being childless.

That said, cut the cake, eat your pieces, put the plate down, and move away. After the photos, the banquet directors should have the cake taken into the kitchen to be cut quickly and efficiently without showing the guests the mess this work of art becomes during slicing.

Some places levy a cake-cutting fee — usually $1 a slice — ostensibly to cover the cost of the "set up" (plates and forks.) We find this charge inappropriate, and you should attempt to expunge this clause from your contract.

If the idea of saving your top tier for future consumption strikes your fancy, take precautions to make the cake as palatable as possible one year later — no mold, freezer burn, or other delightful taste treats. Bring a properly sized box, lots of waxed paper, bubble wrap, and an air-tight plastic bag. Leave explicit instructions for airtight wrapping and charge someone — a cryogenics specialist perhaps — with taking this precious cargo home and popping it in the freezer posthaste. Make arrangements to have it transported to your freezer upon your return from the honeymoon. In lieu of this rather complicated procedure, when ordering your wedding cake you may cleverly put in an order for an additional small cake of the same flavor for your first year anniversary. Unless, of course, you like that hundred-year-old mattress taste.

Chapter 10

Cheers!

In This Chapter

- Learning to speak in bar code
- Understanding pricing structures
- Making the most of toasts

According to the Bible, Jesus performed his first miracle at a wedding in Cana, an ancient town in Galilee, by turning water into wine. While miracles are wonderful, we believe in using them sparingly. Fortunately, providing drinks can also be done with a combination of common-sense planning and good taste. This chapter is about alcohol and how to serve it at your wedding. Our place is not to moralize about *whether* to serve it, although we firmly believe that your serving any alcohol must be done legally and responsibly. If alcohol is an issue because of religion, recovery, or expense, consider having a morning wedding with a breakfast reception, where alcohol is neither necessary nor expected.

Bar for the Course

In figuring your way around a bar, a few terms worth knowing are

- **Pouring** or **well:** Generic liquor as in, "I'll have a screwdriver."
- **Call:** A specific brand you ask for, or call, as in, "I'll have a half Stoli-half Absolut screwdriver."
- **Top shelf, premium,** or **super premium:** Call brands that are higher priced, including single-malt scotches, aged cognacs, and rare liqueurs.
- **House wine(s):** What the establishment serves without an additional charge. Depending on the house, the wine can range from perfectly palatable table wine to rotgut.
- **Champagne:** With a capital "C," Champagne is the sparkling wine produced in France's Champagne region. Using the second fermentation in the individual bottle, Champagne has been made the same way for approximately 300 years. While you may enjoy sparkling wines, only Champagne deserves to be called Champagne.

- **Sparkling wine:** Produced using either the Champagne method or a less expensive method and usually made overly sweet by an addition of sugar. To further confuse things, makers sometimes call these champagnes (small "c").
- **Corkage fee:** The amount charged by the site to "remove the corks" from bottles you supply, and serve the wine.

On-premise pricing

Restaurants, banquet facilities, private clubs, and other spaces, where the catering is on site usually hold a liquor license, allowing them to sell alcoholic beverages with food. (See Chapter 2 for more about on- and off-premise sites.) Their offering full bar service is not a humanitarian gesture to make your life easier but rather a large profit center for the facility. Consider the tastes and habits of your guests when planning the bar. If you have only a pouring bar and your favorite uncle's sole joy in life is a particular single malt scotch, he will not be happy. Should you opt not to provide liqueurs and someone orders one after dinner, the waiters will say, as they have been trained, "I'm sorry, but the host has not provided for that."

On-premise places typically price wine and spirits in one of three ways:

- **Per consumption, either by bottle or by drink:** You are charged specifically and only for what your guests consume. Some places charge per *opened* bottle of liquor, although the fairest way to be billed is by tenths of bottles consumed. This pricing does not apply to wine and Champagne, however, which are charged by bottle opened. Sodas, juices, and bottled water may be served at no additional charge or priced per consumption as well.

  This arrangement is a smart choice if you think your guests won't be drinking much. Advise the maitre'd that waiters are not to clear half-empty glasses (and thus send guests back to the bar for a new drink). Also have the maitre d' apprise you (or the wedding consultant) halfway through the party of the consumption level. Doing so accomplishes two things: You have an opportunity to moderate the amount of wine being poured and the house knows that someone else is keeping track.

- **The cocktail reception (one to one and a half hours) included in the price and per consumption after that:** A good option if wine is automatically poured with each course. Unless the wine is truly undrinkable, most guests are usually content to drink it and not request hard liquor. This arrangement also helps you hedge your bets if you aren't sure what your crowd drinks because consumption is heaviest at the beginning of the reception. House wine is generally included as part of the bar at the cocktail reception.

When you have your wine and food tasting, try the house wines as well. Far from being a minor detail, a glass of house wine is the first thing many people put to their lips at your reception.

- **Total price that includes food and beverage:** While the liquor portion may appear hefty, this structure is cost-effective if your guests are heavy drinkers. Wine is included in the bar for cocktails as well as wine service during dinner. You usually choose from a set wine list. If you wish to upgrade your selection, you should receive a rebate on the list price per bottle. A Champagne toast may be included, but pouring Champagne from the bar as well is most likely an additional cost.
- **A corkage fee for wine and Champagne that you bring in yourself:** Calculate this fee carefully because you can wind up paying a huge premium per bottle once the fee is tacked on. If you have your heart set on a wine the establishment does not carry, find out what they would charge you to special order it. Believe it or not, even when they tack on their markup, this route may cost you less.

Go through your guest list and note how many invitees are under drinking age. Have your contract specify that you are charged a lower price for them.

Stocking the bar

One of the main advantages of holding your wedding in an off-premise site where you bring in a caterer — such as your home or a rental space — is that you can also bring in your own liquor. This way you're not locked into an establishment's rigid pricing structure and you can serve what you like, a plus for specialty bars (covered later in this chapter) or if you have specific tastes in wine and liquor.

Some places where you can shop for liquor and perhaps find deals include:

- **Discount warehouses or superstores,** which sell wine at or near wholesale prices, though usually only by the case.
- **Wine shop catalogs,** which often offer lower prices and a larger selection of hard-to-find wines than local markets.
- **Liquor stores,** which sometimes have special purchases or sales (scan local newspapers for advertisements). Quantity price savings can be particularly juicy when buying wine and Champagne. Just follow the guidelines for proper storage so you don't wind up with several cases of salad dressing.
- **Local wineries,** where you can visit and taste the wine before having it shipped to you.

Some local governments prohibit the shipping of wine directly to consumers, so ask your supplier about the law in your area. If shipping wine is legal where you live, the law may dictate that an adult receive the shipment.

When putting your bar together, bear several points in mind:

- Buy more liquor then you think you need.
- Buy from a liquor store that allows you to return unopened bottles. Just be sure to instruct the caterer not to *crack,* or open, the seal on every bottle.
- Whether or not you are paying a per-person set-up fee (usually $3 to $5 for ice, fruit, juices, mixers, and sodas), go over the particulars with the caterer or banquet manager. Don't assume that the bar will be stocked with ingredients and garnishes for Bloody Marys, piña coladas, margaritas, sours, and other special drinks that you may want to serve.
- Double check the amount of ice ordered.

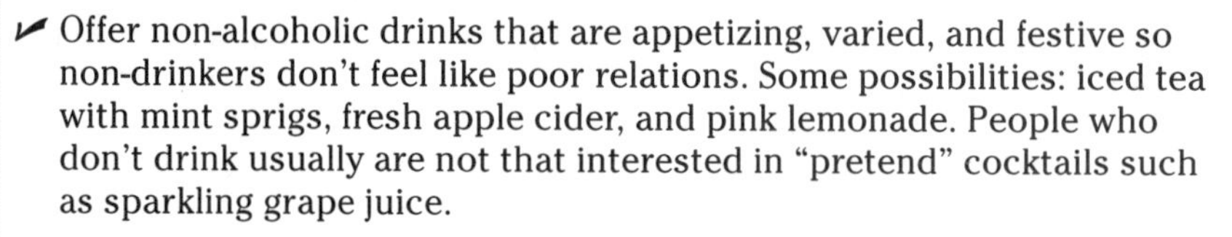

- Offer non-alcoholic drinks that are appetizing, varied, and festive so non-drinkers don't feel like poor relations. Some possibilities: iced tea with mint sprigs, fresh apple cider, and pink lemonade. People who don't drink usually are not that interested in "pretend" cocktails such as sparkling grape juice.
- Make sure that white wine and Champagne are delivered chilled because most off-premise sites don't have enough space — and you won't have enough time — to chill it adequately.
- Specify that not every bottle of red wine is to be opened at once. Neither should all the white wine and Champagne be iced, which causes the labels to soak off, unless you are sure that they will be drunk. Label-less bottles not only look unappealing, but they are also impossible to return, even if unopened.
- To prevent any disappearing surplus, assign a responsible friend to pick up the unopened bottles within a few days after the wedding (when, presumably, you are on your honeymoon).

Chill out

Keep these facts in mind when dealing with ice:

- Figure on 1½ pounds of ice per person and 2½ pounds per person if you are also chilling bottles.
- Although you can ice bottles in about 20 minutes by pouring water in with the ice, doing so makes the labels come off. Otherwise, pack bottles in ice for two hours to properly chill them.
- Crushed ice chills bottles faster than cubes do.

Liquid logistics

If you are at the point where you are not sleeping at all and are obsessing about every detail, here's a little 2 a.m. project to keep you busy: a quick reference for stocking the bar.

Calculating how much alcohol to have on hand is not an absolute science. Several factors come into play — the social habits of your guests, your budget, the time of year, and the time of day. A summer wedding, for example, may require more beer, vodka, and gin than a winter wedding, where people are likely to drink more red wine and whiskey.

When ordering your liquor, take into account the number of bar stations the caterer plans. If you have 200 guests and five bar stations, for example, you need five bottles of bourbon rather than four so that each bar is stocked with the same selection. You may notice that bar arithmetic is akin to doubling recipes. As you can see in Table 10-1, the number of liters needed does not necessarily increase in direct proportion to the number of guests and/or bar stations added.

Table 10-1 How Much Is Enough?

Liquor	*Liters per 100 guests*	*Minimum liters for fewer than 100 guests*
Beer	Varies based on guest list	
Blended whiskey	1–2	1
Bourbon	1–2	1
Campari (optional)	1	1
Champagne	1.5 cases	1
Dry vermouth	2*	1
Gin	4	2
Red wine	1/2 case or 6 bottles**	
Light rum	2	1
Scotch	3	2
Sweet vermouth	2*	1
Tequila (optional)	1	1
Vodka	6	2
White wine	1 1/2 cases (12 bottles per case)**	

* 750 ml bottles

** Refers only to wine served as cocktails, not with dinner.

Equipping the complete do-it-yourselfer bar

If you are setting up your own bar from scratch or insist on driving your caterer crazy by checking over the minutest of details, here's a run-down of non-liquid supplies you need:

- Bar pitchers (4 per 75 guests)
- Bottle openers
- Coasters
- Corkscrews
- Champagne pliers
- Funnels
- Garnish bowls (6")
- Glassware (at least 2 per person)
  - 12-ounce all purpose wine glasses
  - 8-ounce highball glasses
  - 12-ounce all-purpose goblets
- Ice buckets (1 to display Champagne; the others for ice)
- Ice tongs
- Ice tubs (to chill wine and Champagne)
- Knife and cutting board
- Large mixing pitchers
- Lemon/lime squeezers
- Long-handled spoons
- Measuring cups
- Mixing glasses
- Napkins
- Plastic runner (to protect floor behind bar)
- Serving trays
- Shakers/strainers
- Sponges
- Trash bags
- Trash cans

Assuming your wines have corks rather than screw tops, you need a proper opener. Hard to believe but true: Professional waiters do and will arrive at your site without corkscrews. Whether your family is tending bar or you've hired bartenders, it pays to have a half dozen Screwpull corkscrews or Waiter's corkscrews — not the Wing Type Corkscrew. To open special bottles such as Impériales of red wine, you need a bar-mounted corkscrew.

Figure on three to three and a half glasses per person. Caterers generally use "A.P.," or all-purpose, stemmed wine glasses, for mixed drinks and wine served at the bar. These one-size-fits-all glasses make for shorter lines at the bar and are less expensive to rent. Champagne and sparkling wine, however, are always served in a particular glass. If you're having a small wedding or glassware is particularly important to you and your budget can handle it, you might request an assortment of the proper glasses. These include highball, rocks, cordial, and red and white wine glasses.

If your reception is an extended cocktail party rather than a seated meal, you need to modify the formulas for calculating amounts. For a three-hour affair with 100 guests, plan one drink per person per hour, or approximately $1^1/_2$ cases of liquor altogether, comprising in descending order, vodka, scotch, gin, and rum. One liter of liquor yields approximately 18 drinks per bottle.

Not all wine bottles are created equal. French wine bottles hold about $25^1/_2$ ounces (what's known as an American "fifth") and German bottles, which are taller and narrower, usually contain $23^1/_2$ ounces. To distinguish different sized bottles, the French started the tradition of naming them after Biblical kings. With Champagne, for example, a Magnum has the capacity of two single bottles, a Jeroboam four, a Rehoboam six, a Methuselah eight, a Salmanazar twelve, a Balthazar sixteen, and a Nebuchadnezzar twenty. The names and capacities vary slightly for Bordeaux-type bottles. While a Magnum is the equivalent of two single bottles, the rare Marie-Jeanne is about three, a double Magnum four, a Jeroboam six, and an Impérial eight.

Making Things Flow

We cannot stress enough how important traffic flow is to the success of your day. One way to make guests miserable is to have long lines at the bar, making it impossible for them to get that first drink they have been salivating for. An easy and festive solution is to have waiters parked at the entrance of your reception area holding gleaming trays of wine, sparkling water, and, if it's in your budget, Champagne. Most people are perfectly happy to imbibe what's offered and consequently avoid stampeding the bars.

Some people consider serving any alcohol before the ceremony an outrage. In fact, even some banquet facilities are adamant in their refusal to open the bar before the couple is firmly locked in matrimony. We feel, however, that you (and perhaps your officiant) should decide when to serve the first drink. (Obviously, this point is moot when the ceremony takes place in a house of worship or is an Orthodox or Conservative Jewish wedding on the Sabbath.)

Some couples opt to have the full bar open as guests arrive. Arbiters of taste split hairs on the subject, suggesting that to open a full bar is gauche but to serve Champagne and/or wine is fine. Somehow the nuance is lost on us; if you decide to serve alcohol before the ceremony, how much and what kind is a matter of personal style. Just make sure that the guests are ushered to their seats in plenty of time for the ceremony so you don't have an extended cocktail reception before your cocktail reception, and that you have sufficient waiters to whisk away glasses from guests as they take their seats so that the dulcet tones of shattering Champagne flutes do not interrupt the ceremony.

For a cocktail reception that precedes a dinner, the standard ratio of bartenders to guests is one per 50 or 75. Unfortunately, however, you can't count on this. If you are paying per consumption (rather than all-inclusive), some banquet managers load on the bartenders — the better to sell you liquor with, my dears. Conversely, if you are paying an all-inclusive price, guests may feel that getting a drink is like searching for an oasis in the Sahara.

Even if waiters are passing drinks to stave off a crush at the bar as guests are first arriving, contract for extra bar staff during this crucial period. If hiring additional bartenders costs extra, request that some of the waiters (provided it's not a union issue) fill in behind the bar until all the guests have had at least their first drink.

Bar Aesthetics: Set Up and Take Notice

Specify what the bars are going to look like. Determine who is supplying the bar linens — the establishment or your decor person. If linens are an afterthought, you will probably wind up with institutional white ones that are a blight on your painstakingly designed reception. At the very least, the back bar — the table behind the main — should have linens that match the front bar. Glasses, ice bins, and extra set ups should be kept neatly. Sometimes bartenders forget that their workspace is in your reception space.

A few points worth asking about include:

- Will the bartenders *free pour* liquor from open bottles or use *pourers* (bottle spouts that measure per shot)?
- Are pourers silver tone or plastic? (Silver looks more elegant.)
- What are they using as ice bins? If the answer is huge garbage pails (often the case), request that they wrap the pails in a tablecloth. Champagne should be kept in ice buckets.
- What do they scoop ice with? We hope with an ice scoop. Harried bartenders may resort to scooping ice with a glass, sometimes resulting in tasty shards of glass garnish. We won't even discuss bartenders scooping with their hands and we hope you won't have to either.

Having bubba-sized half-gallon bottles sitting out on a bar looks like you're expecting an invasion of Huns. A more aesthetic approach: liter or quart size bottles. If you're serving a variety of beers, a few different wines, or margaritas, display the bottles prominently on the bar so that guests know to request them and the selection is not just a secret between you and the bartenders.

Write a few sentences describing the wines you've chosen and give them to the bartenders so they can speak intelligently about what they are pouring. After you and your fiancé(e) have excitedly chosen the perfect cocktail wines, nothing can make you choke on your 1988 Gevrey Chambertin like overhearing a bartender reply to a guest's query, "Let's see, we got red and we got white."

Grand floral creations on the bar inevitably become a target for the bartenders or guests to knock over. A small, tasteful arrangement of flowers in keeping with the overall theme is plenty. The same goes for candelabra and votive candles. We find nothing as unnerving at a wedding as the constant close calls of dolman sleeves brushing near open flames.

One thing to omit from your bar is a tip cup. We believe that tip cups belong only on cash bars and neither have any place at a wedding. Much to our amazement, we've read in several wedding tomes that a good way to cut your costs is to have a cash bar. Well, so is BYOF (Bring Your Own Food). Remember the purpose of this day: you, your parents, and your future spouse have sent out invitations to have friends and family join you in celebration. We think that this invitation clearly includes food *and* drink. Period.

Specialty Bars: Blithe Spirits

Although they require additional well-trained staff, specialty bars can be a treat for guests even at large weddings. According to Dale DeGroff, the beverage manager of New York City's Rainbow Room and the Rainbow Suites banquet spaces, both known for their signature cocktails, special drinks at parties require special arrangements:

- Serve these drinks at a separate station rather than at the bars.
- Stock each station with the accoutrements needed for the particular drink. For example, a martini station should have martini glasses, matching shakers, and a variety of garnishes, including pickled pearl onions for Gibsons.
- Have bartenders ask guests whether they want the drinks straight up, on the rocks, shaken, or stirred, as appropriate.

Some festive ideas for specialty bars include:

- **Cappuccino and espresso bar:** Doesn't it seem as though coffee bars have taken over the world? Well, weddings are not immune. Some caterers now specialize in supplying coffee bars that offer everything from cappuccino to half-caff double-skim mocha latté. Hot rum toddies, Irish coffee, and hot chocolate spiced with chocolate liqueur also fit in nicely.
- **Dessert bar:** After-dinner drinks are enjoying the same renewed popularity as cigars and martinis. Cordials range from a selection of liqueurs to an assortment of aged cognacs as well as armagnacs and digestifs. Sometimes waiters take orders for these at the table, but if you decide to go all out, carts wheeled to the table with a selection of cordials, and dessert wines — and their proper glasses — are an excellent finale to a sumptuous meal. One catch: Although immensely gracious, the liqueur cart can be a costly proposition as people who would never think of having an after-dinner drink will make an exception when offered one in this situation.
- **Vodka bar:** With the advent of a multitude of unusual vodkas, from flavored to triple distilled, vodka bars are another possibility. Deeply chilled in iced glasses is the only way to serve this spirit. Vodka drinks work well by themselves or as an accompaniment to a food station serving blini and caviar or smoked fish.
- **Wine bars:** Serving a panoply of interesting and delicious wines works especially well for cocktails-only receptions. You can have some fun here based on your tasting experiences of the past couple of months. The wines don't have to be expensive or rare as long as they make a statement. Display each wine with a card or special wine menu explaining the fine points of each selection. Six wines — some whites, some reds — are enough as long as they include a range of grape varieties, perhaps a Cabernet Sauvignon, a Pinot Noir, a Chardonnay, a Sauvignon Blanc, a Merlot, and a Sauterne. Consider selections from Australia, Chile, and South Africa as well as the better known wine regions. For a grand touch, have a couple of Impérials (which are not necessarily more expensive) standing sentry on the bar. To complete the effect, serve each wine in the proper glass.

Certain specialty drinks can look elegant without costing a lot. These drinks lend themselves to premixing all the ingredients, including alcohol, rather than being made as ordered. A few possibilities:

- **Coladas** accented with a skewer of mango, kiwi, and pineapple.
- **Margaritas** poured into V-shaped glasses with salted rims and a wedge of fresh lime.
- **Sangria** made with red wine and a dash of brandy and served from a lovely pitcher loaded with fruit slices.

Wine, Men, Women, and Song

For many people, a good meal by definition is accompanied by wine. The amount of money and time you spend on selecting your wine depends on how important you rate a taste of the grape. Mark-ups on wine and Champagne are typically exorbitant, so this area is one where going for an off-premise site can really make a difference in the cost of your wedding.

One of the most fun aspects of wedding planning is choosing your wine. If you are purchasing the wine yourself, buy several selections in your price range to try at home with dinner. If you are choosing from a banquet wine list, get a copy early in your planning and purchase your top picks at a liquor store to try out. Some establishments include tastings of wine options with menu tastings. Remember, this is a tasting, not a bacchanal. In fact, a wine tasting is probably the only time in your life when you're allowed to sip *and spit* in public. (See Chapter 8 about arranging menu tastings.)

While American wines have come into their own, they don't necessarily cost less than imported ones. Fortunately, a good wine need not be expensive. With the first course, try offering two white wines such as a Chardonnay and a Chenin Blanc as well as two reds such as a Pinot Noir and a Cabernet Sauvignon.

Until recently, when planning a bar, you automatically ordered copious quantities of white wine and a bare minimum of red to satisfy some pretentious eccentric. As good red wines have become more reasonably priced, they've gone mainstream. Order sufficient red wine for everybody to drink it with the main course if A) you are serving meat or a fish in a red wine sauce, B) the wine is particularly delicious, or C) the wedding occurs in the middle of winter.

If you serve white wine (and no red) throughout the meal, half a bottle per person is usually ample. If you serve white wine for only the first course, followed by red or a choice of white or red with dinner, figure on a third of a bottle of white per person.

Should you serve the best wine first or save it for last? Some people believe in the power of first impressions and because guests drink less wine at cocktails, you can afford to serve the best at the start. What's more, after guests are somewhat sated, they won't notice that at some point during the party the wine ceased to impress their tastebuds as much. Others believe that guests only begin to notice what they are drinking after their taste buds have warmed up, so you should serve the good stuff later. One way to circumvent this tangle if you serve more than one wine is to make sure the wines are comparable and complementary.

Many people mistakenly think that serving only wine and beer is less expensive and a way to keep guests from getting drunk. Both are fallacies. First, not every catering establishment charges substantially less for house wine and beer. A better quality wine served in lieu of hard liquor can, in fact, cost you more money. Second, the idea that wine and beer are not as potent as hard liquor is preposterous. Trust us, enough of either can get you good and drunk. Should anyone overindulge, remember the immortal words of Dean Martin: "If you drink, don't drive. Don't even putt."

As the host, you may be liable if liquor is served to minors and if guests drink too much and cause injury to themselves, others, or property. Liquor laws vary from state to state and you should inquire with an insurance company about purchasing a host liability policy.

During Shinto ceremonies in Japan, the bride and groom share three sips of *sake,* a rice wine, from three lacquered cups. This "three, three, nine" ritual known as *sansankudo* symbolizes luck and happiness and solemnizes the marriage.

Don't Worry, Be Hoppy

Beer and weddings date back to ancient times. In fact, the word *bride* is derived from the Germanic *bruths* and the Old English *bryd,* which in turn come from the root word *bru,* meaning to cook or brew. In the 15th century, wedding feasts were called *bride-ales* (an ale being a party), and the drinking of copious amounts of beer — the stronger the better for a robust marriage — was, naturally, a prime activity at these rather rowdy functions. The bride's mother parked herself in front of the church and sold her specially made brew known as *bridal,* to anyone who passed by. The proceeds benefited the bride's dowry.

Today, beer at weddings is not de rigueur, but with the rising popularity of microbreweries and a growing interest in the complexities and nuances of "the liquid bread," beer is no longer considered too roughneck for weddings. Just be sure to serve it in a glass and from a bottle as opposed to a can or a keg unless your reception is doubling as a frat party. If you're offering beer, include a light beer and stock up if it's a hot summer day.

For a special beer bar, you might feature recipes from several microbreweries, a selection of exotic imports, beers from countries representing your families' ethnic heritage, or a "world tour" of beers from every continent (except Antarctica, of course). One way to impress beer aficionados is to get a local microbrewery to make a special batch of its brew for your big day or a pre-wedding party. Print labels with your names and wedding date.

Bubble-Headed Nonsense

Champagne or good sparkling wine have become an integral part of the wedding celebration whether you serve it throughout the reception or just with cocktails, by request, at dinner, or with the cake for a toast. Magnums look dramatic and festive and may actually save you money if purchased on sale.

Avoid serving Champagne in half bottles or splits because they tend not to be very fresh.

Champagnes can be vintage or non-vintage. Any Champagne without a vintage year on the label, which accounts for 85 percent of all Champagne produced, is *NV,* or *non-vintage*. Three or more different harvests are blended for NV. A vintage Champagne consists of grapes from a single year rather than blended with reserves from previous years. Plan on coming into a lot of money if you want to serve vintage Champagne. Whether vintage or non, Champagne is categorized by sweetness and the terms seem like they were coined on Opposites Day:

- *Extra Brut* means totally dry.
- *Extra Dry* is medium dry.
- *Sec* is slightly sweet. (*Sec* in French, however, means dry. Go figure.)
- *Demi-sec* is fairly sweet.
- *Doux* is sweet.

A charming personal touch is a cocktail created just for your wedding. For their rose garden reception, one couple we know served rosé Champagne with a rose petal and a strawberry in every glass. As guests entered, waiters offered the drinks from trays adorned with forest-green leaves and roses and announced, "The 'Rose Cocktail' in honor of Loretta and George."

Rosé Champagne has an undeservedly bad reputation among those who think it is made at the bar by mixing carbonated something and red wine. It is actually made either by adding Pinot Noir in the beginning of the process or by leaving the skins on the grapes during vinification to impart a pink color. Rosés are particularly sensuous and romantic for weddings.

Which glass is best?

Until recently, Champagne was invariably served in wide-rimmed or saucer-bowled glasses called *coupes*. These are fashioned after a glass Helen of Troy (or Marie Antoinette, depending on which apocryphal tale you believe) had made in the shape of her breast, so enchanted was she with the bubbly. Despite its longevity and festiveness, however, this shape is all wrong for champagne. For one thing, that wide rim allows those precious bubbles to escape much too quickly. Secondly, more liquid winds up on the waiters' trays or on the floor than in anyone's mouth.

The preferred glass is either a tall, narrow tulip or flute, both of which enhance the effervescence by allowing the bubbles to rise from a single point at the very bottom. A trumpet-shaped glass poses the same problems as a saucer. In any case, Champagne tastes best when well-chilled but not ice-cold.

If you want to serve Champagne but are concerned about the cost, consider serving an Asti or a domestic sparkling dessert wine with the wedding cake.

One case of Champagne contains approximately 75 glasses, so for a Champagne toast you need one case per 75 guests. For the cocktail hour, figure on $1\frac{1}{2}$ cases per 100 guests. Some flutes or tulip glasses can be deceptive in that they hold less than they appear to, in which case you may get closer to 85 glasses per case.

After your Champagne has made its bumpy journey from store to wedding, let it rest for several hours before opening, as you would any other carbonated drink. Never remove the wire cages before you're ready to open the bottle unless you want spontaneous cork popping. For the same reason, never use a corkscrew, which releases the carbonation suddenly and much too forcefully. While the "correct" procedure for opening Champagne is to gently ease out the cork so it emits a teeny sigh, if you don't mind losing a portion of the contents and are hooked on the Hollywood image of Champagne corks going "Pow!" give the cork a good hard pull. In any case, point the bottle away from decorations, yourself, and any other living creatures to avoid implanting the cork in someone's forehead.

A Few Words about Toasts

Wedding toasts have in the past adhered to a more or less strict protocol. The best man goes first, followed by the groom, who responds with a toast of thanks to his parents and in-laws and perhaps to his bride. Then the bride may make a toast, followed by the bride's parents (mother first), the groom's parents, and the rest of the guests. Frequently these days, however, the groom and the best man give the honor of the first toast to the father and/or mother of the bride if they are hosting the reception. Often the bride's parents offer a short welcome toast and save their extended sentiments for later in the reception.

When to propose the first toast depends on what kind of reception you have. If you serve a meal, wait until everyone has been seated and served wine. In the past, people have often served Champagne for the first toast. We feel, however, that Champagne can be saved for a toast with the cake, with which it goes so well. At a standing reception, you can begin toasting once everyone has a drink in hand. (For specific options on when to toast, refer to the wedding day schedule in Chapter 18.)

Rapping a glass with a fork to get people's attention or to induce the bride and groom to kiss is not only grating but also hazardous. However, the custom of touching your glass to others at the end of a toast originated to produce a bell-like sound to repel the devil. Another explanation holds that wine is meant to be enjoyed by all five senses: taste, touch, sight, smell, and — with the clinking of glasses — sound.

In some cultures, such as Laotian, after the couple takes their wedding sips, they pass the glass from guest to guest around the room. While this custom may trigger your germ paranoia, refusing a sip is a grave insult to your hosts.

Some things you can do to make the toasting go trippingly:

- Nominate someone to act as master of ceremonies to introduce each toaster. You want someone who is witty, wise, and capable of gently giving long-winded toasters the hook. Having a stentorian voice doesn't hurt either as it eliminates the need for a drum roll, strobe light, or puff of smoke to command people's attention. If you don't assign this honor role, the job falls to the band leader who may not strike the tone you want. We've known some couples to act as their own emcee, introducing each speaker with an apropos comment to create a personalized, intimate mood.
- Apprise the people who will make toasts several weeks in advance so they have time to figure out how to be amusing and articulate.
- Be thoughtful about whom you choose to propose toasts. We might even encourage you to cheat a little. In other words, someone may be a fabulous speaker but not very close to you. Honoring a new step-child or sister or brother-in-law by asking them to speak may make all the difference in your relationship going forward.
- Specify that toasts are to be short and sweet. Anything longer than three to four minutes belongs at a coronation not a wedding reception.

- Be clear about the tone you expect. Inside jokes or private anecdotes may be lost on many of the guests.
- The person making the toast should go to the front of the room and face the crowd. The emcee then introduces the speaker and demonstrates how to use the microphone. Few things are more embarrassing than watching the bride's father deliver an obviously heartfelt toast, blotting his copious tears with his handkerchief, as all the guests mouth to each other, "What did he say?"
- Even if you have an entire family of elocutionists, sign up no more than eight for toasting duty. While close friends and family may be entertained, you may begin to hear the distinct sound of snoring emanating from other tables.

A wireless hand-held microphone is a wonderful invention. Most people are more relaxed holding something and the toasts come off less stilted if the emcee hands the mike to the toaster, who can then stand naturally while speaking. If possible, have a *small* table or a podium that can be wheeled on and off the dance floor so that toasters can lay down their notes. A waiter should always deliver a glass to the toaster.

According to the rules of "polite society," during toasts at formal gatherings, everyone should rise but the recipients. Due to the plethora of toasts at a wedding, however, making guests jump to their feet every time someone raises a glass is ludicrous. Tradition also holds that drinking to yourself is gauche, akin to applauding yourself. If you wish to follow the well-mannered path, refrain from imbibing when toasts are made to you. The exception to this rule is often the Champagne toast that accompanies the cake-cutting. Nobody seems to mind the bride and groom sipping along in the moment.

The magic words

While people have presumably toasted since they had drinks to toast with, the first *recorded* toast was uttered in 450 A.D. by a woman at a Saxon feast. "Lord King, be of health!" announced Rowena, daughter of the Saxon leader Hengist, to British King Vortigern, who was so impressed that by evening's end he had made her his bride.

Chapter 11
Setting the Stage

In This Chapter

- Taking the decorator's tour
- Playing with your food (to great effect)
- Discovering your inner flower child
- Solving ceremonial situations

Barely knowing the difference between a pickle and a pin-spot, you and your fiancé(e) have entered the lair of the Flying Whoozamawhatzies, a renowned wedding design team. Hours later, having finally figured out that a pew bow is not a smelly ribbon, a runner is not the fastest waiter who dashes for ice, and a bud vase is not a beer container, you realize you should have learned to speak Decorese before getting engaged.

Decking out your venue to suit your tastes does not require a Ph.D. in the Pedagogical Paradigms of Peonies. You need only educate yourself in the particulars of the space and in the myriad elements that may or may not need a creative touch. First step: Do your homework. Amass ideas and tips, learn the venue's ground rules for decorating (see Chapter 2 for other points to scope out as well), and refine your own personal vision. At that point, you should be in good shape to meet with a wedding designer or begin constructing your wedding fantasy yourself.

What You Should Contemplate Before You Decorate

No doubt with every passing day the wedding you've concocted in your heads has morphed many times over. Be forewarned: You haven't seen anything yet. As your reconnaissance gathering goes into full-tilt boogey, make sure that you:

- **Get a floor plan** (as in Figure 11-1) of your reception space that shows, based on your estimated number of guests, the location of the tables, dance floor, bars, buffet stations, stationary pillars, furniture, kitchen, and architectural features that may affect the set-up of your party.

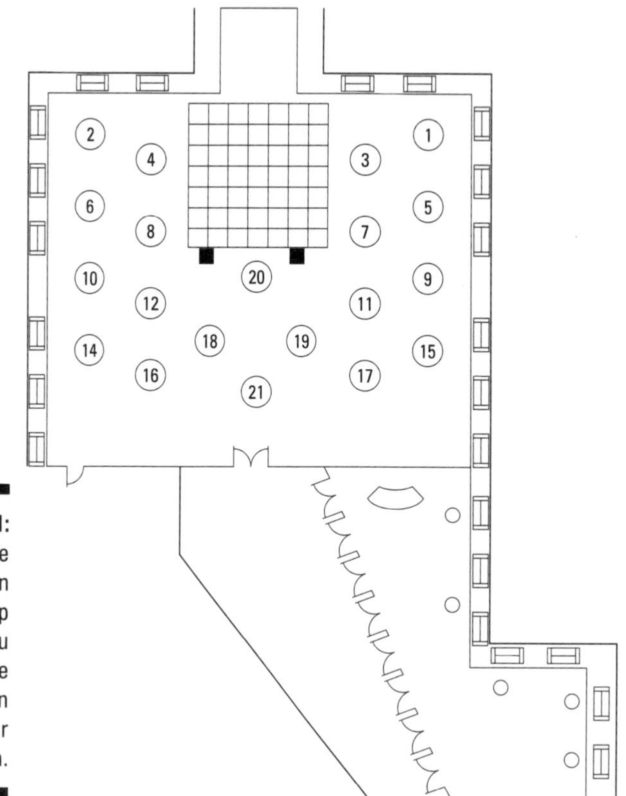

Figure 11-1: A simple floor plan can help you visualize and design your reception.

- **Try out different florists** every time you have an occasion to send flowers. Pay a call on the store or design studio in person and, more importantly, casually drop in on the recipient to inspect the results. Even better, order flowers for yourself. For florists in your area within the U.S., call the American Institute of Floral Designers (410-752-3320) or Teleflora (310-826-5253).
- **Collect swatches, clippings, sketches,** and anything else that helps you describe what you have in mind. Going through local bridal magazines is just the beginning. Peruse bridal magazines from other countries, shelter and food magazines, art books, and classic movies. You may be inspired by something as minute as the way a curtain hangs or a vase is set on a table. If a window display at your favorite boutique catches your eye, find out whether the stylist is available to do weddings.

- **Keep a "Not in *My* Wedding" list** that may include odoriferous flowers such as Rubrim lilies, narcissus (paper whites), and daisies, or any kind of ticky-tacky, cutesy-wootsy ideas that turn your stomach.
- **Solicit the input of the banquet manager or the caterer,** but differentiate between their opinion and fact. They may know what has worked in the past in that space — and they may be right most of the time — but you should feel free to make suggestions and ask questions.

A common pitfall of wedding planning is a lack of communication about your wedding decor with the powers that be at your reception venue. Before things get too far along, meet with the banquet manager and go over the ground rules. Among the things you want to get straight:

- What are the decor givens?
- How much time is allotted for setup and breakdown?
- What can be affixed to what? Some places have strict rules about stringing garlands, hanging things on walls, using nails, and the like.
- What, if any, are the restrictions regarding prop rentals, candles, additional lighting, or fabric draping?
- Do they have a list of recommended and/or dictated floral designers who can work there?
- Where do the bars, buffet stations, and dance floor go?
- Where is the best spot for the bride and groom's table, and what are the best and worst spots for other tables?
- Can you remove or cover decor elements you find objectionable such as taxidermied animal heads, pieces of furniture, and lighting fixtures?
- Do the fountains and fireplaces work? Can they be made to work in time?
- When will renovations (painting, cleaning, and so on) promised in the contract be made?
- Are any new renovations or decor changes in the works before your wedding?
- Are any public or shared spaces off limits for decorating?
- Is the room being turned between the ceremony and reception? How long does that take? (See Chapter 2 for room-turning concerns.)
- Does the venue have air conditioning and is it sufficient?

Decor rapport

For the purposes of this book, we use the term *designer* to refer to any person involved with the decor. You see, once upon a time there were only florists. They supplied flowers for parties and weddings, and you may have called them to send a dozen red roses to your sweetheart for Valentine's Day. Now we have floral designers, party designers, event planners, event producers, happenings specialists, space stylists, and even lifestyle consultants. You cannot tell from the title alone whether they design the entire decor (including flowers, linens, lighting, and props), design solely flowers, or even know a poppy from a popsicle. Look for a designer known for working with a large variety of flowers, including many of the new hybrid breeds (such as coral peonies and mini-calla lilies in burgundy, yellow, and other intense shades), as well as the old standbys.

The classic cautionary wedding tale is that designers, when hearing you are shopping for a wedding, gleefully rub their palms together and start planning their winter vacation to St. Bart's. We think this rap is undeserved. After all, everybody deserves to make a living (or have you forgotten that?) and in our experience, the majority of designers who work with weddings care about both the clients and the results. If anything, they are inclined to give a little extra toward an occasion that's so much more momentous than the usual dinner party.

The first meeting with your designer(s) can take place either at your reception venue or at their shop or workspace. Set the parameters and be up front about your budget; there's no reason to waste your time and theirs by trying to lowball them or having them suggest outrageous concepts you could never afford. Ask to see sketches of possible room treatments. Even if your designer is familiar with your space, take a walk-through *together* as early in your planning as possible.

You should be able to see a sample centerpiece a few weeks before your wedding. If possible, have the designer create a sample table replete with linens, place settings, candles, and table numbers so you have a clear idea of the total effect. Be flexible: When it comes to flowers, what you see is not always what you get. When possible, get a photo of the centerpiece. Your contract most likely stipulates that because of unforeseen events such as frost, seasonal changes, and shipping problems, certain substitutions can be made. Find out what those may be.

To prevent any misunderstanding, here are some other logistical questions to ask your designer(s):

- Do they change the setup and breakdown fees?
- How early will they need to start setting up and how long will it take to break down? (Important for avoiding overtime rental fees.)
- Can they arrange to deliver leftover flowers to your home? For what fee?
- At the end of the event, what materials such as tablecloths, vases, napkins, and table numbers do you own and what does the designer own?

What's in a Room?

Consider every aspect of your space that could use some decoration. The following overview provides ideas and solutions for design dilemmas whether your wedding is in a hotel, a banquet hall, or loft. (For particulars about theme weddings, see Chapter 6.)

When you enter

First impressions count, so as guests enter, give them something to remember:

- An arched trellis adorned with flowers
- A pair of large fiberglass urns faux finished to look like jade, pink marble, or granite and stuffed with flowering branches
- A sign welcoming guests to your wedding done as a whimsical garden plaque, a sports-type pennant, or an illuminated medieval-looking scroll calligraphed in gold paint — especially in lieu of the generic black-event-board-with-white-plastic-letters used in many hotels and conference facilities
- Waiters bearing trays of drinks just inside the door for an immediate display of hospitality

The driveway

Even before you hit the entrance, you can convey a celebratory air without spending a great deal of money. Create a glowing path of footlights by using *luminarias* (votive candles in small paper bags). Either color or plain-brown paper bags will do. Make sure you have a few inches of sand in the bottom of the bag to stabilize it. For an even more festive touch, cut out patterned windows in the bags symmetrically by folding the bags in half as if making paper snowflakes.

Tiki torches, often found at gardening shops, are dramatic as well as inexpensive. When filled with citronella, these have the added bonus of repelling things that go buzz in the night.

For daytime weddings, use potted plants, staked balloons, or Burma Shave–style signs along the drive to guide the way.

The gift table

Except in certain cultures, people seldom bring presents to the wedding anymore, so you may not need to have a fancy table waiting to be piled with packages. But for guests who haven't figured out that gifts brought to the reception are just more stuff for the bride and groom to schlep home, assign a waiter whose sole job is to whisk away the packages and check them in the coatroom. Do so out of courtesy to those guests who sent their gift directly to your home but may, upon seeing a few ribbon-festooned boxes waiting to be joined by more ribbon-festooned boxes, fear that you expected them to inundate you on the spot.

Designate someone to gather up the gifts at the end of the reception and hold onto them until you and your spouse can arrange to pick them up when you return from your honeymoon. (Different traditions for displaying gifts are covered in Chapter 14.)

Up, down, and all around: Ceilings, floors, and walls

Look at the big picture. What parts of the space are crying out for help and need to be disguised? What has potential and should be accentuated? Can you live with the bare acoustic ceiling tiles or should you divert precious centerpiece funds to camouflage them? Does the space contain a singularly exquisite architectural feature — a cathedral ceiling, a sweeping banister, a fountain? You can create an entirely different environment by draping the walls, ceiling, and every possible feature, but if your space requires such a total transformation, why did you book it in the first place?

When it comes to decorating, choose your battles. Neutral walls and even patterned wallpaper may "disappear" depending on the time of day. If the walls are decorated in a flamboyant way, go with it rather than trying to do a complete overhaul. Similarly, the flaming-orange carpet may be distracting during a day wedding, but inconsequential at night once the tables are set up and the lights are low.

Whether you're going for high drama or you simply must turn a sow's ear into a silk purse, borrow an old theatrical technique and drape away. On a lesser scale, you might try hanging strips of sheer fabric emanating from one point over the dance floor to the sides of the room, swagging the entrance way with fabric, or festooning one wall behind the head table. But keep in mind that although the materials are generally inexpensive (usually muslin, tulle, theatrical scrim, or parachute silk), a room swathed in billowing clouds of fabric does not come cheap. Draping is not a do-it-yourself project. Pros know how to do it right so your room looks like a splendid gift-wrapped box rather than a parachute caught in the treetops.

Fabric and other decorating materials must adhere to fire ordinances. Fire marshals have been known to spring surprise inspections at even the most glamorous locations and insist that everything be removed. Speaking of fire safety, by law lighted exit signs and fire sprinklers cannot be covered.

Trees or huge plants such as ficus, palm, or philodendron cover a multitude of sins for comparatively little money because you can rent them from nurseries.

Lighting

People often don't realize how much lighting influences the look and mood of an evening event. A few shades can make the difference between intimate and institutional. You don't want lights dimmed to such a "romantic" level that waiters have to set off flares. Nor do you want the room so "brilliant" that sequin dresses spontaneously combust. However, a pin spot can make even a modest centerpiece "pop," and something as simple as dimming the chandeliers for the first dance can conjure an aura of mystery and suspense.

Visit the space at the time of day your wedding will be. Even for afternoon events, where supplemental lighting is often a waste of money, you need to take into consideration the level of light. Is the light blinding so that shades need to be drawn? *Are* there shades? Should you change the time of your wedding because the light looks best at a certain time of day? Do the lights have dimmers? What are the requirements or restrictions for a lighting designer? Ask your designer to detail the most appropriate light settings for your reception and mark them for the maitre d'.

Hiring a professional lighting company may seem extravagant — and it is — but creative lighting can transform a room in ways you never dreamed. Properly up-lit, an urn filled with branches not only appears larger but also throws dramatic silhouettes on the wall, turning a single arrangement into a forest. Think about restaurants and homes where you feel extremely comfortable. Chances are, the lighting is very pleasing to both your eye and your psyche.

Some designers offer lighting services; others subcontract with companies that supply the equipment. Either way, here are some terms you may hear bandied about:

- **Ambient or diffused light:** The main light in the room, coming from either natural or artificial sources. This light should soften and flatter; use accent lighting to make specific areas or architectural features stand out.

- **Bee, fairy, or twinkle lights:** Strings of tiny lights like Christmas lights. Used behind diaphanous fabrics, on banisters, or in trees, they add a magical touch. An inexpensive lighting trick is to drop strings of these like vines from the ceiling.
- **Gobos:** Custom-made or rented stencils that go over lights to project patterns such as stars, moons, snowflakes, or musical notes onto walls, dance floors, or draped fabric.
- **Pin spots:** Narrow beams that target centerpieces, the cake, or anything demanding special attention. Hung from the ceiling or directed from light poles, they are frequently used in pairs to give cross-directional light. The darker the room, the more dramatic pin spots look.

- **Up-lights and down-lights:** Also known as light-cans, which are usually painted to match the space. Used to project beams of light upward from the base of an urn or tree or down onto a mantel or altar. A recent trend is to put battery-operated up-lights under tables to create a surreal glow.
- **Washes:** Colors (usually pastels) projected over large spaces such as bars or dance floors that bathe the area in a particular light.

To de-emphasize unattractive areas without spending a penny, simply remove some of the fluorescent tubes in the bathrooms or unscrew light bulbs in wall sconces. If you need *some* light, replace the bulbs with pink or frosted bulbs.

Props

By *props* we don't mean big theatrical pieces. Consider incorporating unique items you own such as ceramic pitchers, silver bowls, candelabras, and vases into your decor scheme. Antique stores often rent out items that are not precious, and many cities have prop shops where you can find all sorts of goodies. Caterers and hotel banquet departments often own props that they wouldn't have thought to use for a wedding but that you may be interested in, such as huge fans, paper lanterns, or even backdrops. (Props are, of course, a critical component of theme weddings, which we cover in Chapter 6.)

To symbolize good luck a thousand times over (and over), Japanese couples fold 1,001 origami cranes — a bird that takes only one mate in life — and scatter them on tables and in glasses around the reception. Sometimes the tiny paper cranes are arranged into patterns such as family crests, or characters such as *konji* (long life) and *kotobuki* (good luck).

The cocktail area

A secret to a lively party is keeping guests constantly amused. One way to accomplish this feat is through the decor. Who says that if the dining room is romantic and classical, the cocktail area cannot be glitzy? Whether cocktails are served before dinner or are the main event (see the reception-as-cocktail-party in Chapter 8), don't mimic a dining room with overly large centerpieces and tables for eight. You want guests up and mingling, not planted like carrots.

Cocktail tables

Cocktail tables should be small and seat no more than four people. No matter whether the tables are 28, 32, or 36 inches in diameter, you should provide seating for a third of the guests — but *only* a third — during cocktails. Having seats for, say, 75 percent of the guests is not gracious; it's silly, and makes people think you forgot to rent chairs for the other 25 percent.

A trend of late is bar-height pedestal tables for guests to lean on (rather than sit at) as they chat. Many rental companies offer bases that turn 30-inch-high tables into "high tops."

What goes on your cocktail tables depends on the mood you want to create. Things that seem a bit twee for a dining room may work perfectly in a smaller cocktail area. For example, theme *elements* such as gold and silver lamé linens, Christmas tree topiaries replete with baby garlands, or scooped out mini-pumpkins holding flowers or candles, give a room levity without making your reception singularly thematic. One particularly whimsical cocktail set up for a couple from the Southwest United States featured cacti terrarium centerpieces and black-and-white "cow spot" chairs. Their dining room, on the other hand, was the height of formality.

Escort card table

An escort card is not the same as a place card. If you are serving a seated meal, an *escort card,* picked up before the meal, tells guests at which table they are seated. A *place card* (at the table) informs guests which seat at that table is theirs.

A professional trick: Escort cards work best when they are sets of miniature envelopes with guests' names on the outside and inserts with table numbers — as opposed to having both names and numbers on "table tents" (folded cards) — because the numbered inserts can be done beforehand and changed at the last moment without having to rewrite the entire name. As you can see in Figure 11-2, the envelopes also look quite elegant propped up on their little flaps in rows on the escort card table.

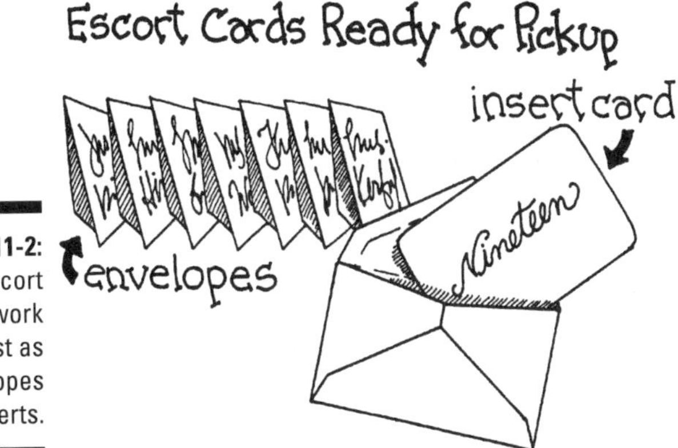

Figure 11-2: Escort cards work best as envelopes and inserts.

In order not to scare the wits out of Korean, Mexican, or Chinese guests, don't calligraph their names in red ink. Although red is a good-luck color in many other cultural situations, particularly for Asians, writing someone's *name* in red is tantamount to making a death threat.

Because the escort card table stands alone, usually in the cocktail area or in another prominent place (but not where you'll cause a bottleneck!), consider swagging or rouching the table cloth as well as having a tall, striking centerpiece. A single fabulous prop, a portrait of the two of you, or an antique lamp also works well. (See the upcoming section "Swagging Like a Pro" and, for tips on designing the escort cards themselves, see Chapter 13.) The table size should be in proportion to the number of cards you have. A table that's too large looks like a bunch of guests are no-shows; a too-small table creates a domino effect when guests start removing cards. A lovely touch is to put framed photographs — the older the better — of parents and grandparents on the escort card table. Guests love to look at them.

Rather than leaving your guest book on the escort card table, ask a friend to pass it around at the reception (as well as be responsible for retrieving it at the end of the party) and encourage people to share their thoughts on the day. Buy a hard-bound album with blank pages (a photo album may work) that matches the style of your wedding. A truly meaningful guest book is more than a list of signatures. Besides, you presumably already have your guests' names and addresses from your invitation list, so you don't need them to sign in as if at a hotel.

You may want to skip a table altogether and use a mantel, an accessible nook, or a shelf on which to place the cards. Or you may use the human card table: a waiter holding a silver tray filled with neat rows of cards.

Post either a waiter or a friend with an alphabetized list and table numbers to troubleshoot should a card go astray or someone brings an unexpected guest. (Rude, yes, but you still have to find an extra seat.) The list-keeper should also note cards that aren't picked up so that extra place settings can be removed before guests enter the dining room.

You may be advised to place the escort card table between the ceremony and cocktail reception or between the cocktail reception and dining room. In most instances, however, we find having the escort card table in the cocktail reception to be most efficient, allowing guests to pick up table numbers at their leisure without creating a traffic jam.

Bars

A banquet table can serve as a bar or you can rent high wooden bars. In either case, avoid bottlenecks at the entrance by making sure the bar — and waiters passing drinks — are far enough inside so guests can grab a drink and keep on moving. Bar linens should be either skirted or "boxed" so the table legs don't show and the colors should work with your scheme. (For a full discussion of bars, see Chapter 10.)

Being a high-traffic spot, the bar is not the place for large centerpieces or candles.

Seat and you shall find

While place cards are optional, we believe that assigning tables for a sit-down meal is a necessity. Even for a buffet meal, unless you are lucky enough to have an entire guest list composed of a jolly group of people who all know and love each other, you must assign tables. Otherwise, one table inevitably has 30 chairs crammed around it while your two oldest school chums eat in a corner by themselves.

When ordering escort cards, you usually need only about half as many as the number of guests because couples seated at the same table have their names on one card. However, if your cards are printed or blind embossed with your names or monogram, you may want to order more to use as gift cards later.

As shown in the illustration below, to compose a seating chart, take a large piece of poster board and sketch in the floor plan with numbered tables. Take a pad of self-adhesive notes and write the names of guests who have confirmed their attendance. Place the names around the tables, trying to fill one table at a time while taking into account whom guests may know at their table and at tables closest to them. Your parents probably want to sit near your table and their friends near them. Conversely, you don't want to antagonize your feuding aunts by seating them next to each other.

By about a week before your wedding, the seating chart should be firm, so you can make an official chart with the names written on it. A charming option for a smallish wedding is a calligraphed seating list framed and propped on an easel in lieu of escort cards. Guests enjoy seeing where everyone is sitting and after the wedding you have a beautiful memento.

Doing Your Seating Chart

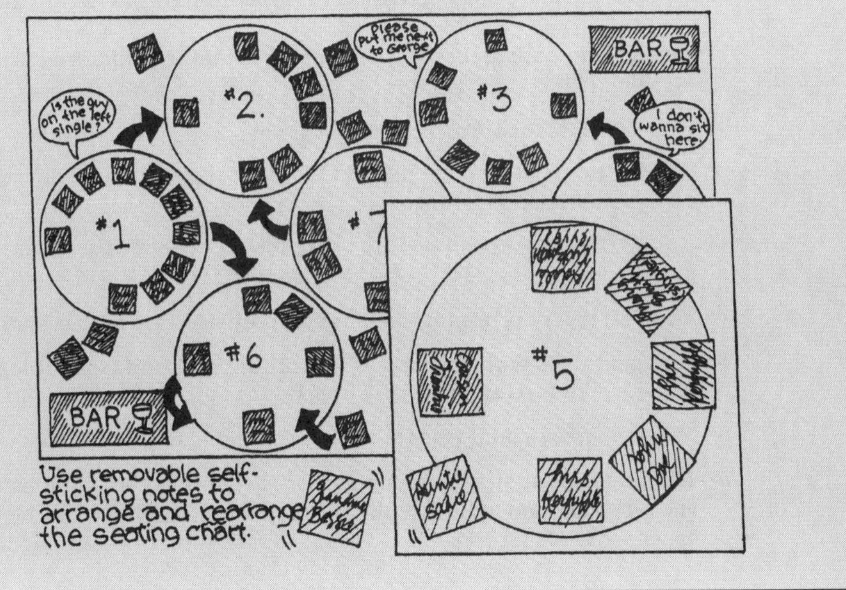

Passed hors d'oeuvres

If hors d'oeuvres mean to you heavy silver trays passed by white-gloved waiters, miniature floral bouquets are an appropriate garnish. If you're willing to experiment, the possibilities are limitless, from "cigarette girl" type boxes with savory puff pastry "cigars" to flats of grass in which blanched vegetables have been "planted." (For more hors d'oeuvre ideas, refer to Chapter 8.)

Passed hors d'oeuvres should be bite size. That's *one* bite. No knives, forks, or spoons. A toothpick or skewer may be okay. Portions of food served at cocktail stations should be small as well. If necessary, a small plate with a small fork is permissible.

Food stations

Whether for cocktails or the main meal, food stations provide a great decor opportunity, so have fun. You and your designer need to involve the chef in creating the concept so the food and decor fit harmoniously. You don't want, for example, the designer's Japanese fan display occupying the same spot on the sushi station that the chef picked out for his Godzilla ice sculpture.

The food itself on stations serves as a decorative element. (For tips on selecting colors and textures, refer to Chapter 8.) Food is more appetizing when everything is laid out at different heights or in different vessels.

You especially want to pay attention to table topography. Some ideas to try:

- Buy a bolt of inexpensive fabric and "puddle" the material around serving dishes.
- Use painted backdrops, creative signage, and simple props.
- Display foods at various heights by using tiered candy trays or specially constructed props.
- Create "peaks and valleys" by using linen-covered dish racks, milk crates, and bus boxes.
- Tilt platters by propping them up with upside-down plates underneath.
- Garnish tables with bunches of beautiful fruits and vegetables such as grapes, artichokes, and crab apples.
- Make *topiaries* (mini trees) out of foods such as lemons, figs, or nuts.
- Thread eggplants (sliced lengthwise), asparagus, or scallions on wire and wrap around cylindrical containers that may hold salads or sauces. (See Figure 11-3.)

Decorating Vessels with Vegetables

Figure 11-3: Vegetable-wrapped cylinders make attractive food vessels or vases.

- Pile round tables high with dried fruits, nuts, olives, marinated vegetables — anything that guests can help themselves to without creating a mess — to make interesting walk-around stations.
- Add a touch of showmanship with food cooked or finished in front of the guests. Pasta, carved meats, grilled chicken skewers, fajitas, and other foods are all the more tantalizing when prepared on the spot by a chef.
- Create mini-vignettes such as a sushi station designed as a Zen rock garden with a tiny fountain and bonzai trees.

For hors d'oeuvres stations, park your decorative touches at eye level and above. Because most guests stand during cocktails, they may not appreciate the welting, fringe, or other decorative finishes on the hems of buffet or bar cloths.

Full-meal food stations are composed of several serpentine, half moon, or rectangular tables placed strategically around the room. Each should have its own supply of china and silver. Some people may carry the same plate around the whole reception while others pick up a fresh one at each station, so if you are renting plates, figure on an average of three per person.

Dining areas

Even if you've had to shoehorn in more than an ideal number of tables, leave adequate room both near the entrance and between tables so guests can make their way gracefully without snagging tablecloths in their wake. Upon entering, guests should feel they are in a completely different atmosphere than the one they just left.

Position one or two waiters as "traffic cops" near the entrance of the dining room with a floor plan that indicates table numbers and locations. Otherwise, Aunt Myrtle may still be looking for her table when you return from the honeymoon.

If one of the first questions a designer asks you is "What color are your bridesmaids' dresses?" think twice about hiring that person. Your main concern should be the gestalt — not whether someone's dress matches the tablecloth.

Dance floor

TIP

A built-in dance floor makes life easy, but if you must rent one, interlocking 3 x 4–foot parquet squares are superior to the flimsy rolled-up variety. For a Deco look, you may consider a floor of black and white vinyl checkerboard tiles; for a classical look, faux marble.

An extraordinary but expensive proposition is a hand-painted dance floor (see this book's color section), a specialty of many designers. One popular design is a couple's monogram in script surrounded by a painted wreath of flowers.

Bandstand

If you're having trouble fitting a large band directly on your dance floor, you simply don't want to give up precious dance floor space, or you just want drama, you can rent platforms to be used as a bandstand. Even though these "risers" generally run only eight inches high, your designer should cover the gap between floor and platform with stapled material. Specify who is erecting the bandstand — the house, the rental company, or your designer.

You can't do much about camouflaging speakers because they need to be placed between the musicians and the audience. Mixing boards are big and ugly no matter what, so place them as discreetly as possible on a table with a boxed cloth that matches the dining tables.

Lighted music stands are often emblazoned with the band's name. If having this free billboard for the band does not jibe with your decor, specify that you'd prefer the band use generic music stands or none at all. For more band information, see Chapter 7.

Cake table

Place this table prominently in the main dining area and decorate accordingly. (See Chapter 9 for a complete cake table report.)

Dining tables

Round tables make a room look more festive than do rectangular tables, which remind people of their grammar school cafeteria. (Exceptions do exist; we've seen receptions with 75 or fewer guests successfully seat everyone at one incredibly long, dramatic table.)

Seating eight to ten guests at a 54- or 60-inch round table works best. Having the same number of guests at every table, however, is virtually impossible. Still, you want to keep the number of people at each table and the table sizes in close range. You may have eight tables of ten and two tables of eight, for example, but not two tables of four, two tables of seven, three tables of ten, and so on. This is a party, not a nightclub; people at smaller tables feel like the odd folks out. Once you have your final guest count, ask the banquet manager or whomever is laying out the seating whether you should do fewer tables because space is tight or more tables because you have room to spare. If you do use different size tables, apprise the tablecloth and centerpiece suppliers as soon as possible so everything is in proportion.

CAUTION

Before you decide on heavy or tall centerpieces, make sure your venue uses real tables, not *toppers* (rounds placed on top of smaller tables to create larger tables). Toppers tend to tip when leaned on, and the crashing of crystal and flowers is not the decor drama you're after.

Head table

Wherever the bride and groom sit is called the *head table.* The most important aspect in planning the head table is where you put it because everyone wants a view of the bride and groom. Two things affect the size of your head table: the size of your space and who you want to sit with you. For the latter, you can do one of two things:

- Seat both sets of parents, the officiant, grandparents, and/or extremely close relatives such as aunts and uncles with you. Then you can sprinkle the wedding party and their significant others around the room, making them mini-emissaries for you.
- Give parents their own tables with friends and seat the wedding party and their significant others at your table. Traditionally, the bride sits to the groom's right, and the best man on her other side. Attendants are alternately male, female.

Seating significant others at separate tables may result in wistful looks and goo-goo eyes from across the room, making other guests feel uncomfortable as well.

Don't assume you're a seating psychic. If your parents are divorced or you have some other family drama that may erupt, ask before you blithely place them where you please. Even if you play the peacemaker at family events, remember that this is not the normal family dinner. Your attention will be elsewhere during the reception. Are you brave enough to leave contentious relatives to their own devices?

Until recently, seating the entire wedding party on a *dais* (a raised platform) on one side of a long table so they faced the room was standard operating procedure. As many couples now find the long head table either unattractive, silly, or impossible to plan seating for, they are opting to use a round table. If as a matter of diplomacy or personal taste you use a rectangular head table, you can make it a focal point, swagging the cloths, planting floral gardens down the length of the table, or situating the table under an airy arbor or gazebo-type structure.

Some couples, perhaps out of the sheer frustration of determining who should sit at the head table, have a table for just the two of them. Some even go so far as to put the table on a riser and sit on throne-like chairs. We consider this a fascinating study in self-aggrandizement that bemuses guests more than it impresses them.

Chairs

Hotels and restaurants often spend a great deal of money on their chairs, which are designed to work with the room's decor as well as to seat the optimum number of people around each table. If you need to rent chairs, in most parts of the country wooden and plastic folding chairs are available in various colors. A more elegant option are Chiavari (faux bamboo) chairs, which are smaller — though less comfortable — than most chairs and can seat more people at a table. Although Chiavaris cost more to rent, you may actually break even because you need fewer tables, tablecloths, and centerpieces.

If your venue's chairs are particularly hideous or your taste is phantasmagoric, you might rent chair-back covers, full slipcovers, and/or simple sashes. Materials range from polyester-cotton blends in various colors to space-age-looking Spandex. A ribbon of tulle covered with a floral garland on the backs of the bride's and groom's chairs adds romance. For a funky chic look, swathe chairs with a few yards of diaphanous fabric such as crystal organza or tulle that is ultimately tied into a gigantic bow in the back.

Table tops

A centerpiece alone does not a table make. The flavor and spirit of an event are conveyed through many details, which, repeated seat after seat, table after table, form a delectable impression as guests enter. After guests are seated, they have time to note and appreciate each and every nuance, from the color of the napkins to the placement of the wine glasses. Consequently, the hours you invest planning these elements are well spent.

Before the guests file into the main dining room, have the head waiter or your wedding consultant do a table–by–table inspection to make sure the correct number of chairs and place settings have been set at each table, the tables are where you want them, every place is set correctly, the glasses have no spots, the candles are lit, the chairs are straight — in short, that every decorative detail has been taken care of. Then, and only then, should the meal begin.

Tablecloths

As you probably know, anything you can dream up for your wedding can be rented — for a price, of course — and tablecloths are no different. Many companies rent nationally as well as locally, happily shipping linens anywhere in the country. The typical white restaurant tablecloth, darned and dingy, is best used as an under-pad. You can make just about any tablecloth look more festive, however, with a little creativity:

- A thick band of satin edging on a table square
- Block-painted or stenciled designs
- A rolled hem or cording sewn into the hem for a formal "petticoat" effect
- Swagged tablecloths (see Figures 11-4 and 9-1)
- Fringe and/or tassels sewn on a square top-cloth or used with swagging
- Hand–painted designs, which you can create with inexpensive materials yourself (Having your designer custom-make these is pricey, so you may want to limit this technique to the cake or escort card tables.)
- A solid color under-cloth that shows through a lace top-cloth
- A tablecloth of leaves — made by gluing green leaves onto the cloth
- Mixed patterns such as floral chintz top-cloths over striped under-cloths
- One-of-a-kind cloths such as patchwork quilts, antique lace, or vintage shawls for a special table
- Overlays made of organza or panne, or cut, velvets
- Damask or brocade runners down the center of the table
- Each table a different shade of the same color so the room appears as a sea of blues, for example
- Table squares with silk or fresh flowers, tassels, or rings sewn on the corners (To calculate what size square you need, see Table 11-1.)

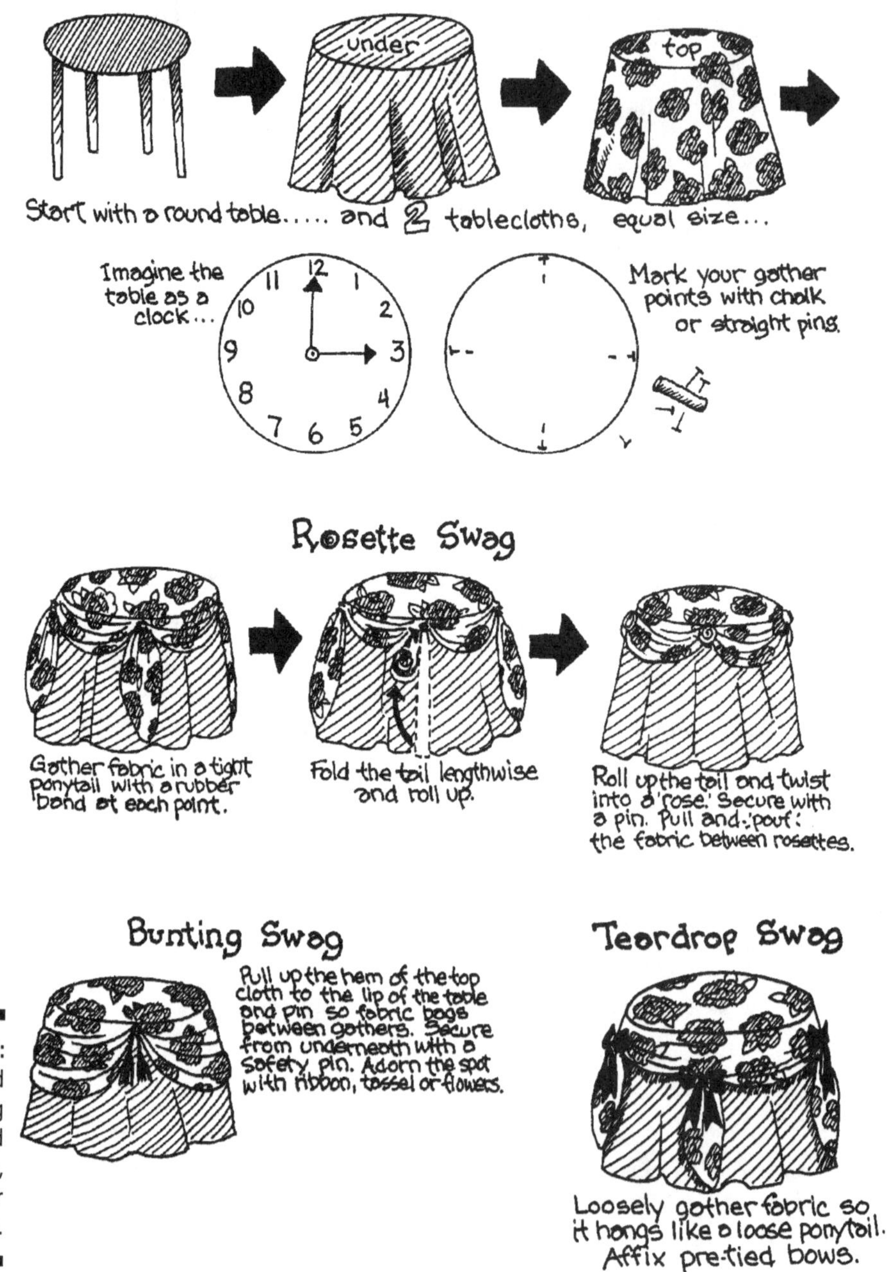

Figure 11-4: Instead of renting pre-swagged tablecloths, do your own.

Table 11-1 What Size Tablecloth Square?

Rectangular Table Length	Square Overlay Length (Point to Point)
127″	90″
119″	84″
101″	72″
85″	60″
76″	54″
64″	45″

Something about bare table legs draws people's attention away from the splendor of the rest of the room. Try to use floor-length cloths at all costs. For rectangular buffet and bar cloths, add 60 inches to both the length and width to get a floor length cloth. To calculate the size cloth you need for a round table, see Table 11-2.

Table 11-2 What Size Round Tablecloth?

Table Diameter	Round Floor-Length Cloth
72″	132″
66″	126″
60″	120″
54″	114″
48″	108″
36″	96″

The clunking of cutlery and china on wood can feel harsh, so place a foam pad or another linen between the table and linen.

Napkins

A subtle part of the decor, napkins can go on the service plate (see Figure 11-8) or directly on the tablecloth, but don't work well fanned out in glasses when a low centerpiece is on the table.

Rent plenty of extra napkins for waiter's service and to replace dropped or soiled ones. For cocktail napkins, order at least three per guest.

Tying napkins with wire-edged, satin, or raffia ribbons is a lovely finisher and less expensive if you (and your helpers) do the tying. That means picking up the napkins a few days before your wedding if possible. For a couple of lessons in creative napkin folding, see Figures 11-5 and 11-6.

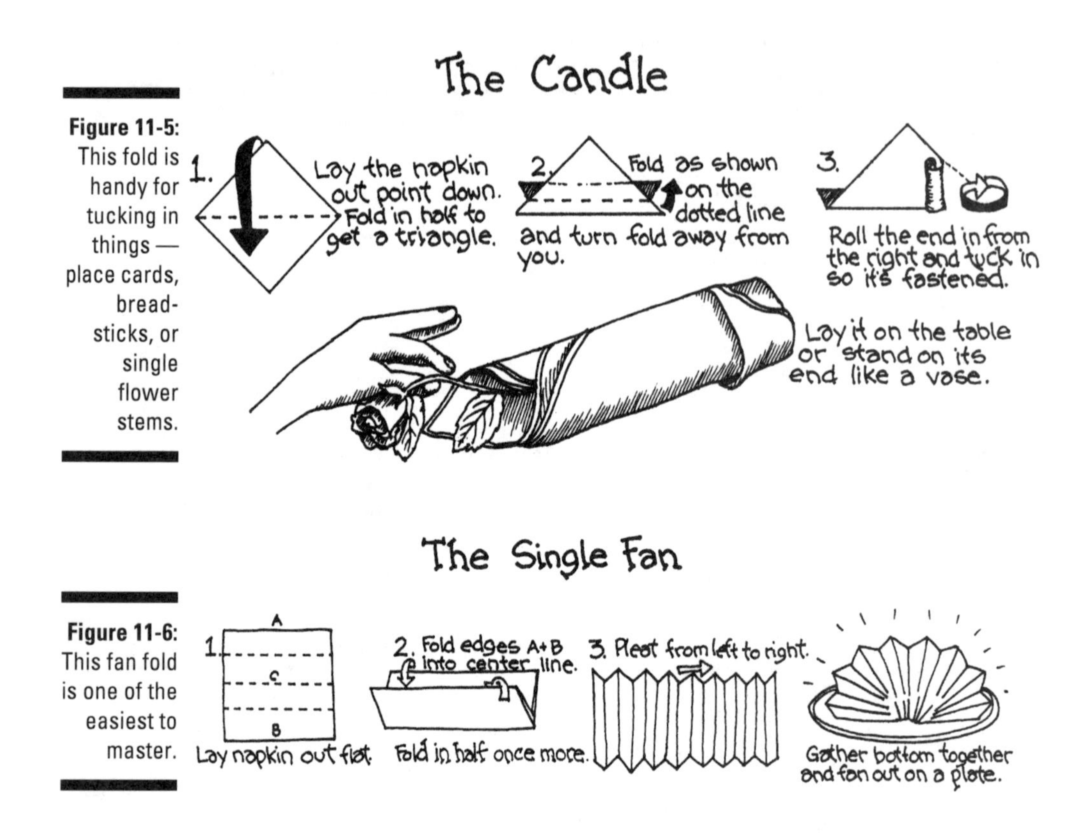

Figure 11-5: This fold is handy for tucking in things — place cards, bread-sticks, or single flower stems.

Figure 11-6: This fan fold is one of the easiest to master.

When it comes to cocktail napkins, starched linen is elegant and formal but not inexpensive to rent. A standard monogram on paper napkins is fine, but creating your own logo by hand or computer and having it printed on paper cocktail napkins and hand towels may be more in keeping with the style of your reception.

Candles

Candles have long held a mystical appeal and perhaps as an outgrowth of New Age trends have become, if you'll pardon the pun, hot, hot, hot. Where once you may have seen two elegant tapers guarding each centerpiece at a reception, you now find a virtual conflagration composed of hundreds of candles in all shapes and sizes. (A few types can be seen in Figure 11-7.)

Tall tapers can turn into wax-spitting demons in rooms with cross-directional air currents. Even "dripless" candles can be hazardous. If you're at all unsure, ask the banquet manager if you can come in with some test candles and see what happens.

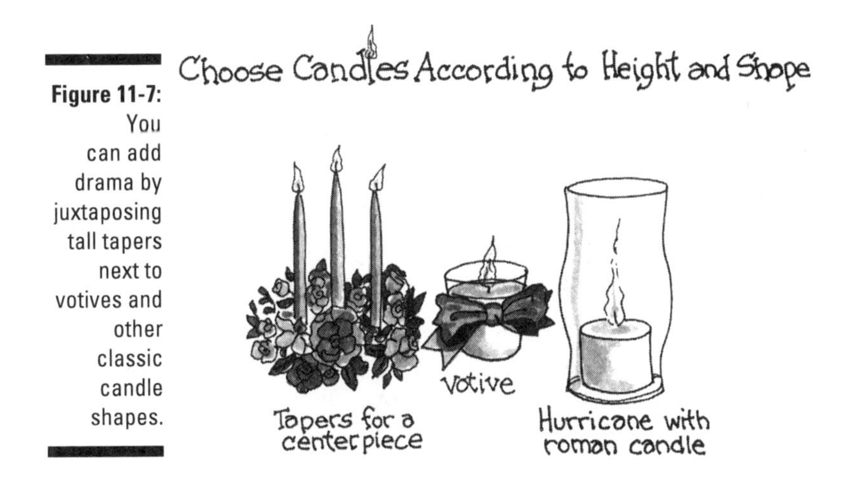

Figure 11-7: You can add drama by juxtaposing tall tapers next to votives and other classic candle shapes.

Some places do not allow open-flame candles. Two ways to circumvent this limitation (as well as the air-current problem) are to use either hurricane lamps or "mechanical candles" in which a steel spring pushes up wax through a metal candle-shaped casing as it burns. From a distance, these look fairly natural, making them suitable for ceremonies and chandeliers.

The glass holders for votive candles provide a base for decorating. They are frequently gold or silver leafed, covered with galax or lemon leaves and tied with raffia, beribboned, covered in mesh or fabric, planted in tiny terracotta pots, or hung from precisely engineered centerpieces.

Some ways to wax romantic include:

- Chunky Roman candles of different heights grouped together
- Hand-dipped spiral candles
- Candles shaped as orbs, squares, and pyramids
- Floral-shaped tea candles floated in rose bowls
- Taper candles, which can be as high as three feet, placed in short, ornate holders or in the tops of tall centerpieces
- Scented candles in the bathrooms (but never around food)
- Candles in votive holders placed on mirrors set in table centers to reflect more light
- Votive candles, grouped together and/or set in wreaths of flowers, lemons, or branches
- Table lamps that hold candles, with beaded or silver shades

Dishes, cutlery, stemware, and so on

Frequently in hotels and restaurants you don't have a choice in china and silver. Ask to see what they use as a service plate, or *charger* (the empty plate that is part of the place setting when you enter the room). If you hate the pattern, skip the service plate and put a napkin in the center of each place-setting instead.

For rentals, choices abound. At the inexpensive end of the spectrum are heavy, white china, flimsy silverware, and soda-bottle-thick glassware. Attractive options do exist at various price points and if you and your caterer can agree that one plate can be used for two courses (in other words, washed in between), renting attractive china can be affordable. Just make sure that every element works with the overall table design. As you can see in Figure 11-8, outfitting a place setting for a five-course meal means a lot of rental charges.

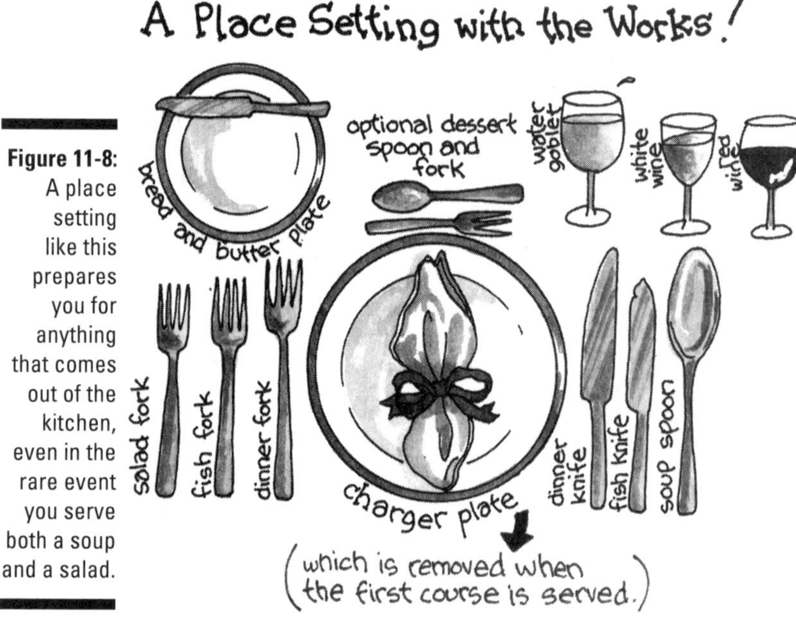

Figure 11-8: A place setting like this prepares you for anything that comes out of the kitchen, even in the rare event you serve both a soup and a salad.

Table accoutrements can be practical as well as enchanting:

- Individual salt and pepper shakers or cellars for each person
- Placing butter on lemon leaves
- Tiny silver tongs for sugar cubes
- Victorian silver toast holders

- Metallic or faux jewel napkin rings
- Knife, spoon, or chopstick rests

If you're serving meat, be sure to order sharp knives. Regular rental knives are usually not serrated, forcing guests to engage in eating olympics.

Table numbers

Make table numbers easy to read but refrain from billboards. And put some thought into creative ways to avoid using generic table number stanchions. These ways may include:

- Rococo frames displaying calligraphed numbers
- Leaves painted with numbers, affixed to a long tube, and planted in the centerpieces
- Numbers on table tents that match escort and place cards
- Use different flowers or props on each table and assign guests to table names — "Gardenia" or "Tango" — rather than by number

Table numbers should be removed at the beginning of the meal — the table is probably too crowded as it is and, once guests are seated, numbers are unnecessary.

When numbering the tables (as in Figure 11-1), do evens (2, 4, 6, ...) on one side of the dance floor and odds (3, 5, 7...) on the other rather than what you think is a consecutive arrangement. The odd-even split makes narrowing down the location of a table that much easier for waiters directing guests. Keep in mind that some people have an aversion to the number 13, so you may want to skip that table number.

Use low numbers at the least desirable tables and high numbers at the best tables. This makes those at the low-numbered tables feel important even if the table is behind the palm tree.

Place cards

Place cards tell guests where at the table they are seated. You can use table tents, centered at 12 o'clock above each plate, or flat cards set on top of each napkin.

In times past, place cards were a must at seated meals. They went out of fashion during the '60s and '70s but made a comeback in the '80s. Fortunately, place cards are increasingly — and sensibly — less formal, using first names and even nicknames so members of the table know how to address each other.

Assigning tables is difficult enough and, admittedly, assigning seats is an even bigger pain. But guests really appreciate your having thought about whom they may have to talk to for several courses.

Menu cards

Nice menu cards don't have to be expensive. You can design them yourself on your computer and have them either offset by a printer or photocopied on card stock by a professional copy shop. Many stationery shops carry artistically bordered cards specially made for laser printers. If you're having your wedding at a restaurant or hotel that laser prints its daily menu, they may be happy to do yours in the same fashion. While you may have one menu per person, two or four per table is sufficient. When you have food stations, menu cards are a must. Otherwise, after the party you will hear, "I didn't know there was filet."

Rest rooms

Women, in particular, get a kick out of bathroom baskets filled with goodies. We suggest throwing in everything from hairspray to breath mints to emergency pairs of stockings in various sizes. In off-premise spaces, the bathrooms can be dreary at best, so bring in your own hand towels, scented candles, soaps, and even toilet paper to replace the particularly torturous variety found in institutional rest rooms.

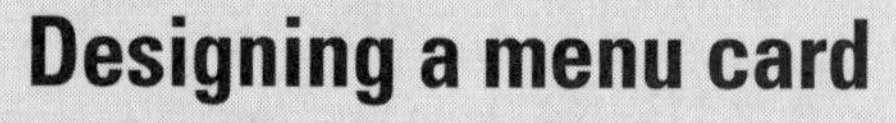

Designing a menu card

A handsomely printed or calligraphed menu card makes a nice memento. Here are some tips for making yours special:

- Put your names or monograms, the wedding date, and the site at the top of the menu.
- List the wines to be served to the left of each dish — but only if they are interesting enough (this doesn't mean expensive) to mention.
- Use colorful and descriptive adjectives, but don't use foreign words unless normally used for the dish or your meal calls for it. "Vanilla Butter Cream Wedding Cake filled with Hazelnut Truffle Mousse" makes sense; "*Mousse de Noisettes*" seems over the top.

Transitional spaces

You don't have to bedeck vestibules, foyers, and spaces between the cocktail and dining rooms in flowers and finery, but they should at least look like they are a part of the same event. Even if you've already blown your budget on more pressing design details, try to save a few bucks to place some votive candles around on ledges and tables, or to cover spare tables and chairs with tulle, the all-purpose wedding material. Potted plants in plastic garden containers can be covered in tulle or other fabrics and grouped together to soften otherwise neglected spaces.

Flower Power

As the most important aspect of your reception's design, flowers are likely to eat up the bulk of your design budget. Flowers themselves are generally expensive, and then someone has to select, prepare, transport, and arrange these precious blooms — and that costs money. To last through your reception with heads up and color intact, flowers cannot be just plopped in a vase. They must be conditioned — stems denuded of thorns, anthers, stigmas, and extra leaves (which may decay in water, producing a foul odor), ends snipped or crushed, and stems wired. If you desire a certain look such as fully opened roses, these must be "blown" open just enough but not one iota too much. Even the seemingly homespun wild-flowers-in-a-pitcher look is not as simple as it appears. Studied casualness takes *work*.

An oft-heard bridal refrain is, "Can't we simply use some heavenly wildflowers flowers that we pick ourselves?" Sure you can — if you want to begin your wedding by getting arrested. Federal law prohibits the picking of wildflowers, so if you want them, grow your own or find a supplier who does.

At some point, your designer should communicate with your cake maker. If your cake is to have a flower design, you may want it to coordinate with the centerpieces or the bridal bouquet.

In a spirit of magnanimity, many couples consider having their leftover flowers donated to a local hospital. It's a nice thought, but, frankly, most hospitals don't want them. Sometimes you can arrange with the florist to provide wax floral paper and an assistant to wrap bouquets for your guests to take home.

Reception flowers

Many hosts are obsessed with centerpieces being no higher than eye level when you are sitting at the table. While this raises manic arguments between designer and client, keep in mind that people tend to converse with those seated next to, rather than across from, them. People like to be able to at least nod at the smiling faces across the way, but in our opinion, as long as centerpieces are airy, you don't have to worry about partially obscuring the cross-table view. You just don't want a mini privet hedge bisecting the table.

If you are fixated on giving guests a clear view across the table, use the elbow test. Rest your elbow on the table and raise your forearm perpendicular to the table, fingers extended. Centerpieces on the table should end below your fingertips (about 14 inches) and elevated centerpieces, where the flowers are above eye level, should start above your fingertips.

Use filler such as trite flowers and greenery sparingly. Ideally, greenery consists of leaves removed from the flowers themselves and used only to balance an arrangement.

Shaped centerpieces use floral mechanics — floral foam, chicken-wire cages, tape, wire, and wired tubes — to add height and breadth. In any centerpiece, no matter how elaborate or simple, these materials should never show.

One of the most refreshing trends in floral design has been dispensing with the centerpiece assembly line. Designers create rooms as a whole, using similar colors and/or flowers but different approaches for each table. Some tables may have low arrangements with tapered candles, while other tables feature the same flowers in elevated centerpieces with votive candles. You may also change the color palette and flowers from table to table.

Flowers in the center of the table should be finished 360 degrees around. Arrangements that go against a wall can be "flat backed," requiring only the fronts and sides to be finished.

Different cultures ascribe different meanings to flower colors. Iranians and Peruvians give yellow flowers to their worst enemies, and Mexicans use them for funerals and Day of the Dead celebrations. Similarly, white flowers are a sign of mourning for the Chinese.

Centerpieces can be designed in various styles and configurations:

- **Breakaway:** Several dainty posies in individual glass containers arranged to look like one big bouquet. At the end of the party, each person at the table takes home one of the pieces. For a twist,

Decor by Renny; Photo by Sarah Merians

For this ceremony in the round, uplights transform flowering branches into a wedding arbor (top). In an ornate church, you don't need more than a red carpet runner and simple pew bows as decoration (right).

Photo by David Hechler

Decor by Atlas Floral; Photo by Andy Marcus

Suspending bouquets from the ceiling by strings of bee lights in tulle allows guests to see each other across the tables (top). The unlikely occurrence of an indoor swimming pool as a "dining room" called for a clear Plexiglas floor on top (bottom left). A simple room is turned into a fantasy with the addition of strands of tiny lights (bottom right).

Floor by Stanford Tent Company; Photo by David Hechler

Decor by Martha Meier Design; Photo by David Hechler

DECOR BY ANTHONY FERAZZ DESIGNS; PHOTO BY ANDY MARCUS

DECOR BY ROBERT ISABELL; PHOTO BY ANDY MARCUS

A New Year's Eve wedding uses hundreds of gold, white, and silver balloons to festive effect (top). Damask tablecloths, chair covers, and rose topiaries complement a Baroque room (left). Grandeur reaches new heights with scores of tapers in imposingly tall centerpieces and platform "candelabras." Votives cast a flattering light, and the hand-painted dance floor brings all the elements together (bottom right).

A hand-painted satin cloth offset with hydrangea garland and roses makes a spectacular chuppah. The garlanded standing candelabras heighten the drama.

Decor by Anthony Ferrazz. Photos by Andy Marcus.

Photo by Andy Marcus

Photo by David Hechler

A destination wedding in Jamaica includes a rehearsal dinner on the beach (top). This gazebo trimmed with a garland of greenery and flowers was the setting for an interfaith wedding. The sound was carefully orchestrated, with microphones wired into the top of the gazebo, so that the ceremony participants could speak in conversational tones and still be heard by the guests (left). A few infrared shots can look as ethereal as you feel on your wedding day. Printing the two frames from an enlarged contact sheet imparts a film verité feeling (bottom).

Photo by Laurie Klein Gallery

This tent reception incorporates several clever design elements: Tall centerpieces and candles are mixed with low ones for variety and interest. Standing light fixtures throw light upward and direct pin spots highlight specific areas. Branches intertwine overhead to give guests the feeling of being in a forest while a painted dance floor provides a focal point for the room. Note also how the tables are spaced to promote interaction among guests without crowding them. The chiavari chairs, made of gilded faux bamboo, look festive and allow you to fit more guests around a table comfortably. The table linens, in deep rich colors, complete the effect.

Photo by Terry DeRoy Gruber

Photo by Alex Kirkbride

Decor by Preston Bailey; Photo by Alex Kirkbride

The smallest details can convey the emotion of the day.

Photos by Maureen Edwards DeFries

Accessories by Jan Kish; Photos by Lambert Photographs

You can serve hand-decorated fondant miniatures in a variety of designs, some even painted with gold leaf (top left). Hand-painting sugared almonds is a new twist on an old tradition. They make perfect after-dinner treats (top right) or, wrapped in metallic tulle, party favors (bottom).

1
Cake by Sylvia Weinstock; Photo by Andy Marcus
2
Cake by Bijoux Doux
3
Cake by John and Mike's Amazing Cakes
4
Cake by John and Mike's Amazing Cakes
7
Cake by Jan Kish; Photo by Lambert Photographs
6
Cake by Colette Peters; from
Wedding Cakes
Photo by Colin Cooke
5
Cake by John and Mike's Amazing Cakes
8
Cake by Montclair Baking
9
Cake by Montclair Baking
10
Cake by Montclair Baking
11
Cake by Ana Paz Cakes

1. Tiered cake with a plethora of sugarpaste flowers in shades of white and ecrus: calla lilies, roses, tulips, and lilies of the valley. Note the cake table decor – fresh calla lilies, orchids, and greenery. **2.** A cake covered in marzipan, with royal icing delicately piped to resemble dotted Swiss lace is finished with a cascade of gumpaste flowers. **3-5.** With the exception of the bridge, all of the elements for these cakes are completely edible, mostly done with white modeling chocolate. The water is made of buttercream. **6.** This one-tier cake is the perfect size for a small wedding. The design is made from run-in sugar (thinned royal icing). **7.** Lemon cake with lemon curd is made to look like a Chippendale planter box. The unique and exquisite flowers have been crystallized. **8.** Hand-molded gumpaste gardenias, jasmine, plumeria, and fresh greenery accent textured white chocolate draped over fondant. **9.** Pale yellow fondant decorated with avocado green grosgrain ribbon and daisies (both made of sugar) give this cake a retro look. **10.** This tiered cake, both stacked and separated, features gumpaste fabric swags and flowers, including the quintessential bridal flower, orange blossoms. The lace and floral swags are white chocolate. **11.** A tiered cake, iced in fondant and decorated with pastillage flowers, is designed to be served on an antique English plate and incorporate antique silver placques. This beautiful cake happens to be kosher. **12.** Five cakes with basket weave of buttercream; some have piped buttercream roses and others have molded sugar fruit in an ultra-realistic style. **13.** Shaker box cake adorned with sugar daisies, perfect for a country-theme bridal shower.

Decor by Preston Bailey; Photo by Alex Kirkbride

Photo by Andy Marcus

Work with the architecture of your venue, not against it. In this case, a few strategically placed flowers look like many, with the help of face-to-face mirrors (top left). Cinderella's glass coach at Disney's Fairy Tale Weddings is one of the most romantic ways to make an entrance (top right). A wedding tent that could be a ballroom. Note how the pin spots of light make the centerpieces "pop." The sides of the tent and ceiling are draped in pleated fabric, and the chandeliers and sconces add elegance (bottom right).

Lighting by Frost Lighting Inc.; Photo by Don Laurino

At a Moroccan-style wedding, one of several resting areas invites guests to relax (top), while fabric sails draped from the tent ceiling give a feeling of movement and make the space feel more intimate (bottom).

It Figures by Melanie Wynne

Modeled after a photograph of the couple, this 6-inch-high figurine makes a whimsical cake topper or decorative element for an escort card or head table.

incorporate grapes, pears, and other fruits for breakaway cornucopias. (When you make your rounds to all the tables between courses, you can inform guests that they can take part of the centerpiece.)

- **Candelabra:** A tall candelabra that has four to six arms holding tall tapered candles. Flowers start at eye level, emanating from an elevated bowl in the center of the candelabra.
- **Fish bowl:** Round glass bowls stuffed with one kind of flower such as roses for a fairly low centerpiece.
- **Garden:** An abundance of flowers and foliage such as cabbage roses and ivy tendrils that look as if a small garden is growing in the middle of the table. The greens either completely obscure the container (which is therefore nothing fancy) or allow at most a peek of the container, such as a pretty basket or patterned pitcher.
- **Ikebana:** A Japanese style in which each element is meticulously and artfully placed with a strong sense of space, proportion, and scale.
- **Pavé style:** European-style arrangement composed of flowers whose stems have been cut almost down to the head and arranged in low, mounded patterns. Well suited for side tables as well as centerpieces.
- **Still life:** Arrangements that have not only flowers but also colorful fruits and vegetables such as asparagus, artichokes, china berries, crab apples, grapes, green apples, kale, kumquats, nuts, vanilla beans, or whatever's in season.
- **Topiaries:** Either natural ivy grown around a metal frame and trimmed to resemble something as simple as spheres or as complex as cupids, or topiary "trees" made of Styrofoam balls covered with moss and finished with flower heads fruits, ribbons and so on.

Flanking the band or bordering the dance floor with floral pieces is generally a waste of money as these have to be removed when the music starts.

Listening to your flowers

Since Roman times, people have ascribed various meanings to flowers and herbs. The Victorians took floriography to new heights, producing several books on the subject, the most famous being *La Langue de Fleurs*. A man might send a woman a red chrysanthemum (I love you) only to have the object of his affection respond with a striped carnation (refusal). Of course, both parties needed to refer to the same book in order to prevent any misunderstanding. Today the language of flowers is spoken most often at weddings and encompasses the language of herbs as well. Since the times of ancient Greece, when brides carried herbs and grains as signs of fertility, many a bride has slipped sprigs of herbs in her bridal bouquet either to convey a special meaning or to fool the evil eye.

Personal flowers

Personal flowers include not only the bride's bouquet and groom's boutonniere, but also all the flowers worn by attendants, family members, or others you wish to honor. Men often have preferences, some quite specific, for the boutonniere they sport on their wedding day. For brides, though, the flowers they carry as they walk towards married life are more than an extension of their dress — they are a symbol of how they see themselves and wish to be seen by others.

Specify exactly where you want your flowers delivered and that you want them all labeled to avoid even the slightest chance that an usher may try to pin the flower girl's tussy mussy (see Figure 11-10) to his lapel.

Bride and attendants

At the beginning of this century, brides and bridesmaids carried such elaborate bouquets that the women practically needed a wheelbarrow to transport them down the aisle. Bouquets should be striking but not distracting; you want all eyes on the carrier, not on her bouquet. As an accessory, the bouquet should complement the dress as well as the size and shape of the wearer. Bridesmaids' bouquets need not be dwarf versions of the bride's, but can be mini works of art in themselves.

Antique lace, organza, or wired ribbon wrapped around the stems finish a bouquet beautifully, although not inexpensively. One of our favorite looks is having each bridesmaid carry a different vibrantly colored bouquet finished with matching ribbon streamers.

For years only one style of bouquet was considered appropriate for formal weddings: all roses, stephanotis, and lily of the valley. No longer. At even extremely formal ceremonies, brides now carry a variety of flowers and colors (see Figure 11-9).

Flowers, however dazzling and pure, can cause you grief if they aren't prepared with meticulous care. Before handing them to attendants, have bouquets checked for leaking holders, smashed stems, unraveling ribbons, and droopy blooms.

Hold your bouquet by placing your elbows at your hipbones and grasping the stems or handle with both hands in front of your belly button. You should be able to do this while linking your arm with one person, but you may find it difficult while linking both arms with two escorts. Therefore, who is walking you down the aisle and how you walk together affects the kind of bouquet you can comfortably carry. Some of the following examples are illustrated in Figure 11-10.

Figure 11-9: Traditional bouquet and centerpiece elements.

- **Biedermeier:** Tightly composed concentric circles of individual colors, wired into a lace collar or other holder.
- **Cascade or shower:** Classic, elaborate shape with ivy and long-stemmed flowers that are wired or pulled out to droop gracefully in a "waterfall" effect.
- **Composite:** A flower constructed of hundreds of real petals wired together to look like one enormous flower.
- **Crescent:** Composed of one full flower and a flowering stem, often orchids, wired together to form a slender handle that can be held in one hand. Designed as either a *full-crescent,* a half circle with a central flower and blossoms emanating from two sides, or as a *semi-crescent,* which has only one trailing stem.
- **Nosegays:** Round bouquets (16 or 18 inches in diameter) composed of flowers, greenery, and occasionally sprigs of herbs, all wired or tied together.
- **Posies:** Smaller versions of nosegays. Ribbons and silk flowers are often integrated into them.
- **Presentation:** The pageant bouquet — long-stemmed flowers cradled in your arms.
- **Tossing:** A bouquet used for tossing so the actual wedding bouquet can be saved for posterity. No need to duplicate the original.
- **Tussy mussy:** From the Victorian era, a posy in a small metal hand-held vase. Some have attached ring chains for easy carrying.

Bouquet–building basics

A bunch of flowers can almost never be left to its own devices. Creating floral sculptures and even simple arrangements requires the skills of a few magicians. Here's how some of the most spectacular arrangements are created:

- **Individually wired:** Stems are cut down and taped to wire so the flowers are more malleable. For greens such as ivy, the leaves have first to be stitched with a fine silver wire. This technique is complicated, time-consuming, and, consequently, expensive.
- **Arranged in holders:** Floral foam soaked in water is placed in a bouquet holder — a plastic cone with a handle. Flowers are then stuck into the foam.
- **Tied in bunches:** A natural bunch of flowers tied together with ribbons, which are prettiest when French braided or finished with love knots. For a more natural look, leave the stems showing.

Figure 11-10: A bouquet's shape and style are as important as the kind of flowers it contains.

Instead of a bouquet, consider these additional ways to bloom:

- An heirloom prayer book accessorized with flowers
- A single long-stemmed flower such as a calla lily, rose, or Casablanca lily
- A wreath of flowers worn in the hair
- A hat adorned with fresh flowers
- A comb, barrette, or headband covered in lace, ribbon, and flowers
- A border of flowers on your veil or hem of your dress
- A cloche made of flowers

Mothers, stepmothers, fathers' girlfriends, and others

Say corsage and many women think "blue hair," not to mention pin holes in their fancy silk frock. Alternatives exist, including tussy mussies, flowers pinned to a handbag, or a floral bracelet, much like a mini garland — not to be confused with wrist corsages, which can be as dowdy as the pinned version.

Grooms, ushers, stepfathers, mothers' boyfriends, and others

No longer the standard-issue white senior-prom carnation, the groom's boutonniere may look like one of the flowers in the bride's bouquet — as if plucked from there. The ones he chooses for his ushers and other gentlemen to be honored should reflect his personal style and be appropriate for their outfits. These flowers should neither brown around the edges nor wilt in the heat and be hardy enough to withstand hours of hugs.

A few replacements for trite lapel pins:

- Corn flowers
- Acorns
- Vibrant-colored roses set with a sprig of herbs
- Berries backed by a galax leaf
- Variegated ivy, fern, and pine
- A stem of hydrangea

Boutonnieres are worn on the left side and pinned on the underside of the lapel so that no part of the pin shows.

Order extra boutonnieres because they are relatively inexpensive and one or two may not survive hamfisted attempts at pinning. Besides, it's good to have extras for any forgotten menfolk.

Little touches for little people

When dealing with flower children (or any children, for that matter), keep accessories in proportion to the child's size. You don't want your flower girl to look like an ungainly flowering plant moving down the aisle. Some simple floral alternatives to the traditional flower basket include:

- **Circlet:** A ribbon or twig band that is accented with blossoms and worn on girls' heads.
- **Garland:** Birch vines covered with smilax and flowers and carried in tandem by two or three very young children. This arrangement looks adorable and also keeps them together.
- **Hoop:** Made of vine strung with flowers and carried like a tambourine.
- **Pomander:** A styrofoam ball, covered in lace and tulle and trimmed with floral heads, which hangs on the wrist.

Fresh petals can be slippery. If you wish to follow children strewing petals from baskets, show them how to sprinkle them, alternating sides of the path rather than straight down the danger zone.

The ring bearer's main accessory is the ring pillow, which may be sewn of luxurious fabrics such as satin, silk, velvet, or organza. These pillows are sometimes embroidered or trimmed with silk, natural flowers, or ornate tassels. The rings are tied on with attached ribbons. As special as the pillow is, the ring bearer may be more interested in wearing a boutonniere identical to that of the ushers.

We suggest the ring pillow never have the real rings on it. To protect the child's ego, attach fake rings and have the best man make a display of untying them. The real rings are, of course, safe in the best man's breast pocket.

Keeping flowers forever young

If you choose not to toss your real bridal bouquet, you may want to preserve it, which can be done in one of several ways:

- **Air dry:** Hang the bouquet (and the boutonniere as well, if you wish), upside down in a ventilated dark space, separating the flowers by type for best results.
- **Freeze dry:** Professionally done, this keeps the colors more vibrant than air drying does. The flowers can then be displayed in a glass dome or shadow box.

- **Desiccants:** Simple but time-consuming, this is an arts-and-crafts project that requires you to bury the bouquet in silica gel, available at hobby shops.
- **Potpourri:** Dry the flowers and remove the petals, which are mixed with fragrant oils, herbs, and spices. Put in an airtight jar and shake once a day for six weeks.

An In-Tents Experience

We have seen the sad results of people who erected grand tents but ran out of money to decorate them. While their fantasy may have been to dine in a palace that had somehow magically dropped into their backyard, the reality ran more toward dining inside a great white laundry bag. If the tent itself puts such a gaping hole in your budget that you can't afford to hang a piece of greenery, you need to reconsider your choice of venue.

Some crucial aspects of tent decorating include:

- **Banners:** Wide bands of fabric that cover part of the ceiling and are less expensive than a full tent lining, but serve the same purpose in drawing the eye away from the ceiling.
- **Fabric linings:** Most tent companies rent pleated fabric linings that cover the ceiling and/or the walls. Linings are rather pricey.
- **Flooring:** If you opt for the floor, carpet is a tony touch that also muffles sound. A less-costly floor covering is black or green AstroTurf. (See Chapter 2 regarding floor issues.)
- **Interior lighting:** If your wedding is in the evening, the tent requires lighting. Options include chandeliers, "starlighting" (bee lights), track systems, inexpensive globes, or carriage lights (which look like old-fashioned gas lamps).
- **Landscape lighting:** Used to emphasize natural features such as ponds or trees, as well as to guide guests to necessities such as rest rooms and driveways.
- **Poles:** Depending on the pitch of the tent, for a large tent, poles can be up to 42 feet tall. When planning tent seating, take into account how poles affect sight lines. Poles are metal and ugly and need to be covered somehow. Besides painting them, you may wind them in floral garlands or rouche and tie fabric around them. For a touch of organic whimsy, cover the poles in cheap fabric and glue leaves in overlapping rows pointing upward to completely camouflage the metal. For a country theme, corn husks work well.
- **Windows:** Tent sides are clear plastic, opaque plastic, or cloth, depending on the season, and often stenciled with windowpanes, arches, and shutters.

To Love, Honor, and Embellish

Whether your nuptial site is an old church with Byzantine arches, a yarrow-dotted bluff overlooking the sea, or a white-washed photography studio, you want to convey your personal spirituality. That may mean letting a grand site speak for itself with little or no embellishment, enhancing the most eloquent aspects of the space through equally eloquent decorations, or undertaking a major overhaul to evoke the solemnity and dignity of the occasion.

Visit your ceremony site with your designer and think about the chronology of your ceremony in relation to what needs decorating. What do guests see as they arrive? What's the view from where they sit? Can they hear what's going on? Where are the musicians positioned? Where does the bridal party enter? Where does everyone exit?

The great outdoors

Some outdoor sites, such as public gardens, do not allow chairs to be placed on the grounds. If this is the case, keep your ceremony short so guests are not forced to stand for an inhumanly long period of time. In any case, renting dainty Chiavari chairs for an outdoor ceremony can be a mistake because their spiky legs tend to sink into the ground.

Never plan on an outdoor wedding without having a reasonable backup site unless you intend to spend your wedding heavily tranquilized. By reasonable we mean an indoor or sheltered spot where everyone can be seated and the ceremony can retain most of its intended flavor.

Outdoor ceremonies should be about the outdoors. Wrapping gardens in tulle and fabric is usually gratuitous and incongruous. Let nature speak for itself.

Candlelight ceremonies

Mystical and awe-inspiring, candlelight ceremonies can take place in late afternoon or early evening. From the moment guests arrive, they fall under a spell.

Unity candles usually consist of three candles at the altar. The bride and groom take the outer two, which are lit, and together light the center one to symbolize the joining of two hearts and their shared commitment to the marriage. Other guests may also be given candles and the couple walks down the aisle, stopping at each row to light the nearest candle, which in turn is used to light the next and so on. In other cases, only parents or other family members join in the candle lighting.

African-American couples who marry in December are lucky to have the drama of the seven candles of Kwanzaa as an option for their ceremony. The bride and groom start at opposite ends, working their way toward the middle, noting the significance of each candle: *umoja* (unity), *kujichagulia* (self-determination), *ujima* (collective responsibility), *unia* (purpose), *kuumba* (creativity), and *imani* (faith).

Outdoor ceremonies and receptions often attract a few unwanted guests — flies, mosquitoes, gnats, and the like. Some people feel strongly about not poisoning the environment with pesticides. Citronella candles and tiki torches are your best bet. If you insist on spraying, however, you must do it both the day before the event and again several hours before the guests arrive. (Cough, cough.)

Aisle runners

Some limousine services and florists "throw in" complimentary paper aisle runners. Even if these withstand the ushers' unfurling them before the ceremony, they will most certainly be in shreds by the time the bride makes her way down the aisle. Canvas or fabric runners are a more durable option and can be beautifully painted. When in doubt, skip the runner altogether.

Houses of worship

Typically, churches and synagogues have someone on staff who is responsible for specifying and enforcing the rules as to how you may or may not decorate, what time you can begin decorating, and when things have to be removed. Houses of worship can be particularly strict about decor, so heed their rules carefully.

Before you consider lugging your altarpieces to your reception to do double duty, check the rules. Some churches like you to leave the flowers behind for the congregation to enjoy.

If your house of worship has booked another ceremony either before or after yours, consider splitting the cost of decorating with the other couple. The powers that be at your site are usually happy to put you in touch with them.

Seating

Without the formality of pew or within-the-ribbon cards (see Chapter 13), ushers are usually in charge of seating relatives and others the couple wish to have in the first few rows. The rehearsal dinner is often an opportunity to familiarize ushers with the VIPs. Once at the ceremony, guests often feel it looks presumptuous to let ushers know they deserve front-row seats. If you don't apprise ushers ahead of time, you may find yourselves looking at rows of empty chairs during your ceremony. You may also mark reserved seats with little cards.

The marriage ceremony can be held in a variety of configurations if you are not in a religious setting and therefore not bound by "house" rules. You may arrange seating "in the round" or in a semicircle. Or you may face the guests as you take your vows.

Make each row short enough to provide easy access and egress. Long rows across inevitably mean that 15 people have to get up so one person can take a seat in the middle. ("Excuse me. Excuse me. Excuse me. Uh, were those your toes?") Also, have an even number of seats in each row because most people come in couples. For seating in the round, break up the rows with extra aisles that are smaller than the main one. (You can see an example of seating in the round in this book's color photo section.)

Row or pew markers

Simple ribbons tied into beautiful bows and elaborate rose topiaries seemingly in full bloom may go on the ends of rows along the aisle — typically every two or three rows — and be free standing or attached to benches with floral holders.

Keep the size of the space in mind when choosing these arrangements. An exquisite country church with a diminutive altar should not be overpowered by flowers appropriate for St. Patrick's Cathedral. A house of worship's ambiance should remain intact after your design wizards alight.

Altar or bimah flowers

Usually an altar is flanked by arrangements. Delicate blossoms disappear at a distance so these arrangements should be composed of large flower heads. Greenery and filler flowers can be used in these pieces advantageously because the arrangements can be quite airy. Because churches and synagogues tend to be dimly lit, use either light or vibrant hues, but keep the flowers in one palette. The flowers should enhance the couple and surroundings, not call attention to themselves.

Other flower positions

In churches the baptismal font may seem the perfect piece of architecture for the wedding touch, but check first to make sure you can decorate it. If you can, filling the font with multi-colored rose petals or garlanding around the base adds a charming note to the surroundings. Garlands or small pots set on windowsills complete the vision.

A floral and ribbon marker of some sort, attached either to the door frame or on the entrance banister, or threaded through a trellised gate, guides guests who are driving, welcoming them to the celebration.

Chuppahs

While religious law requires Jewish weddings to take place under a *chuppah* (see Chapter 5), and it cites no specifics regarding size or decoration. Generally, a chuppah is a canopy open on four sides and constructed just for the wedding. Some chuppahs are designed to be free standing, and others are carried and held up by four people the couple wishes to honor.

Chuppahs can be very beautifully simple (as in Figure 11-11), covered with a fabric that's meaningful to the couple such as a tallit, or prayer shawl, given to the groom by the bride and her family or a material richly embroidered with symbols of married life or other personal notes.

Chuppahs can also be quite elaborate. These have come into vogue as Jewish or interfaith ceremonies often take place in off-premise sites or hotel ballrooms. Some appear to float above the congregation amid billows of tulle, ivy, and flowers suspended by invisible wires. Others are topped with baskets of leaves and set within garlanded columns of wisteria and branches to evoke the feel of a country garden.

If you make the canopy for your chuppah by hand or have an elaborate one made for your wedding to be passed on, you may suspend it over your bed (to symbolize the chuppah's original meaning), frame it, or use it as a wall hanging after your wedding.

Take into consideration the size of table and cloth to be used under the chuppah. It is an eyesore in a beautiful setting when this small table on which the officiant places the wine goblet and wine, and rests the prayer book has been covered with something in hot pink a busboy has thrown on at the last moment.

Chalices and kiddush cups

In many cultures, the ceremonial drinking of wine is a part of the wedding ceremony and the vessels in which the wine is served can be highly symbolic in their own right. Traditionally, Europeans used a matched pair of goblets or a cup specially created for the wedding, which then became part of the couple's household to be used on other religious occasions.

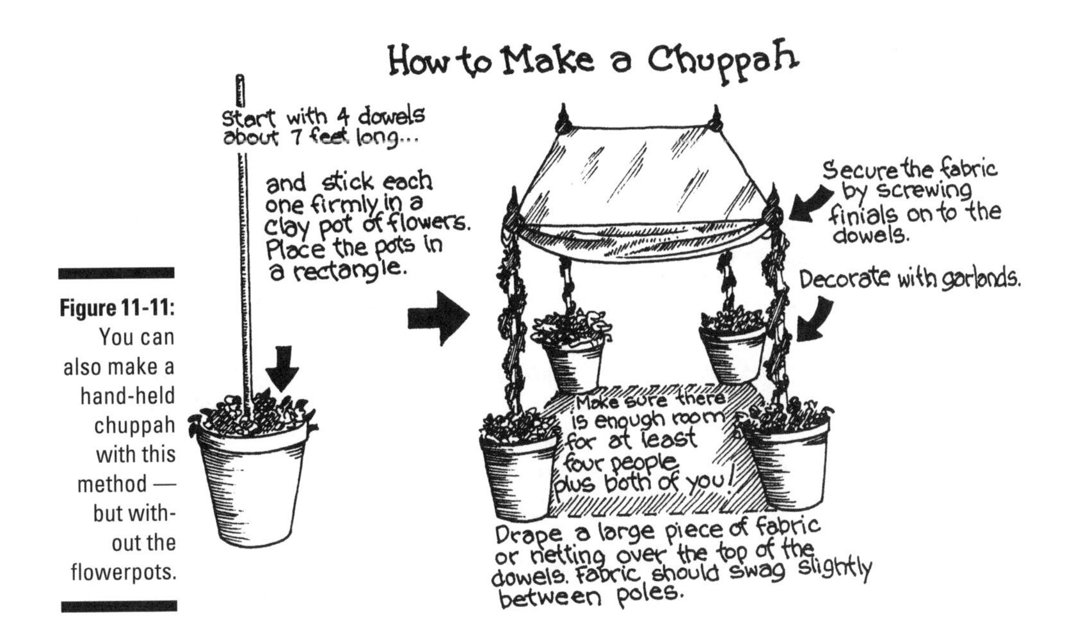

Figure 11-11: You can also make a hand-held chuppah with this method — but without the flowerpots.

The Christian *chalice* is a goblet used during the sacrament of marriage. These can be specially monogrammed silver cups that become heirlooms for later generations.

In Jewish ceremonies (see Chapter 5), the rabbi says two blessings over wine, which the bride and groom drink from either one or two separate kiddush cups. (*Kiddush* is the Hebrew word for sanctification and the betrothal ceremony.) The cups, sometimes monogrammed silver goblets, are placed on a table under the chuppah.

If you have an heirloom kiddush cup or chalice, make sure that it's polished and ready to use.

Ketubah

The ketubah, the Jewish marital contract, can be a plain scroll but more often is a richly painted, or illuminated, Hebrew and English manuscript that is read during the ceremony and displayed during the reception. (See Chapter 5.) Many couples then hang their framed ketubah in their homes. Some Judaica stores sell pre-made ketubahs on which you fill in your names. Most synagogues keep a list of ketubah makers who can customize one for you.

Things to throw

Releasing a tide of helium-filled balloons and watching them drift up and out of sight seems romantic but is in fact environmentally unfriendly. The balloons eventually deflate and become random litter, get hung up in trees, or wind up in lakes and oceans, where animals such as whales, birds, and dolphins ingest them and die. Rice has also fallen out of favor because it expands in the stomachs of birds and other creatures and can be fatal.

Here are some creative alternatives:

- **Birdseed:** A popular rice alternative that's inexpensive and a nice treat for our feathered friends.
- **Bubbles:** Order little jars of soap bubbles and hot-glue lace, leaves, and flowers to the outside (see Figure 11-12).
- **Butterflies:** Setting free hundreds of painted lady butterflies has become a trend. Companies now specialize in raising butterflies in various stages of development and ship them ready to hatch.
- **Hearts of rice:** Companies now offer "designer wedding rice" — rice without the hull, which is safe for birds.
- **Petals:** Fill cones made of paper or doilies with fresh or dried flower petals. Dry the petals yourself by using the potpourri recipe given earlier in this chapter or buy them pre-packaged from a florist.

Figure 11-12: In lieu of throwing rice or birdseed — bubbles!

Photo by Terry deRoy Gruber

Chapter 12

For Posterity: Photos and Videos

In This Chapter

- Catching every moment on film
- Rethinking the video vanguard
- Timing is everything

Long after you return from your honeymoon, the last thank-you note has been written, and your wedding garb has returned safely from the dry cleaner, you may wonder if it was all a dream. Until, that is, your photographs and/or video arrive. These images are the key to keeping each memory as sharp as if you were married this morning. The way the photos and video are shot should reflect the overall mood and effect you have in mind — and that depends on who does the shooting, what kind of film and equipment they use, how they develop and edit the film, and how the images are displayed. Figuring out your options — and you may be surprised at the new technologies available — is what this chapter is all about.

As your wedding takes shape, you will probably (we hope) have a great many moments that are touching, humorous, or even weird enough that you want to remember them. Chronicle these by taking photos, saving notes, and jotting down conversations. All this may go into one big annotated album — with your professional pictures — when it's all over. You may also put together a wedding time capsule that contains mementos from your engagement through the first year of marriage, including letters from friends and loved ones that are left sealed until you open the capsule a decade or two later.

Your photographer and videographer are two of the team who must painstakingly go over your wedding day schedule . Send it to them early and then go over any questions or important details with them to make sure they have read it. (See Chapter 18 for tips on creating your schedule.) If you want either of them to capture every millisecond of your day, arrange for them to travel with you if your ceremony and reception are in different venues.

If your photographer and/or videographer have not seen your site before, they should agree to scout the space and surrounding grounds before the wedding. (You should think twice about hiring someone who assures you that the site visit isn't necessary because "I like to be spontaneous.") Your first choice should be to see the spot with them in the same season and time of day as the wedding so they can arrange to shoot any outdoor photos where the light is best. Photographers and videographers often have smart ideas about selecting the best spots for posed and portrait shots, positioning background floral arrangements, arranging chair groupings, and refocusing lighting fixtures. They are also responsible for getting the guidelines for photography/videography in the church or synagogue.

Shoot to Thrill

Highly reputable professional photography studios abound throughout the world. The problem is that a studio itself does not shoot your wedding. The studio's sample album may be full of stunning shots, but they're probably the very best culled from thousands taken by the studio's stable of pros, who may number anywhere from one to 100. Even assuming that everyone is identically trained and, consequently, shoots in the same style (as the studio may assert), we strongly suggest that you meet with and see the work of the specific photographer assigned to your wedding. For one thing, photographers are artists and no two are stylistically identical. Secondly, this person is going to be with you all day, so you had better have an excellent rapport with him or her.

Clicking with your photographer

Good wedding photographers, especially those who specialize in particular styles, book up early, so start your search in plenty of time. To find a good photographer:

- Call up recently married couples whom you know well enough to ask to see their wedding photos.
- Call catering professionals, banquet directors, and wedding consultants (even those you are not using). They are usually quite willing to recommend someone whose work they respect.
- Look at the wedding portraits printed in your local newspaper and other newspapers. If you love the way a couple looks, check for the photographer's name in tiny print under or alongside the photo.
- Check out "real wedding" features in bridal magazines. Often these have been shot by talented photographers, which is why they are being featured.

- Obtain a list of wedding photographers in your area by looking online or calling a trade organization such as the Professional Photographers of America (888-97-STORY x 333). ***Note:*** These are usually just regional referrals, not a recommendation.
- Consider flying a photographer in from another area. Airfare and room rates, depending on the season, may be reasonable — some photographers may even agree to stay in someone's home. Because many photographers enjoy traveling, their rates may also be negotiable.

Interview as many prospective photographers as time and energy permit before you hire one. If you are looking for a particular style, ask about their ratio of *candids* to *portraits* (see the upcoming section "Shooter styles" to find out the difference). More important, do the photos they show you reflect the style you want? It may seem obvious, but if people tell you they are adept at black and white and you have seen only color shots, something is amiss.

Ask questions that bring out their feelings about weddings. Notice how they refer to brides and grooms — warmly or with great eye rolling? Do they badmouth past clients? Do they seem enthusiastic about their work or burnt out? Among the questions you may ask:

- What are their favorite moments to photograph? Which weddings have been their favorites and why?
- Do they come with an assistant? More than one? What exactly does the assistant do?
- What do they wear?
- What sort of lighting equipment do they use?
- How many weddings have they shot? What is their background?
- How do they charge and what is included?
- Do they always come with back-up equipment?
- Will they shoot in color, black and white, or both?
- Do they charge for travel, parking, or other expenses?
- Are they used to working with videographers? Do they have a plan of action for working together?
- Do they charge *twilight fees*? (These are extra fees charged if the job takes time from what they could book as either a day or evening wedding.)

While looking at a photographer's album of great picks, you may notice that all the photos are of a particular venue, such as a hotel's various ballrooms. Ask to see shots from weddings in a variety of locations. You also want to see film from weddings in various stages — from proofs or contact sheets to completed wedding albums.

If you like a photographer but feel you need to do more homework, say so. Ask the photographer to hold the date for a short while or at least give you the right of first refusal. Then make your decision as quickly as possible.

If relatives or friends who are photography buffs suggest that they want to photograph everything as well, tell them politely you prefer them to be a true guest and enjoy themselves. Flash from other cameras may set off lights that the photographer has set around the room, ruining the professional shot and producing a continuous disco light show. If you prefer to have no flash photographs during your ceremony, state your wishes in the program.

Getting focused

Professional photographers understand that their main function is to "cover" the wedding: They can do the classic shots in their sleep — the first dance, the cake cutting, the bouquet toss, and so on. It's up to you, however, to decide the style and format. To figure this out, think about how invisible you want the photographer to be, the number of formal shots you want, whether you want close-up portraits or candid action shots, and whether to get a photograph of every guest. The goal is to get a style that makes you feel good every time you look at your photos for years to come.

Shooter styles

Many photographers specialize in one or more styles. If photographs are at the top of your priority list (in other words, you've appropriated a large chunk of your budget for them), consider hiring more than one photographer. For example, have one photographer do the formals and another photographer who specializes in candids shoot the rest of the wedding. Among the styles you may consider:

- **Candids:** Results appear unposed and natural. Positive aspects include the photographer being less intrusive, capturing some unexpected wonderful moments, and everyone looking like their true selves. Downsides include everyone looking like their true selves (if you have a less than movie-star profile, you can't hide it), unexpected décor elements showing up such as balled-up cocktail napkins and cigarettes floating in half-empty drink glasses, and unidentified bits of food captured in people's teeth for posterity. The photographer needs to shoot extra exposures to ensure that enough desirable ones turn out.
- **Classic or traditional wedding photography:** The best photographers in this genre pose their subjects artfully and use creative set ups: for example, a spontaneous-looking shot of the bride and groom stopping to share a hot dog at a city cart as opposed to a trite shot of the bride gazing at her train as if looking for moth holes. Their "candids" are obviously more posed than spontaneous but the subject looks natural and comfortable nonetheless. Couple's portraits are taken with great care. Photos are retouched and custom-cropped.

- **Formals:** These include line-ups of family, attendants, and friends, posed singly and in groups. A good classic photographer is very exact, arranging the subjects as a painter does a still life. Photojournalists tend to be more "seat of the pants," and the lighting or staging may suffer.
- **Photojournalistic approach:** The photographer chronicles the day as it unfolds, rather than staging situations. Styles vary — some look for natural situations to occur, then stop the action to get a good shot; others just look for great moments and capture them discreetly. Unfortunately, as this style has become more in demand among couples who have an aversion to classic wedding shots, some photographers who really don't get it are marketing themselves as photojournalists. An attempt to capture the mood of the day by taking a shot of your cat, ragged ribbon around her neck, plopped on a bridesmaid's bouquet, and obviously dying to scram, somehow lacks that sweet, spontaneous feeling that a good candid captures.
- **Portraits:** Close-up photographs of the bride, groom, or both. Staged, such as the bride posed on a staircase with her train trailing down the steps as she gazes into the camera. Also the term used for head shots submitted to newspapers.
- **Set-up or stock shots:** Classic photos taken during a wedding such as the groom and best man toasting each other, the bride and her attendants lifting their legs can-can style, or the two mothers with their arms around each other.

Figuring out the film

To get the look you want, you should be familiar with the basic speeds and types of film, such as:

- **Black-and-white:** Very much in vogue. Photographers with a photojournalistic approach take a majority of their pictures in black and white. Processing and reprints require precision and are consequently more expensive than color. Black-and-white photographs should be shot with black-and-white film; those shot using color film and converted to black-and-white actually look gray-and-white and fuzzy.
- **Color:** Traditional photographers shoot mostly in color with a few rolls of black-and-white upon request (and often for an extra fee). If you plan to buy the proofs and/or negatives and develop your own film, it is important that you go to a quality photo lab that specializes in expert processing of these kinds of photographs.
- **Digital:** Images are stored on computer chips, as opposed to paper film, and printed through a computer. Improvements in equipment may soon produce wedding-quality photos. (See Chapter 21 for more on this new technology.)

The corner photo booth

We're not crazy about leaving disposable cameras on tables for guests to use, but renowned New York photographer Terry deRoy Gruber has developed an original alternative. At weddings he sets up a truly candid "self-portrait" studio with a customized canvas back-drop (which can be anything from an ocean scene to faux marble). Adding props and shooting in sepia tones can create a vintage look. Guests pose and pop the camera themselves by using a cable release. As the party picks up speed, the various formations can be hilarious. The couple is supplied with two sets of proofs so they can keep a proof for themselves and send the other to a guest in the photo.

The self-portraits may be made instantaneously by using Polaroid film. That way you can give pictures to guests on the spot. Or have the pictures placed in frames for guests to pick up as they leave.

- **Medium format or 2 1/4:** This format is generally better for formals and portraits, although some adept photographers use the film to take candids. Superior for details — the twinkle of diamond earrings and the draping of the bride's dress — as well as color shots, it allows for really big blow ups if you want fancy murals of yourselves.
- **35 MM:** Zoom lenses enable you to stay farther away from subjects, which makes it better for candids. Thirty-five millimeter works best when photos are not going to be enlarged bigger than 8 x 10. This film generally results in better black-and-white photos than it does in color.

Looking over the shots

Because developing every shot from your wedding in full size and on quality paper would cost a fortune, you look at all the frames in a less-expensive format and choose only the ones you really want developed. These preliminary formats include:

- **Contact sheets:** This is a compilation of the shots from a roll of film in miniature, which you then examine with a magnifying glass or photographer's loupe. Mark the photos that you want with a grease pencil, perhaps indicating where you would like the photo cropped. Some photographers give clients enlarged contact sheets that are easier to see.
- **Prints:** Photographs that have been cut and blown up from the negatives but not cropped or retouched.
- **Proofs:** A preliminary set of simply developed photos, all numbered and cataloged, from which you choose your album shots. They may be arranged in "proof books" or boxes. The ones you choose are then enlarged, custom printed, and cropped to your specifications.

Making the camera lie (just a little)

By using special lenses and processing techniques your photographer can create unusual photos for your album. If any of these techniques interest you, ask your photographer if they are available. Some of those ways include:

- **Colorized:** This method involves hand painted detailing of black-and-white shots, usually with soft colored pencils. This technique works well with infrared shots to beautifully fill in such details as bouquets.
- **Fish-eye lens:** This technique distorts a photo, almost as if shot through a magnified key hole. These shots are bizarre, but including a few can be fun.
- **Infrared:** Outside photos are shot with black-and-white film that reads heat instead of light, giving a dramatic, other worldly feel. Photos are high contrast — grainy black and white — with no middle tones.
- **Panoramic:** Pictures are shot with a wide angle or *rotation* lens. Photos are long and horizontal, covering a large expanse.
- **Soft focus or portrait lens:** Traditional photographers use this technique to make people look younger, "vaporizing" wrinkles. Pictures look slightly out of focus.

Putting a little light on the subject

Film needs light to work. If your photographer does not understand how to work with light in a variety of settings, you'll have photos with dull colors and no highlights. Candid shots may need no more than a flash, but formal shots — even outdoors — may look completely amateur without the aid of professional lights. Here are some tools that may seem unwieldy to have carted around your wedding, but can make the difference between getting back crisp photos with color that "pops" out at you, or rectangles of fuzzy darkness:

- **Flash:** The light on a camera that enables photographers to shoot outside quickly using ambient light without having to use a light meter between each shot. To get people shots as well as the background of a ballroom for example, the flash must be used with additional light such as light poles or strobes placed around room that are set to go off when the flash goes off.
- **Natural light:** "Open shade," or natural outdoor shade, is the ideal light for shooting. Because natural light is difficult to capture quickly, many photographers fill in with a flash and reflectors as well.
- **Time exposure:** An efficient method for photographing ceremonies if you are adverse to the distraction of flash, or if the house of worship prohibits it. The camera is set on a tripod; it takes a second or so to expose the film (you hear a soft click) so any movement blurs the photo.

- **Umbrellas:** Large black lighting umbrellas are placed on tripods. Umbrellas are used for group formals, and they produce a less harsh effect than a flash.

Dark colors absorb light, so dark-skinned people should be photographed with more light and the photographs taken with more exposure.

If you want to be photographed at a public space such as an atrium, garden, or park, you may need to apply for a special license from a government office such as a parks commission. Also, don't be surprised if a beautiful public site is crowded with other couples taking wedding photos at the same time.

Celluloid scheduling

One of the most hotly contested wedding day details is whether to take photos before the ceremony or after. Wedding photographers almost universally prefer taking formal shots before the wedding because they can take their time to make them perfect. But don't let anyone pressure you one way or another. Here's the true picture, based on the facts, so *you* can decide which time works for you.

Photos before the ceremony

The main advantage of shooting before the ceremony is that faces aren't streaked with tears yet, your hair is as perfect as it's ever going to look, and nobody is impatient to get to the reception. As we discuss in Chapter 18, pre-ceremony photos are necessary if you have a receiving line at the reception. On the downside, however, these shoots can be fatiguing and can take away the magic of seeing each other dressed as bride and groom for the first time when the bride approaches the altar. The sense of anticipation may in fact be dampened for everyone involved.

In general, unless your wedding is very small, pre-wedding photos take about one and a half to two hours. Parents and close relatives from both families, the two of you, and your wedding party should arrive dressed, coifed, and made-up. Distribute bouquets and boutonnieres. Then, using the efficient "hit list" that you have provided, the participants pose and smile until their faces and feet ache.

If you choose to take your photos before the ceremony, consider these points:

- Arrange for the two of you to have some quiet time alone to see each other before the mayhem of the photo session begins.
- Remember that shooting too early means you rush to get dressed hours before your ceremony. Cutting it too close, however, means that your guests are left waiting.
- Have *stainless* drinks such as ice water and club soda for the group.

Prioritizing your photography punch list

You have probably chosen a photographer because his or her style matches your style. Still, just to be sure, you should specify types of photos you do and don't want. While some couples love boudoir shots, others are deeply offended by the suggestion. Table shots, where half of the guests are asked to get up and pose around the other half of the table are horrendous to some, an integral part of a wedding album to others.

For formal shots, give your photographer a very specific list of the groupings you want, such as the bride and groom and her family, and the order you want them in (and do so under the advisement of the photographer). Be certain to include those groupings that may not seem obvious, such as the bride and groom with the bride's stepmother and step-brothers.

Sharing family dirt with the photographer is not indiscreet. Not doing so may cause you far more embarrassment. If your parents are acrimoniously divorced, one or both of them is with a second spouse or "friend" that the other detests, your sister hates your new spouse's brother — whatever the case may be, full disclosure is the best course of action. Otherwise the hapless photographer or assistant may naively attempt to take an endearing photo and wind up with an altercation.

If you don't have a wedding consultant, appoint an attendant or close friend to show the photographer the guests who are important to you, so the photographer can make a point of including them in candids. Do so in advance so that your designee can put faces to names of new acquaintances at the pre-wedding events. Your appointed picture police should also be prepared to gently advise the photographer of whom does not merit major camera time, such as the new hunk or hunkesse your ex has in tow.

You may want to hire your photographer to shoot the rehearsal dinner, where many of the most poignant moments may transpire. Doing so helps loosen up the subjects for the next day and familiarizes the photographer with the key players to be shot. The rehearsal dinner usually requires the photographer to be there for only two hours at most.

- Avoid rumpling, crumpling, and smudging by instructing everyone to air kiss until after the ceremony.

Asian-Americans often include large, formal family portraits on their photography lists. Couples also frequently pose in traditional dress several weeks before the wedding so they have photos in costume without having to change clothes at the wedding.

Photos after the ceremony

Shooting formals in the short window of time between ceremony and reception precludes having a receiving line — unless you want your guests to wait four hours to eat. The wedding party and families must make a fast getaway after the ceremony to the spot where the formals are to be taken and, unless you spend the money for an assistant photographer, you must wait for the photographer to set up. On top of that, people are usually quite emotional after the ceremony and need a little while to pull themselves together and focus.

But the merits of waiting to shoot formals are many. We believe that no moment in your life compares to that instant when you lay eyes on each other for the first time from opposite ends of the aisle on your wedding day. The sacrifices are worth this magical experience. Even though taking as many photos before the ceremony as you can manage (you and your attendants, and parents, and siblings, for example) will expedite things somewhat for after the ceremony, the shots that you will most likely want to put in your album are those that include both of you.

If you wait to take photos until after your ceremony, we suggest:

- Plan the session to be short and efficient. The best way to do so is by providing a list of specific shots you want and indicating any groupings that can be taken later during the reception, such as the two of you.
- Arrange your photo session from the largest group to the smallest so that people can be dismissed to join the reception as soon as possible.
- Skip the "return shots" at the altar or bimah. Coordinating everyone once again to reenact your ceremony takes up too much time.
- Have the photographer's assistant (if you've spent the money for one) set up the lights or other necessary equipment, so it's ready as soon as you are after the ceremony.
- Have a waiter serve drinks but unless your wedding party is ravenous, refrain from serving hors d'oeuvres — waiting for people to swallow between shots holds things up.
- Realize that you (and others in your wedding party) can't have your hors d'oeuvres and eat them too! You may miss part of your cocktail hour. Your guests should not be punished by being forced to drink and nibble for two hours so that you can be photographed after the ceremony *and* get your full cocktail time in too.

Request that the photographers and their assistants and/or video person eat at separate times so someone watches for a spontaneous toast or other photo-worthy occurrence.

Photography fees: Comparing apples, rocks, and bird cages

Photographers use so many different pricing structures that comparing them dollar to dollar or photo to photo is impossible. While asking how many rolls of film a photographer typically shoots at a wedding can help you gauge the value, knowing what percentage of the photos shot are "keepers" is more important. Because candid shots are less controlled than posed ones, the photographer must shoot substantially more film to get the same number of usable pictures.

You may be surprised to learn that in most areas, bottom line price differences for wedding photographers, with the exceptions of superstars, may be negligible. Photographers generally charge in the following ways:

- **Flat fee, no frills:** You pay a single fee for the photographer's time, film, and expenses. The fee is usually based on an estimate of the amount of film to be shot during the event. The photographer gives you proofs and negatives, but the rest is up to you. That means that if your photos need retouching or custom cropping (trimming the photo to emphasize the main action by removing extraneous people or background), you must find a lab to do it. You also put together your own album, which requires a great deal of time, creativity, and energy. If you are not up for a big project, be prepared for your wedding photos to remain in their lovely paper envelopes from the film store for years to come.
- **Flat fee, including albums:** The albums may be one large and two smaller ones or a combination of albums and enlarged, matted photos. Although the shooting is less expensive up front, additional prints cost dearly. The album may be of good quality but a standard configuration. If you prefer to supply your own album, the photographer may give you a rebate. Some photographers retain ownership of the proofs, meaning that you must return them after choosing the images you want. Some photographers may sell you the negatives for a nominal price after a year.
- **Hourly fee or flat fee, including contact sheets, proofs, and (usually) an album:** Photojournalists often charge this way. The up-front (hourly or flat) price is hefty, because they don't make much money selling you additional prints at a great mark-up. You typically contract for a specific number of hours and pay extra for overtime. Negotiate a generous time frame in advance so you don't feel rushed.

Just one look

Because my favorite moment in any wedding is when the groom first sees the bride coming toward him down the aisle, I knew I wouldn't want to dilute the drama by having photographs before the ceremony. Michael and I even spent the night before the wedding in separate hotels to avoid seeing each other and thus heighten the intensity of that first glimpse. I was so focused on that part of the wedding, however, that I ironically neglected to draw (yes, yes, Marcy did insist that I make one) up a detailed punch list for the photographer. Although the photographer was a pro and got some amazing shots, we later felt we were missing a few key ones. So my advice is: don't assume the photographer can read your mind — take the time to write out a shot list and be specific about certain groupings and angles that you want.

Photographers may take three months or longer to prepare your custom album after you have chosen the shots you want. Be patient. The photographer has to go through every photograph carefully to ensure the quality of color and cropping.

Ask your photographer to shoot a special roll — perhaps with everyone posed in a special way — and give you the film to develop right away. You can easily have these turned into glossy postcards for thank-you notes, amusing announcements, or holiday cards.

Wedding albums: Putting it all together

Wedding albums come in many styles. Classic photographers often include a "flush" album, where the photograph and the page are one. These are most often 8 x 10 inches, but some offer 10 x 10 inches. Often, at least one photo spans two full pages. Candid-style photographs are usually compiled in books that have different size matted photos on each page. If you are designing your own album, go through your photos with your photographer and specify the size you want each one to be.

A particularly exquisite and memorable album that one bride created included calligraphy surrounding tiny photos, artwork and doodles around larger photos, shots in color as well as black and white, newspaper clippings of amusing events that happened the day of their wedding, and the couple's invitation and announcement.

Assembling a dozen or so highlights from the wedding in individual albums for family and attendants can earn you major points. Mat the photos or mount them with photo corners in petite hand-made albums or accordion-fold albums that tie with a ribbon, often available in stationery and art stores.

If you are buying your own album, note that an archival-quality album features:

- Covers made of quality materials such as leather, fine fabrics, wood, or metal.
- Acid-free pages, double-sided archival tape, mats, or photo corners as opposed to rubberized pages covered in cellophane.
- A durable spine with raised ribs.

If you are getting your own film processed, insist that each print have the number of the roll and the negative stamped on the back to facilitate ordering. *Never* cut the negatives yourself.

Lights, Camera, Tape!

If you want your ceremony and/or reception videotaped, but you are worried about ruining your professional lighting scheme or hate the idea of having your reception lit up like a basketball court, don't despair. The art of video has evolved greatly in the past few years. Unlike old tape, which required floodlights, new super light-sensitive equipment means that you need much less light than you needed in the past.

While it's true that the newer equipment requires less light, that doesn't mean that ultra-dim lighting will achieve the best results. Many reception halls have virtually no lighting — they consider "mood lighting" a room as making it a place where bats would feel at home. This total lack of lighting assures that both photographs and videos will come out poorly. Individual guests may be illuminated by the videographer, but the room itself may film as a large, black hole. Design your room so that the lighting works to create the mood you want without compromising the quality of your video.

Many of the new-style videographers also specialize in subtlety, sensitively capturing special wedding moments without getting in everyone's way — and with exceptional results.

If your photographer and videographer have not worked together before, the three of you should have a meeting either in person or by conference call. You don't want them falling over each other in their zeal to capture key moments such as the cake cutting. At one wedding we know of, a knock-down, drag-out fight ensued between the two and the unfortunate groom got injured attempting to break it up. Most professionals, though, are used to choreographing their movements in tandem so they can get the shots they need. Be sure to tell the videographer very clearly that, when in doubt, the photographer's shot comes first.

Use the same criteria in finding a videographer as you would a photographer: state-of-the-art equipment, an aesthetic style you like and can agree to in writing, and a good rapport. In short, you want a professional videographer who works with professional equipment, not some hack who ran into a deal at Camcorders-R-Us and videotapes weddings on weekends when his aluminum lawn furniture business is slow.

Ask photographers who are not affiliated with a video company to recommend a videographer. Because many photographers have an aversion to working with any video person, any recommendation they make is probably a stellar one. Also ask banquet managers — they know who their clients have been enamored of and who they have complained about.

Safekeeping the past for the future

Heat, light, and fumes can damage photographs and videotapes. Taking a few precautions can ensure that they're still around for your great-grandchildren to see:

- Store photos and videos in a moderate temperature and humidity away from any direct light.
- Store videos upright on end in plastic cases away from electromagnetic fields produced by household electronic equipment such as stereo speakers, which have magnetic coils at their centers.
- Remove the clip at the back of your video so you don't record over it by mistake.
- Keep a second copy of your video and the negatives of your photos in a separate place, preferably in a fireproof box made especially for photographs and negatives.

Equipment check

Find out what kind of film and equipment the videographer shoots and edits with. Specifically ask what kind of format you receive. Professionals shoot in broadcast quality with "three chip" cameras that can sort colors, as opposed to "one chip" cameras, which can't. Editing should be done on professional equipment in either S-VHS industrial format or the more expensive Betacam. Unless you have some souped-up home system that requires another format (and if you do, you most likely don't need to read any of this), your finished video should come to you in VHS (Video Home System).

Some helpful terms to know include:

- **Super VHS:** Most videographers in the mid-affordable range shoot in super VHS. This was the state of the art until very recently and produces a perfectly fine video.
- **Betacam:** These cameras are the cutting edge, producing the highest resolution and requiring little light. Television stations use them to shoot the news. The only downside is that each tape is only 30 minutes long.
- **Hi band 8 MM or High 8:** This tape is being phased out, but many videographers still use it. A viable format, not to be confused with the consumer version, which is 8 MM.
- **DV cam:** This is a very new and expensive system, so it's not yet widely used. The tape runs for three hours and requires minimal light. The zoom feature captures intimate details unobtrusively.

Editorial license

Ask to see complete videos — not composites — that the videographer has recently shot. In evaluating the work, note whether the image is sharp, in focus, and steady. Is the sound clear? Are the shots varied? They should include: long shots, which give a sense of setting from afar or panning horizontally; medium shots, which are a little closer, showing, for example, the entry way to the reception; and close up shots of the guests. The video should tell a chronological story rather than bombard you with random, disconnected images (unless you *want* your wedding video to look like an early David Lynch film.)

No matter how talented someone is at handling a camera, unless the finished product is edited stylishly and cohesively, the video won't be fun to watch. Pacing is crucial. Does the video open with an *overview* — a sense of the action to come, such as a montage of the city where the wedding was held, or a Harry-and-Sally sort of interview with the bride and groom? Do the special effects look like an amateur music video? For that matter, is the music in sync with the action? Does the end of the tape consist of a recap of the best parts of both ceremony and reception? Do the editors use *time-shifting* techniques, the method Hollywood uses to put scenes that are shot out of order in the proper sequence? If you want to splurge, you may have computer-generated graphics, animated titles, interspersing of still photos, and quick cut techniques, making your wedding video look like a major theatrical release.

You can contribute to the unique flavor of your video by choosing meaningful music that is dubbed in to cover up background noises, adding photos from your honeymoon, scripting wit-provoking questions for on-camera interviews with guests. You may also want to create a continual reel that includes video footage or stills from your shower, rehearsal dinner, bachelor/bachelorette party, and honeymoon. Most videographers do not allow clients to participate in the editing process, so you need to be very clear about all the elements you want and how you want them used.

While most videographers (like photographers) do retain the rights to their own material, you may save money if you can negotiate with them to give you a first-generation tape that you then have duplicated. Look in the Yellow Pages under audio/visual services for companies that reproduce videos.

Sounding out the talent

For a ceremony in a church or temple, the optimum place for the microphone is within three to five feet of the bride, groom, and officiant. When that is not feasible, your videographer must get creative. In a church or temple that does not permit recording near the altar or bimah, the videographer may be able to put a microphone near the p.a. system to pick up the ceremony, although doing so can produce inferior results. For an outdoor ceremony, hiding a wireless microphone in the chuppah or in a tree or other stationary element works best.

Because most wedding gowns have no lapel or collar, putting a wireless microphone on the bride is virtually impossible. If your videographer wants to "wire" the groom or officiant, be aware that in some areas, these microphones may pick up outside radio signals — and you may end up having random cellular phone conversations and radio transmissions punctuating your ceremony.

Although your family and friends may say they care deeply about reliving every moment of your wedding with you, asking them to wade through four hours of real-time video is pushing it. At most your tape should be an hour and a half. Ask your videographer to create a *highlight tape,* and, if it's affordable, make duplicates for your fans. Also, negotiate to retain your *master tape* (the unedited version). The videographer really has no need for it, and you may find this uncut version contains parts you are happy to have in later years.

TIP

Getting ready for your close-up

Many people underestimate the degree of stage fright they may suffer at their wedding. If being thrust into the starring role unnerves you, your photos will show it. The most important — and sometimes most difficult — thing is to relax. Continually remember to breathe from your diaphragm, particularly when the camera is on you. Be aware of your shoulders — are they hunched up around your ears? Shake your arms out and loosen your shoulders. Also watch your posture; you want to neither slump nor stand at formal attention. And whatever you do, don't lock your knees.

During your formal shots, appoint someone to keep guests away. You don't want them distracting you or the photographer. Don't feel you have to converse with the photographer during the shoot — your mouth will look strange in the photos while your eyes are making contact with the camera. Remember that looking up at the camera for affirmation during candids or while being filmed ruins the sense of spontaneity.

If at all possible, have a friend take Polaroids of each of you in complete wedding gear (brides should definitely have photos when their hair and makeup rehearsal is done) weeks before the wedding. You may very well find things that you want to change — the tiara that looks so good in the mirror may look like a Barbie accessory on film, or the *very* white sleeves that seemed just a smidgen long peeking out from the tuxedo jacket look like gauntlets in a portrait shot. If you will be kneeling at the altar during your ceremony, consider blackening the bottoms of the groom's shoes with an indelible marker, so they don't pop out in the photos. You may even want to practice smiling, as silly as that sounds. Although scars, pimples, and wrinkles can be expunged from your photos after the fact, a frozen grimace cannot. (For hair and makeup tips, see Chapter 3.)

Part IV
Marital Minutiae

"I told you we should have registered."

In this part . . .

Pop quiz:

- How do you phrase your invitation if your parents are divorced?
- When and where should you register for gifts (or what if you don't want to receive gifts)?
- What constitutes a quality diamond and how do you know you're getting what you pay for?
- When and where do you get your blood tests? Do you even need them?

These are the types of details that can cause you to hit the panic button during your wedding planning. In this part, we cover those details so you don't have to lose any sleep.

Chapter 13
Getting the Word Out

In This Chapter

- A word to the wise
- Perfecting the presentation
- Announcing the nuptials

The invitation is meant to convey the necessary facts about your upcoming ceremony and the celebration following. If things were as simple as who, what, when, and where, we could do away with this chapter and you could save a bundle by relaying the salient information via telephone calls, e-mail, or paper airplanes.

As you are well aware, this is not the case. The wedding invitation — from its wording, form, and addressing to its printing style and ink color — is the subject of etiquette controversies, long, long chapters in wedding books, and dictatorial outlines. To flout the rules that these sources imply is to risk massive embarrassment, if not complete social disgrace.

Such scare tactics are not our m.o., but we do believe you should be familiar with what the social wags consider proper before you venture into the realm of creativity. Therefore, the first part of this chapter covers all the rules for writing traditional, formal invitations. The second part contains tips and ideas for both those who want to be very traditional and those who want to mix it up a bit. Either way, your invitations should reflect the style you want for your wedding.

Opening Volleys

Play it safe. Order your invitations three months — and send them no later than six to eight weeks — before the wedding. Guests coming from abroad should be sent invitations ten weeks in advance. If you plan on getting married over a holiday weekend, send out invitations to everybody eight to ten weeks ahead of time.

In figuring the number of invitations you need, a classic mistake is to think that if you're inviting 200 people, you need 200 invitations. Guess again. Look at your list. Chances are that a good number of those people are couples, which means you need send only one invitation, not two. However, you do want to order extra envelopes in case you mess up a few addresses.

Ordering your entire stationery wardrobe — from invitations to thank-you notes — at the same time may save you money and, more important, helps ensure consistency in color, paper weight, and ornamentation (monograms, floral motifs, clip art, and so forth).

If a large number of guests need to make special travel arrangements in order to attend your wedding, you may want to send out *save-the-date cards* several months to a year beforehand. Save-the-date cards can be playful, short, and sweet. You might send a picture postcard of the area where you plan to marry with:

Larkin and Gilbert are getting married!
August 11th
Bar Harbor, Maine
Please save the date
Invitation and details to follow

Guest who?

Before you can figure out how many invitations to order, you need to get a grip on your guest list. The complete guest list can represent the merger of a minimum of four lists — the bride's, the groom's, and that of both sets of parents. The recipe for the final number should comprise one part realism (budget and logistics) and two parts graciousness and hospitality. Consider this a casting call for all the supporting players in not only your two individual lives, but also in the lives of your two families together. Being obstinate now about someone who is important to your future mother-in-law may strain relations for eternity.

Be as tolerant as possible of your parents' requests. Nostalgia is a major draw for weddings and later you may be very touched that your parents' oldest friends and long-lost relatives care enough to reconnect as you realize that they in fact do make your circle complete.

If you're looking for where to draw the line, remember that weddings are not an opportunity to pay back social obligations or recoup your investment on wedding gifts to others in the past. And never make the mistake of sending invitations to people you really don't want to come on the assumption they won't. Those are often the very first souls to accept.

Some people may never speak to you again if they're not invited. If you can live with that, leave them off the list. Otherwise, add them and don't look back.

For a wedding held in a tourist area during peak season when accommodations are at a premium, a longer letter may be in order, detailing travel and lodging options. (See Chapter 19 for details on destination wedding newsletters.)

The year is considered mandatory on announcements, and optional on invitations. You may wish to include it on the invite though, particularly if you are the sentimental type and will be framing your invitation as a keepsake. Including the year will also be very helpful as a reference in years to come for those who are anniversary-challenged.

The Write Way (But Not the Only Way)

What constitutes a traditional, formal wedding invitation? It is written in the third person, engraved on folded paper or heavy card stock in black ink, and mailed inside two envelopes. The inner envelope has no glue. The invitations are usually ecru although some couples prefer the look of pure white. For invitations engraved on card stock, the edge may be beveled with gold or silver. The rules of composition for such an invitation are quite specific:

- **Abbreviate and punctuate (almost) nothing.** That means you spell out words like Doctor, Street, Road, Apartment, and state names (including District of Columbia). The exceptions are Mr., Ms., Mrs., and Jr., which are abbreviated and take periods.
- **Use commas in only two spots.** Between days and dates (Saturday, the nineteenth of July) and between cities and states (Spur, Texas).
- **You may omit the state if the city is well-known,** such as New York City, Dallas, or Seattle.
- **Employ British spellings of favour and honour.**
- **Use *the honour of your presence* for ceremonies in a house of worship.**
- **Use *the pleasure of your company* for ceremonies in secular locations,** such as a home, hotel, club, or other non-religious venue, or solely for the reception.
- **Write out the numerals for long numbers in street addresses,** unless the numbers are particularly unwieldy.
- **Write out times including the word "o'clock."** For example, *two o'clock.*
- **Use *half after* or *half past* in lieu of *-thirty* for half hours.** For example, *half after five o'clock* or *half past five o'clock,* not *five-thirty o'clock.*

Attention!

On invitations, enlisted personnel and non-commissioned officers may be listed with their military branch beneath their names:

Frederick Homer Cooley
United States Army

Senior officers (above captain in the army and lieutenant senior grade in the navy) appear with their rank before their name and their branch underneath:

Commander Troy William Sloane
United States Navy

The titles of junior officers go on the second line with the branch:

Melinda Anne Turner
Second Lieutenant, United States Air Force

- **Write out years.** In the tradition of needless nuptial debates, whether to capitalize the year ranks as a biggy. We like the look of capitalizing it, but whatever you choose is correct. While we're on the subject, the new millennium may appear as *Two thousand and one* or *Twenty hundred and one,* capitalized or not.
- **Always put the bride's name before the groom's.**
- **Note that while *Mr.* is always used with the groom's name, the bride's name does not take *Miss* or *Ms.*** In the case where the groom's parents are hosting the wedding, the rule is reversed.
- **Use military titles for brides and grooms on active duty.** Fathers may use their military titles whether on active duty or retired.
- **Use professional titles (*Doctor, Judge*) for grooms.** Ditto for fathers.
- **Do not, however, use professional titles for brides or mothers.** The one exception for brides is if you both are issuing the invitations.

The crux of traditional formal invitations lies in meticulous placement of names to convey who is related to whom as well as who is hosting the wedding.

If the bride's parents are hosting the wedding:

Mr. and Mrs. Garthwaite Stubbs Kerfuffle
request the honour of your presence
at the marriage of their daughter
Ida Hortense
to
Mr. Wylie Beauregard Blandsky
Saturday, the eleventh of August
Two thousand and one
at half after four o'clock
Saint Agnes Church
Wigglebury, Vermont
and afterwards at the reception
The Neptunian Society Pavilion
Forty-two Sweetbirch Drive

RSVP

If the wedding is not in a church:

Mr. and Mrs. Garthwaite Stubbs Kerfuffle
request the pleasure of your company
at the marriage of their daughter
Ida Hortense
to
Mr. Wylie Beauregard Blandsky
Saturday, the eleventh of August
at half after four o'clock
Town Green Gazebo
Wigglebury, Vermont

RSVP

The most formal invitations contain the name of the recipient written in by hand:

Mr. and Mrs. Garthwaite Stubbs Kerfuffle
request the honour of
Mr. and Mrs. Franklin B. Langley's
presence
at the marriage of their daughter...

Calligraphy courtesy of Glorie Austern

If the bride's mother is a widow or divorced and goes by her ex-husband's surname:

Mrs. Cassandra Kerfuffle
requests the honour of your presence
at the marriage of her daughter...

If the bride's mother is divorced, she may combine her maiden name and married surname:

Mrs. Bloomberg Kerfuffle
requests the honour of your presence
at the marriage of her daughter...

Although etiquette mavens have always maintained that no such person as *Mrs. Annabelle Kerfuffle* — in other words, Mrs. with a woman's birthname — can exist, as more women are combining their first name with Mrs., the rules seem to have been relaxed of late. We can simply shrug our shoulders. It's your call.

If the bride's father is a widower or divorced and he is hosting the wedding:

Mr. Garthwaite Stubbs Kerfuffle
requests the honour of your presence
at the marriage of his daughter...

If the bride's mother is remarried and she and her new husband are hosting the wedding:

Mr. and Mrs. Malcolm Holliday Harglow
request the honour of your presence
at the marriage of her daughter
Ida Hortense Kerfuffle…

Note: You can use the words *Mrs. Harglow's daughter* for *her daughter.*

If the bride's widowed father has remarried and he and his wife are hosting:

Mr. and Mrs. Garthwaite Stubbs Kerfuffle
request the honour of your presence
at the marriage of his daughter…

Note: You can substitute the words *Mr. Kerfuffle's daughter* for *his daughter.*

If the bride's father is deceased and her stepmother gives the wedding:

Mrs. Garthwaite Stubbs Kerfuffle
requests the honour of your presence
at the marriage of her stepdaughter
Ida Hortense Kerfuffle…

If the bride's parents are divorced, both are remarried, and all are sponsoring the wedding:

Mr. and Mrs. Malcolm Holliday Harglow
Mr. and Mrs. Garthwaite Stubbs Kerfuffle
request the honour of your presence
at the marriage of
Mrs. Harglow and Mr. Kerfuffle's daughter
Ida Hortense Kerfuffle
to…

The name of the bride's mother and her new husband goes first. If you think your guests can assume whose daughter she is, you may omit the line before the bride's name *(Mrs. Harglow and Mr. Kerfuffle's daughter,* in this case.)

If the bride's parents are divorced and her mother goes by her ex-husband's name:

Mrs. Garthwaite Stubbs Kerfuffle
and
Mr. Garthwaite Stubbs Kerfuffle
request the honour of your presence
at the marriage of their daughter
Ida Hortense Kerfuffle...

Listing the parents on separate lines, as shown above, indicates that they are divorced or separated.

If the bridegroom's parents are giving the wedding:

Mr. and Mrs. Edgar Montague Blandsky
request the honour of your presence
at the marriage of
Miss Ida Hortense Kerfuffle
to their son
Wylie Beauregard...

Note: In the preceding case, use *Miss* for the bride and omit *Mr.* for the groom.

If the groom's father is deceased and the groom's mother is hosting the wedding:

Mrs. Edgar Montague Blandsky
requests the honour of your presence
at the marriage of
Miss Ida Hortense Kerfuffle
to
Wylie Beauregard ...

If you are hosting your own wedding:

The honour of your presence
is requested at the marriage of
Miss Ida Hortense Kerfuffle
to
Mr. Wylie Beauregard Blandsky...

or

Miss Ida Hortense Kerfuffle
and
Mr. Wylie Beauregard Blandsky
request the honour of your presence
at their marriage...

If the ceremony is very small, you can invite people either by phone or include a ceremony card with the reception invitation for the few invited to both:

The honour of your presence
is requested at the marriage of
Miss Ida Hortense Kerfuffle
to
Mr. Wylie Beauregard Blandsky
Saturday, the eleventh of August
Two thousand and one
at half after four o'clock
Saint Agnes Church
Wigglebury, Vermont

You do not need to put *RSVP* on invitations that are for ceremonies only. It's unlikely that the church or synagogue will not accommodate all guests.

If the recipient is invited only to the reception:

Mr. and Mrs. Garthwaite Stubbs Kerfuffle
request the pleasure of your company
at the wedding reception of their daughter...

This type of invitation is useful for belated receptions held, for example, after the couple has returned from their honeymoon or if the ceremony was held in another town (see Chapter 19 for far-away weddings). This invitation also works for extremely small ceremonies consisting of just family or just you and witnesses. Bear in mind, however, that anyone you care enough to invite to the reception would probably love to see you walk down the aisle. Think twice before depriving them of this pleasure.

If the reception and ceremony are in different locations, or you can't fit all the information on the invitation, you may have a separate reception card:

Reception immediately following the ceremony
Neptunian Society Pavilion
Forty-two Sweetbirch Drive
Wigglebury, Vermont

RSVP

You ask for a reply by printing one of four things under the text or in the bottom left corner: *Kindly respond, The favor of a reply is requested, RSVP, Rsvp,* or *r.s.v.p.* The abbreviation RSVP is short for *Repondez, s'il vous plait,* which is French for respond (if you please). Include the address where the response is to be sent because the return address on the envelope is often blind embossed, which is hard to read, and recipients often discard the envelope.

In countries where double invitations are customary, two complete sets of text are printed side by side with the bride's on the left and the groom's on the right. This is the perfect solution to invitations printed in two languages. A similar concept known as a *French-fold invitation* — folded in half twice, once horizontally and then vertically — is also back in vogue and useful for weddings hosted by both the bride and groom's parents. The bride's information appears on the left, the groom's on the right, and the where and when is centered beneath:

Mr. and Mrs. Jaime Puente
request the honour of your presence
at the marriage of their daughter
Juanita
to
Mr. Antonio Jicama

Mr. and Mrs. Geraldo Jicama
request the honour of your presence
at the marriage of their son
Antonio
to
Miss Juanita Puente

Saturday, the fourteenth of November
at two o'clock in the afternoon
Our Lady of Angels Church
New York

Thought you should know . . .

Address and stamp announcements before the wedding so that they are ready for a friend to mail the day after. Announcements go to anyone you did not invite to the wedding but would like to inform of your nuptials.

Wedding announcements can be from the bride's parents or both sets of parents:

Mr. and Mrs. Garthwaite Stubbs Kerfuffle
and
Mr. and Mrs. Edgar Montague Blandsky
have the pleasure of announcing
the marriage of
their children
Ida Hortense Kerfuffle
and
Wylie Beauregard Blandsky...

Extra, extra

If you get really stationery happy, you may end up with more enclosures than the Publishers' Clearinghouse Sweepstakes. Use them only if they serve your purposes, not because you think the bulkier the invitation, the more important it appears.

- **Rain cards:** If you are having an outdoor ceremony, you need to have a back-up site in case of inclement weather. If that location is not near the original site, a rain card informs guests where to show up. Because people have differing definitions of a monsoon, you may post someone at your original site to send weather-oblivious guests on to the alternate sight.
- **Pew cards:** Small cards that say, *Pew Number___* to tell close friends and family in which pew they are to sit. Cards may say, *Within the ribbon,* meaning that several pews (designated by a ribbon along the aisle) are reserved for special guests but no specific pew is assigned. You may include pew cards with invitations or send them later after receiving replies. In the latter case, cards must be large enough to meet postal regulations — at least 3½ x 5 inches in the U.S.
- **At-home cards:** Traditionally used to tell guests of the couple's new address once they moved in together after the wedding. As many couples today are living together before marriage, these cards have a new purpose: to tell people how the bride and groom want to be known after the wedding.

The happy couple may announce their marriage themselves:

Ida Hortense Kerfuffle
and
Wylie Beauregard Blandsky
have the pleasure of announcing
their marriage...

In response, you should expect nothing more than a note of congratulations.

When things don't go as planned

If the wedding is canceled after invitations are mailed, you (or your maid of honor, close friends, or relatives) must call each guest personally if time does not permit you to send written word. If you do send a formal announcement, you are under no obligation to explain your decision.

A cancellation announcement may read:

Mr. and Mrs. Garthwaite Stubbs Kerfuffle
announce that the marriage of
their daughter
Ida Hortense
to
Mr. Wylie Beauregard Blandsky
will not take place

If a wedding is postponed due to death or other unforeseen circumstances after the invitations have been mailed, you may call with the information or print a formal announcement of the change:

Mr. and Mrs. Garthwaite Stubbs Kerfuffle
regret that
[owing to a death in the family]
the marriage of their daughter
Ida Hortense
to
Mr. Wylie Beauregard Blandsky
has been postponed
[to Saturday, the eleventh of September]

If the invitations have been printed but not mailed, you may enclose a card (rush printed), saying:

Kindly note that
the date of the wedding has been changed
to
Saturday, the eleventh of September

How Else Shall We Put This?

You may feel that the style for your invitation lies somewhere between the (dare we say) anachronistic style of the ages and the wit and wisdom of a Dilbert cartoon. You're up for something more creative, more ambitious, more *you.* In that case you may adapt traditional wordings to your own means. Feel free to break the rules as long as your guests are not left scratching their heads or guffawing.

For starters, consider these alternatives to the tried and true wedding invitation formulas:

- **Use American spellings.** *Honor* and *favor* not *honour* and *favour.*
- **Better yet, consider not using *honor of your presence* or *pleasure of your company* at all.** (See examples later in this chapter.)
- **Use first person (*We cordially invite ...*) as opposed to third (*Mr. and Mrs. William Dinkel request the pleasure...*)**
- **Use *Ms.* instead of *Miss*:** Or omit social titles altogether.
- **Skip *Mr. and Mrs.*:** Use the first names of both parents and step-parents instead.
- **Use professional titles for brides and their mothers, just as you would for the guys:** The fact that they are doctors, dentists, judges, or active military is not a state secret.
- **Include a stamped, addressed envelope with an RSVP card:** In addition, put *Kindly respond* in lower left corner of the invitation.
- **Put *Respond by [date]* on RSVP cards:** If you're planning on issuing more invitations after you receive regrets, have some response cards printed without a date. Remember, however, that yesses generally come in early, while nos delay their responses as long as possible.

Invitation turn-offs

The social haiku of invitations is intended to prevent you from over-sharing. Some things to avoid in your creative frenzy include:

- Cloying poetry and trite, drippy sentiments
- Bad art
- Tiny messy things such as Day Glo confetti, glitter, and adorable metallic musical notes that spill forth as you remove the invitation from the envelope and which surface in carpets, chair cushions, underwear drawers, and even more exotic places for years to come despite the use of industrial-strength cleaning contraptions
- Where you are registered and what particularly you are hoping to receive (see Chapter 14)
- That children are not welcome (pointedly excluding anyone on an invitation is hostile)
- So many names as hosts that guests know without a doubt who is on the "committee" that is paying for the wedding

Some variations if your parents are hosting:

Mr. and Mrs. Garthwaite Stubbs Kerfuffle
invite you to join us at the marriage of
our children ...

or

Jane and Kermit Winkler
would be delighted to have you
join them
as their daughter
Melissa Hope
and
Harry Crichna
pledge their love to each other ...

If you host your own wedding, the invitation may read:

Ida Hortense Kerfuffle
and
Wylie Beauregard Blandsky
would be delighted
to have you share
in the joy of their marriage
Sunday, the twelfth of August
at half after one o'clock
Temple Beth Israel
Tel Aviv, Texas
and afterward at the reception
K-Brand Ranch
Cricket, Texas

Another variation:

Ida Hortense Kerfuffle
and
Wylie Beauregard Blandsky
invite you to celebrate with us
at our wedding...

When the ceremony and reception take place in the same venue, you may think it's unnecessary to mention both events. After all, you assume, guests know you wouldn't drag them all this way without feeding them. But you know what happens when you assume, don't you? To be absolutely certain that guests won't be making a fast break for the nearest restaurant after the ceremony, try:

Ida Hortense Kerfuffle
and
Wylie Beauregard Blandsky
invite you to witness our vows
and join us afterward for dining and dancing
under the stars
Saturday, the eleventh of August
six o'clock in the evening
K Brand Ranch
Cricket, Texas

If the couple and both sets of parents host the wedding:

Ida Hortense Kerfuffle
and
Wylie Beauregard Blandsky
together with their parents
Mr. and Mrs. Garthwaite Stubbs Kerfuffle
Mr. and Mrs. Edgar Montague Blandsky...

Many couples of all religions are adopting the Jewish custom of listing both sets of parents on the invitation, not necessarily because the groom's parents are helping foot the bill but simply out of respect:

Mr. and Mrs. Garthwaite Stubbs Kerfuffle
request the honor of your presence
at the marriage of their daughter
Ida Hortense
to
Mr. Wylie Beauregard
son of Mr. and Mrs. Edgar Montague Blandsky...

If you wish, out of respect, to include the name of a deceased parent, make sure that it doesn't read like a dead person is giving the wedding:

Mrs. Garthwaite Stubbs Kerfuffle
requests the honor of your presence
at the marriage of
Ida Hortense
daughter of Mrs. Kerfuffle
and the late Mr. Garthwaite Stubbs Kerfuffle
to
Mr. Wylie Beauregard Blandsky...

RSVP Remedies

Even if you don't have other events to worry about, a fill-in-the-blank reply card is the most expedient method for the wedding itself:

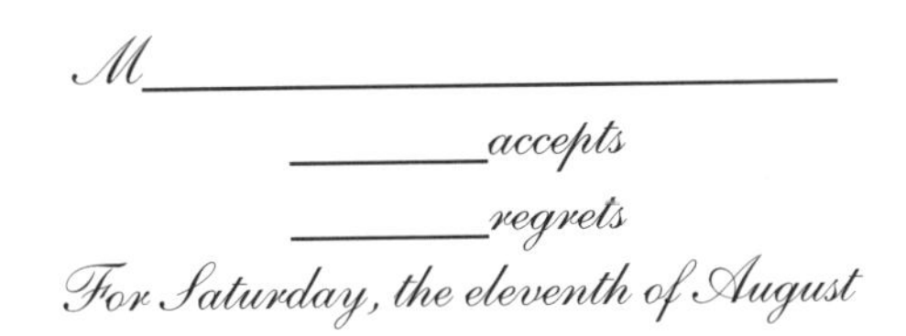
M______________________

________accepts

________regrets

For Saturday, the eleventh of August

Another variation:

Kindly reply by the eleventh of July

*M*______________________

will ______ *attend the wedding*

Response cards never ask the number of guests coming. Guests should assume that only the people listed on the envelope are invited. They then write in only the names of the invitees who can make it.

A compromise between the traditional lack of reply card and a fill-in-the-blank reply card is a card that says, simply, *Kindly respond by [the date]* or *The favor of a reply is requested.* Guests then write a gracious note in the blank space. If the thought of leaving your friends and relatives to figure things out scares you, consider adding *for [your wedding date]* at the bottom.

The date on the response card should be three to four weeks before your wedding, depending on how early you mail your invitations.

In light pencil, number the back of each RSVP card to coordinate with your numbered guest list. Doing so enables you to cross-reference cards of guests whose handwriting requires a Scotland Yard decryption unit.

GAME RULES

Dress codes: Now wear this

One of the most difficult decisions among many couples is whether to dictate guests' attire. An invitation that is engraved for or after 6 p.m. does not automatically direct people to dress in black tie. If it's important to you to see every male guest in a tuxedo and all the women in their fanciest dresses, print *Black tie* on the invitation.

If you want to stress the formality of the occasion but not compel friends to spend money on tuxedos consider *Black tie optional* on the invitation. Despite its recent popularity, the phrase *Black tie invited* seems actually to confuse the issue. *Business attire* is appropriate only for corporate events.

Other dress codes you may specify include *Dress for an evening in the country* (hopefully a hint for women to leave their spike heels at home), *Garden party attire*, or *Festive dress.*

The non-printed invitation

If you're having an extremely small wedding, you may invite guests via a handwritten note:

Dear Prudence,

Wylie and I are getting married Saturday, August 10th. We would be delighted to have you join us for the ceremony at 3 p.m. on the town green in his hometown, Wigglebury, Vermont, and afterward for tea at the home of his aunt, Hazel Twig, 42 East Bean Street.

Affectionately,

Ida

Rehearsal Dinner Invitations

Traditionally, the groom's parents host the rehearsal dinner. If the rehearsal dinner is small, you may simply let invitees know when and where by word of mouth. These invitations may have a touch of whimsy (see Chapter 17) or you may rely on a classic format:

Edgar and Sally Blandsky
invite you to a rehearsal dinner
[or prenuptial dinner]
in honor of
Ida and Wylie
Friday, August 10th
7 p.m.
Wick's Steak Palace
777 South Beaumont Avenue
Spur, Texas

RSVP
516- 555-1234 (Sally Blandsky)

Extracurricular Events

Often the bride's parents, grandparents, or close friends host a brunch the morning after the wedding, particularly if several of the guests are from out of town (see Chapter 17 for other parties). If the same guests are invited to the rehearsal (or other pre-wedding event), wedding, and brunch, for efficiency and economy, you may combine the before and after events in one invitation:

Please join us for a
pre-nuptial cruise and jam session
Saturday, August 11th
The Sabine Queen
boarding at 6:30 p.m.
setting sail at 7 p.m. sharp
Pier 20, Port Gusher
Bring instruments

— Ida and Wylie

~

Gladys Cossaboom
invites you to join her for a
post-wedding brunch
Sunday, August 12th
at her home
45 Pansy Way
Spark, Texas

To make things easier, you may use one RSVP card for several events. The card is sent back — in a stamped, pre-addressed envelope — to whomever has the most time to keep running tabs on the various head counts.

Please respond by July 11th
M ______ will attend the wedding
M ______ will attend the cruise
M ______ will attend the brunch

Alerting the Media

The only way to announce an engagement to the multitudes is through the newspaper. Many papers, however, have abandoned listing engagement announcements because they discovered that vendors deluged couples with solicitations. What's more, engagements are often broken. The papers figure it's better to run an announcement once the couple has crossed the finish line.

To get your wedding announcement in the newspaper, send in your vital statistics at least six weeks in advance. If you send a picture, be prepared for some rather odd photo composition requirements — that the couple's heads must be at the same level, eyebrows in the same plane, in formal or business attire, and so on.

Perfecting the Presentation

Marc Friedland of Los Angeles-based Creative Intelligence is renowned for invitations that immediately make guests feel that they are invited to something incredibly special. "Long gone are the days when only an ecru and black engraved invitation was suitable for a formal wedding," he says. "Using ink colors such as copper, eggplant, and moss — which are very popular — as well as textured papers and letter press printing, today you can create invitations that are elegant and formal, but which have a lot more personality and individuality."

Many couples choose truly original invitations designed by graphic artists or advertising firms. These range from customized logos (that are then used on everything from the invitations to cocktail napkins) on hand-bound booklets to videos or compact discs with hand-painted gift boxes.

Printing methods

The way your invitation is printed conveys as much about your wedding style as the words themselves. You may choose among several printing methods to suit your invitation, including:

- **Blind embossing:** Letters are etched into metal plates, which are pressed against paper without ink so that you just see the imprint, no color. Usually used for monograms, borders, and return addresses.
- **Calligraphy:** Handwritten with special pens and inks, usually for addressing. Can be done in a print style to match the invitation or use a calligraphed original to make a plate for an engraved invitation or as the prototype for an offset invitation.

- **Computerized calligraphy:** Done by a special machine with mechanized pen and laser printer. Meant to look hand-calligraphed; some fonts are more successful than others. Used for both invitations and addressing.
- **Engraved:** Letters are etched into a metal plate, which is then rolled with ink, and wiped off. Ink remains in each etched letter. The paper is pressed onto the plate, leaving a raised image and a "bruise" on the reverse side. Engraving in black ink is considered the appropriate mode for formal invitations. You may need to include a sheet of tissue paper over the type when mailing to prevent it from smudging.
- **Letterpress:** Until recently, the most common form for printed invitations. Created on an old-fashioned movable type machine. Raised type is inked and stamped on the paper. Although printers that still use this method are difficult to find, the antique effect can be quite beautiful. Unlike other processes, letterpress works well on handmade paper.
- **Lithography, offset, or flat printed:** Produces a crisp, flat image. An inked impression is made on a rubber-blanketed cylinder and then transferred to paper.
- **Thermography:** A popular, less-expensive alternative meant to mimic engraving. Heat-sensitive powder is sprinkled onto ink, which is heat-treated to form letters that are raised but not indented. Can be shiny.

Paper

Paper is measured in *bond weight.* Cards are three-ply stock; sheets are 32- to 42-pound bond. The most desirable paper is acid-free, 100 percent cotton rag as opposed to paper that contains a high percentage of wood pulp.

Most invitations come in one of two standard sizes: *embassy,* which is $5^1/_2$ x $7^1/_2$ inches; and *classic,* which is $4^1/_2$ x $6^3/_4$ inches. An invitation may be a single, heavy card or a single-folded sheet with printing on the outside or a double-folded sheet with the printing on the inside. In either case, the words can run horizontally or vertically. If you depart from these standard sizes, you may have to buy hand-made envelopes, which can be pricey.

If you opt for a non-traditional style, you can use special papers to creative effect. *Vellum* is a strong translucent paper resembling parchment and used either as an overlay or as the actual invitation. Gilt-edged vellum, which is rimmed in gold ink, is expensive yet beautiful. Sold by the sheet, special handmade papers may have nubby textures and be embedded with leaves, dried wildflowers, or metallic threads. Often impossible to print on, they make beautiful backgrounds for mounting invitations printed on plain card stock. If these options prove too expensive, consider using them for a smaller event such as the rehearsal dinner, a brunch, and so on.

Fonts

Although some printing companies invent their own names for specific type styles, or fonts, they are all variations of the same styles. You may choose from several printing styles (see Figure 13-1) ranging from what is usually called Antique Roman, a fairly staid but respectable looking block print, to Copper Plate, a swirly script. Many typefaces come in shaded versions that add a three-dimensional look to the font. Discuss the merits of various point, or letter, sizes with your printer.

As shown in Figure 13-2, professional calligraphy can add a nice touch. If you use a calligrapher to address your envelopes, you must provide an accurate, alphabetized guest list. If you don't know all the zip codes, don't expect the calligrapher to. Look up zip codes in a directory (available at libraries or on CD-ROM) or call the post office. Some calligraphers are conscientious enough to catch mistakes and correct them free of charge. Mistakes that are your fault, however, will cost you in both fees and extra envelopes.

ENGLISH SCRIPT — Mr. and Mrs. Paul Dillon, 2nd

OPEN ANTIQUE ROMAN — Doctor Paul Ireland Hamilton

ITALIC — Mr. and Mrs. Neill Fraser Simmons

GEORGIAN — Miss Adelaide Wainwright

SOLID ANTIQUE — Admiral Sir George and Lady Richards

MONARCH — Mr. and Mrs. Leslie Robinson

Figure 13-1: Engraved typefaces come in a multitude of styles, some fancier than others.

Courtesy of Cartier

Ink color

Aside from the traditional dark black, many colors are available from deep gray to violet. If you want the type on your invitations to be the same shade of cornflower blue as your beloved's eyes, you can find a matching PMS (Pantone Match System) color at your printer.

Envelopes

If you use double envelopes, and you choose to spiff up your invitation with a lining, it goes in the inside envelope but not the outer. Linings can be anything from black satin moiré to tie-dyed papers.

An invitation to remember

I have a weakness for beautifully engraved stationery, and I thought I would surely go the traditional route with formal engraved wedding invitations. But when Marcy showed me an invitation for a country wedding she'd done, I turned around 180 degrees. The invitation was calligraphed and engraved in forest green ink on an ecru card, which was mounted on a rectangular piece of crinkly green crepe-like paper, which was in turn mounted on a piece of hand-made paper embedded with dried flowers and ferns. This second piece folded over to form a cover.

Michael loved the invitation too, but this version was beyond our budget, so we set out to create a facsimile — at about half the cost. To save money, we had our invitation offset instead of engraved (nobody could tell the difference once the card was mounted), shopped around for less expensive hand-made papers, and did some of the labor ourselves — with the help of our wedding party. First we "deckled" the flower paper to look as if the edges were hand-torn. To do this, you use a deckling ruler (available at crafts and stationery stores), which has a wavy, sharp edge. You lay it on the paper and tear-cut the paper along the sharp edge.

The deckled sheets were then fed into our invitation assembly line to be folded, mounted (tip: buy at least a dozen glue sticks), stuffed into envelopes (with four other inserts for our destination wedding), addressed, sealed, and stamped. The whole process took a total of 12 hours, but this "package" set the tone for a very special weekend.

Mr. and Mrs. Alexander H. London
Mr. and Mrs. Tyler E.R. American
Mr. and Mrs. Albert F. G. Daley
Mr. and Mrs. Kenneth Saint James
Mr. and Mrs. Raymond A. Shaw
Mr. and Mrs. Jackson S. Italic
Mr. and Mrs. Charles F. G. White
Mr. and Mrs. Franklin B. Langley
Mr. and Mrs. Sean Antique Roman
Mr. and Mrs. Randolph K. Tucker
MR. AND MRS. ROMAN B. CAPITAL
MR AND MRS SLANTED V. TALESWORTH
Mr. and Mrs. Samuel F. O. Bartholomeuw
Mr. and Mrs. Benedict S. Canyon
Mr. and Mrs. Parker Terrace Hamilton

Figure 13-2: The beauty of various calligraphy styles, or "hands," lies in the quirks and flourishes of each letter.

Calligraphy courtesy of Glorie Austern

Tradition has dictated that the return addresses on outer envelopes are blind embossed at most, but you won't win any friends at the post office this way. Calligraph or print the return address — with no name — on the back flap. The address should be that of whomever is hosting the wedding. Traditionally, even if the bride's parents are hosting the wedding in name only, the reply cards go to them. If you are keeping track of regrets and acceptances, the parents then pass on that information, or merely drop off the weekly returns in a pillow case for you to tabulate.

If you have oversized invitations, you may mail them in oversized boxes (similar to a scarf box) with the invitation wrapped in tissue. Many companies sell transparent mailing tubes perfect for scroll-like invitations.

Besides taking into account special postal costs, (not just for weight but for non-standard sizes as well) consider where the invitations are being mailed. Your exquisite packaging may get karate-chopped and crumpled as it's crammed into a tiny apartment mailbox.

Other enclosures and embellishments

You can dress up your invitations in many ways. In cases where you can do at least part of the labor yourself — inserting ribbons, applying sealing wax — you can create a highly customized look without it costing a fortune.

- **Borders:** Possibilities range from blind-embossed trailing ivy to antique letterpress repetitive patterns.
- **Die cuts:** Expensive if custom designed, but ready-made possibilities are available. The front of the invitation is cut out in a pattern, such as a wedding cake, to reveal writing behind, or the edge of the invitation itself is cut into a pattern, such as a skyline or church steeple.
- **Green, growing things:** You may include a real sprig of herbs or a miniature bouquet of dried flowers in the bow, to suggest a country or at-home wedding.
- **Maps:** May be hand-drawn and offset, but should be in keeping with the style and ink color of the invitation. Top them with a heading that says, *Directions to [your first names'] Wedding.* If you don't want to overwhelm your pristine invitation, send maps separately or include them in the rehearsal or other invitation. If you have maps from the ceremony to the reception, have extras to give out after the ceremony. (See Chapter 21 for help in finding maps on the Internet.)
- **Monograms:** For the invitations themselves, a monogram would be used only if the two of you are hosting the wedding, and because you are not yet married, comprise the four initials of both names. (See Chapter 14 for a discussion of monograms.)

- **Motifs:** With the advent of computerized clip art, a motif or what the printers call *ornaments,* can be used on all your stationery items. These can be almost anything imaginable, from a tiny etched sailboat to a gold embossed topiary. An artist's sketch of your home or the place where you are getting married, reproduced on the front of your invitation is a truly personal statement.
- **Ribbon:** Wired ribbon either in subtle tones that complement the ink used or shaded in pale to dark color, can be tied around the invitations and finished with an artfully tied bow.
- **Sealing wax:** Comes in an array of colors to match your invitation. Sealing envelopes on the back is tedious but not difficult.

When recipients open the envelope, they should be able to read the invitation without turning it around. Folded invitations go in the envelope fold first. You may put the enclosures either on top of the invitation or in the fold. Tuck reception response cards under the envelope flap, not inside the response envelope. Don't put the response card behind the invitation because some guests may not see it.

Addressing Tradition

As with other aspects of traditional formal invitations, inner and outer envelopes subscribe to precise rules of decorum. For starters, address envelopes by hand or have them calligraphed. Never use laser printers or labels. The following rules apply:

Outies

- **Use formal names.** If you use middle names, you must use them in full. Middle initials do not suffice; if you don't know the middle name, skip it.
- **Spell out all words such as Apartment, Avenue, Street, and state names.** Although the U.S. Postal Service prefers you to use two-letter state abbreviations and no comma between cities and states so letters can be scanned by machine, they won't send it back to you if you do otherwise.
- **Abbreviate only Mr., Mrs., Ms., Jr., Messrs., and Esq.** Write out professional titles, including Doctor.
- **Address envelopes to both members of married couples even if you know only one: *Mr. and Mrs. Travis Twig.***
- **Address envelopes to unmarried couples as *Mr. Huck Porter and Ms. Wanda Guernsey* with the names on separate lines.**

Proof it all night

After ordering invitations, you receive a proof of the text. Read this proof over very carefully; any mistakes you overlook are not considered the printer's fault. Then have someone else — preferably someone who knows nothing about your wedding and thus doesn't have the same blind spots you do — proofread everything. Obvious typos are often the easiest to miss.

With engraved invitations, the proof is made from the actual printing die, on which all the text appears backward and requires a mirror to decipher. After the invitations are printed, if you can get the die from the printer, you may want to turn it into a small tray or have it mounted, a custom popular in Victorian times.

- **Send separate invitations to children over 13.** (***Note:*** Some experts say children over 18; use your discretion.)
- **You may send joint invitations to siblings of the same sex younger than 13.** Address them as *The Misses Twig* or *The Messrs. Twig.* If you're sending to both boys and girls, write the names on the same envelope like this:

  The Messrs. Twig
  The Misses Twig

- **You may write *Miss Daisy Twig* or *The Misses Twig* under *Mr. and Mrs. John Twig,* but *The Messrs. Twig* receive a separate invitation.**

- **Because adults should receive their own invitation no matter what, the phrase *and Family* may be used only when everyone under the same roof is invited.** Such open-ended generalizations can, however, get you in trouble; some people have very large families and you may not want to meet all of them on your wedding day.

Innies

If you also use inner envelopes, address them as follows:

- Address married couples as *Mr. and Mrs. Twig* with neither the first names nor address.
- Use only first names for children: Pearl, Pablo and Gus.
- Put a young daughter's name below her parents' if the outer envelope is addressed to both the parents and her: *Miss Felicity Twig.*
- You may address intimate relatives as, say, *Aunt Hazel and Uncle Woody* or *Grandfather.*

- If you ask a friend to bring a guest, write *and Guest* on the inner, but not the outer, envelope. Better yet, find out the guest's name.

Fit to Be Titled

As if you don't have enough rules to remember in writing a simple address, professional titles can put you out of your tree. Traditionally, the rule has been very simple: Women, no matter what, are never listed with professional titles or, if they are married, their own first names. That's simple enough, yes, but these days, ignoring a woman's professional and personal identity strikes many people (including us) as sexist to say the least. The fact that many women are keeping their names after marriage complicates things even more.

We believe that you should use professional titles for either everyone or no one. If you're stumped about how to list the names, go with this simple rule: alphabetical order unless superseded by title. For example:

Judge Jane Silk and Mr. Ty Bickle

In the preceding example, although *Bickle* would normally go before *Silk*, because Jane Silk has a title — judge — she goes first.

However, if the partners have different names and each has a title, list them alphabetically by last name:

Judge Felix Bipp and Doctor June Pickle

If the couple has the same last name, put the titled person first:

Doctor Whit Fink and Ms. Camela Fink
Doctor Mathilda Burr and Mr. Rip Burr

It's in the Mail

Don't forget to send invitations to your officiant and parents. You'd be amazed at how often these very important people get overlooked. Also send an invitation to yourselves a few weeks before the others go out so that you can see how long it takes to arrive and in what condition.

In calculating the cost of your invitations, be sure to include postage. Once you have a sample, including response card, direction card, map, and all other inserts, take it to the post office to have it weighed (twice). Be prepared to put up to three stamps on each envelope. Don't pinch pennies here: Go for all matching stamps, which look more "finished" even if you have to pay a few more cents to mail it.

When you're at the post office, inquire about commemorative stamps. You can sometimes find designs that tie in with your theme or color scheme. If you're really lucky, you can get a design you like in the new self-stick stamps, which eliminates the odious task of stamp licking.

Putting stamps on the response envelopes encourages your lazier guests to mail them in. However, stamping reply envelopes for guests abroad is useless — they must use their own postage.

After you've gone to all the trouble of painstakingly inscribing each envelope and choosing special stamps, you don't want the effect ruined by having your invitation run over by the post office's vicious canceling machines. A hand-canceled envelope looks more elegant and keeps calligraphy and sealing wax intact. In many areas, unfortunately, you must promise your firstborn to get the post office to hand stamp anything. However, the look of a hand cancel is worth your most charming powers of persuasion.

One for the record

The simplest way to preserve your invitation is to mat and frame it, or include it in your photo album. If you have a lot of time on your hands, you may decoupage it on a plate, serving tray, or hope chest in which you keep other wedding mementos. Or save time by sending it to a company that backs invitations with velvet and mounts them in shadow boxes.

Chapter 14

Gimme, Gimme

In This Chapter

- Registry rules and rigmarole
- Please, just throw money
- Thank you, thank you, thank you

The "getting" part of getting married is like winning *The Price Is Right, Wheel of Fortune,* and *Let's Make a Deal* all at once and then — if you have a wedding registry — personally dictating the prizes you receive. All that's required of you is a credible demonstration of appreciation in the form of a well-written thank-you note. Far from being an unseemly show of greed, registering is the accepted method of making your wish list public to those who care to know.

Registering As a Preventative Measure

Christofle claims to have invented the bridal registry in 1856. The French silver manufacturer apparently figured out that wedding guests appreciate some guidance on what to get the happy couple — or it grew tired of couples exchanging their umpteenth set of sterling silver toast tongs. Many stores recognize that wedding registries are not only an entree to the lucrative bridal market, but also a way of winning couples' shopping loyalty for life. Consequently, retailers have gone to great lengths to make the process painless, from dedicating a team of consultants who steer you through the aisles to equipping you with bar code scanners to zap any item your heart desires onto your list.

All this consumerist sophistication, and all the glee that comes with choosing gifts that you would never buy for yourselves, however, does not mitigate the emotional trauma of the process. Suddenly, you're shopping for "our stuff," attempting to meld your personal tastes into one — and that can be very unnerving. If you doubt this, just go to the housewares floor of any department store on a Saturday afternoon and watch while one couple after another morphs from browsing Jekylls into snarling Hydes as they decide which china pattern to live with *for the rest of their lives.*

In spite of this, registering remains a brilliant concept — your defense against a deluge of this year's hot gift item as well as grotesqueries from well-intentioned but hopelessly taste-challenged relatives.

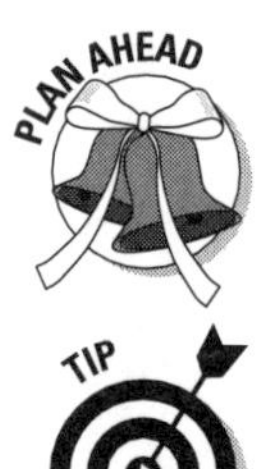

To give yourself enough time to choose your items carefully, begin planning your registry soon after you are engaged. Some people like to consult your registry for shower gifts, so you may want to register before those invitations go out.

TIP

Before you show up wearing your comfortable shoes and clutching your wish list, call the stores to find out whether you need to make an appointment. A few questions worth asking:

- In what format does the store keep your registry — computer, online, a sales clerk's small black book? Do other store locations use the same format? How easily can other branches access your list?
- Are you assigned a customer service representative who oversees your particular registry?
- How quickly after you fill out the paperwork is your registry "up and running" for people to order from?
- Does the store have a toll-free number? (Try the number a few times at different times of day to see whether your guests may have to endure rude operators, being put on hold interminably, or other annoyances.)
- How quickly does the store update your list when someone buys something? How does the store avoid sending duplicate gifts?
- How can you add items to your registry?
- What are the store's return policies?

You can't always get what you want (but sometimes you get what you need)

Don't get carried away by the thought of choosing all sorts of free loot. Whether you are just starting out, are merging two households, or have dreams of trading in the wine crate you've been using for a dining-room table, approach registering methodically. Take a careful inventory of what's missing from your lives and use that list to begin selecting items for your registry. You may discover that while neither of you owns a single frying pan, you actually have 6.2 sets of china between you. That doesn't mean china should definitely be off your list, if that's what you really want, but you may want to direct those precious gift dollars toward other more urgently needed or unusual goods.

Take notes on items and patterns that appeal to you. You may want to scope out the merchandise in person at least once before actually signing up for it (although you can always go back and change your choices). Collect lots of brochures and magazine ads to assist in those late-night discussions about non-stick cookware and percale sheets.

Apart from stores where you can register for traditional items such as flatware, china, and crystal, you have a wide world from which to outfit your future life together. Registering with several stores gives you and your guests more flexibility, particularly if you register with a national chain or two so out-of-town guests can easily shop for a gift. Another possibility is a non-traditional registry, such as:

- **Charity:** For non-materialist types and previously married couples. Guests are directed to make a tax-deductible contribution in your names to one or more charities of your choice.
- **Hobby:** For the couple who either has everything or cares more about keeping their inner children happy than having matching sets of towels. Ranges from sporting goods to wine to compact discs. Look for these in specialty stores, travel agencies, and mail-order catalogs.
- **Home improvement:** Not just a guy thing, this category includes tools, lawn mowers, gardening paraphernalia, Jacuzzis — anything a couple of fledgling homeowners may need. Check out hardware stores, large home improvement centers, and garden shops.
- **Mortgage:** Monetary gifts go toward a down payment on a home or to a mortgage payment fund. Some banks in their zeal to promote this creative approach to building a house fund automatically send out letters to your "prospective donors." That's a bit much; make it clear that you will take care of notification.
- **Services:** These can include spas, massages, steak-of-the-month clubs, housecleaning — use your imagination.
- **Travel:** Arrange with a reliable travel agent to accept contributions to your travel fund for your honeymoon or future trips. Again, clarify that the agent is not responsible for notifying guests of your registry.

You may feel that not all of your guests can appreciate a non-traditional registry, so you may want to suggest them to only close friends or relatives in addition to the more traditional options you announce to others.

While your eyes may widen at the thought of owning the most elegant designer china and golden flatware, be realistic. Unless your friends and family have collectively won the lottery, you may find yourselves owning no more than a single teaspoon and a gravy boat from the pricey patterns you have selected. If your needs really are limited to a state-of-the-art sound or video system, or something equally unaffordable for one person or a couple to bestow upon you, hint broadly to a close friend that a group of your friends chip in for a large item.

If you already own a set of china, crystal, or flatware but it's incomplete, consider registering for the missing pieces rather than a whole new set. Replacements, Ltd. stocks thousands of patterns, some up to a century old. In a similar vein, Wedgwood guarantees that if your pattern is discontinued within five years of registration, the company will exchange your dinnerware at full value toward a new set or assist you in completing your set.

Try to register at stores that give you a discount after your wedding on anything left on your registry.

Psssst . . .

After you sign up for all those goodies, you may have to keep reminding yourself that you only registered for them — they're not yours until people purchase them for you. And you certainly want to ensure that they do! We sympathize, but try to restrain yourself from shouting the store's toll-free number from the rooftops, renting out a freeway billboard, or listing the various places you have registered on your answering machine. If you're wondering whether you can "be helpful" by printing your registry info on your wedding or shower invitations, the answer is an unequivocal *no.*

That's right. We believe that under no circumstances should an invitation mention a gift in *any* way. Nor should you have the store send catalogs, cards, or other notices to guests. We even disagree with having a store name or two discreetly calligraphed at the bottom of your shower invitations.

Look what I brought

Before the days of wedding registries and Victoria's Secret, women spent years tatting doilies, needlepointing pillows, and embroidering monograms on bedclothes for their daughters' hope chests. The real excitement came when the girl got engaged. Suddenly her *trousseau* (French for the "little trusse" or "bundle" the bride carried to her husband's house) expanded to include frilly lingerie and enough new clothes to get her through the next year. She might even get a few saucepans to boot.

Today the bridal hope chest and trousseau seem quaintly anachronistic (although who wouldn't like any excuse to go out and buy an entirely new wardrobe?) However, if you've already started stockpiling sheets, tablecloths, and tumblers for your wedded life, you may be wondering whether and how to monogram, or "mark," them. As shown in the upcoming figure, the best spots for your initials are as follows:

- **Crystal:** Can be etched anywhere, though are usually centered.
- **Flatware:** Engraved on the front, near the tip of the handle, or on the back to leave the integrity of a sleek, classic pattern intact.

Ornate flatware styles may take the monogram on the spine of the handle.

- **Napkins:** Embroidered diagonally in one corner or centered on a rectangular fold. You may use just one initial centered on a cocktail napkin.
- **Pillowcases:** Embroidered centered two inches above the hem.
- **Sheets:** Embroidered in the center so the monogram shows when the top of the sheet is folded down.
- **Tablecloths:** For a rectangular one, embroidered in the center of a long side, where the cloth hangs down. For square ones, embroidered in one corner so it shows on the top of the table.
- **Towels:** Embroidered in the center of one end, so the initials show when the towel is folded in thirds lengthwise and hanging on a towel rack.

Which initials, then, to use for your monogram? Traditionally, brides have used their birth surname monogram on their stationery and a combination of their birth and married surnames on their linens (which they theoretically pass down to their daughters). For example, Lydia Scooter marrying Michael Blip may use *LB* or *LBS* (with the *B* larger) or *S*B*. Other items such as flatware and crystal would take the husband's last name initial. But that's changing; a bride and groom may choose any combination of their initials, perhaps intertwined, on an angle with the bride's initials overlapping the groom's, or incorporating some symbol of their lives together such as an acorn or leaping salmon.

Note: Hold off on monogramming anything until you decide what name(s) to use after you're married, and request that your registries do the same, because engraved items are obviously not returnable.

Is once enough?

If you or your future spouse have already been married (and presumably cleaned up the first time around), you may feel uncomfortable registering this time. If so, trust your instincts. But, in our opinion, just as a previously married bride may wear white if she chooses, so may an "experienced" couple register. You can't stop people from giving you gifts, and they may appreciate your guidance all the more because they don't know whether you or your ex got custody of the lead crystal decanter.

The only exception may be if your last marriage was extremely short-lived. If you go through spouses the way some people go through coffee filters, perhaps you should register for pre-marital counseling.

The only graceful and acceptable way to get the message out is by word of mouth. But never volunteer the information; someone must first inquire, "Where are you registered?" Then you or your mother or your attendants can respond, "My, that is so sweet of you to ask," while whipping out a card with the store's name and phone number. For those who phrase the magic question as "What do you need?" or "What do you want?" don't be coy. Give them some general parameters and then direct them to your registry.

While your intentions are certainly the best, be aware that to many guests writing something like "No gifts, please" on an invitation is both presumptuous and offensive. Doing so is actually likely to backfire as people who feel they must give you something rely on their own devices and taste.

What We Really Want? Well, It Rhymes with Honey . . .

The very idea of checks as gifts makes some etiquette mavens apoplectic, but we think money is a very thoughtful gift. Usually only close relatives are likely to give you money and, depending on your family, you may have to have a little bird (of the close-friend species) mention your wishes. As with gift registries, posting your checking account number in conspicuous places is considered quite rude.

Most money gifts come as personal checks or U.S. Savings Bonds, which some people like to slip to you in envelopes during the reception. Before you leave for your honeymoon, endorse all the checks and write "For deposit only" on the back. Then fill out a deposit slip and have someone you trust deposit them while you're away.

Show us the money

In some cultures, giving money for weddings is a revered custom:

- A Nigerian tradition carried on by some African Americans is showering the bride with money during the reception. The bride carries a specially decorated money bag into which guests slip envelopes with checks.
- The parents of Japanese grooms present a cash gift (about three months of the groom's salary) to the bride's family in a special envelope. Knotted gold and silver strings, which are supposed to be impossible to undo, adorn the envelope, which is called a *shugi-bukero.* The amount and giver's name is written on the back of the envelope.
- Chinese brides serve a ritual tea to their new in-laws, who then give them money in lucky red envelopes called *hung boas.*
- At a Polish wedding, in order to dance with the bride, guests pin money to her dress.

Problem Presents

If a gift arrives damaged, take or send it back to the store from which it came. (Returns and exchanges should not be a problem with reputable stores, which want to keep you happy.) If the giver personally shipped the present, check the wrapping to see if it was insured so that the person can collect the insurance and send a replacement.

Sometimes in spite of registering and making sure everyone is notified of your registry, you receive perfectly nice gifts for which you have no use, but exchanging them is more trouble than it's worth. You put the present in a drawer, with the idea that one day you'll find someone who can truly appreciate it. *Regifting,* as it's known, seems like a harmless way to recycle, but we've noticed that these gifts tend to have a vibe (perhaps it's guilt) that can come back to haunt you. And you have to remember who gave it to you and whether that person would ever come across it in the secondary recipient's home or notice its absence from yours. In a world where everyone nods when you say "six degrees of separation," regift at your own risk.

Returning gifts for exchange, however, carries with it no guilt penalty. You don't need to inform the sender of the switch, although close friends usually don't mind and even enjoy keeping up with your gift list. In any case, thank the giver of the original gift — lie a little if you must — and let the matter rest.

Return to sender

The only time you return items to the giver is if the wedding is canceled. If you have already used the gift, you must send the giver an identical replacement. Of course, waiting to use gifts received before the wedding until you are legally a couple seems overly superstitious to us. We say go for it; if you don't make it to the altar, you'll have bigger problems to worry about than whether you already slept on the sheets Aunt Priscilla gave you.

Banking debunked

Exchanging gifts is one thing, but trading them all in for one fat check to blow on something else that is so outrageously expensive you would be embarrassed to register for it is taking advantage of your guests' generosity. This distasteful scenario, known as *gift banking,* is actually promoted by some stores. You register for a slew of phantom gifts; as guests purchase the items (or so they think), the store notifies you but instead of sending the presents, adds the value of the gifts as cash credits to your account. Later, the credits are tallied and you get the funds for a shopping spree. One caveat (surprise, surprise): Most stores do not give cash refunds — you must spend the credit in the store.

Some gifts never make it to their destination. Weeks after you receive a notice from the store or a friend has mentioned that a present is on its way, you realize that something is wrong. First, call the store, if possible. Then notify the giver, who is no doubt wondering whether you just hated the gift or are too inconsiderate to write a thank-you note.

Keeping Track of the Loot

The minute you receive a present, write down what it is, who gave it to you, and the date. This information can go on an index card with the guest's other vital information. If you're keeping your guest list in a spreadsheet such as Excel, just make two more columns — for the gift and the date you sent a thank-you.

Also save the paperwork (such as a receipt, which probably does not list the price). You may need this to prove the item's origin if you return or exchange it. Receipts are also helpful if the store sends duplicates or fails to send out the gift because of some oversight.

Displaying the gifts is an integral part of wedding tradition in some cultures. In 1893, for example, when Princess May and the Duke of York married, their wedding presents were displayed at Marlborough House — all 3,500 of them! In the U.S. South today, friends and relatives may drop by the home of the mother of the bride a few days before the wedding to see the gifts arranged in all their glory. (Companies there even specialize in creating a tableau of gifts amid damask linens and cut flowers.) Some people like to keep the cards with the gifts; others feel that doing so is indiscreet and clutters up the effect. Checks, it seems, should stay in their envelopes if displayed at all.

Giving Thanks

People may give you a gift any time from the moment you announce your engagement until one year after your marriage. Although opinions vary, we feel that you have a month to send a thank-you note. (Honeymooners get cut some slack, but only a few weeks' worth.) If you fall behind, triage the situation: Send notes first to people such as Aunt Myrtle who is probably losing sleep wondering if the vase arrived intact; send the next batch to folks whose checks you've already deposited; and then take care of the rest — but don't procrastinate too long. You and your spouse may actually enjoy this opportunity to relive certain moments of the wedding and mention them to gift givers. (Okay, we tried!)

A well-written thank-you note mentions the gift, how much you like it, and how you intend to use it. You may also add a few words regarding how much you enjoyed (or missed) them at your wedding. For example:

> *August 11*
>
> *Dear Aunt Beatrix and Uncle Hal,*
>
> *Thank you so much for the exquisite hand-painted vase. It looks like it was made for our mantle and we have already put it to use holding a bouquet of daffodils. We were thrilled that you came all the way from Pucktawket for our wedding — your presence made this an even more memorable family event.*
>
> *Again, our deepest thanks. We are crazy about the vase.*
>
> *With love and affection,*
>
> *Crystal & Howie*

Both of you may sign the note. A sweet touch is for the other spouse to append a brief post-script such as: *P.S. I so enjoyed meeting you after hearing Howie say such nice things about you for so long. Thank you again. We hope to see you soon. — C.T.*

If the gift is actually quite hideous and destined to be exchanged or donated to charity, brush up on your euphemisms — *unusual, unique, bold, conversation piece* — and focus on the thought behind the gift.

Thank-you notes for money gifts are exercises in the oblique. Do not mention the words cash or check — refer to it as *your gift* or *your generous gift* — and never mention the exact amount. You may, however, indicate how you intend to use the money: *We have earmarked it for our house fund. . . .*

Thank-yous in general should be short, sweet, and uncomplicated. (See Chapter 13 for proper stationery.) For people who send you gifts before you've sent them an announcement or invitation, don't stuff everything in one envelope; send the other missives via separate post. You are not obligated to invite people to your wedding just because they send you an early gift.

Although we encourage you to deputize whenever possible, thank-you notes are not one of those situations. You must write them yourselves. By hand. ASAP.

Some etiquette gurus advise using printed acknowledgment cards when you don't have time to pen the real McCoy right away. These cards say that you received the gift and will send a personal note of thanks soon. In other words, they are an elaborate form of procrastination. Simply get on with the thanking and if you have a legitimate delay — the gifts were sent to your parents' home and had to be re-shipped long-distance or you both are taking the bar exam — so be it. No need for lengthy explanations or excuses; even the most cryptic scribbled message is better than none or a generic printed one.

Send thank-you notes to all those people who got you through your day — the hairdresser, caterer, photographer, the florist, and so on. As we say in Chapter 16, service professionals rely on letters of reference for their business, and a laudatory letter often means more to them than a monetary tip does.

Chapter 15

Left Hand, Fourth Finger

In This Chapter

- Telling carats from karats
- Searching for the perfect setting
- Doing the loupe-de-loupe

Even if your idea of commitment is matching nose rings, you may want to devote special attention to finding the right engagement and wedding rings. For one thing, they undoubtedly qualify as major purchases for most couples. For another, you will wear them for the rest of your life.

Despite the cliché of the man proposing by springing open a jewelry case under his beloved's nose or surreptitiously sinking a ring in her champagne glass, many brides and grooms prefer to shop for the engagement and wedding rings together. Or at least "pre-shop" together so the groom doesn't buy something that is his taste, not hers. When you do go looking, consider your lifestyle. For a woman who runs stockings by just looking at them, a pointy pear or marquise shape would be a disaster. For a mechanic, a ring of any kind may constantly get in the way or get damaged. We suggest trying on many different rings before you buy anything. Using the guidelines here, you may develop an eye for quality stones and craftsmanship, but your final choice is extremely personal and should reflect your taste, feelings for each other, and, as unromantic as it sounds, your budget.

The Diamond C-saw

A diamond is nothing more than a hunk of carbon, yet in its pure, crystallized form is the hardest transparent substance known to man, one hundred times harder than ruby or sapphire. Only another diamond can cut a diamond. This durability, along with its light, has made diamonds an enduring marriage symbol.

The first diamonds came from India 2000 years ago, but credit for the first diamond engagement ring may go to Archduke Maximilian of Austria — much to the delight of his intended, Mary of Burgundy. The year was 1477 and her ring featured a diamond in the rough; it wasn't until the late 15th century that jewelers figured out how to cut diamonds to unlock their brilliance and "fire" — rainbow colors that vary in intensity. Discoveries of diamond supplies in Brazil and South Africa in the 18th and 19th centuries made the stones more widely available, affordable, and popular.

Today, most engagement rings in the U.S. feature diamonds, so you probably haven't gotten this far in your engagement without having heard about the *four Cs* — cut, color, clarity, and carat weight — by which all diamonds are judged. Chances are you're even sick to death of the four Cs, but just in case you've been hiding under a rock, read on.

Orthodox Jews believe that wedding rings should be plain with no jewels or stones that may impede the eternal, heavenly circle of life and happiness.

Cut

A diamond's *cut* and proportion determines its brilliance and fire, making the cut perhaps the most important factor in a diamond's beauty. Because each facet acts as a light-dispersing mirror, more facets generally mean greater beauty. To appreciate a stone's cut, you should be familiar with the anatomy of a well-proportioned diamond, as in Figure 15-1.

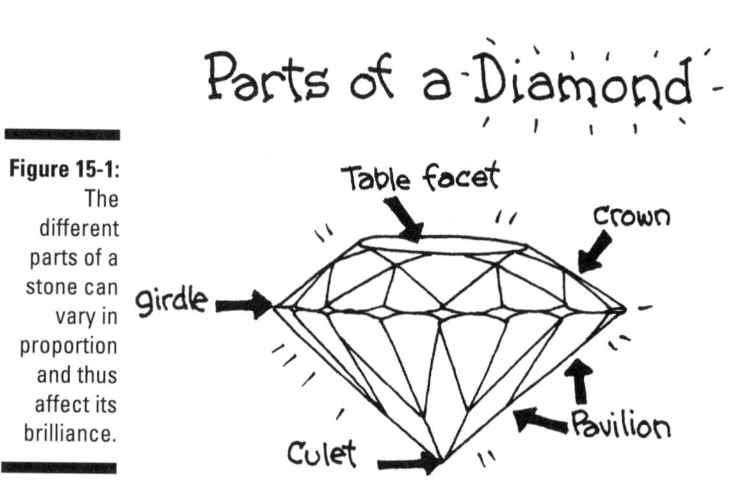

Figure 15-1: The different parts of a stone can vary in proportion and thus affect its brilliance.

A modern round, brilliant-cut diamond has 58 facets, which makes it more brilliant than other shapes. When light enters an ideally proportioned diamond, it is reflected from facet to facet and back up through the top, maximizing its fire and sparkle. In a well–proportioned diamond, the crown appears to be roughly one third of the pavilion depth. In a diamond that's cut too deep, light is lost through the sides and the center appears dark. A diamond that's cut too shallow to make it look larger appears dull.

Don't confuse cut with shape. Figure 15-2 shows various shapes: oval, pear, round brilliant, emerald, baguette, and marquise. (However, just to confuse you, a diamond may be emerald cut and an emerald may be cut like a round brilliant typical of diamond solitaires.)

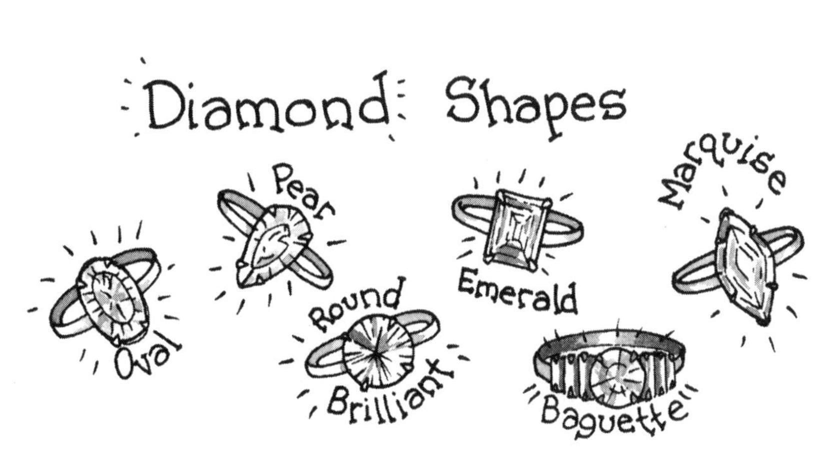

Figure 15-2: A few traditional diamond shapes. Note that straight and tapered baguettes are often used to surround and complement center stones.

Color

For some people, a diamond can never be too "white." The Gemological Institute of America (GIA) grades color starting with the letter "D" (colorless) through the alphabet to "Z" (progressively more yellow).

Some diamonds possess natural *fluorescence,* which produces a yellowish, bluish, or whitish glow when viewed in daylight or under fluorescent lights. Professional gemologists test for fluorescence to ensure that the diamond color is graded properly — otherwise a strong fluorescence may throw off the color. A stone that fluoresces blue can mask a yellow tint or make a white diamond look blue-white — a kind of bonus, actually. A white diamond that fluoresces yellow, however, can make the stone look less white, decreasing its value.

In nature, diamonds occur in virtually every color and shade — blue, pink, lavender, yellow, green, red, and even black. Known as *fancies* in the trade, colored diamonds are increasingly popular for engagement rings, and some rare colors are quite pricey.

Dirt and grease deposits can collect in and around a diamond setting, making the stone appear more yellow than it is. An old diamond ring may clean up whiter than you expect.

Clarity

Internal imperfections such as small cracks, whitish dots, or dark spots, are called *inclusions.* External flaws, such as naturals, nicks, pits, and scratches, are *blemishes.* Generally speaking, the fewer the inclusions and blemishes, the clearer and more brilliant the diamond, the rarer it is, and, of course, the more it's worth.

You can find, however, slightly imperfect stones that actually have better color and more brilliance than some flawless stones. In fact, even an I_3 diamond — the lowest category of the imperfect grade — is 97 percent clean. A perfectly "clean" stone is less important than a well-cut one. Many jewelers stress that you should *never* sacrifice cut.

While you may not be able to determine a stone's clarity with the same precision as a professional, you can judge brilliance and light and see certain imperfections by using a ten-power jeweler's *loupe,* a small magnifying glass that covers the eye.

Most jewelers in the United States grade flaws according to the GIA system, which has a large range of classifications:

- ***FL:*** *Flawless,* meaning without any surface characteristics or internal imperfections. Extremely rare.
- ***IF:*** *Internally flawless* with only minor external blemishes that can be polished away.
- **VVS_1** and **VVS_2:** *Very, very small inclusions* that are difficult for a qualified observer to detect.
- **VS_1** and **VS_2:** *Very small* inclusions visible only under magnification. Usually a good buy. As a point of reference, Tiffany sells only VS_2 diamonds or better.
- **SI_1** and **SI_2:** *Small inclusions* that are readily apparent under magnification, but not to the naked eye, making them desirable.
- **I_1, I_2,** and **I_3:** *Imperfect* grades in which the flaws may or may not be visible to the naked eye. Much lower in price and generally do not appreciate in value.

Carat weight

Gemologists measure the size of diamonds in terms of weight, specifically in carats (ct). A carat contains 100 points. Therefore, if a jeweler says, for example, that a stone weighs 25 points, it is 1/4 carat. ***Note:*** Don't confuse carats with karats (kt), which in the United States refer to gold quality.

If you ask jewelers *how large* a stone is and they tell you it has, say, "a 2-carat spread," watch out. Many diamonds are "spread," or cut with thin proportions, to maximize weight rather than brilliance. Therefore, a diamond that *spreads* 1 carat is not the same as a stone that *weighs* 1 carat. The correct way to phrase the question is, "What is the stone's exact actual weight?" The jeweler should then give you the number of carats — with no mention of the word *spread.*

We won't go so far as to say that size doesn't matter, but size is virtually meaningless outside the context of cut, clarity, and color. A large stone that's dull, flawed, or improperly cut is worth less money than a perfect little diamond. The larger a good quality diamond, however, the more it's worth.

The fifth "C" — cost

The jewelry industry has very thoughtfully devised a formula to determine how much you should spend on a diamond ring. If you really love her, they say, spending the equivalent of two months' salary is quite reasonable. While that doesn't seem outrageous to us, it does seem rather arbitrary. You surely have your own priorities and can figure out for yourselves what is appropriate.

If knowing the "norm" is of any help, you may be interested to know that according to *Modern Bride* magazine, couples spend $2,909 on average for an engagement ring, $768 for the bride's wedding ring, and $391 for the groom's.

Does CZ count?

Many imitation diamonds have appeared over the years and some have gained a large following. Known as zircon, GGG, Fabulite, and Wellington Diamond, these fakes have proven soft and/or brittle compared to the real thing. Since it was introduced in the 1970s, however, the most popular imitation has been *cubic zirconi* (known as CZ) because it was more durable and less prone to scratches and cracks than other synthetic and imitation stones. Now, however, CZ has competition from a new substance called *synthetic moissanite,* which is the second hardest gemstone next to — and more brilliant than — diamond. Synthetic moissanite has even fooled thermal testers, the standard way jewelers detect CZ.

However, synthetic moissanite costs only 10 to 20 percent less than real diamonds, making it significantly more expensive than CZ. So if wearing several thousand dollars on one little finger makes you nervous, CZ is a good alternative — at least as a back-up for day-to-day use. (We actually know many Park Avenue women who wear CZ copies of their most expensive baubles while the real thing sits in a safe and no one is the wiser.) If you want more diamond than your budget allows, but you can't bring yourself to wear CZ, synthetic diamonds, which are grown in a lab not in nature, are a good alternative.

If diamonds aren't your best friend

Although the overwhelming majority of American brides wear diamond rings, colored gemstones such as emerald, garnet, ruby, and sapphire have become increasingly popular. In fact, since ancient times, people have prized colored gems, believing they endow their owners with power, status, luck, and good health. Various stones were associated with each of the twelve tribes of Israel and the twelve apostles; Hindus and Arabs ascribed stones to the signs of the zodiac. In 1952, the jewelry industry adopted a list of birthstones, which has become the standard in America, although there are actually lists of stones for days of the week, hours of the day, states of the union, and each of the seasons. In short, if you like a stone for its color, you can find many kinds of meanings attributed to it through the ages to further justify your purchase.

While clarity is an important factor in buying a gemstone, flawlessness is a harder characteristic to find than in diamonds. A far more important consideration is color. The closer a stone comes to a pure spectral hue, the higher the quality. In other words, in a red stone, the purer the red, the better. To accurately assess a stone's true color, look at it in several types of light. After examining many ruby rings, for example, you may notice they range in hue from bluish-red to brownish-red to pink with several gradations in between. In fact, while a true ruby is corondum, some of those "rubies" may actually be from other gemstone families — beryl, garnet, spinel, tourmeline, or zircon – and (should be) priced accordingly. Certification for gemstones is not as institutionalized as with diamonds, but a jeweler should be able to verify the stone's color grade and whether the stone is natural or synthetic.

What's in a ring?

In some parts of the world, a marriage is not valid without a gold ring, but in the United States, a ring is not required nor does it validate a marriage. The majority of couples exchange them anyway. The tradition, after all, goes back as far as the Pharaohs of Egypt, who used a circular band as a symbol of eternity, which like love and happiness, has no beginning and no end. In many cultures, in fact, a circle is a sacred shape, symbolizing perfection, wholeness, the feminine, and the cycle of life.

The earliest rings were made of braided grasses, leather, bone, ivory, and lumpy bits of metal. By the middle ages metalsmiths were turning out ornate settings, and in the Renaissance rings reached new levels of complexity and intricacy.

A development in the sixteenth century was the betrothal ring, which often took the form of a gimmal ring. The ring, which is still popular today, consists of two hoops that slide together perfectly to form a single ring. Upon becoming engaged, the prospective bride and groom each take one half. The hoops are reunited at the wedding and placed on the bride's hand, symbolizing two lives coming together as one. If a third hoop is included, it symbolizes the presence of God in the marriage, and is usually entrusted to a close friend who wears it until the wedding.

Gimmal rings were often quite detailed in design, with sculpted forms representing life and death. These rings gave rise to the *fede* (or faith) ring, which featured two small gold hands clasping when the rings were joined. A third loop may have a heart or key, which the hands appeared to grasp together.

Setting Pretty

A ring's setting is like the right picture frame that sets off a masterpiece to its best advantage. The ring must also be in proportion to your hand. An elaborate setting may camouflage flaws in a stone. In fact, an illusion setting (as shown in Figure 15-3) — which looks like a little box in which the stone sits — is almost certainly a sign that there's something to hide. Particularly distinctive settings, however, may bear the designer's insignia inside the ring, whether the design is elaborate or minimalist.

Classic settings include:

- **Bezel:** Streamlined setting with no prongs. The stone sits close to the finger. May reduce appearance of brilliance because light cannot enter from the sides. Works well with two different metals such as yellow gold and platinum.
- **Carved scroll:** Victorian setting that became an international trend. Elaborate scroll work surrounds the stone.

- **Channel:** Used in mounting a number of smaller stones of uniform size in a row. (See Figure 15-3.)
- **Cluster:** A large stone surrounded by smaller stones.
- **Gypsy:** Stone lies flush with the band. Metal around the stone is much heavier than around the shank. (See Figure 15-3.)
- **Invisible:** No visible metal prongs or channels. Stones are cut and fit so precisely that no gaps exist between them. These cost more because stones must match very closely.
- **Pavé:** Small stones set together in a cluster with no metal showing through.
- **Prong:** Four or six metal "claws" grasp onto the gemstone. A six-prong setting is often called a Tiffany setting.
- **Silver cups:** Edges crimped beneath the stones to reflect light. This design originated in the late 1700s.
- **Solitaire:** A single gemstone mounted without ornamental side stones, usually with four or six prongs.
- **Tension:** Diamond appears to be almost floating, barely held in place at the girdle.
- **Tiffany:** Uses six prongs.

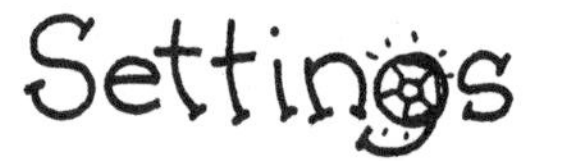

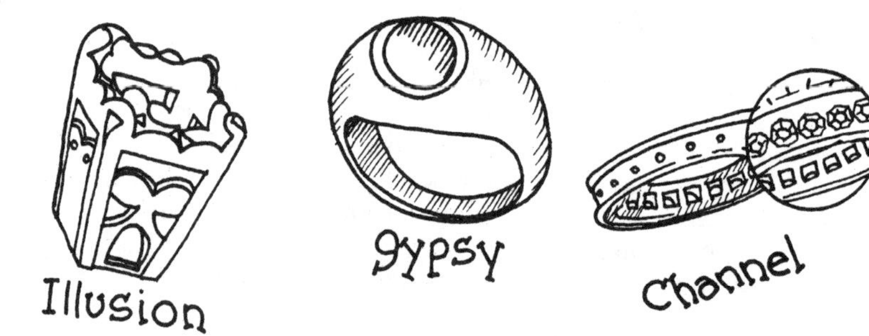

Figure 15-3: A stone can look vastly different depending on what kind of setting it is in.

Metal Matters

The metal of your ring should flatter both your skin tone and the color of the stone. You may need to weigh aesthetics against practicality. For example, 18-karat gold is a brighter yellow than 14-karat, but more expensive and not as hard. On the other hand (so to speak), 18-karat white gold is white, less likely to cause allergic reactions, and more affordable than 14-karat white.

If you can't decide whether you like yellow, white, or pink gold the best, tri-color "rolling" rings feature all three.

Whatever metal you choose, you may have the ring designed with a matte or satin finish, patterns such as delicate flowers or swirling paisleys, or detailed edgings such as *milgrain* (like tiny beads) or a soft bevel known as *comfort fit.*

One Ringy Dingy, Two Ringy Dingies

Despite the invention of gimmal rings, men rarely wore wedding rings until after World War II. Even the romance-obsessed Victorians preferred a plain gold band for women and no ring for men. Today, 98 percent of all weddings are double-ring ceremonies.

The groom's ring is usually a larger, wider version of the bride's. Although his ring may be a completely different style, like hers, his ring should slip easily over the knuckle and hug the base of the finger, leaving just enough room to slip a toothpick through to account for fingers swelling when the temperature changes.

Finding the Right Ring

Whether you decide to buy a brand-new, never-worn wedding set, or if you opt for a set with some history, searching for a ring can be an exciting experience. Like the wedding gown and the groom's ensemble, the rings you choose should be distinctly "you."

In the loop

Many couples have a special message engraved on the inside of their engagement or wedding rings. This inscription may be their initials or wedding date. Others are downright tomes requiring a fairly wide and large band. Here are some classics:

- *DODI LI V' ANI LO* (Hebrew for "I am my beloved's and my beloved is mine")
- LOVE ~ HONOR ~ CHERISH
- CONSTANCY AND HEAVEN ARE ROUND AND IN THIS EMBLEM FOUND
- I DOE RECEIVE IN THEE MY CHOYCE (from a 17th century ring)
- MAY THIS CIRCLE BE UNBROKEN
- WHOM GOD HAS JOINED TOGETHER LET NO MAN PUT ASUNDER
- PUT IT BACK ON

Actually, any finger will do

Through the ages, every digit of the hand — including the thumb, in the 17th century — has been used as the wedding ring finger. The Egyptians used the fourth finger of the left hand, believing that the *vena amoris* ran straight from that finger to the heart. That no such vein exists has not deterred people from favoring that finger for wedding rings. In fact, the English Prayer Book of 1549 specifies the left hand. Perhaps that explains why Roman Catholics used the right hand until the eighteenth century.

Buying new

As with most things in life, when it comes to buying a diamond, beware of deals. If a price sounds too good to be true, it probably is. Although you're usually safe when buying from a reputable retailer, scams do abound. These range from counterfeit or altered certificates to bait and switch advertising to deceptive pricing schemes. A legitimate jeweler should have no problem with having a ring checked out by an appraiser of your choosing.

The appraiser should be a Graduate Gemologist (G.G. degree) from the Gemological Institute of America or an F.G.A. (Fellow of the Gemological Association of Great Britain). Certification from the American Gem Society or the American Society of Appraisers is also worthy.

Whether based on an hourly rate or per carat for diamonds, appraisal fees should be posted in your face. The appraisal should be conducted in your presence and provide:

- The millimeter dimensions, quality, weight, and identification of each stone
- Cut, color, clarity, and carat weight of the diamonds
- The hue, tone, intensity, transparency, and clarity of colored stones
- Identification and assessment of metals used in mounting
- A thorough description or photograph of the item
- The estimated value of the piece

You need an appraisal for insurance. In addition, take photos of all your precious jewelry and store them in a photo-quality fire-proof box. (Color photocopies of your ring are also a good record with the added bonus that you can write on them.) Keep this photograph with a GIA grading report (often erroneously called a certificate), which is issued when the stone is finished by the diamond polisher. The report does not evaluate price, but does describe the characteristics of an unmounted diamond.

If you have a diamond, you may go a step further and get a Gemprint, a special laser image that "fingerprints" your stone. A copy is then registered with the Gemprint Central Registry in Chicago. The process takes only a few minutes, usually costs under $50 — and some insurance companies offer a 10 percent discount on annual premiums for Gemprinted diamonds.

Choosing your heirloom

Recognizing the appeal and value of antique jewelry, many jewelers have introduced *estate jewelry* departments. Bear in mind, however, that estate jewelry is not necessarily the same as *antique* (at least 100 years old); jewelry that once belonged to someone else may actually be only a few years old. The easiest and surest way to know is to check a diamond or colored gemstone certification.

If no certificate is available, the cut may date a stone. Developed in the 16th century, the *rose cut* was characterized by a flat base and facets in multiples of six. In the 18th century, the *old mine cut,* which had unprecedented brilliance and fire, was popular, and by the mid-19th century, the *old European cut* proved even more brilliant. Like today's modern brilliant cut, old mine and old European cuts (see Figure 15-4) have 58 facets. But they are not as brilliant as stones cut after the 1920s and therefore are typically appraised for less.

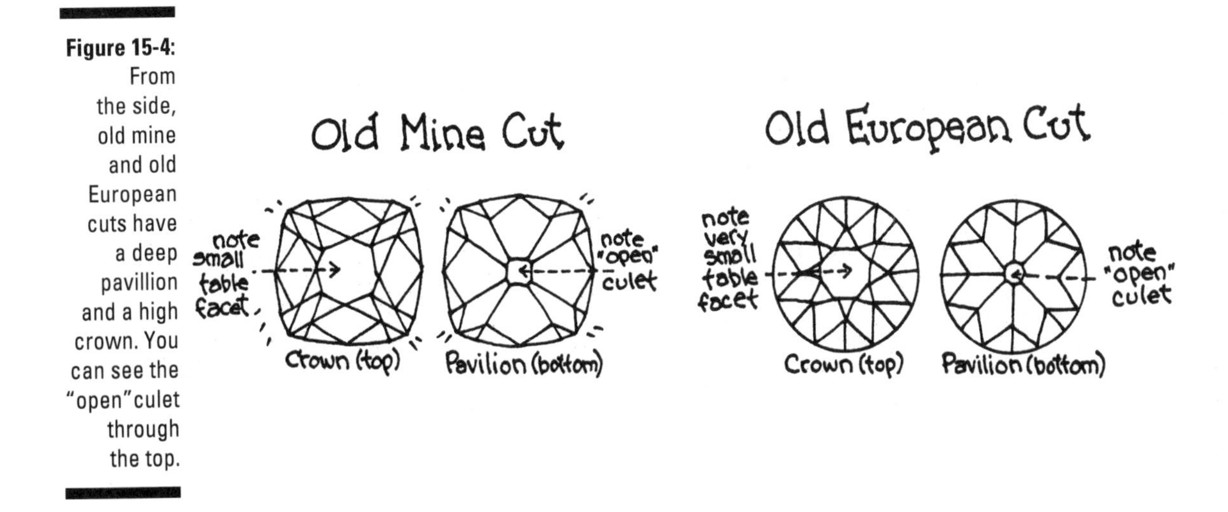

Figure 15-4: From the side, old mine and old European cuts have a deep pavillion and a high crown. You can see the "open"culet through the top.

An antique diamond ring may be an antique all right, but not a diamond. It was common in Victorian times to use paste or leaded glass gems in precious metal settings and you may need an expert to determine a stone's true identity.

While an heirloom ring may hold great sentimental value, it is not necessarily a paradigm of great taste. If the style looks dowdy, you may be able to strike a compromise by having the stones reset in a more contemporary or flattering setting. First have the stones appraised; you not only want to make sure the stones are legitimate, but you also want to check for any damage that may affect what you can do with them.

If you opt to have a new setting designed, choose a jeweler who specializes in styles you like. Unless you're absolutely sure of what you want and can provide detailed sketches of the top and side views, try on many rings of various weights and styles and clip magazine photos of rings you like. As you work with the jeweler, request a wax model so that you can make any last-minute changes before your ring is permanently cast.

Making Your Ring Last

Although it is harder than a rock, a diamond can chip or break if hit hard enough from certain angles or if the girdle is cut too thin. Avoid wearing your diamond while playing rugby, repointing your fireplace, spelunking through subterranean caves, or doing anything else where you may inadvertently whack or sully the stone.

Natural skin oils, lotions, perfume, and hair spray can gunk up your stone, etch colored gemstones, and discolor pearls. Always apply these products before putting on your jewelry. Although you can clean diamonds in a solution of equal parts water and ammonia, avoid letting other jewelry come in contact with chlorine, which can pit and discolor precious metals. To clean most jewelry, soak for a few minutes in warm sudsy water using a mild detergent, then gently scrub with a soft, small brush. Rinse and dry with a lint-free cloth. In a pinch, you can "huff" it — blow hot breath (saying, "Hah!") on it—then defog it with a lint-free cloth. Polishing or cleaning your ring ultrasonically every year greatly reduces its lifespan, but it's not a bad idea to have a jeweler check the setting every so often.

Give your rings a good dip in cleansing solution the day before your wedding so they shine like new.

Store your jewelry in separate pouches or compartments in your jewelry box, so the pieces don't collect dust or scratch or tarnish each other.

Chapter 16

Nuts and Bolts and Loose Screws

In This Chapter

- Making it legal
- Playing the name game
- Handling money matters
- Inviting children – or not

Ah, marriage — a union that is cerebral, spiritual, emotional, and mystical. As you enter this agreement with each other (and God, if you so believe), you are bound as well to the community, which means that you must plow through a mountain of paperwork, from contracts with caterers, party planners, and florists to legal documents for the town clerk, social security, and the Internal Revenue Service.

The following tidbits should help you finesse changing your names if you choose, negotiate contracts that are mutually equitable, and generally enter the marital state with some sense of what's going on. Billions of people have traversed this same path, but that doesn't mean you should take anything at face value. When in doubt, ask questions. And don't sign on any dotted lines until you're satisfied and can recite the fine print in your sleep.

License to Thrive

Like driving, fishing, or hunting, within the United States you need a state license to get married. Call the clerk of the town or city *where you're getting married* to find out about application procedures, age requirements, and familial restrictions.

Typically you can apply a few days to a couple of months before you get married, but you must have the license in hand the day of the wedding. Some states, such as New York, have a waiting period (also known as a cooling off period) from the time the license is issued to when the wedding may take place, so don't leave the license to the last minute unless you are coming to a screeching halt in front of a Las Vegas wedding chapel. (Nevada is the only state in the U.S. with no cooling off period.)

Pick up the application or have it mailed to you a few weeks ahead of time, so you can fill it out at your leisure and, if necessary, have it notarized. You both must appear in person before the town clerk, who types up the official license, which you sign in the clerk's presence. You may need to provide one or more of the following:

- **Proof of age:** This may be a birth certificate, baptismal record, passport, driver's license, life insurance policy, employment certificate, school record, immigration record, naturalization record, or court record.
- **Information regarding previous marriages:** You may have to tell how many times you've been married, the date, and why the marriage(s) ended (death, divorce, annulment), whether the former spouse is living, and when, where, and against whom the divorce or divorces were granted. You may also have to present a certified copy of your divorce decree or death certificate of your former spouse.
- **Results of blood tests or pre-marital medical examination:** Most states within the U.S. still require blood tests before you can obtain a marriage license. Ask your doctor or a local clinic for a "standard pre-wedding" blood test. What are they testing for? Mostly venereal diseases. Some states test for such varied diseases as rubella, sickle cell anemia, and infectious tuberculosis. If you don't like needles, head to a state that doesn't require blood tests: Arizona, Arkansas, Delaware, Iowa, Kansas, Kentucky, Maine, Maryland, Minnesota, Missouri, Nevada, New York, North Dakota, South Carolina, South Dakota, Tennessee, or Texas.

Before you pay your nominal license fee, check what form of payment is accepted; some states, for example, take only money orders, others take only cash. At the wedding, your witnesses sign the form, which the officiant then sends back to the town clerk, so the official certificate can be completed.

Solving Your Identity Crisis

Deciding what to call yourselves after your marriage is not the simple wife-changes-her-name-to her-husband's scenario it once was. Although most newspapers still feel compelled to note when "the bride is keeping her name," upon marriage a woman's surname does not automatically change to her husband's, nor is she legally *required* to change it. A woman must choose to change it and then take certain measures to make the change official (that is, legal). A woman who retains her birth name is still entitled to a portion of her husband's pension, social security, or other rights associated with the marriage contract the same way as a woman who changes her name.

Names are important symbols of our identity. Before changing yours, consider what the change means. At one end of the spectrum are traditionalists who insist that a woman's taking her husband's name is an honor and a privilege and any woman who doesn't is selfish, subversive, and probably not such good wife material. At the other end are people who find the idea of a woman dropping her birth-name to become Mrs. So-and-So tantamount to erasing her identity and creating an imbalance of power in the marriage. In the middle are people who feel that getting married is such a transformative act that creating a new name for both the bride and groom is properly symbolic of their identity as a married couple. These days a variety of options are both possible and socially acceptable. These include:

- The bride takes the groom's name.
- The bride keeps her birth name.
- The bride keeps her birth name for professional circumstances, but takes her husband's name in all other cases.
- The bride and groom use both their last names, with or without a hyphen.
- The bride uses both her birth and married surnames, with or without a hyphen.
- The bride and groom append each other's name to their own.
- The groom drops his name and takes the bride's.
- The bride and groom meld their names.
- The bride and groom pick out a new name altogether.

The Spanish solution to married names is to link the husband and wife's names with *y*. For example: Maria Hinojosa y García and Roberto García y Hinojosa.

You should decide by the time of your wedding what names you will use legally, professionally, and socially. If you change your names, start with social security to make it official — it's hard to get any other institution to acknowledge your new identity until Big Brother does. You can apply for a new card in person or by mail. In the U.S., call your local social security office (800-772-1213) for instructions. The next stop after that should be your driver's license.

Before you're married, when you get your marriage license, order an extra copy or two because you must submit an original copy — not a photocopy — when applying for a new social security card and driver's license. That way, if you mail your marriage certificate in with your social security form, you don't have to worry about your only bona fide copy returning to you in several pieces or stained with coffee rings or forever disappearing into the bureaucratic black hole.

Once you have your new social security card and driver's license, you're ready to update all your other legal and financial records. Just when you think you've changed every last one, you're sure to discover another. After you start, you must change everything, otherwise you leave yourself vulnerable to such annoyances as nasty notices from the IRS and canceled plane tickets because the name on your passport doesn't match. Here are a few things you need to change:

- Bank accounts (order new checks, too)
- Business cards
- Credit cards
- Frequent flier programs
- Income tax forms
- Insurance policies (again, change your beneficiaries)
- Passport
- Retirement accounts (change your beneficiaries as well)
- Stationery
- Voter registration card
- Your employer's accounting office and office manager

If your marriage coincides with one or both of you moving to a new address, update your address where necessary.

Take a copy of your marriage license with you when you travel or have to sign anything official, such as the papers in closing a home sale.

Handling Those Wedding-Bell Bills

For every vendor you hire for your wedding, you should have a *written* contract that specifies the deposit paid and the amount due. If you are dealing with professionals (which we hope you are), the contract should contain a list delineating the specific services agreed upon. If you are dealing with a friend or relative, have at the very least a letter of agreement spelling out the service(s) to be provided. Make no exceptions. Verbal agreements are legally binding, but subject to amnesia and harder to prove in court. At any rate, the point is certainly not to prepare for possible lawsuits but rather to make your wedding day as flawless as possible.

Contracts should be as specific as possible. Instead of "rose bouquets" say, "three nosegays of yellow and orange roses, hand-tied with pale yellow satin ribbon; one hand-tied bridal bouquet of pink, yellow, and ivory roses, hand-tied with ivory satin ribbon." List any possible substitutions as well. For example, "If roses are unavailable we will substitute a yellow flower of similar size."

Most businesses have their own formal contracts, but if a vendor fails to produce one, you may want to take it upon yourself to draft a letter or contract detailing the goods or services you have ordered, the pertinent details of your wedding, and the amount you expect to pay. Ask the vendor to sign a copy; if the vendor refuses, find a new one. You don't want to do business with people who are not willing to take responsibility for their work.

Before signing a contract, read it carefully and don't be shy about writing in additions or changes. However, ask vendors how they want that done so that a legal feeding frenzy does not ensue. The vendor and you must both initial all changes before signing. Never sign a partially or entirely blank contract. A vendor may try to expedite things by saying the details can be filled in later. Don't assume they have criminal motives — they may just in fact be trying to expedite matters — but you are nonetheless better off waiting or finding a different vendor.

If you and a vendor discuss changes by telephone or e-mail, you need to follow up with an actual letter reiterating the changes. Keep a copy for your files. In fact, keep *all* receipts and copies of contracts in your wedding file. You will need to refer to them several times before and after the wedding.

Depending on the type of vendor, your contract should include:

- Business name, address, and phone number
- Contact person
- The person responsible for your event
- A complete description of the product or service
- The quantity you are ordering
- The number of people to be served
- Date and time service or product is to be available
- Exact prices for product
- Date and time service is to end
- Where and at what time product is to be delivered or set up
- Fees for delivery and set up
- When overtime begins and the fee per hour or half hour

- Policies regarding returns, postponement, or cancellation
- Price escalation policies and when quoted rates expire
- Payment plans such as layaway or three payments
- Acceptable payment methods (check, cash, credit card, or certified cashier's check)
- Whether gratuities are included or expected
- Business representative's signature and date
- Your signature and date

Fork over a little at a time

Giving a deposit is actually in your interest: It tells vendors that you're serious and further commits them to your event. While most contracts you've probably encountered don't require you to pay in full until all goods or services have been delivered to your satisfaction, the event world runs a little differently. Many suppliers insist on full payment before the day of your wedding and specify so contractually.

After you pay a deposit and sign a contract, you are legally bound to pay in full.

As you make deposits, update your wedding budget. If you pay with a check, make a note on the memo line exactly what the deposit is for. For example, "50% of wedding cake." Paying deposits with credit cards is also a good idea because if the vendor fails to deliver, goes out of business before your wedding date, or commits some error— and you can convince the credit card company of that — the charges may be reversed. Buyers' remorse does not qualify for a reversal of charges.

If you cancel or postpone your wedding, don't expect a full refund of your various deposits. Some businesses charge 50 percent of their estimated fee regardless of the reason you cancel. They may have turned away other business on your wedding date; your deposit compensates them for this loss. Some vendors return deposits if you cancel because of a death in the family or if they are able to rebook the date and recoup the revenue. If you don't cancel but merely postpone, you may face a price increase.

Are gratuities gratuitous?

Rare is the person who does not appreciate a little something extra. Any service person who soars beyond your expectations — such as a waiter who loads and unloads a truck at your tent site — deserves more than a "Thanks, pal" at the end of the event. Even those who merely meet your expectations should get a token of your gratitude.

If you really appreciate the job someone does for you, put it in writing. Most vendors make their living based on referrals and recommendations. A letter of praise or recommendation may help a vendor get the next job or a service worker get promoted. Often these are more valuable than a cash tip. But if there is some unfinished business you also need to take care of — some overtime fees, for example, or a small complaint ("Please, however, do something about that leak in the ladies room. . . .") — put that under separate cover. Such non sequiturs make the letter unusable for a media kit unless the vendor gets busy with the correction fluid.

Houses of worship usually require a fee or "donation" that covers the use of the facilities. In addition, the best man should give something extra to the officiant. Rabbis or ministers who perform ceremonies outside a house of worship almost always charge a fee, which should be paid before the ceremony, if possible, to avoid any awkwardness.

Judges are allowed to accept money for performing wedding ceremonies, although every county and municipality has its own regulations regarding how much they can accept. Tipping judges seems rather odd, but you may show your appreciation by making a donation in their name to the charity of their choice, or by buying them an appropriate gift.

Only in Florida, Maine, and South Carolina can Notary publics perform marriages, and they generally do so for a small fee. As with judges, a charitable donation in their name may be appropriate.

For such vendors as caterers, florists, photographers, and wedding planners, a monetary tip may seem inappropriate, especially if the person also owns the business. In such cases, you're better off giving something that is both useful and luxurious, such as a silk scarf or wine.

Several top catering managers we've talked to feel adamant that tipping should be based solely on merit and that a percentage standard is not only degrading for head waiters and banquet managers, but also detrimental for consumers because it can lead to subtle forms of pre-wedding blackmail: "If you want your wedding to go well, you better tip these five people *x* amount." They say that if you are really blown away by someone's performance (and only then), you may tip.

Before you start palming bucks and extra checks, read over your contracts and final bills to make sure that a gratuity is not already included. Union operations, for example, have a built-in gratuity that is distributed equitably among the waiters, bartenders, bus boys, and so on. Ask your banquet manager how the gratuity is distributed before you dump tips on people willy nilly.

You won't find any hard-and-fast rules regarding how much to tip. In fact, this topic is highly subjective. Table 16-1 provides some guidelines, which may vary depending on your area, the level of service, and the number of people served.

Table 16-1: Tipping Guidelines

Recipient	*Amount*
Banquet captains	$50 to $150 based on merit and number of guests
Banquet manager	$100 to $300 based on merit and number of guests
Bathroom attendants	$1 to $2 per guest or a flat fee arranged with venue management
Bride's dresser	15 to 20 percent of fee
Caterer	15 to 20 percent of food cost, to be split among staff, for extra special service
Chef	$0.50 to $1 per guest
Civil ceremony officiant	$15 to $25, if appropriate
Clergyperson	$25 and up, depending on the size of the wedding
Club manager	$100 to $300 based on merit and number of guests
Coatroom attendants	$1 to $2 per guest or a flat fee arranged with venue management
Cooks	$20 each
Hairdresser	10 to 20 percent of fee, depending on number of heads
Hotel chambermaid	$1 to $2 a day
Maitre d' or head waiter	$50 to $200 based on merit and number of guests; or 20 percent of the total bill to be distributed among all the waiters and captains
Makeup person	10 to 20 percent of fee, depending on number of faces
Musicians (ceremony)	15 percent of fee
Musicians (reception)	$25 to $50 per member, especially if guests make a number of requests
Parking attendants	$1 to $2 per car; or 15 percent of bill for valet parking
Photographer	$100 for extraordinary service if service is on a flat rate with no overtime fee
Tailor	10 percent of fee

Recipient	Amount
Transportation driver	15 percent for bus; 18 to 20 percent for limo
Waiters and bartenders	$15 to $25
Wedding planner	15 percent of fee; 15 to 20 percent if charged hourly or just for the wedding day

Plan your tip distribution scheme beforehand and bring along extra cash or checks for surprise niceties. Ask your wedding planner to distribute both payment checks and gratuities for you. If you don't have a planner, give checks for everyone who expects to be paid before they begin (bands, for example) to the banquet manager or another person in charge, and gratuities to your best man or maid of honor. As we previously explained in this chapter, withholding payment until afterward is not only legally worthless, it is also logically silly. You will look rather graceless sitting down at the end of your wedding, as the band is packing up and waiters are stripping the tables, to scribble a bunch of checks. Such a scene can also be detrimental to your bottom line: It's easy to get carried away when you're on the spot, not wanting to look like a cheapskate.

Tip bathroom and coatroom attendants ahead of time with the understanding that they should refrain from accepting any gratuities and should politely explain that the matter has been taken care of by the hosts. (Some places put a sign up to this effect.) And under no circumstances should you have a tip jar anywhere on the premises. This should go without saying, but just in case, reiterate to the powers that be how crazy the sight of one would make you.

The sky is falling! The sky is falling!

If you are the sort who always sees the glass not only half-empty but also cracked in six places, you may consider taking out a wedding insurance policy. The Fireman's Fund Insurance Company underwrites Weddingsurance, which covers postponement, photographs, dress/attire, gifts, additional expenses, personal liability, and medical payments.

Is the one-time premium worth it? Like all insurance, it may seem like money down the drain until something goes horribly wrong. But read the fine print. Weddingsurance, for example, pays for postponement or cancellation only in cases when nonrefundable expenses are incurred due to circumstances beyond your control. These include sickness or bodily injury to the bride or groom or anyone *essential* (whatever that means) to the wedding party, damage or inaccessibility to the premises where the wedding or reception is to be held, loss or damage to the bridal gown or other wedding attire, corporate or military posting, or job loss. Change of heart, not surprisingly, is not covered.

Kiddie Komplications

One of the wonderful things about weddings is that they can bring many generations together under one roof. On the other hand, you may not be delighted to have screaming infants punctuating your vows, or paying for even the most adorable Shirley Temple clone to take up a seat at your reception.

Whether to invite children to your wedding is one of the more emotional issues you may face during your pre-marital meanderings. As you may have noticed, people can get positively fierce when it comes to their little darlings. So what are your choices and once you make your decisions how do you impart them most graciously?

While you may have committed Chapter 13 of this book to memory, don't count on your guests being versed in the nuances of invitation addressing. (In other words, that they will realize that if children's names are omitted, they have not been invited.) Once you have made your decision, be firm when people call and ask if the exclusion was an oversight. The easiest way to start an all-out family war is to cave in and make an exception for some children but not others. Specifying an age cut-off is difficult. If you have young ladies and gentlemen involved in your ceremony as junior ushers and bridesmaids, they will undoubtedly be crushed if they are not invited to the reception. What's more, depending on your families, you may be pressured to invite other relatives of the same age if you are including these kids. And for an evening reception, trying to have any children whisked away at their "witching" hour without having to bid farewell to their parents is next to impossible. One solution may be to arrange a small room adjacent to your reception where this age group can be deposited to nap until their parents are ready to leave.

After you have put together your preliminary guest list and before you embark on your venue search, count the possible number of children and adolescents. When interviewing caterers or banquet managers, find out what kind of a price break you can get for these "non adult" meals. But do this early in your negotiations — you may not be able to change the terms of your contract at the last minute.

Banning children at destination weddings is tricky. Many people will not travel without their children, and consequently may refuse your invitation. One way to please everyone is to include children at surrounding events (see Chapter 17) and hire a babysitter during the wedding itself. It is up to you to pick up the tab for this sitter as well as arrange to have the children in one place, fed, and properly cared for.

Just in Case the "For Worse" Part Kicks In

What lovelier time to think about accidents, catastrophes, and even death than when you're getting married? But being responsible for someone else and doing everything you can to protect that person is a big part of marriage. We're not saying that you have to sell the motorcycle and give up bungee jumping, but you do need to think about what may happen should you or your spouse become disabled or die. The sooner you square away your insurance coverage and wills, the better you can sleep at night — resting up, no doubt, for that bronco-riding contest.

Run for coverage

Insurance protects you from catastrophic expenses (accident, illness, or death) as well as from the cost of day-to-day curve balls life throws you (fire, theft, and broken legs). If you've been operating in the adult world for a while, you may be covered in one way or another. But getting married may qualify you for savings or make some policies redundant. Review them all, comparison shop for better deals, and update your beneficiaries. The major types of insurance you should consider are:

- **Auto:** Rates are usually lower for married drivers, so put all your cars on one policy. Consider taking high deductibles to keep your premiums low.
- **Health:** If you're both covered by employers, compare your costs and benefits. Doing so is especially important if you plan to have children or already have them.
- **Life:** Should you or your spouse die, you need enough coverage to replace your after-tax income, and perhaps pay for major debts or expenditures such as mortgage and college tuition for your children. Low-cost term life policies, where you pay an annual premium for a set amount of insurance, are generally better deals than more expensive cash-value policies, which combine life insurance with a putative "savings account." You're usually better off paying a modest premium and having a separate tax-deferred savings plan such as a 401(k) or IRA that earns you more money.
- **Property:** All those wedding gifts and new furniture — and don't forget rings — need to be figured into your renter's or homeowner's policy. Besides protecting your assets, you also want to be insured for liability in case someone is ever injured or killed in your home.

While you're updating your renter's/homeowner's policy, document your property by photographing or videotaping rooms and valuable items. Keep a written inventory of your belongings on a computer or in a folder with receipts for major purchases and other vital documents. Keep copies at a location away from your home.

Where there's a will

If you have children, you must have a will to name a guardian for them, but you don't need (and shouldn't) wait until the first junior comes along to prepare a will. You don't need an attorney; you can hire a paralegal or do it yourself using a software package such as WillMaker or Nolo's Living Trust. To make it valid, just have three witnesses sign the document. If you update your will, which you should from time to time, you need to have it signed again.

This is also a good time to discuss a *living will,* which gives power of attorney to someone you trust to decide with a physician your medical care options, including whether to withhold extraordinary life support measures.

Love means never having to say, "You owe me"

Believe it or not, prenuptial agreements are not just for the Ivana and Marla and Donald Trumps of the world. They may have a bad rap, but prenups need not (and should not) be a divorce rehearsal. The main purpose for premarital contracting is to sort out financial issues — the percentage of your incomes you both will contribute to a mutual savings account, inheritance rights, control of assets you owned before marriage. Some people even use them for setting guidelines for merging step families, having children, and delegating household duties.

Such delineations may seem like overkill, but some couples find that putting issues in writing helps them communicate their own needs and desires before they become unresolvable problems. Sometimes, many of the issues hashed out in prenup preparation become simply private pledges rather than part of a legally binding document.

That said, don't underestimate the possible psychological repercussions of a prenup. Before you broach the subject, ask yourself whether such an agreement is worth the effect it may have on your relationship.

If you decide to negotiate a premarital contract, instruct your lawyers to write the agreement in plain English as opposed to legalese and include an amendment clause. Sign it before you're swamped with wedding preparations because an agreement signed under duress may not hold up in court. And remember that you're not auditioning for *LA Law;* be flexible and certain that every negotiation reflects your love for each other.

Part V
3-2-1, Blast Off!

"After all that planning and preparation it seems inappropriate to have a sign that says 'JUST' married."

In this part . . .

When the time comes for attending your various parties and showers, creating your actual wedding-day schedule, or planning your honeymoon (or wedding!) get-away, some expert advice may be just what you need. The chapters included in this part can help you comprehend the protocol and handle even the most trying details with grace.

Chapter 17

Warming Up, Cooling Down, and Looking Back

In This Chapter

- Lathering up for your shower
- "Batching it" one last time
- Favoring your guests

Your wedding reception is the culmination of a joyous time of feasting and festivities. You may find yourselves being honored at several events, including engagement parties, showers, and bachelor/bachelorette parties. In this chapter, we help you figure out the rules and invite you to invent traditions of your own.

Life would be grand if all you had to do was bask in the glow of your engaged state. But you are, of course, in the throes of planning a wedding, and one of the many things on your To Do list is coming up with unique guest favors. In this chapter, we also offer ideas for mementos that guests are sure to treasure.

Send a note and a gift thanking anyone who hosts a party for you.

Opening Rounds: Engagement Parties

Making it official that you are going to get married can be as formal or informal as you wish.

Although you (or your parents) may announce your engagement in a newspaper (see Chapter 13), mailing printed engagement announcements may be seen as a "send gifts" alert, and neither engagements nor engagement parties are occasions for gifts. Writing personal notes to or calling friends and relatives you want to inform personally, however, qualifies as a sign of affection.

Under no circumstances should you place a newspaper announcement of your engagement if either of you is still legally married.

Traditionally, the bride's parents held the first engagement party. If that wasn't feasible, the duty fell to the groom's parents. Nowadays, friends of the couple often honor the couple with a shindig, particularly if the couple lives far away from their parents or if complicated family relationships make it awkward for the parents to throw a party.

Everyone who is invited to the engagement party should be invited to the wedding, if the same people are hosting both. (Otherwise guests may wonder what they did at the first party to keep them from being invited to the wedding). Exceptions can be made in two circumstances: when the engagement party is significantly larger than the wedding; and when friends or relatives who have no control over the wedding guest list host the engagement party. Such events may be as simple as an at-home dinner with your families followed by a round of toasts. Or they may be a major to-do, complete with themed entertainment and foods. The most common scenario is a party at someone's home. Invitations, which may be formal or stylized, should not use the words "engagement party," but rather invite guests to a party "in honor of" (see Chapter 13).

Shower Power

The bridal shower is said to have started a few centuries ago with a poor yet beautiful girl in Holland whose father had betrothed her to a prosperous pig farmer. Her father, miser that he was, refused to give her a dowry if she married the honorable but penniless miller she was in love with. Although the community wasn't exactly loaded, people were so touched by the couple's obvious love for each other that they took matters into their own hands. They "showered" the bride with small, useful gifts, adding up to even more than her dowry would have been, so that she and her beloved could marry and set up house.

The bridal shower today has evolved from this endearing apocryphal anecdote into a dreaded social obligation. For most women we know, shower invitations bring to mind not an exhilarating time of female bonding but rather an afternoon or evening spent bored to tears. But your shower doesn't have to be a dud. Assuming that you can be perfectly honest with your maid of honor, you may offer these alternatives:

- **Interactive shower:** Make the shower interactive and co-ed. For example, put together balanced teams for a volley ball, softball, or touch football game. Or have a modern "barn-raising" by chipping in for some funky furniture for the couple — two end tables and a coffee table for example — and spend an afternoon sanding, staining, and stenciling as a collective gift. Accompany with finger foods, beer, and wine.

- **Progressive dinner shower:** The host rents a mini-van to take everyone to a different restaurant for each course. Presents are sent ahead of time to your last stop, where the opening of the gifts is the finale. Hint: Make reservations at all your stops.
- **Theater shower:** Everyone chips in for block of theater or concert tickets. After the show, you all descend on your favorite pub or coffee bar for a critique and dessert.

According to tradition, the maid of honor throws the bride a shower. (We like to see the other attendants chip in, but as the bride you usually should keep your nose out of such intricacies.) For a relative to host this party is way un-cool; it looks as if your family is conspiring with you to amass booty. Consequently, if a relative such as your sister or mother is your maid of honor, someone else needs to throw the shower. (Your family may have other opportunities to host events closer to the wedding.)

Unless a surprise shower appeals to you, make it clear from the outset that you are not being coy — you really prefer not to be surprised. After the hostess tells you of her plans, be as helpful as possible, supplying a typed guest list with correct names, addresses, and phone numbers. If you are going to be "showered" more than once, cross-check the lists so the same people are not invited and consequently not overburdened with buying too many gifts.

Showers are thrown three to six weeks before the wedding; invitations for the shower should go out after those for the wedding.

Unlike engagement parties, showers do call for gifts, so invitations should go only to people who are invited to the wedding. The exception is when people from your work, school, club, or other part of your life throw a shower. In these cases, the groom may also be the guest of honor. In fact, many women who boycott girls-only showers are happy to attend co-ed ones.

On the Saturday before the wedding, some Jewish communities have an *ufruf* or *aufruf* — a "calling up" for the groom. In synagogue, the groom is given the honor of being called up to read the blessings before and after the Torah (Hebrew Bible) readings. Many congregations have modernized their services to call up both the bride and groom. Afterward, the congregation sings a congratulatory song as they shower the couple with small packages of candy, nuts, and raisins.

Letting Down Your Hair

Drink, my buddies, drink with discerning
Wedlock's a lane where there is no turning;
Never was owl more blind than lover;
Drink and be merry, lads; and think it over.

— Bachelor party toast

The original bachelor parties were thrown by a group of unmarried friends to give the poor soul about to be incarcerated a stipend of drinking money for the future, when his new wife would make him account for every cent. Before the party ended, they nonetheless offered a toast in honor of the bride, and smashed their glasses so they would never be used for a toast of less import.

The best man now is responsible for throwing the bachelor party (usually with the ushers), but it does fall to the groom to dictate the sort of event he feels comfortable attending. Clichés abound that you're supposed to take this one last shot at freedom to the extreme, making crude jokes about the female gender, playing air guitar in your skivvies, mooning passing cars, ogling strippers, swigging beer till you puke, or doing things your buddies may blackmail you with for the rest of your married life. Perhaps because women have made good on their threats to have equally raunchy bachelorette soirees or because many men today have reached a higher state of consciousness, this kind of primal exhibition has become less popular.

Men have other options with which to "send off" one of their own — options that can actually be more fun. You may even include your father and future father-in-law to join the fun and chronicle a PG-rated episode of male bonding on film or video to show the grandchildren — and you don't have to hide any evidence or change any names to protect the innocent. Here are some possibilities:

- **Road trip:** Take a train or rent a mini-van and drive to a nearby city for a weekend of museums, galleries, movies, rock concerts, and junk food.
- **Team spirit:** Really take the plunge by jumping out of a plane together (take skydiving lessons the first day and a group dive the second day). Or go on a wilderness trek with an experienced guide over a long weekend. Or learn to cook a seven-course Chinese banquet, and then sit down to an extravagant table.
- **Tennis tourny:** Participants are "seeded" and trophies are awarded during dinner at a clubby restaurant.
- **Virtual reality round up:** Start with pizza and beer, then head for a virtual reality arcade. A great way to get those pre-wedding ya-yas out of your system.

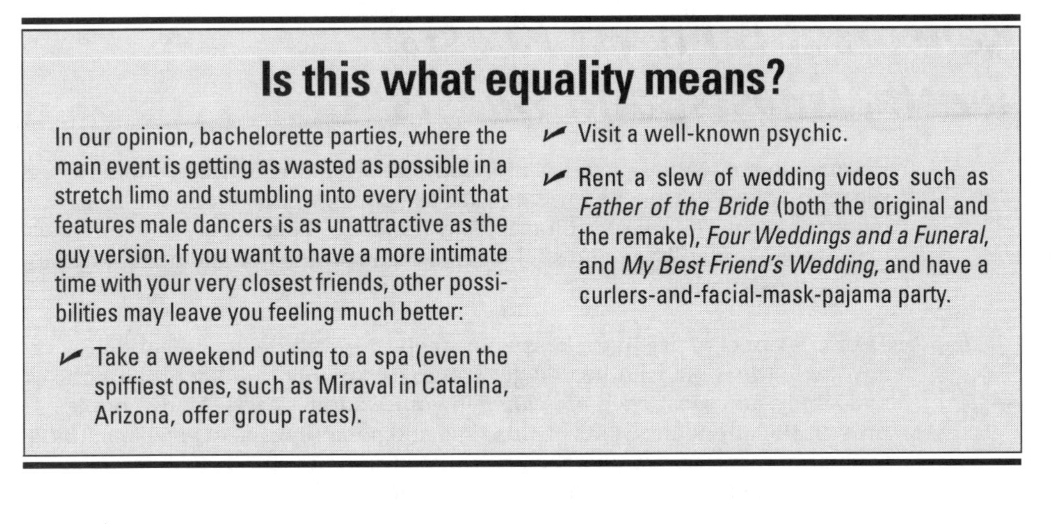

Is this what equality means?

In our opinion, bachelorette parties, where the main event is getting as wasted as possible in a stretch limo and stumbling into every joint that features male dancers is as unattractive as the guy version. If you want to have a more intimate time with your very closest friends, other possibilities may leave you feeling much better:

- Take a weekend outing to a spa (even the spiffiest ones, such as Miraval in Catalina, Arizona, offer group rates).
- Visit a well-known psychic.
- Rent a slew of wedding videos such as *Father of the Bride* (both the original and the remake), *Four Weddings and a Funeral,* and *My Best Friend's Wedding,* and have a curlers-and-facial-mask-pajama party.

Waiting until the night before your wedding to have a bachelor party is risky (unless you like the idea of getting married completely exhausted), but having your bash any earlier is a problem when ushers and other close friends are coming from out of town. An alternative is to have the bachelor party the day of the wedding — a softball game and barbecue, a golf outing ending with a club lunch, or a treasure hunt of the town, ending at a great brunch spot. These activities are also a terrific antidote to the groom's wedding day anxiety attacks.

Attending to Your Attendants

Brides often hold an intimate luncheon or tea to thank their attendants for their services. Inviting both your mother and the groom's as well as a few close female relatives is thoughtful. Holding this party the week before the wedding or on the afternoon of the wedding (if the ceremony and reception are in the evening) is usually the most convenient. Whether you have this event at home or at a restaurant, you can go all-out on the table decor as you have only one table to worry about.

A myriad of antique or pottery teapots paired with hand-painted cups and a few tiered cake stands filled with truffles, cookies, petit fours, and tea sandwiches — all served on a quilt or over lace, puts the group in a most divine lady-like mood. Invitations may even ask the group to "Come to the Mad Hatter's Tea Party." A table of Alices In Wonderland can be a charmed afternoon for a stressed-out group, if they are willing to play along. You may prefer to give your attendants their thank-you gifts at this event rather than at the rehearsal dinner.

Rehearsal Dinners: Roasts, Toasts, Ghosts, and Boasts

Because the rehearsal dinner is more intimate than the actual wedding reception and everyone is buzzing with anticipation, this meal can be an emotional tour de force, with both teary toasts to the memory of loved ones who are no longer living and slightly ribald anecdotes not suitable for more public consumption.

Take this opportunity to express your deepest gratitude and affection to anyone in the room who helped get you to this point. Thank your parents and family, and toast each *individual* in your wedding party. Many couples present the attendants' gifts at this time and sometimes also give something to their parents. Sometimes the bride and groom present these gifts in tandem, to make clear that it is from both of them.

Showing a this-is-your-life video or slide show (that friends have put together) at the rehearsal dinner can make the whole evening, especially if the video includes secret interviews with your dry cleaner, personal trainer, parking garage attendant, grammar school teachers, and so on. You may also turn the idea around with a slide show of candid photos of family and friends taken over the years.

The guest list for the rehearsal or pre-nuptial dinner can be as complicated as that for the wedding. This gathering may be limited to just the wedding party and very close family members or it may comprise all of the out-of-town guests. If people are traveling a great distance to be with you, show them the utmost hospitality, entertaining them the night before the wedding and perhaps the day after with a farewell brunch. Putting welcome baskets in their hotel rooms lets them know how pleased you are that they made the trip. (The welcome baskets we describe in Chapter 19 work perfectly for this situation.)

Because the guest list — and the expense — for the rehearsal dinner can balloon out of proportion, and because you don't want this event to compete with the wedding itself, you may want to keep the rehearsal dinner very informal. Some ethnic cuisine restaurants such as Mexican, Chinese, or Italian can be an economical way to feed a lot of people in a festive atmosphere. The dinner may also be a simple barbecue or picnic. Offer such touches as personalized fortune cookies or chopsticks with your names and wedding date (both items made by novelty companies). On another theme, napkin "wedding" rings made of bread and a menu of exotic, colorful pastas can be festive.

Having it both ways

Because we live in New York, our getting married in Maine meant that all of our guests were coming from far away, many of them descending on Bar Harbor the night before the wedding. We wanted our wedding weekend to be, more than anything, a chance to spend time with family and friends, some of whom we hadn't seen in years (decades, even). Inviting 100 people to a rehearsal dinner seemed redundant, so we scheduled the rehearsal two nights before the wedding (Thursday) and took our guests out on a Friday-night boat cruise. Although this arrangement put a little more pressure on the wedding party to come a day earlier, once they were there, they didn't mind at all. And the boat ride accomplished our goal of "warming up" the crowd — people drank beer, ate good food, sang songs, made new friends, and reconnected with old ones as we sailed, literally, into the sunset.

In the past, if the bride's family picked up the tab for the wedding, the groom's family did so for the rehearsal dinner. Now the rehearsal dinner cost may be split, depending on the other financial arrangements, who is being invited, and whether you (or a friend) have arranged an alternative event for any out-of-town guests while you are with the wedding party and close family at the rehearsal dinner.

The invitations for this dinner may be straightforward or cute. Because many of the guests may not be rehearsing, you may invite them to a "pre-nuptial" dinner or ask them to *"Celebrate with us the night before Beany and Cecil's wedding . . . ."* (See Chapter 13.) Making the rehearsal dinner a bit funky can help loosen you up for the big day — consider sending beach party invitations in the shape of a large shell, tucking invitations to a Chinese dinner in colorful take-out containers, or wrapping an invitation for a barbecue around a can of baked beans and sending it in a padded envelope or box.

Wrapping Up

Often, if you have a large number of out-of-town guests catching planes or driving long distances home, a relative may host a goodbye breakfast or brunch the day after the wedding. These are best planned as light buffets — breads, cheeses, fruits, juices, omelets, individual quiches and the like. The invitation may be included with your main wedding invitation if the same guests are invited (see Chapter 13), or simply be a phone call. Because people are on different schedules (and you may drop by for only a short time if at all), schedule these events over a few hours — *"Drop in and have a bite 9:30-1:00,"* for example. Obviously, seating is not assigned and tables should be constantly cleared and re-set.

Do Your Guests a Favor

While sending guests off from your reception with a small gift is a lovely gesture, finding the right item that is neither too cheap nor too grand can be difficult. With wedding memorabilia, the line between cute and kitsch can be mighty thin. We were reminded of this not long ago when we came across an ad for the "perfect wedding favor" in the back of a bridal magazine — a customized air freshener with the couple's invitation reproduced on it. If you either can't or don't decide to spend the money to give your guests something they may actually save until they get to their car, you should forego giving anything at all — it's not necessary. With a little creativity, however, you can probably find or make the perfect party favor. Our suggestions:

- The traditional candied almonds, symbolizing the bitter and the sweet of marriage, but packaged creatively to evoke your own wedding style (for example, small tins with calligraphed "labels" that double as place cards)
- Dream pillows, a Native American concept, with a handwritten note explaining their use (to be kept under your pillow to invoke specific dreams) and thanking guests for coming
- If your wedding has a floral theme such as daisies or roses, a full-size plant in a terra-cotta pot with a note on care and treatment
- Herb plants such as basil or sage in a terra cotta pot, with a printed card of your favorite recipe
- Whole miniature wedding cakes, large enough to be a dessert portion, packaged in white glossy boxes and tied with chiffon ribbons
- Small boxes made of sugar filled with tiny chocolates and packaged in beribboned white boxes
- A tin of assorted homemade cookies in the shapes of tiered wedding cakes bells, and rings
- A two-, four-, or six-pack of boutique beers with a label dedicating the brew to the bride and groom
- Homemade preserves or chutneys in Mason jars with hand-written labels
- Bottles of wine with a custom label from a small vineyard (these should be full size bottles; what can a couple do with a half bottle or split — rinse their mouths?)
- A framed portrait of each couple or single guest to take home with them (See "The corner photo booth" in Chapter 12.)
- A ceremony program with a leather bookmark or a metal page-keeper that is embossed with your wedding date
- A pair of hand-painted champagne flutes
- Small topiary trees in faux antiqued pots

Certain party favors must come in pairs. Giving guests (whether couples or single) a lone champagne glass or bottle of beer is beyond useless — it's too sad to contemplate.

If favors are not part of your tabletop decor, the best way to distribute them to guests is as they are leaving the reception. Put the favors in small shopping bags with pretty tissue paper, and have a waiter hand one to each guest. In cold weather, the coatroom attendant may hand them a bag with their coats. Putting the bags on guests' chairs is rarely convenient; the bags end up on the floor, getting trampled every time someone gets up from the table.

For a wedding that ends in the wee hours of the morning, send your guests off with a special favor — a goody bag containing the early edition of the next day's newspaper and some ready-to-eat breakfast fare. Bagels and cream cheese, a mini-loaf of sourdough bread and a wedge of good cheese, or tiny croissants, breakfast pastries, and a small pot of jam are sure to be appreciated.

Nobody goes home empty-handed

Michael and I spent months scouring flea markets (our favorite pastime) and amassing elegant but inexpensive antique flower vases, candlesticks, and picture frames (for the table numbers) to outfit our "funky rustic chic" table tops. Every table at our wedding dinner glowed with a different combination of pressed and cut glass, pewter, and wrought iron accessories. Each setting had a menu and on the back of three menus at each table I wrote discreetly, "Vase!" or "Candlesticks!" or "Frame!" We assigned guests to tables but not to specific seats at each table, so everyone had an equal chance of going home with a memento.

Chapter 18

The Wedding Day: Spontaneity on Schedule

In This Chapter

- Creating a seamless flow of events
- Cueing the players
- Laying it out in black and white

Whether you have hired a wedding consultant, are arranging things yourself, or have put yourself totally in the hands of a banquet manager or caterer, you must compose a wedding-day schedule that is so detailed it makes Napoleon's datebook look sketchy.

The schedule tells all the players — members of the wedding party, vendors, and staff — what they are to do and when they are to do it. More important, just as you are overtaken by amnesia (a prime symptom of panic), the schedule serves as your personal prompter and keeps you moving in the right direction through the most terrifying parts. (Most brides and grooms return to their senses at some point after the ceremony.)

Schedule Basics

Create two versions of this Wedding Day Schedule:

- The first version is a master list, delineating every teeny detail that makes up the entire day. Give this list to everyone on the team involved in making your day happen — caterer, band, florist, cake maker, banquet manager, and anyone else who needs to know all the players and how they interconnect.

- The second is an abridged version focusing on the ceremony. Give this list to the attendants, your officiant, parents, and other ceremony participants. Distribute this schedule at the rehearsal and go over it carefully. Also bring copies to the actual ceremony — few people are like soap opera stars, able to get their next scene down cold in one reading.

The rehearsal should not be the first time you apprise everyone of the way you want things. You should do a preliminary schedule and have key people give it a once over, offering suggestions for improving the flow and timing. You may revise it up to the last minute, but make sure that everyone keeps up with the latest version. Leaving your parents waiting at the ceremony site for a receiving line that you nixed long ago is a bit of a faux pas.

The comprehensive schedule includes:

- Names and times of arrival for everyone involved
- Phone numbers, including those for beepers and cell phones
- Directions to sites
- Specifics for ceremony
- Guesstimated timing for each activity, including toasts
- Specific notes or addendums for each vendor, if applicable
- Highlighted list of important details
- A separate sheet of transportation specifics

Planning a Wedding, Minute by Minute

To give you an idea of what you may include in a typical wedding schedule, we've planned a fairly complicated day, which includes an interfaith ceremony, two separate venues for the ceremony and reception, and many of the sticky situations that can arise. Although some of the information may seem like overkill, trust us — the more precise you are, the less chance things will go haywire. This wedding is a composite of many weddings, and no matter how much your day differs, this sequence of events should give you some idea of how to budget your time and adapt this formula for your own purposes.

In this case, Charlotte Russe (Reform Jewish) is marrying Edward Pandowdy (Protestant). Although neither of them are religious, they're honoring some of the cultural and religious aspects of their backgrounds because of personal feelings and out of respect for their parents. The Gazebo, where the ceremony is being held, is a nonsectarian ceremony venue. Beecham Manor, an inn with in-house catering, is where the reception is being held and where many of the guests are staying.

Who's Who in the Russe / Pandowdy Wedding:

Bride: Charlotte Russe		*555-7894*
Groom: Ed Pandowdy		*555-7894*
Bride's Parents: Sylvia and Ken Russe		*555-5663*
Groom's Parents: Grace and Robert Pandowdy		*555-8185*
Best Man: Mac Pandowdy		*555-4050*
Maid of Honor: Trudy Heller		*555-3981*
Bridesmaids:	*Peggy Dane*	*555-7775*
	Penelope Pistachio	*555-6840*
	Lisa Woodruff	*555-5960*
	Bernice Babcock	*555-9090*
Ushers:	*Paul Bigwater*	*555-2314*
	Gordon Goforth	*555-8310*
	Rodney Rafter	*555-8907*
Rabbi Tend		*555-3222*
Reverend Fend		*555-7089*
Hair & Makeup: Boom and Trix, Mr. Randy Salon		555-0897
Dressmaker: Patience Saintly		555-9080
Ceremony music: Joy		555-0662
Bandleader: Stix Hendrix		555-0800
Beecham Manor		555-2829
	Wren T. Gouger (banquet manager)	555-6655
	Roscoe (captain)	555-6652
Rentals: Party Hardy Inc., Ann		555-9880
Photographer: Cody Ak		555-8050; 555-4000 (beeper)
Car Service and Limos: Wheelz Iz Us		555-6666

Russe/Pandowdy Wedding Transportation

Car # 1 (town car)

1:45 p.m. Picks up Mrs. Pandowdy and Bernice Babcock from home (312 Elm Street) and transports them to hotel (Beecham Manor). Car dismissed.

Car # 2 **(limousine)**

3:20 p.m. Picks up Mr. Pandowdy from 312 Elm Street and transports him to Charlotte and Ed's apartment (222 Fifth Avenue).

5:45 p.m. Takes Ed, Mac, and Mr. Pandowdy to Gazebo.

7:15 p.m. Takes Mr. and Mrs. Pandowdy, Mr. and Mrs. Russe, Bernice, and Peggy to Beecham Manor. Car dismissed.

Car #3 (limousine)

5:15 p.m. Picks up Mr. Russe at home (3355 Corby Avenue) and transports him to Beecham Manor.

6:10 p.m. Leaves with Mr. and Mrs. Russe, Charlotte, and Trudy for ceremony. Waits there until after ceremony.

7:15 p.m. Takes Lisa, Penelope, Mac, Trudy, Paul, and Rodney to Beecham Manor. Car dismissed.

Car # 4 (limousine)

6 p.m. Takes Mrs. Pandowdy, Bernice, and Peggy to Gazebo for ceremony.

7:15 p.m. Takes Charlotte and Ed Pandowdy to Beecham Manor. This car remains until after reception.

Car #5 (town car)

6 p.m. Takes Penelope and Lisa to Gazebo. Waits there until after ceremony.

7:15 p.m. Takes Rabbi Tend and Rev. Fend to Beecham Manor. Car dismissed.

Note to drivers: Please check your trunks and take any items belonging to wedding party to hotel's coat room. Notify banquet captain that you have brought things there.

When scheduling limos, the cost to retain a limo for several hours is usually the same as having it return to pick you up (because it's unlikely they can book a job in between). Negotiate rates with the booking agent and ask about cheaper rates on less-luxurious limousines. (Some companies actually charge less for untinted windows.) Be specific about the number of guests cars hold and whether the cars have *jump seats* (extra fold-down seats).

WEDDING DAY SCHEDULE

Charlotte Russe and Ed Pandowdy

September 10, 1998

(6:30 p.m. ceremony)

The following is an approximate schedule for the wedding day, so we're all are on the same wavelength. The timing is guesstimated, and although this may look overly regimented, don't worry. In reality, weddings take on a life of their own and we will adjust accordingly. Most important, enjoy yourselves!

10 a.m. If it's raining, Trudy calls caterer to secure coatroom staff and golf umbrellas.

12 noon Bridesmaids arrive at Beecham Manor on their own. Bridesmaids who are staying at the inn overnight should check in this afternoon. Changing room is under Russe/Pandowdy. Bridesmaids should bring stockings, shoes, undergarments, makeup, personal toiletries, and carry-all bags for street clothes. Their dresses for the wedding will already be in room.

Charlotte and Trudy have already arrived.

In many hotels, check in is at 2 p.m. so the bride should either stay in this room (perhaps with her maid of honor) the night before the wedding or negotiate with the hotel for an early check-in. Even couples who are living together often spend the night before the wedding in separate places.

12:30 p.m. Hair and makeup stylists to bride's room. Start with Trudy, followed by Peggy.

1:30 p.m. Hair and makeup begin on next two bridesmaids, Lisa and Penelope.

Mrs. Russe arrives. (She's having her hair and makeup done elsewhere beforehand.)

2:15 p.m. Mrs. Pandowdy and her daughter Bernice arrive in car #1 (town car), which is released after they arrive.

Bernice has her hair and makeup done here.

2:30 p.m. Light lunch from room service.

Whether or not you provide transportation for some or all of your wedding party depends on your budget. If you do provide transportation, a limousine is certainly not a necessity. Other far less expensive possibilities range from yellow cabs and car services to "executive vans" that hold up to 22 passengers. You should also offer transportation to grandparents and elderly guests.

Whether the attendants are getting dressed in a hotel or at someone's home, always arrange for lunch or tea. They won't be eating for hours and the combination of starvation and the first glass of champagne can be explosive. Also, the bride should always be last to have her hair and makeup done so that she waits the least amount of time "done up" before the ceremony.

3:15 p.m.	Charlotte has hair and makeup done.
	Photographer arrives at Ed and Charlotte's apartment and set up to take pre-wedding photos. Ed and his brother Mac (best man) are there and dressed.
3:30 p.m.	Paul, Gordon, and Rodney (ushers) arrive at apartment fully dressed.
	Floral assistant arrives with boutonnieres.
3:45 p.m.	Mr. Pandowdy arrives. Car #2 (limousine) remains.
3:45 to 4:45 p.m.	Photos of Mac, Paul, Gordon, & Rodney, Mr. Pandowdy, and Ed.

Note that the bridesmaids outnumber the ushers — a no-no of the manner matrons of the past — but sometimes that's just the way your friends balance out.

4 p.m.	Photographer's assistant arrives to set up at hotel room for pre-wedding photos.
	Bouquets arrive at hotel suite and are distributed before photos.

If the weather is very hot or the bouquets are delicate, have them delivered to the ceremony site and forego taking photos with them at the hotel.

5 p.m. Photographer arrives at bride's hotel suite for "getting dressed" shots and shots of mothers and bridesmaids.

Ushers leave for ceremony at the Gazebo. If it's raining, call car service (see phone numbers on attached list). Otherwise walk or take cabs.

Attention ushers: You must arrive at The Gazebo by 5:45 — no later! Ceremony starts at 6:30. Do not seat guests before 6:10 unless they request to be seated. Show early arrivals where rest rooms and bars are. Bar will be open for soft drinks and sparkling water. Give each guest a program. Give men a yarmulke if they request one. Welcome guests, be chatty and charming. C'mon guys we know you can do it!!!

5:45 p.m. Ed, Mac, and Mr. Pandowdy leave in car #2 (limousine) for ceremony.

Mr. Russe arrives at hotel in car #3 (limousine) that takes him, Charlotte, her mother, and Trudy to ceremony.

6 p.m. Bridesmaids leave for ceremony as follows:

Mrs. Pandowdy, Bernice, Peggy in car #4 (limousine)

Penelope and Lisa in car #5 (town car)

Ed, Mac, and Mr. Pandowdy arrive at the ceremony. Ed and Mac go to the room where Reverend Fend and Rabbi Tend are waiting.

Because Ed and Charlotte are not seeing each other before the ceremony, Rabbi Tend has Ed and Rodney sign the ketubah first. Then Rabbi takes it into Charlotte and Trudy, who both sign it. Reverend Fend has the couple sign the civil marriage license before the ceremony as well.

Normally, the best man and maid of honor sign the *ketubah* (Jewish marriage contract) as witnesses. However, if they are related to the bride and groom, Jewish law forbids them to do so.

In strictly legal terms, the marriage license is not to be signed until after the ceremony, but many officiants allow the couple to sign beforehand to save time after the ceremony.

6:10 p.m. Charlotte, Mr. and Mrs. Russe, and Trudy leave for ceremony in car #6 (limousine).

Ushers begin seating guests.

Note to ushers: There is no bride or groom's side. Except for the reserved seating that follows, guests may sit on either side for the ceremony.

In this case, although ushers are not asking guests, "Bride's side or groom's side?" the bride and groom have decided that they themselves will stand according to the Jewish ceremony style — with the bride and her attendants on the right (facing the front) and the groom and his attendants on the left. Therefore, their immediate families follow suit in the first few rows.

6:15 p.m. Prelude begins with harp, flute, and violin trio playing:

The Rites of Spring

Water Music

Jesu, Joy of Man's Desiring

Upon arriving, Mrs. Pandowdy joins Mr. Pandowdy and they wait for Ed at the rear of the ceremony. They greet guests as they arrive. Mr. Russe greets guests along with the Pandowdys as they arrive. Mrs. Russe prefers not to see guests until after the ceremony. She is with Charlotte, Trudy, and the bridesmaids.

6:30 p.m. Ushers have seated guests in front rows and left seats open as follows:

1st row, left side, from aisle (7 seats): Aunt Hannah Borak; Uncle Ben Borak; Ned Borak; Brenda Borak; Grandma Borak; first two seats on the aisle are for Mr. and Mrs. Pandowdy.

2nd row, left side, from aisle (7 seats): Mac's wife, Coco; her sister Delores, Delores's husband, Bill; Aunt Plum and Uncle Bruce Pandowdy; their daughters Emma and Christine.

1st row, right side, from aisle (6 seats): Mr. and Mrs. Russe, Grandma Russe, and Grandma Royale, Aunt Betty Royale, and her son Sherman. Be sure to save the first two seats closest to the aisle because Mr. and Mrs. Russe won't sit until later.

During the rehearsal, tell ushers to fill in rows directly behind the reserved ones because people are shy and deserted front rows can be disconcerting to a bride and groom gazing out at the guests.

6:30 p.m. Ned Borak seats his wife and Grandma Borak and takes his seat.

Paul seats Grandma Russe and then joins the other ushers in the back.

Rodney seats Grandma Royale and then returns to back.

Paul seats Grandma Russe and returns to back.

Rabbi Tend and Reverend Fend take their places under the Gazebo.

Paul and Rodney unfurl the aisle runner, and then take their places in the ushers procession.

6:35 p.m. Procession music starts:

6:45 p.m. *Trumpet Tune* (Purcell).

Ushers walk down aisle in the following order and take their places at the Gazebo on left side (if you are facing the Gazebo):

Paul (farthest left) and Rodney (next left).

Gordon (walks alone) stands closest to the Gazebo.

Mac (walks alone) and stands *under* the Gazebo, left side.

Ed and his parents walk down the aisle. Ed takes his place under the Gazebo. Mr. and Mrs. Pandowdy take their seats on the left aisle.

Bridesmaids proceed in the following order:

Bernice (goes to far right of the Gazebo)

Penelope (goes next to Bernice, further in)

Lisa (goes next to Penelope, closest in)

Trudy (walks alone) and stands *under* the Gazebo, opposite where Mac is standing.

Music changes to:

Trumpet Voluntary (Clarke)

Charlotte walks down the aisle, her mother on her right and her father on her left.

When they reach the second aisle, Charlotte's parents lift her blusher, kiss her, and replace it over her face. They take their seats in the front row as Ed steps forward and escorts Charlotte to her place under the Gazebo.

Trudy adjusts Charlotte's veil and takes her bouquet.

Brenda Borak reads a poem Charlotte has chosen and Christine Pandowdy reads a poem Ed has chosen (approx seven minutes total for both).

6:55 p.m. Ceremony is performed.

The two clergymen bless the couple.

Final moment (cue for musicians, *et al.*): Ed and Charlotte both step on and break the glass.

7:15 p.m. Recessional:

Charlotte and Ed

Trudy and Mac

Mr. and Mrs. Pandowdy

Mr. and Mrs. Russe

Penelope and Paul

Lisa, flanked by Gordon and Rodney

Ushers return for grandmothers.

Wedding party gets in cars immediately.

If you want the photographer to follow your every move, have him or her ride in your car. Also offer to provide transportation for your officiant(s) to the ceremony (to make sure they arrive on time) and to the reception (to be especially gracious).

Please note: Everyone needs to hustle into their cars so we can leave for the reception venue A.S.A.P. We want to get photos done promptly so you can attend the cocktail hour!!

Rodney and Lisa are responsible for putting the appropriate people in their cars per the attached transportation schedule.

Also note: We will have no receiving line — so once we finish with photos you can party!

Although we discuss whether to take formal photos before or after the ceremony in Chapter 12, one thing is certain: if you have a receiving line, and your guest list is anything but teeny, you need to take your formal photographs, including those of the bride and groom together, *before* the ceremony — unless you want to make your guests wait three days to eat.

If you have 125 guests and allot each one 30 seconds, you're looking at an hour-long receiving line. In spite of this fact, many wedding manuals consider receiving lines a must. A receiving line does ensure that the couple greets all the guests, but that can be done by making your rounds at the reception, which is more hospitable, anyway.

If you feel you must have a receiving line, keep it short. You don't need to have all 24 of your attendants glad-handing the guests. The fastest way, if possible, is to hold the receiving line at the door of the ceremony site as guests are leaving. Even that, however, does not prevent traffic jams. Having the line at your reception should not mean torture for your guests. Make sure they are offered drinks and hors d'oeuvres while waiting.

An ample receiving line includes, from left: the mother of the bride, the mother of the groom, and the bride and groom. A longer one has, from left: the mother of the bride, the father of the bride or groom, the mother of the groom, and the father of the bride or groom. If time is not an issue, you may include the maid of honor and, even though it's not considered part of the standard line up, the best man. Anything longer is for the Rockettes. If issues exist with divorced parents, be kind. Don't force people who cannot bear each other to stand side by side, smiling through clenched teeth.

The receiving line is like a good game of telephone. Guests introduce themselves to the mother of the bride, who then introduces the person to the mother of the groom, who introduces the person to the bride, and so on. Of course, by the time Harriet Luce gets to the end, she has become Marion Tooth.

At Beecham Manor

7:10 p.m. Cocktail music sets up, bars open, hors d'oeuvres stations ready in anteroom.

Reminder to Roscoe (captain): Please check — votive candles (4 per table) and imprinted cocktail napkins. **Make sure that music is playing as guests arrive!!** Also we need a hand-held microphone and a small table near the stage so we can move it in front of the band when it's time to make toasts.

7:30 p.m. Cocktail music begins.

Wedding party and family assemble on the south terrace of Beecham Manor.

Follow photo schedule. ***Note:*** Take photos of grandmothers first so they can go to cocktail party.

7:40 p.m. Guests begin arriving at Beecham Manor and are directed to north terrace, away from wedding party and photographer.

8 p.m.	Photos to be finished, ending with shots of Ed and Charlotte, any photos still to go will be done during the reception. Wedding party joins the reception.
8:20 p.m.	All three musicians leave for dining room.
8:30 p.m.	Roscoe takes the Russes, Ed, and Charlotte to see the dining room. Final sound check completed. Band begins to play.
8:40 p.m.	Cocktail reception is over; guests are escorted to the dining room.

Note to Roscoe: Please remember to post two waiters with seating chart at dining room entrance.

Note to Stix (bandleader): No announcements will be made. Bride and groom will enter and take their seats with the rest of the guests. Please play lively upbeat music (selections from list A) until guests are all in dining room.

8:50 p.m.	Guests are all seated.
	Uncle Borak blesses and cuts the challah bread.
	Reverend Fend blesses the meal.
	Waiters pour wine (White — *La Fleur du Maison*).
	Mr. Russe proposes a welcome toast.
9:10 p.m.	Waiters serve appetizer.

If guests want to get a little dancing in before the first course, they should feel free to kick up their heels. The bride and groom should dance with each other before dancing with other people.

Classically, the best man proposes the first toast, but you may prefer to have the host welcome everyone first. In any case, having the best man (or some other special person) introduce the first dance is more personal than having the bandleader do it.

9:25 p.m.	While waiters clear appetizer, Mac proposes his toast.
	Mac introduces first dance: "And now, Charlotte and Ed, for their first dance as a married couple."

Note to Roscoe: Please make sure that lights are dimmed.

Ed and Charlotte go to the dance floor. Music is "Let's Stay Together" (by Al Green).

Note to Stix: The couple wishes to dance the entire song before you switch for cut-ins. Again, make no announcements for the cut ins. Music changes to "Crazy Love" (by Van Morrison) as Mr. Russe cuts in and dances with Charlotte.

Ed escorts Mrs. Russe to the dance floor halfway through "Crazy Love." Mr. Russe cuts in on his daughter. Mr. Pandowdy dances with Mrs. Russe while Mr. Russe dances with Mrs. Pandowdy.

Mac cuts in on Charlotte.

Stix invites the guests, including the rest of the wedding party, to the dance floor to dance with whomever they want.

This dance set lasts approximately 15 minutes.

The do-si-do of the first dance and cut-ins becomes infinitely more complicated if you have myriad sets of parents who don't speak to each other, widowed parents, or hypersensitive mothers. If the groom's mother feels she should be first to dance with him — after the bride, hopefully — then do so. If a parent is partnerless, be sure to pair him or her with someone and give them top billing in the dance order. If the entire situation seems too complicated, give up and invite everyone onto the dance floor simultaneously after your first dance.

9:45 p.m. Guests are seated. Waiters serve main course and *offer* red wine (*La Tour de Change*) as well as white wine to anyone who prefers continuing with that.

Note to Stix: Background music only — very subtle — three musicians.

Now is a good time for the rest of the band, the photographer, the videographer, and the wedding consultant to eat. Assistants should eat when the others are finished so someone is watching the room for any spontaneous toasts and so on. Arrange with your caterer ahead of time to serve them something appetizing even if it's not exactly what you serve your guests.

10:30 p.m.	Waiters clear main course.
	Mr. Russe proposes his toast, followed by Mrs. Russe.
10:40 p.m.	Band plays a short Hora and swing set for next 20 minutes.

Note to Stix: Begin with a short Hora, followed by Swing set (list B). Before guests are seated please announce, "The bride has requested the presence of all single men and women on the south terrace for the bouquet toss."

Note to Stix: We will not perform a garter ceremony. Even if a guest asks for one, explain that the bride and groom have requested that there not be one.

Note to Roscoe: Please make sure that throw-away bouquet is given to Charlotte.

Charlotte tosses her bouquet. Guests are then seated.

In lieu of a wedding planner, a captain should be prepared to choreograph the bouquet toss. Participants should be several yards behind the bride, arranged into a semi-circle. If possible, gather participants on a softer surface than a dance floor; competition can be ruthless and people have been known to go down.

The bride stands with her back to the crowd, in a place with no chandeliers or other possible impediments to a high, vigorous fling. To the sounds of a drum roll, if possible, the bride bends ever so slightly at the knees and tosses the bouquet over her head, aiming high. If the bouquet collides with the ceiling or other stationery object, the toss results in a foul and she must attempt again.

If you don't have a critical mass of single friends at the wedding, you may want to simply present the bouquet as a memento to a favorite aunt or other person you want to honor.

If you're having ethnic dancing such as a Hora or Tarantella, schedule it after the main course to get guests moving again after eating and drinking.

11 p.m. Guests are seated as cake is wheeled to thc middle of the dance floor and band plays reprise of first dance music.

Note to Stix: Please do not have band on break at this time. You must be prepared to begin again immediately after toasts.

Waiters OFFER champagne and bring four glasses to cake table. Mrs. Pandowdy proposes toast. Trudy proposes toast. Ed and Charlotte cut cake. Waiters wheel away cake table to finish cutting in kitchen.

Ed and Charlotte toast.

Band immediately kicks in.

11:20 p.m. Waiters offer coffee and de-caf; place silver trays of chocolate truffles on tables.

11:30 p.m. Cake served.

11:45 p.m. Guests begin to leave.

Note: Town cars for Mr. and Mrs. Pandowdy have been reserved for 12 a.m.

Ushers load gifts into Pandowdys' car.

Note to Roscoe: Remember to put cake top in Russes' car.

Ed and Charlotte's limo takes the grandmothers home and returns for Ed and Charlotte.

Someone should keep the gifts until the bride and groom get back from their honeymoon. They also should freeze the caketop if the couple wants to eat it on their first anniversary. (See Chapter 9 for freezing instructions.)

12 midnight ***Note to Stix:*** Please check with bride or groom if they wish to go into overtime.

12:15 a.m. Band announces last set; finishes at 12:30.

Note to Roscoe: Make sure that the picnic basket, utensils, champagne, and glasses have been put into the bride and groom's car.

12:45 Ed and Charlotte leave for their hotel.

Traditionally, the bride and groom gracefully disappear after the cake cutting, and then reappear shortly in elegant street clothes, bid farewell, and take their leave amid tears and waves in their shaving-cream-and-tin-can festooned limousine. Many couples today, however, after having spent vast amounts of money and time planning this event are not willing to miss a second of it. Rebellion against the early exit has come so far that many brides and grooms are not only the last left standing on the dance floor, but are also the last to leave the reception, often with a close group of friends who then accompany them to their suite for "last call."

In Ed and Charlotte's case, they are staying someplace else where they can be alone because many guests are staying at Beecham Manor. Early the next morning they leave for their honeymoon while guests convene for a farewell breakfast.

Chapter 19

Let's Get Out of Here

In This Chapter

- Planning a hassle-free honeymoon
- Getting wed far, far away
- Pampering out-of-towners

The Owl and the Pussycat went to sea
In a beautiful pea green boat,
They took some honey, and plenty of money,
Wrapped up in a five-pound note.

— Edward Lear, "The Owl and the Pussycat"

This isn't right, you keep thinking, as the sun drops behind the lush mountains on Day Three of your South Seas honeymoon. You had such ambitious plans. For months you and your beloved dreamed about parasailing on the aquamarine bay, tromping through the verdant jungles like Indiana Jones, and dancing with abandon under the stars until the wee hours of the morning. But so far, after flying for 28 hours (including two puddle jumpers and a ferry) to get here, you've both been too exhausted to do much more than drag your weary carcasses to the pool and park them side by side in chaises longues. Though you would never admit it to anyone nosy enough to ask, you were even too tired on your wedding night to consummate your marriage, which made you both feel a little inadequate, to say the least. This was supposed to be *Endless Love,* but now it feels like *The Big Sleep*. Is this a harbinger of married life? The sound of your spouse slurping another piña colada interrupts your panicked reverie. At least, you shrug, you can be zombies together.

Second only to the wedding day in unrealistic expectations is the honeymoon. The ubiquitous image of carefree newlyweds frolicking in the surf of some developing island nation has skewed the expectations of many a couple. Yes, a honeymoon is a once-in-a-lifetime sojourn. It's an intimate time for bonding with each other and easing into your new life together. But that doesn't mean you're going to Fantasy Island, so don't read too much into your honeymoon if it's less than total perfection. (And, incidentally, very few couples actually have the energy to make love on their wedding night, and those who say they do are probably lying.) Like your wedding, a successful honeymoon owes much to careful planning and budgeting. So shop around, consider the options, and allot realistic funds.

Some couples, because they want either the path of least resistance or to get married in Never-Never Land, plan their nuptials some place other than where they live. These weddings, or in some cases wedding and honeymoon packages, call for some innovative approaches, which we cover in this chapter as well.

Paradise or Bust

Devising your honeymoon itinerary is much like planning your wedding. You and your spouse-to-be should start by sharing your fantasies of where and how you've pictured yourself on a honeymoon. If you've never given it much thought, try to remember the last photograph in a travel magazine that knocked you out. What would be the vacation of your dreams? Is it exotic, inspirational, hedonistic, or simply immobile? Hold off on financial and other realities for this first part of the discussion; just let your imagination go. Once you have some sense of what would be heaven for each of you (and hopefully there are enough common denominators to at least get you both on the same continent) look at the financial, spatial, and time-frame realities. Get as many of the essential pieces from your REM state to fit into your REAL state. Some general advice:

- **Keep it simple:** Trust us, you have never been as bone-tired as you will be the day after your wedding. This doesn't mean your jaunt has to be boring; just don't plan on extremes. Unless you have a full staff attending to your wedding and your job is only to get dressed and appear at the altar, you may feel like you've run eight marathons. While it may sound great now, actually sitting on a plane for 12 hours after the emotional high of the previous 24, only to land in a sweltering country where nobody speaks English and the unemployment rate is 400 percent, may feel like honeymoon hell.
- **Know your physical limitations:** If you've never climbed a mountain or scuba dived before (and you haven't been training for a recent Iron Man competition), now is probably not the best time to start. We realize that getting married makes you feel like a new person, but do you really think that you've become bionic? If your goal is to do something totally new and exhilarating together, take time before the wedding to prepare, whether that means training in a particular sport, getting in shape, or buying the proper gear.

- **Give yourself enough time:** In scheduling, too little realism can spoil the romance. If your idea of fun is to follow the Silk Road from Xi'an to Khunjerab Pass, or dine with maharajahs in India, you need more than a week away. And don't compromise quality for quantity: Whizzing through 22 countries in nine days is hardly conducive to focusing on each other — one of the main points of taking a honeymoon. If you can't afford the time now, scale back your plans and make the grand tour a goal for later.

It's a big world after all

The possibilities for your first married vacation are virtually limitless. With the exception of the most rarified venues, created and maintained solely for the rich and famous, world travel has become not only affordable but also efficient. The United States has kept up by offering a stunning variety of honeymoon choices as well. Most American newlyweds flock to places where the living is easy — places synonymous with sun and surf. (Florida and Hawaii are the top destinations, followed by the Caribbean and Mexico.) A trend that follows the rise in the urban health-club frenzy is the action-adventure honeymoon. Couples who find sitting like lumps on a beach as exciting as learning their multiplication tables are devising post-wedding trips that get their adrenaline pumping. This book is not a travelogue and providing a comprehensive list of honeymoon destinations (at least all the specific places we wouldn't mind spending a few weeks) would take at least three other volumes. Still, as you're sorting through various ideas, think about these postcards you could send home:

- **Adventure:** Itineraries that are pre-packaged or customized to the exact specifications of your super-hero aliases. Consider white-water rafting in Colorado and Utah; game-viewing safaris in Kenya or Tanzania; climbing Mt. Kilamanjaro; exploring the Galapagos Islands; or ascending the Mayan ceremonial city Chichen Itza in Mexico's Yucatan. You can even take a high-performance driving school for two in Arizona.
- **Asia and Australia:** As long as you're going to the other side of the world, what's another continent? After you walk along rice-paddy trails and venture into elephant caves in Bali or bed down in luxury in the Amanwana tent camp on a private nature reserve on Indonesia's Moyo Island, you may lunch with kangaroos and wombats in the Australian Outback.
- **Europe:** Park yourselves in a wondrous city — Madrid, Paris, Rome — and immerse yourselves in the culture. Tour France's Burgundy wine regions and Loire Valley chateaus — by hot-air balloon, setting down at a different inn each evening. Rent a honeymoon villa on the Amalfi coast in Italy. Charter a private yacht (with other couples) in Greece. Cycle the Irish countryside, staying at medieval castles.

Great expectations

It's not uncommon to feel blue on your honeymoon. We've even known some newlyweds to go on an inexplicable three-day crying jag. Going from the biggest emotional high of your life, surrounded by family and friends, to a quiet one-on-one journey with your new spouse can send you straight into post-partum depression. Even if you're not that bad off, you probably are processing a backlog of emotions ranging from rapture to nostalgia to fear. At some point you may even look at your spouse and think, "Who *is* this person?" Welcome to Honeymoonland! Take this time together to discuss these feelings, get closer, and adjust to this new state of being.

One way to sabotage this precious time is to get hung up on the myth of the perfect honeymoon. Yes, you are bound to have the occasional squabble. Yes, you are normal if you don't make love nine times a day. Yes, you really are married. So enjoy.

- **Sporting:** Some people just don't feel right unless they exercise every day. Stables in Vermont offer week-long horseback tours. Or check out the California wine country by bicycle. You can enroll in sailing schools on the Gulf Coast of Florida and tennis camps that offer romantic accommodations in addition to daily instruction. Combine two loves in one trip by kayaking and hiking through the rain forests of Hawaii.
- **Tropical isles:** The Caribbean islands include Jamaica, Grand Cayman, Turks, and Caicos (just over an hour's flight from Miami), as well as the British Virgin Islands, Puerto Rico, and a slew of others that offer perfect beaches and innumerable hotels in various price and pampering ranges. Consider Belize, known for its mesmerizing diving experiences, including Jaguar Reef Lodge, the world's first C-Breathe Center, where untrained divers can safely go to 25 feet under water without oxygen tanks. You may want to go to the Bahamas with pristine white beaches and the Atlantic Ocean or to the South Pacific Republic of Fiji with more than 300 islands and resorts comprising thatch-roofed cottages and miles of unpopulated beaches.

"Ecotourism" and "responsible tourism" are buzzwords used by travel companies in marketing photographic safaris (you shoot game with cameras, not weapons), exotic diving expeditions, rain forest treks, and archeological expeditions that are sensitive to the environment.

If you like the idea of a truly meaningful, philanthropic honeymoon — and hard work and very unglamorous conditions don't scare you — consider taking a trip with a non-profit organization such as One World Workforce, which organizes trips, for example, to save endangered sea turtles and pelicans in their Costa Rican and Mexican habitats.

If you honeymoon in the Caribbean, consider scheduling it during *Carnival,* the party to end all parties. In many Caribbean countries, Carnival precedes Lent, and therefore falls at different times during the year, although some islands hold it at the same time every year (Trinidad in January and February; St. Thomas in April.) July's Heritage Festival in Tobago includes a send-up of a 19th century wedding — "The Old Time Wedding" — with an appearance by a "pregnant" girlfriend and a wedding cake wrapped in mosquito netting.

If you've been someplace extraordinary with someone else, don't go there on your honeymoon. Experiences on this trip are to be shared solely by the two of you, not haunted by other reminiscences.

Smooth exits

Medical school, law school, high-boogie jobs — sometimes a honeymoon just has to wait. But don't deprive yourself entirely. Try taking off just two days. A long weekend in a nice hotel ordering room service may do wonders and ease you back to reality.

Though you may be eager to start your honeymoon, do yourself a favor and spend your first married night in a luxurious place as close to your reception site as possible rather than embarking on your trip. Then you can start your trip refreshed.

Have your luggage brought to the hotel where you are spending your wedding night so you can leave the next day without any hassle. Leave your wedding clothes with the concierge and have someone pick them up so you don't have to drag them along on your honeymoon.

But you can't waterski in a parka

Until fairly recently, all honeymoons were pretty much a surprise for the bride. The groom agonized, researched, and hypothesized in silence and then prayed that his bride would not find his plan abhorrent. While many wise couples now plan their honeymoons together, a good many grooms still feel that this is *their* primary responsibility, which perhaps explains the trendlet toward surprise honeymoons. The groom tells the bride what to pack or perhaps tells her to pack everything from ski suits to bikinis to keep her guessing. He may wait until the last possible moment — often right before fastening seat belts — to disclose their destination. This route is for the fearless and confident. If you've lived together for eons and vacationed together as long, this may be a way to inject the once-in-a-lifetime feeling into your honeymoon.

The first taste of honey

Germanic tribesmen in ancient times, after capturing their future wives, would join them in drinking *mead,* an intoxicating beverage made of fermented honey. This resting period (or perhaps hiding-out period until the bride's family gave up their search for her) usually lasted for a month — or "moon" and thus became known as the honeymoon.

If the pressure of thoughts of intimacy on your wedding night has gotten to you — even if you have been living together long enough to be sharing one bathrobe — you may empathize with the plight of the poor medieval bride and groom. Friends and relatives escorted them into their bedchamber to help in "bedding the bride" — loosening her garments and tucking the two of them in, then sticking around during lovemaking to bear witness that the bride was a virgin. The marital bedroom was festooned with ribbons on the bedposts to represent the marriage knot and other symbols of a successful deflowering. People crammed in to cheer on the couple and grab at the tossed-off stockings and other undergarments in the same manner they reach for a tossed bouquet today.

If Aunt Myrtle is throwing a farewell brunch for all your out-of-town guests the day after the wedding, you usually are not obligated to stay. In fact, doing so may delay your honeymoon departure up to an entire day, depending on your flight, cruise, or train schedule. Just make it clear to such hosts at the start of their planning so you don't disappoint them later on.

Accommodating yourselves

While for some honeymooners the destination is the deciding factor, for others the style in which they lay their heads counts more. Many different styles of accommodations are available to suit your taste:

- **All-inclusive resorts:** Braco Village, Club Med, Sandals Resorts International, and SuperClubs are just a few of the highly rated all-inclusive resorts that exist in different parts of the world. Some are truly all-inclusive — no surprises on your credit card — where you are hard pressed to spend extra money even if you try. Others require diligence in keeping track of what's included and what's à la carte. Find out to whom the resort caters — couples, singles, or families.
- **Cruise ships:** Whether your ship is a mini-city with 3,000 people or a private yacht with motorized sails and a capacity of 150, cruises are best booked through a travel agent who specializes in them. Voyages may include daily ports of call or long stays at sea. As cruises are enjoying a return in popularity, you may find just about any sort of theme on board, from sports with professional athletes to haute cuisine orgies for foodies to self-improvement seminars. Choose a cabin

carefully by looking at the ships' deck plan. If you like to sleep late, don't take a room by the promenade deck, where joggers may take their morning runs

- **Inns and bed & breakfasts:** Although the terms are often used interchangeably, the two can be very different experiences. B&Bs are often private homes that rent a few rooms to guests and include breakfast but usually no other meals. You may not have your own bathroom. Many offer folksy touches, such as milk and cookies at bedtime or a cat to sleep on your bed, but other amenities or activities are unlikely. You may also be under the watchful eye of an on-premises landlord. Inns on the other hand are usually larger, grander, and have more rooms, programs, and amenities. They may have not only a charming dining room but also excellent cuisine to match. Inns and B&Bs can range from very rustic to very luxe, so research carefully before reserving. For more information, check out *Country Inns Magazine,* the Recommended Country Inns Guidebook Series, or the Independent Innkeeper's Association.
- **Grand resorts:** For some, these mega-complexes are the answer to their relaxation prayers, for others they are like terrariums. These hotels, which often have more than a thousand rooms, may offer some packages relating to sports or ritzy meals, but are usually play and pay. These properties are designed to include everything you could conceivably want — 24-hour room service, stores that are open until the wee hours, multiple nightclubs and restaurants, twice-a-day room service, and day camps for the kiddies. They also may cater to large business groups during certain seasons, so find out if these times coincide with your plans. (Also ask what percentage of guests are families and whether children have separate pool and beach areas, if that matters to you.)
- **Spas:** Perhaps just what you need after a few months of wedding stress, spas may be part of a large resort or hotel or a self-contained destination. As with resorts, find out whether the spa caters to couples or singles, men and women. Are you expected to follow a regime or can you plan your days as you go? Are the bedrooms posh or in monastery mode? Are classes, beauty treatments, and sports lessons included in the fee? Does the dining room serve solely spa cuisine or does it offer choices for the ravenous? You may want to spend the last few days of your honeymoon decompressing at a spa before returning to planet Earth. A spa may also be the perfect solution if you just have a few days off after your wedding and plan to take a longer vacation later.
- **Villas, condos, or other rental properties:** You may be surprised to learn that renting a private home (especially during off season) or part of a villa in the Caribbean or the Mediterranean, a palazzo (apartment) in Venice, a motor home in France, or a lighthouse or estate cottage in the United Kingdom may be quite affordable, particularly if you buy alcohol and groceries at a local market and prepare most of your own meals. Of course, if you've decided to throw financial caution to the winds some private villas come complete with a cook and chauffeur. Either way, this option is an exciting way to feel like a native in another place.

As you call around to get price quotes on rates for lodging and accommodations, ask whether the price includes tax — all tax. (In addition to sales tax, some places charge a room tax, which can be over 20 percent.)

It pays to advertise. When you make your hotel reservations, and then again when you arrive, make a point of telling the reservationist and/or concierge that you're on your honeymoon. Better hotels like to do something special for honeymooners to encourage them to come back for anniversaries and vacations. Letting everyone know that you're just married (without being obnoxious about it), may result in little perks, ranging from extra solicitous service to discounts at attractions to a bottle of champagne in your room.

Asking for a king, queen, or double bed usually gets you just that in the United States or Caribbean. Cruise ships have a limited number of cabins with double beds and they must be reserved well ahead of time. In other parts of the world, double beds mean two single beds. Unless you're impersonating Lucy and Ricky Ricardo, specify a large matrimonial bed.

Check to see whether you need to reserve tours or appointments for special services before your arrival. Even if it is not mandatory, do so. You don't want to be playing tennis at 3 a.m. because the courts are booked for the rest of the day.

This ain't Europe on $5 a day, but . . .

Your honeymoon need not be a money vacuum to be memorable and romantic. The more astute you are about the financial variables, the less money you may spend. Keep in mind, however, that after the fact you may regret having "cheaped out" on some of the frills. You are, after all, going to do this only once. Some smart ways to save money are to:

- Ask your travel agent about off-season and package rates.
- Exchange money at banks or cambios. They typically have better rates than hotels, which often add a surcharge.
- Take advantage of student discounts. A few youth hostels have private rooms that may be nice enough for a few honeymoon nights.
- Compare package rates with à la carte rates. Paying as you go may be cheaper than pre-paying for amenities and services you don't use.
- Limit your phone calls, especially overseas. Many hotels charge significantly higher rates than normal. If you must use the phone, a calling card billed to your home number may be cheaper.
- Stock your mini bar with your own snacks, soft drinks, bottled water, and (preferably duty-free) spirits. Ask the bellman or room steward for ice and glasses.

- Bring enough sunscreen and toiletries to last the whole trip. Hotel and cruise gift shops charge outrageous prices to captive guests.
- Limit the number of shore excursions on cruises or else plan your own with the help of a good guidebook and travel agent.
- Buy cruise tickets far in advance — you may save up to 50 percent off brochure rates and be more likely to get the cabin of your choice.
- Set a limit for how much to gamble and stick to it. Better yet, don't gamble. Every game favors the house.
- Even if you rarely fly, join the frequent flyer club of the airline you take most often. Ask for an application when you reserve your flight; it doesn't cost anything and the miles add up to upgrades and free trips. Also check out telephone programs that offer free miles for a certain amount of long distance usage and charge cards where you receive miles for dollars charged.
- Check out discount air tickets vendors such as Global Travel in Nevada and 1-800-FLY-ASAP. You can find other deals in *Best Fares* magazine.

Driving off into the sunset

You may decide to drive to a not-so-far-away destination. If you're renting a car and your licenses don't have the same address yet, tell the agent that you're just married so you don't have to pay an extra driver fee. (This announcement seems to melt even the toughest of hearts.) Know ahead of time whether you need to buy extra insurance from the car rental company. Chances are if you already have comprehensive homeowner or renter, car, and health insurance policies, you're set. Also, some credit card companies extend coverage when you pay with their card.

If your travel plans include driving in the United States, the three big companies — Hertz, Avis, and Budget — all require a minimum age of 25. Alamo rents to drivers between 21 and 24 years old for an additional $20 per day. Otherwise, if you're younger, you may have to rely on small, unknown rental companies.

Often renting a car rather than taking a tour bus can be cheaper in other countries, so compare the two. For the best prices, prepay through a travel agent to avoid fluctuating rates. Whether you travel in the U.S. or abroad, return rental cars with a full tank, which is usually less expensive than the rental company's per-gallon charge.

When in doubt, bring it

Should you bring stationery to write thank you notes? Absolutely not. Sure, you'll have all the more to write when you get home, but nobody expects to hear from you now.

However, you may not think to throw a few items in your suitcase as you're swept into the swirling wedding vortex. Our suggestions:

- Adhesive bandages
- Antacid
- Aspirin
- Birth control
- Blow dryer
- Bottle opener
- Camera, film, batteries
- Candles
- Diarrhea medicine
- Ear plugs
- Electrical adapter
- Feathers
- Flashlight
- Hats
- Insect repellent
- Journal and pens
- Lingerie and new sexy underwear
- Liquid detergent (small bottle)
- Manicure set, nail polish, remover
- Massage oil
- Mini steamer
- Music (favorite tapes, CDs)
- Resealable plastic bags
- Spot remover
- Sunscreen
- Tickets for planes, trains, or boats
- Travel neck pillow
- Vitamins
- Water booties

And Away We Go

You may be thinking, weddings are stressful enough — why would you make it even harder on yourself by planning one hundreds of miles away? One reason is cost; destination weddings usually attract fewer guests and you can often get more bang for the buck in a small town than in a major metropolitan area. (Some places, however, are so inaccessible that saving money is impossible.) What's more, having your wedding in an exotic location or someplace that's especially meaningful for you makes it all the more memorable. In spite of the complicated logistics, destination weddings provide ample opportunity for originality, freedom, and intimacy. You also have the advantage of neutral territory if you're worried about family feuds or power issues. In fact, what used to be called eloping is increasingly referred to as a destination wedding-honeymoon for two, *sans* guests.

Destination weddings are generally one of three kinds:

- **Back Home:** You both live in one town but you're having the wedding where one or both of you grew up, your parents and friends live, the family officiant lives, or you have some other long-standing tie. Even though you have a core group of people in town, you're basically planning long distance and have many guests coming from out of town. Because one of the main reasons to have this kind of wedding is to make parents and relatives happy, you trust someone — a mother or other relative — to either plan the wedding or work with a coordinator. This kind of wedding is not usually an option for the must-be-involved-in-every-detail couple; be prepared to give up major control before you commit. Because this wedding is often held over a weekend, it's called a *weekend wedding;* you probably want to schedule some extracurricular activities or get-togethers for guests.
- **Honeymoon-Wedding:** Some people call it *eloping,* Walt Disney World in Orlando has dubbed it the *Intimate wedding,* and Sandals Resorts has trademarked the term *WeddingMoon* — a wedding *à deux*. You've decided the whole planning ordeal is too much, or you've done it before and you want this wedding to be about only the two of you, or you simply want to cut to the chase — the honeymoon. This approach may be a custom-designed combination wedding and honeymoon in a far-away place, which involves a level of planning that makes D-Day look like a trip to the grocery store. Or you may simply tack on a wedding ceremony to your honeymoon. Because resorts are in business to sell room nights, these "add-on" weddings are often inexpensive — even free at some resorts. Perhaps unsurprisingly, the weddings are pretty formulaic, held in only certain areas on the properties with a set style and length of the ceremony, and topped off with some fizzy stuff and a cake product. Ask the wedding department at your destination to send you full details on how they do these ceremonies and mini-receptions. If you want something different and you are willing to pay for special plans, notify your destination in advance — in writing. Arrive a few days early to arrange things the way you want them. An on-site wedding coordinator should be able to assist you in whipping your wedding into shape.
- **Spin the Globe and Pick a Place:** The true destination wedding. You've been to more weddings than you can stand to think of. No matter how beautiful, innovative, or romantic, they all run together in your mind as one big flower-studded rendition of "Feelings." The thought of hosting one of your own makes you gag. Or perhaps you did a very preliminary guest count and between both sets of parents and your combined lists you may have to rent the Astrodome. The solution may be a wedding some place far away where you've always wanted to go — where you can have a ceremony that combines native customs and your culture in a setting that is so spectacular you don't even need to decorate. The number of guests (perhaps only close friends and relatives) and the portion of their tab you pick up depends on what *you* decide to spend.

Finding and working with a travel agent

Trying to plan such an important trip without the help of a good travel agent is a good example of penny-wise-and-pound-foolishness. Yes, they work on commission and some may charge a fee or even expenses depending on the sort of place you are interested in. Nonetheless, the good ones steer you to exactly where you want to be and at the very least get you the most for your money. If you are planning a destination wedding, their services can be invaluable. Have all your guests book through them, so you don't have to be a travel clearinghouse.

Unfortunately, membership in a professional organization such as the American Society of Travel Agents is no proof of competence. The best way to find a travel agent that suits your needs is through word of mouth — get the name of the particular agent, not just the agency.

If you already know where you want to go, or what kind of trip you want your task is slightly different: Hire an agent who is a DS (destination specialist) in that particular site or one that specializes in a type of travel such as adventure trips. To find a specialist, call the Institute of Certified Travel Agents.

When interviewing a travel agent, bring a list of your wishes, possible venues, and desired amenities such as a Jacuzzi, ocean view, or four-poster bed. Have a good handle on your budget parameters. The more work you do before you start your chat, the more helpful they can be. Some questions to ask:

- Based on what we have told you, what are the options you would recommend?
- Have you personally stayed at the site, done the tour, flown the route, or sailed the line that you are suggesting?
- Do you have guidebooks or videos we could look at?
- How quickly can we expect you to return our phone calls when we are working together?
- Will you supply us with references of other couples whose honeymoons you have planned, preferably those with similar budgets and interests?
- Can we expect you to deliver all tickets, vouchers, and necessary papers to us a few weeks before our wedding?
- Will you help us to obtain visas, passports, and other documents we will need?
- If something goes awry with our trip, what will you do to straighten it out? Do you have a 24-hour help line we can call?
- Where are the deals? What kind of discounts can you get? Will you research special honeymoon packages?

- What sort of vacations are your specialty? Do you usually work with individuals rather than businesses or groups?
- How do you work in conjunction with tour operators?
- For destination weddings, do you work with a wedding coordinator or does the venue have one on site? If not, can you recommend one?

Aside from a travel agent, destination weddings really call for the services of a wedding coordinator. You may hire someone where you live to travel on a site inspection or hire someone who specializes in weddings at the destination. To find such a coordinator, look in the back of *Honeymoon* magazine, an excellent source for all kinds of honeymoon info, or call the tourist board of your destination. Incidentally, *Honeymoon* also features a magazine within the magazine, *Destination Weddings,* a decent Web site (`www.honeymoonmagazine.com`), and a travel-query e-mail address at `www.romint.com`.

Ceremony solutions

When getting the marriage license, check out the length of the "cooling off" period, the residency requirements, and the number of witnesses you need to sign the certificate. In some countries, you need to have lived there six months or more, while others allow only citizens to marry! Also find out the business hours of the office where you apply for the license; you may need to arrive a few days early to process this paperwork. While you're at it, determine whether you need a blood test and if one from your doctor back home will suffice. (For more information regarding marriage licenses and blood tests, see Chapter 16.)

Destination wedding innovations

Two destination wedding pioneers have come up with new twists for nuptial bliss:

Sandals Resorts — the people who invented the WeddingMoon — have recently opened Beaches hotels in Jamaica and on the Turks and Caicos Islands. Their new Sunset Version of the WeddingMoon includes such amenities as a celebration dinner for six. Most interesting, however, is that Beaches caters to singles, families, and couples — making a destination wedding for a group far more feasible than it is has been at the couples-only Sandals. As an added convenience, several packages now include airfare.

Disney has experienced immense success with its Fairy Tale Weddings, which can be intimate affairs for two or extravaganzas for hundreds, and Fairy Tale Honeymoons, which has made Walt Disney World the top post-nuptial destination in the country. Now the Disney Cruise Line's inaugural ship, *Disney Magic*, ups the ante for the honeymoon-wedding. A seven-day package begins with a ceremony at Disney World, followed by three or four days there. Then couples board this very innovative ship for a voyage to Disney's private island, Castaway Cay, in the Bahamas.

Getting the gown there

One of the hairiest feats of planning a faraway wedding is transporting your gown with a minimum of wrinkles (to either you or it) or other damage, especially if you have a poufy ball-gown the size of Nebraska that can stand up by itself with no one in it. After your final fitting, have the shop pack it in acid-free tissue paper — and lots of it — and a special hanging bag. If you're flying, try to take an off-peak flight when you have a better chance of getting an empty seat for your "companion." Most airlines charge you, but others may give you a break because you're a bride.

Another option is to pack the garment bag in reams of bubble wrap in a large box and either ship it overnight or 2nd day air. We don't suggest that you check the dress with your baggage. Ditto with your headpiece and veil(s) — despite its airiness, tulle can actually crease, so don't scrunch it into a suitcase. To be totally safe, bring a portable steamer or find out if the hotel has one. Even better, try to find a professional cleaners or tailor who can steam your dress — as you watch. Never, ever let anyone with an iron near your dress unless you have ordered the special asbestos model. Also, if your dress is heavy, avoid hanging it for more than a day or two; the weight may stretch it out. Pack other clothes in plastic dry cleaning bags, leaving them on the hanger.

Some countries such as Mexico require a civil ceremony before a religious one; in others, a religious ceremony is legally binding. To be married under U.S. law, your wedding must comply with the laws of the place you get married. That's fairly easy if your wedding is on U.S. soil or in a place like Jamaica or Bermuda, which have relatively simple stipulations. But Italy, for example, is notoriously bound in red tape. Before you decide on a country, consult its consular office in New York or its embassy in Washington, D.C. The U.S. State Department can provide marriage requirements and lists of U.S. consular offices abroad, where you should have your marriage certificate authenticated.

If you plan to have a Catholic ceremony, you may need a letter from your parish priest confirming that you've been through pre-Cana counseling and requesting that the wedding be performed in another church. If you want the wedding outdoors or in secular setting, you need a special dispensation. Similarly, for a Jewish wedding the rabbi may require a letter or phone call from your hometown rabbi, or have practices that are more or less reform than you're used to.

Getting married on a cruise ship is not a matter of having the captain perform the nuptials. (Such marriages are not legal and last only as long as the cruise.) Most cruise lines offer special wedding packages, which include a civil ceremony either on embarkation day while the ship is docked, on board, or in a port of call.

TIP

Essentials for getting married afar

In addition to our list of honeymoon goodies, you may need the following for a long-distance or destination wedding:

- Birth certificate (authenticated)
- Confirmation, baptism, and pre-Cana records (for Catholic weddings)
- Immunization and other health records
- Passport
- Proof of economic solvency
- Proof that you're free to marry, such as a divorce decree or death certificate (authenticated and perhaps translated)

Playing travel agent, cruise director, and concierge

Honeymoon-weddings can be the simplest to carry off — wedding-planning companies all over the world can get you the necessary documents, find an appropriate place for your ceremony, and supply bouquet, boutonniere, Champagne, and even witnesses. At most, you send out announcements when you return.

Back-home and spin-the-globe weddings, however, both involve extra planning, hospitality, and organization. Some of the areas that need special attention include:

- **Dietary requirements:** If you have kosher or vegetarian guests, informing the kitchen in exotic environs may not be sufficient. Unless you want the kitchen to translate "string beans cooked" into "creamed beef stock," be *very* specific with food requests.
- **Hair and make-up:** Whether you are getting married back home or off in paradise, having someone you don't know at all do your hair and make-up for the main event is risky, particularly in areas where stylists justify their fee by spraying your tresses with copious amounts of lacquer. In such cases, take some lessons in advanced blow drying and face-painting and give it your best shot.
- **Hospitality suite:** Either reserving a special suite or designating a public gathering place at the resort has a two-fold benefit: It builds camaraderie and guests won't be gathering in your room at odd hours for lack of another place to go.

- **Multiple activities:** Whether you are all going to some new place or you are inviting guests to your home town, you must plan on entertaining them during their stay. (See Chapter 17 regarding other events.) Barbecues, softball games, picnics, hikes, cruises, and other types of group events give everyone a chance to meet and spend quality time with each other. One way to encourage group spirit is to plan for some team events during your days together. Beach volleyball, or, if you are in a city, a treasure hunt with clues in different ethnic areas, or even a softball game in a public park. T-shirt prizes with the name and date of the wedding are fun mementos.
- **Newsletters and questionnaires:** Send guests a newsletter updating them on your plans. Make it festive; if you're all going to an island, for example, toss in a couple of small seashells and mail the whole package in a bubble-wrap envelope. If you are going to a resort, include a questionnaire that asks whether they are interested in spa services, or sports such as sailing, tennis, or diving. This way you can inform the management in advance so they can staff properly.
- **On-site concierge:** If you have a large number of guests and they are all staying at one place, a very spiffy touch is a separate, on-premise concierge just for your party. If that is not feasible, ask the management if you may pay the concierge extra to have a list of activities, items, and special considerations for your group.
- **Photography/videography:** Because finding a first-rate photographer in an out-of-the-way spot is often impossible, some couples "import" a photographer and/or videographer. You may even be able to barter some vacation time after the gig for part of the shooting fee. Be sure to schedule your check-up trip(s) when you can meet with several photographers.
- **Reconnaissance trips:** Plan on making at least one site-inspection trip (and probably more) to meet with your on-site wedding consultant, (even if she's your mother) see the accommodations for your guests, and meet with as many vendors as possible.
- **Save-the-date-cards and special invitations:** The earlier you inform guests the better. A save-the-date-card eight months before is not unreasonable. A missive with all the particulars may go out four months later. This should include all hotel information if they need to reserve themselves. Mail the invitation eight to ten weeks before the wedding. The final invitation for a destination or weekend wedding works beautifully as a booklet with all the information detailed.
- **Tuxedos:** You may either transport your party's tuxes to and from your location, or contract with a tuxedo-rental establishment at your destination and pray to the gods of formal wear. Good tuxedo rental shops have the "ushers from around the world" thing down pat. They send out measurement cards and can do alterations within a day if necessary. Yet you should consider what is sensible — do the guys have to wear tuxedos at all?

- **Transportation:** If possible, retain at least one mini-van and driver if you are having a small destination wedding, or lease them per event if you need to get the guests around to a rehearsal dinner, the ceremony, reception, brunch and a few cocktail parties. Doing so may save you an enormous amount of turmoil.

- **Wine and liquor:** On many islands in the Caribbean that are popular for destination weddings, prices for good wines and champagnes are through the roof — better to forego the undrinkable options and come up with a wonderful signature drink.
- **Welcome baskets:** If guests have traveled a long way to join you for your wedding, one of the loveliest expressions of thanks is something in their room upon their arrival. A truly welcoming gift includes a note from the two of you thanking them for making the trip, a schedule of the events to come, some indigenous food or drink from the region along with the proper utensils or glasses, and a map or guidebook of the area with highlighted places and activities that you recommend.

One of the biggest issues regarding long-distance and destination weddings is whether to pay for all your guests. If you have the means, you may want to rent out an entire resort or inn for your family and close friends, and pay their travel expenses. Investigate group rates for hotel rooms and charter flights. If you can negotiate a special rate, guests should mention they are with your wedding when they make reservations. Some hotels provide response cards that you can include in invitations. They may require you to pay a deposit or guarantee with a credit card if you can't guarantee that the rooms will be rented. If you know that different guests will have different needs (bathtubs for children, small budgets), highlight a variety of accommodations.

Planning a wedding 475 miles away

I picked my wedding spot two years before I got married or even knew whom I would marry (although I had a hunch). My boyfriend, Michael, and I were visiting his alma mater, the College of the Atlantic, in Bar Harbor, Maine. We strolled through a terraced garden that overlooks the bay and is framed by handsome dry-stack stone walls. "This," I thought, "would be a great place to get married."

A year later, when Michael proposed, we happened to be back in Maine and spent the rest of our vacation touring hotels and inns and interviewing banquet managers. By the end of the trip, we had a place, a caterer, and a plan.

We returned a few months later to scope out lodging options for our guests. In the summer, Bar Harbor is a tourist town and the high concentration of inns, bed & breakfasts, upscale hotels, and moderately priced motels book up early. I toured them *all* with my future mother-in-law. We also made preliminary arrangements with a restaurant for the rehearsal dinner, and outlined a wedding menu with our caterer, who turned out to be

(continued)

(continued)

an old friend of Michael's. One advantage of getting married in a small town is that your choices are limited. After asking around, you quickly find out who are the best (or only) caterer, florist, baker, and band — and they've usually all worked together before.

Our third (and final trip before the wedding) was during a bitterly cold week in early spring. The trip started on a less-than-auspicious note when some bagpipers we'd gone out of our way to audition turned out to be mere amateurs with no wedding experience and a less-than-friendly attitude. Well, better to find out now than on our wedding day. Besides, we had many more important — and pleasant — matters to attend to. We had dinner with our officiant (another old friend of Michael's) and discussed our thoughts about marriage and the ceremony. Our caterer did a private tasting for us, in which we felt like pashas, nibbling so many exquisite delicacies. (As it turned out, we paid like pashas too; cooking 15 dishes for two, as we point out in Chapter 8, is not cheap.) We also chose the place settings and chairs at the rental company. We then met with our baker to decide that we preferred chocolate decadence cake with Grand Marnier Italian meringue to lemon poppy with buttercream frosting.

Marcy also came up and braved the cold to "block" our wedding processional at the college, as a director does scenes of a play, and figure out the floor plan at the reception hall, which was not heated on that 16-degree day. (What are co-authors for?) By this time, Marcy and I had been working on this book for almost a year — talk about anxiety! I had been dutifully making mental notes of every possible wedding glitch and necessity, which may explain why I had already begun having the classic recurring wedding nightmares.

In the following weeks and months, we traded e-mail with our caterer and phone calls with the band, who ended up playing the ceremony as well. We arrived in Bar Harbor several days before the wedding to unwind and make last-minute preparations such as getting the marriage license. Two things I was glad I brought: a laptop computer, which made revising the seating chart (in Excel) a cinch, and a stack of large manila envelopes, which came in handy for leaving instruction sheets and schedules at hotels for people and for stashing all the cards and checks we received over the weekend. Of course, nobody's perfect: I did forget to bring my blow dryer and sneakers.

The morning of the wedding, I found myself at the reception site, tying napkins, unpacking candlesticks and table numbers, making luminarias — generally getting in the caterer's way. But at a certain point I realized it was time to turn the execution of all my months' planning over to the pros. My job now was to go get dressed and be the bride.

Part VI

The Part of Tens

"It was the only tent they could get on such short notice. Just watch your step around the trapeze rigging."

In this part . . .

If your taxi ride is only ten minutes long, but you just can't bear the thought of wasting that precious time on (gasp!) *relaxation,* you've come to the right place. This part of the book offers some quick tidbits of useful information — everything from money-saving tips to marriage-saving tips and a useful appendix full of other resources that may help you with your planning. Enjoy!

Chapter 20

Ten Tricks for Saving Money

In This Chapter

- Rent whatever you can
- Fewer guests, more fun
- Music for a song

There are smart ways and not-so-smart ways to save money. Before you start scaling back your grand wedding vision, consider making these surgical cuts to your budget.

Cut the Guest List

With every person you add to your guest list, the cost of your wedding rises exponentially. That's one more meal to pay for, invitation to send, welcome basket to assemble — after 10 or 20 people, that's another table to rent, centerpiece to order, and so on. Soon you're talking big money. Rather than cut back on the amenities you offer your guests, cut back on the number of guests requiring amenities.

Be ruthless in paring your guest list. Whom do you consider an acquaintance as opposed to a friend? You should not feel compelled to add "and guest" to invitations sent to unmarried friends even if they think dating a whole week constitutes "almost living together." And beware the "and family" Pandora's box. Talk about your guest list exploding!

Remember the Old Wedding Adage: To Save a Cent, Rent, Rent, Rent!

Anything you can buy, you can rent. Potted plants, tablecloths, candlesticks, silk garlands, sofas — it's all out there and renting it for a day almost always costs much less than buying it.

Let's Not Do Lunch (Or Dinner)

Consider having a cocktail and hors d'oeuvres reception, which saves you money in food, music, and decor. Be sure to specify "cocktail reception" on the invitation so guests don't expect a full sit-down meal. Brunch, tea, or champagne and dessert receptions are also options.

Avoid Overtime

Be realistic in planning your wedding-day schedule (see Chapter 18) so you don't automatically incur overtime charges. Leave some leeway in case the ceremony doesn't start on time (which it almost never does) and the rest of the schedule gets pushed back. Otherwise, for example, if you're running late and the band is set up and waiting to play, you will be charged for their time even though they won't start playing a single note until the reception starts.

Buy Your Own Liquor

If you have your wedding in an off-premise location (such as a loft or a tent) and you're allowed to bring in your own wine and liquor, take advantage of sales throughout the year to stockpile before your wedding. Buying by the case may also entitle you to discounts, so check with your liquor store.

Ask Before You Pour

If you're paying by consumption, instruct the maitre d' that you want the waiters to *offer* wine and Champagne rather than simply filling any glass within a three-mile radius.

Decor as High as an Elephant's Eye

Spend your decor budget where guests are sure to see the results. That means at eye level and above: entranceways, tabletops, tent poles, and so on. While nothing is wrong with fancy edgings on tablecloths, tassels on chair cushions, garlands on low railings, and the like, they don't have the same punch that an oversized flower-filled urn does. The best bang for your buck for an evening reception are candles — votives, gothic, Roman, tapers — which, wick for wick, can add drama and romance to a room as much as flowers do.

By the same token, don't have your wedding in a yawning abyss that needs a Broadway set design team to make it wedding-friendly.

Orchestra in a Box

In lieu of hiring a few classical musicians for your ceremony, have an entire symphony — all you need is a decent sound system, a few compact discs, and somebody to press the right buttons at the right time. In an offbeat setting, well-chosen music can sound powerful and perfectly natural.

Do Easy Things Yourself

Simple but labor-intensive tasks such as tying ribbons around napkins, sealing wax on envelopes, and baking cookies can end up costing you a lot of money, so enlist bridesmaids, ushers, prospective in-laws, and siblings to help perform them.

Get Married Off-Peak

Depending on your area, you may be able to get a better deal on your reception by booking it on a Friday evening or Sunday afternoon or during a month or on a day that is not prime time for weddings. (See Chapters 1 and 2 for ways to schedule around peak times.)

Chapter 21

Ten Gadgets, Gizmos, and Gimmicks to Make Weddings a Whiz

In This Chapter

- Surfing the wedsites
- Using software for hard decisions
- Getting the kinks out

Modern weddings call for modern tools that make planning easier and the process more fun. We assume that you have enough taste not to e-mail thank-you notes or to answer a cell call at your ceremony, yet the more open you are to new technologies, the better you'll be able to breeze through the next few months. Some of the items here are still in their infancy, but the way things are going, by the time you celebrate your first anniversary, these may look like dinosaurs.

The World Wide Wed

Because the World Wide Web is evolving at such a mind-boggling pace, we realize that just about anything we write about it could be obsolete in a few nanoseconds. The following information is therefore on the general side. We've come across intriguing Web sites that exist for one cybermoment, never to be found or updated again. And, of course, a good deal of self-indulgent and misleading junk is floating around out there. But as more companies, magazines, services, and governmental agencies go online, the depth, diversity, consistency, and reliability of information improves.

You can buy more and more things over the Web, often with a credit card. As people have raised concerns about privacy, many sites have started offering secure servers, which scramble your credit card number as it travels along the wire. Others allow you to place your order and then phone in your credit card number. Most Internet experts consider these methods just as safe as handing your card to a sales clerk in a store — so you really don't have any reason to be more paranoid than usual. As with any transaction, keep track of verification numbers and save (or print out) the order form or other pertinent information regarding your purchase.

We personally like sites that offer more than pretty pictures and obvious tips. In general, the most comprehensive sites are magazines. These include magazines that have put up a site — such as *Modern Bride* (www.modernbride.com), *Town & Country* (www.tncweddings.com), and *WeddingBells* (www.weddingbells.com) — as well as magazines made just for the Web such as *Today's Bride* (www.todaysbride.com) and *UnGROOM'd* (www.ungroomd.com). By far, the most comprehensive, and therefore the most visited, Web site is The Knot (www.theknot.com).

Quirkier wedding Web sites are popping up all the time, and you can find information in lots of places that aren't tailored to getting married. The best way to get started is to do a search of the Internet using the key words "wedding and planning." You may need to type http:// before some specific addresses, and you may require a search engine such as Yahoo!, Excite, or Alta Vista. Other topics to plug in are honeymoons, travel, catering, and churches — the more specific you are when trying to shake a subject needle out of the Internet haystack, the greater the chance you'll hit on something useful. Here are some wedding-related things you may use the Internet for:

- **Budgeting:** The Knot (www.theknot.com), for example, is a wedding-specific site that provides, among many other things, a worksheet in which you input your estimated costs to find out which types (or brands) of stationery, rings, dresses, and so on fall in your price range.
- **Dresses:** The Canadian *WeddingBells* (www.weddingbells.com) features designer gowns, complete with style numbers, fabric information, and retail sources. The Knot also offers a library of thousands of "gown pix" and designer information.
- **Maps:** Just type the word *maps* in your search engine to get hundreds of maps. Doing so is still kind of a crapshoot — not all cities are listed and those that are often lack the kind of detail you need to figure out exactly how to get where you're going. One of the better cartology sites is Maps On Us (www.mapsonus.com).
- **Phone books:** Local telephone directories are available online through sites such as Nynex's www.bigyellow.com and Who Where Connect Now at wwcn.whowhere.com.
- **Stationery:** If you want to put your personal artistic stamp on thermographed or offset invitations, letterhead, or other standard stationery items, try ordering through iPrint (www.iprint.com). You create your own design by using their templates, specify the quantity, paper, and ink (you can even request inks that are safe for laser printers), and zip your order away.

- **Travel:** Just about every city and country has an online address for its tourist bureaus. (Do a search using the name of the city, state, or country.) You can also check out travel health advisories at www.tripprep.com, which includes state department publications among its offerings. And, of course, every major airline, car rental agency, hotel chain, and cruise line has a Web site.
- **Venues:** Many chambers of commerce can be accessed online through www.chamber-of-commerce.com. *Agenda,* a trade magazine for the special events industry, has a site (www.agendaonline.com) through which you can order the publication's directories for Boston, Dallas, New York, Philadelphia, San Francisco, Southern California, and Washington, DC. The National Park Service (www.nps.gov) can provide information on both wedding sites and honeymoon destinations.

Revolutionary Registries

Many companies feature detailed information about their products and registry programs on their Web sites. Some also allow you to update your registry online, where giftees can see what's on your list. A few sites even let people order gifts online. Actually registering online so you never have to set foot in a store is inching along the horizon. The online registry is a key feature of *Town & Country*'s site.

The other big innovation in registry convenience has been the use of bar code scanners — the same dandy devices used in supermarkets. Target (whose registry program is called Club Wedd) and Home Depot are two chains that have pioneered this method. You just amble through the store zapping with your scanner all the items that you want on your registry.

Stationery by Design

With a personal computer, a decent laser printer, and some high-quality papers, you can create perfectly fine invitations, menus, newsletters, place cards, programs, return envelopes, and other stationery. Microsoft Word alone contains enough special features to pull off a good-looking document, but if you want to get fancy, CorelDRAW and PhotoShop enable you to create more elaborate designs with just a bit of practice. New programs are coming out all the time, so check your local computer store or go shopping online.

After you lay out your document, you may simply print copies on your personal printer or make one copy on bright white paper (which makes type look crisper) and have a professional printer offset it on heavy or decorative stock. For informal pieces, high-quality photocopies may be sufficient.

If you are a paper fanatic (welcome to our world), you can find beautiful hand-made specimens through mail-order catalogs and specialty stationery shops. Papers that are ridged, translucent, metallicized, or embedded with wildflowers and such do not take to laser printing but make excellent backgrounds. Print your text on plain card stock and mount that on the more ornate papers. (For details on designing invitations, see Chapter 13.)

If you want to incorporate fancy papers into your invitations or other documents that you're having professionally printed, buy the paper in large sheets, which the printer can then cut to invitation size. Paper stock that has already been cut down cannot go through a printing press.

Stamp-Free, Toll-Free RSVPs

All right, so you've looked at every invitation in the universe — and nothing has even remotely tickled your fancy. Consider this: Instead of paper RSVP cards and return envelopes, send interactive phone cards. On one side of the card is a design of your choosing such as photo of you or the wedding location, the invitation itself, or a cartoon. The other side contains the guest's name, an 800 number, and a "secret code" for activating the card. When guests call in, they use a touch-tone phone to say whether they are coming, how many guests are in their party, the day they are arriving, or whatever questions you want. Roberta and Barry Strom, whose company, Communications Design Group, Inc., produces Telecards for Southern New England Bell, designed a card for their own wedding (the second for both), which parodied Moviefone, complete with celebrity impressions. For $2,000 they give you 100 cards printed in one color, an interactive program with up to four questions, and a weekly report of who has called. This method is, admittedly, not for everyone, but it does save on paperwork and return postage.

Another way to field RSVPs by phone is to hire an answering service. One that specializes in weddings is RSVP Service (800-514-9686). When your guests call this toll-free number and extension, they'll never know that they're calling northern Kentucky. Guests provide whatever information you request such as number of adults and children, which event they are attending, and so on. Two weeks before the wedding, someone from the company calls all the guests who have not yet responded — another headache cured. The cost is about $90 for 100 invitations.

Forget about Film

In case you haven't noticed, the whole world is going digital and cameras are no exception. Most professional wedding photographers have yet to join the digital revolution because printing photographs from digital cameras is more expensive than with regular film and the quality of the prints is less than optimum. But that may soon change — even as we write this, the technology is improving in quantum leaps. In the meantime, *you* can have a blast with digital cameras, documenting wedding festivities from the planning stages to your honeymoon. These cameras don't use film — images are recorded digitally on "storage cards," which look like computer diskettes. You slip a card into your digital camera, snap away, then download the images to your computer. Unlike film cartridges, you can selectively erase any or all of the images and reuse the blank card to take more pictures.

Another variation on the digital theme is to take a regular roll of film and request Kodak Picture Network processing when you take the film to a participating photofinishing retailer. When you get your pictures back, you also get a claim number that allows you to look at your photos online. As a member of the Kodak Picture Network (currently $4.95 a month), you can access your personal online "studio" with a private password. Your pictures are stored in this studio, and you can sort through them, title the roll of film, write captions, and delete all the ones in which you look like a toad. The best part is that you can then create personal picture postcards that you e-mail to friends and relatives. (***Note:*** They must have Internet Explorer or Netscape 2.2 or higher to view these postcards.) For more information, see the Kodak website at `www.kodak.com`.

Digital technology also means new possibilities for the Corner Photo Booth described in Chapter 12. With a digital camera and Kodak Event Imaging Software, companies such as First Hand Images are able to mix photos with digital images, artwork, magazine covers, guest names, and so on. The process takes about 90 seconds from pose to print.

Rub It In

As massage aficionados, we know that a massage is best when it's low-tech — a pair of strong hands (or feet) pushing and pummeling and prodding away at every knot, from your trapezius to your flexor brevis digitorum, until you're as relaxed as a plate of linguini. We do, of course, encourage you to practice on each other regularly during the course of your day-to-day marital existence.

But when you're both stressed out and in the midst of pre-wedding mania, the old I'll-do-you-if-you-do-me-routine means that one of you has to regain consciousness to fulfill your half of the bargain. In the spirit of ultimate self-indulgence, we recommend one of the latest electric massage contraptions (not to be confused with vibrating hotel beds). The Sharper Image sells a 10-motor massage mat with heat that is a pretty good substitute for the real thing. Sharper Image also carries a Shiatsu-style foot massager — and we *know* that has more patience than one's sweetheart. Brookstone offers a gadget called the Tapper/Vibe, a hand-held massage wand that gives you a choice of a tapping or vibrating massage, the effects of the two combined being supposedly very beneficial.

Guess Who's Coming to the Wedding?

People who are super organized often think they know exactly how to get you organized. They invent binders with little pre-made checklists and come up with lots of little adages and mnemonic devices to keep you on top of things. You then feel incompetent or guilty if you forget to record every little piece of data in the proper box.

Now those people have started writing software programs to help you plan your wedding. Although some of these programs have a few useful features, such as seating chart worksheets, summaries of people who still need thank-you notes, and stationery-designing workshops, none of them have everything we would want. Many of them take up precious bytes with insipid etiquette and romance tips as well as pre-conceived timelines that need a great deal of modifying to make them relevant to any individual wedding. And all of them seem to require a lot of input on your part. The better ones seem to be Wedding Planner by Expert Software, Wedding Workshop by MicroPrecision, and My Wedding Companion by Five Star Software. *WedServ* offers a nifty program called WedLink, which you can download from their Web site (`www.wedserv.com`) for free.

If you're at all handy with a spreadsheet program such as Excel, you can customize your own wedding planning system. Your version may not have all the macros and pretty colors of a professional program, but you do have the freedom to include all (and only) the items that you need. You can also see at a glance how many guests have been invited and how many to date are actually coming.

To indicate *who* is coming, boldface those entries. If you're having a far-away wedding and can stand to lug your laptop computer there, you can reorganize the seating chart with a few quick keystrokes.

Following the Money

In addition to keeping track of guests, Excel and other computer spreadsheet programs are good for figuring budgets. You'll probably be adjusting your expenses up until — or past — the wedding day. Doing your budget in a database allows you to compare your estimated costs with actual expenses, create subcategories (delineating all the rentals under catering, for example), track payments, and remind yourself how much you're really spending.

Quicken by Intuit also enables you to create budgets and track expenses for all your accounts, including checking, savings, and credit cards. You can create reports that tell you what percentage you've spent on what and whether you're headed for a wedding deficit.

The more detailed your budget, the more realistic you'll be in the planning. (Unless you get so carried away by your computer prowess that real numbers cease to matter.) See Chapter 1 for a complete list of all the various budget lines you may need to include.

If you have a PC and modem, check to see if your bank has online banking. (Citibank and Chase Manhattan, for example, offer this service for free.) Banking by phone is one of those rare technological advances that really can change your life for the better: no more stamps to buy, checks to write, or envelopes to lick. As you pay those wedding bills (by pressing a few computer keys!), you know exactly how much you have in the kitty at any time.

But Where Do I File the Hors d'oeuvre Sample?

Planning a wedding is like having a second full-time job with countless appointments, errands, and meetings that you must squeeze in among all your other countless appointments, errands, and meetings. Although you sleep with your date book under your pillow, you may want to cut down on the paper trail with a portable electronic organizer, preferably a memo pad, datebook, and phone book all in one. Every few months another company comes out with a smaller, faster, smarter model that can do everything from sending e-mail to tracking expenses. Others have full keyboards and fax capabilities. Most now "dock" with your PC so you can synchronize all your data.

"No, I'm Not Talking to Myself, I'm Talking to — Oh, Never Mind!"

Even if you can remember every meal you've ever eaten since the age of seven and you never forget to send out birthday cards, planning a wedding can make you feel like a pinball machine on TILT. One way to save your sanity is to take notes. Pocket voice recorders are a godsend for those temporary bouts of amnesia or when a wedding epiphany strikes while you're walking down the street carrying two sacks of tablecloth samples, the last part of your thesis, and tonight's groceries. Just grab your teeny voice recorder (they can be worn around your neck or kept in a jacket pocket) and take a memo. One of our favorites is the IQ Voice Organizer, which weighs just over 2 ounces and records up to 200 appointments and 640 phone numbers and recognizes your voice in any language.

Chapter 22

Ten Tacky Temptations We Beg You to Resist

In This Chapter

- Banking the booty
- Groping garters
- Putting down in-laws

We believe strongly that you should do whatever you want at your wedding — almost. As you exhibit your creativity and personal style, you need to keep hospitality foremost in your thinking. When we talk about tackiness, we're really talking about thoughtlessness. Here are a few social land mines to sidestep.

Pre-Wedding Debauches

Embarrassing, drunken, macho/macha, G-string-pulling, divorce-causing, bachelor or bachelorette parties are not a good idea. For starters, you should ask the host to invite your prospective in-laws (mother, father, brother, sister) to join in this prenuptial rite, so if the event being planned would make them blanch, perhaps you should graciously suggest an alternative. While these events can be a time to let down your hair, we suggest that you don't indulge in behavior you'll live to regret. (For ideas on pre-wedding parties, see Chapter 17.)

You Are Cordially Invited to Buy Us Something

We're all for efficiency, and we do believe in registering, but enclosing your registry information with any kind of invitation is gauche. The main agenda appears to be a gift grab with the invitation as an afterthought. We cannot imagine that, between your parents and close friends, nobody has a big enough mouth to pass the word of where you're registered. (For more on this subject, see Chapter 14.)

Thanks for the A) Glasses, B) Towels, C) Other

Realizing that they have Champagne tastes and their friends have diet-soda budgets, some couples, egged by the stores, are resorting to *gift banking*. As we explain in Chapter 14, the couple registers for moderately priced things; and as guests purchase the items, the store keeps the goods and "banks" the money. The couple then uses this credit toward something more extravagant.

This practice begs several questions: Why go to all that trouble of registering if you don't need or want the stuff? What do you say in your thank you note? ("Thank you so much for the glasses. We've never seen anything like them.") How do you explain the gift's absence when the giver visits? As Mark Twain said, "If you tell the truth, you don't have to remember anything."

Turning the Aisle into a Runway

We're not sure which is worse, asking someone's cute daughter you hardly know to be a flower girl just because she'll look adorable or hiring and firing attendants based on their modeling prowess. We're all for pageantry and theater, but don't forget what a wedding is really about. (To review the criteria for selecting members of the wedding party, see Chapter 4.)

Bad-Mouthing In-Laws-to-Be

If your prospective spouse is a frustrated stand-up comic who loves to regale the crowd with his or her "hilarious" anecdotes about your parents, nip this sweet habit in the bud now. Such jokes often veil a certain hostility, and you can only wonder what your spouse will be saying about you in years to come.

Turning Guests into Photographers

Leaving disposable cameras on every table so that guests can augment your scrapbook with their own candid shots is a nice theory, but it rarely works. Inevitably, guests either shoot the film but never get to see the photos they've taken, or they walk off with the camera and you never get to see the pictures. If you want shots besides those the photographer takes, ask guests who know how to take pictures to do so and to send you the developed film later, at your expense. Or set up a corner photo booth, as described in Chapter 12.

The Hacking Cough Hall of Fame

How distressed everyone was years ago when, as dessert was served, all the men promptly got up and went into another room to light up their cigars. That isn't a problem now because many considerate chimneys — including women — light up right at the dinner table. For many guests, however, being enveloped by second-hand smoke is not only decidedly unhip but also life-threatening. We love the idea of no-smoking receptions, but since some of our favorite people would have a nic-fit on the spot, we suggest a designated smoking area.

Do Unto Others

Be kind to those who have gone before you: restrain yourself from criticizing other people's weddings as you plan your own. Catty comments made in passing — "Well, we would never dream of serving *fake* Champagne" — inevitably return to haunt you. Reserve these observations for private discussions with your fiancé(e), best friend, and tight-lipped parents. (Besides, once you add up everything, you may decide that "fake" champagne ain't so bad after all.)

The Great Garter Grab

A holdover from the glorious medieval practice known as stripping the bride, where guests yanked off the bride's underclothes to hasten the consummation of the marriage, the garter toss hasn't lost any of its charm. We realize many people think this bit of vaudeville, with the band playing the theme from *Gypsy,* is jolly fun. How else, after all, will the single men know who is next to marry?

Fortunately, this tradition is dying, although not fast enough. We suggest that all single guests, male and female, compete instead for the tossed bouquet. Don't get us wrong. We love sexy lingerie and garters are no exception. But we feel you should remove them in the privacy of your honeymoon suite.

Squeeze Plays

Inviting more guests than can fit comfortably in your space results in some people either being seated in Outer Slobovia — anterooms, balconies, closets, hallways, pup tents, or rooftops — or being crammed in so tightly at each table that they have to take turns cutting their food. Either invite fewer guests or book a bigger space.

Chapter 23

Ten Ideas to Make a Wedding Special

In This Chapter

- Revving up the welcome wagon
- Notes on thank-yous
- Tackling tasks in tandem

Even if you decorate the room with more flowers than the Rose Bowl Parade, top every table with life-size chocolate cupids, and shoot yourself from a cannon, the most meaningful (and memorable) wedding touches are those that show how much you care for each other and those around you. Here are a few of our favorites:

Dynamic Dances

Instead of swaying and sweating, praying for the first dance to be over, take some dance lessons and strut your stuff. Choreograph this moment complete with dips, spins, and flings. Or escort your mother or father to the dance floor to something hot (rather than the classic maudlin medley) to prove that they're still kicking.

Revive the Language of Flowers

The Victorians, who were mad for horticulture, assigned specific meanings to herbs and flowers, and weddings are the ideal opportunity to resurrect what they called the Language of Flowers. Put a sprig of sweet basil (good wishes) and trails of ivy (fidelity) in the bride's bouquet, and use a red rose (love) for the groom's boutonniere. Gilded sprigs of rosemary (remembrance and friendship) make lovely mementos for guests. On the tables, fill vases with red tulips (declaration of love). Translate this language on your program, so that guests can appreciate all the thought you've put into these details.

Miscellaneous Mementos

In lieu of or in addition to generic favors, give your guests ceremony programs and menu cards, which tend to wind up in scrapbooks and remind guests of your beautiful day. Calligraphed or embossed bookmarks, small pots of herbs or flowers, and flea-market candlesticks are practical as well as memorable.

This Is Your Life

A slide show or video set to music and featuring photographs and mementos of the bride's and groom's lives can be an icebreaker, especially if done as a surprise by the couple's friends. An even better surprise is for the bride and groom to put together their own show — with pictures of their friends and relatives. After all, people are basically narcissistic and prefer gazing at shots of themselves.

Psychic to 'Em

Hospitality often means anticipating guests' needs ahead of time and accommodating them before they have to ask.

- Find out which of your guests are vegetarian, have food allergies, or keep kosher, and inform waiters where they are seated.
- Seat people with similar interests at the same table.
- Instead of writing "and guest" or "guest of so-and-so" on escort and place cards, find out the person's actual name.

"Our Hour"

This day is about both of you, from the planning to the execution (if you'll pardon the expression). Nothing is sweeter than seeing a wedding that bears the signature of both the bride and groom. This means sharing the fun as well as the drudgery, the cake tastings as well as the thank-you notes. Consider these tasks a warm-up to "in sickness and in health."

Winning Welcomes

If you're playing host to a large number of out-of-town guests, show your appreciation by inviting them to either the rehearsal dinner or a less formal event such as a barbecue, boat ride, square dance, hay ride, bonfire, or softball game. Also have something waiting for them in their rooms when they arrive. Guests love a welcome basket stuffed with fruit, souvenirs, a local guidebook, maps, or museum passes. Be sure to include a handwritten note of welcome and thanks. (For more tips on hospitality for guests traveling to your wedding, see Chapter 18.)

The Fall of the House of Ushers and Bridesmaids

Your attendants are not one homogenous group; treat them as the individuals they are. Choose bouquets and boutonnieres for each of them specifically. The same goes for their gifts and garb.

Gifts from the Heart

Choose, commission, or compose a poem or song for your intended. Have a talented friend or the band perform it as a surprise for your new spouse.

Thanks, Folks

Present each set of parents (or multiple sets, if that's the case) with a gift from both of you, thanking them for raising the love of your life and (we hope) for their a$$i$tance.

Chapter 24

Ten Secrets to a Happy Marriage from Couples Who Know

In This Chapter

- Useful phrases
- Strategies in times of love and war
- Timing is everything

As you plan your wedding, you've no doubt had to stop more than once and remind yourself that there is a point to all this work and aggravation. Welcome to married life! Every couple has a recipe for making their relationship work. We delight in couples who have been married for decades and still melt when their spouse walks into the room. So we asked a few the secret to their wedded bliss and longevity. You won't hear these answers on *The Newlywed Game* — these couples have spent a lifetime figuring them out. But you don't have to wait that long: We now offer these gems to you (free of charge!) and guarantee them to last the length of your marriage! If you're not completely satisfied, return the unused portion to Secrets, 4 Theduration, Hope Springs, Eternal 00001.

What You Don't Know Won't Hurt You

"One, separate bathrooms. Two, don't ever ask a question you can't stand to hear the answer to. And three, forbid all conversations from the time you get out of bed until after breakfast. Conversations before you get out of bed are encouraged."

— *George, married to Loretta for 43 years*

Unless It's "Yes, Dear"

"Remember that having the last word is not important."

— Helen, married to Mal for 57 years

Two Words, One Sign

"Perpetual lust."

— Bob, married to Dell for 30 years

"We're both Leos."

— Dell

Special Physical Attributes

"Have an exceptional ability to listen or be deaf."

— Joan, married to Al for 46 years

Compliments to the Chef

"Have a husband who cooks."

— Étel, married to David for 28 years

Twice a Day

"Every night before we go to sleep, even if we've been arguing, we say, 'I love you!' And every morning when we wake up, the first thing we say is, 'I love you, and I'm so happy to be with you!'"

— Helen and Walker, married 52 years

I Scream, You Scream

"We make a date with each other every week even if it's only to go out for ice cream."

— Patsy and Hayes, married 38 years

A Kiss Is Never Just a Kiss

"We always kiss each other hello and goodbye whenever we leave the house or come home."

— Lee, married to Gene for 42 years

Bedside Manners

"When I'm sick, he doesn't tell me to get out of bed, and when he's sick, I don't tell him to get *in* bed."

— Barbara, married to Steve for 14 years

Inertia Kicks In

"If you live together long enough, eventually you become good friends."

— Helen, married to Abe for 46 years

Appendix
References

Chapter 1: The IZE Have It

Weather: *Weatherdata Network* provides forecasts up to a year in advance with 75 percent accuracy; $12.50, including shipping and handling; 800-888-0430. **Wedding/Event Planners:** *Creative Parties Ltd.;* Rita Bloom; Bethesda, MD; 301-654-9292. *Glorious Events;* Diane Harris; Atlanta, GA; 770-455-6600. *Event Planning & Design Consultants, Inc.;* New Orleans, LA; 504-943-1445.

Chapter 2: Space: The First Frontier

Books: *Places: A Directory of Public Places for Private Events & Private Places for Public Functions* by Hannelore Hahn; $24.95; free update information provided by phone to book buyers; *Tenth House Enterprises, Inc.;* Caller Box 810, Gracie Station, New York, NY 10028; 212-737-7536. **Magazines:** *Locations* offers free search service and listings of venues and vendors in New York-New Jersey with plans to expand to other cities; 257 East 72nd Street, New York, NY 10021; 212-288-4745; fax: 212-861-0939; `www.locationsmag.com`. *The Guide to Unique Meeting Facilities;* a Minturn, CO-based directory that offers a free search service to help you match your event with a suitable site; 800-933-3500; `www.theguide.com`. **Travel brochures and catalogs:** *The Innkeepers' Register: A Guide to 315 Distinctive Destinations;* $12.95; updated annually by the Independent Innkeepers' Association; to order, call 800-344-5244. *Romantic Wedding Destinations* by Jackie Carrington; published by Innovanna Corporation; 13839 Southwest Frwy, Suite 217, Sugar Land, TX 77478; 713-242-9835; 800-577-9810. **Travel newsletters:** *Andrew Harper's Hideaway Report;* $125 for 12 issues; $10 for back issues; Box 300, Whitefish, MT 59937; 406-862-3480; fax: 406-862-3486. *Easy Escapes* publishes frank and informative reviews of accommodations in the U.S. and Europe; $47 for 10 issues; $6 for single issues; P.O. Box 120365, Boston, MA 02112; 617-426-7288; 800-221-0878. Also puts out *Interesting and Unusual Hotels,* which includes lighthouses, tree houses, and tugboats. **Bridal fairs:** *The Great Bridal Expo* is one of the biggest, appearing several times a year around the U.S.; 800-422-3976; `www.greatbridalexpo.com`. **Professional associations:** *Association of Bridal Consultants;* 200 Chestnut Land Road, New Milford, CT 06776; 860-355-0464. *International Special Events Society* (ISES); 9202 N. Meridian St., Suite 200; Indianapolis, IN 46260; 800-688-ISES; fax: 317-571-5603; `www.ISES.com`. *Leading Caterers of America* can refer you to its national network of caterers and help you find off-premise sites; 2167 South Bayshore Drive, Miami, FL 33133; 800-743-6660; fax: 305-285-1362; `www.leadingcaterers.com`. **Tents:** *IFAI Tent Rental Divison,* an international trade association, publishes a free worldwide directory of tent rental professionals; 1801 County Road B West, Roseville, MN 55101; 800-225-4324; 612-222-2508; fax: 612-222-9334. *Andy Gump, Inc.;* 26954 Ruether Avenue, Santa Clarita, CA 91351; 800-263-9486; 800-992-7755; 805-251-7721. *Stamford Tent and Party Rental;* 54 Research Dr., Stamford, CT 06906; 203-324-6222. **Portable bathrooms:** *Executive Restroom Trailers;* P.O. Box 172, Annapolis Junction, MD 20701; 800-445-4928.

Chapter 3: And the Bride Wore . . . Whatever She Pleased

Bridal retailers: *Bridal Boutique of Manhasset;* 1681 Northern Blvd., Manhasset, NY 11030; 516-869-8455; fax: 516-869-8655. *Kleinfeld;* 8202 Fifth Avenue, Brooklyn, NY 11209; 718-833-1100. *Michelle Bridal*; 24 West 57th Street, 2nd floor, New York, NY, 10019; 212-245-3390. **Gloves:** *Carolina Amato;* 800-GLOVE-95. **Image consultant:** *Laurie Krauz;* 212-799-7073. **Makeup artists:** *Laura Geller;* 1044 Lexington Avenue, New York, NY 10022; 212-570-5477. *Maria Verel;* 212-889-4110. **Milliner:** *Tia Mazza Millinery*; New York, NY; 212-989-4349. *Susan van der Linde;* 111 East 56th Street, New York, NY 10022; 212-758-1686. **Personal Shopper:** *Gail Kittenplan Associates;* Wedding and fashion consultants; 1165 Park Avenue, New York, NY 10128; 212-348-8401. **Sewing your own dress:** *Bridal Couture* by Susan Khalje; $29.95; 1997; Krause Publications, 700 E. State Street, Iola, WI 54990-001; 800-258-0929; 715-445-2214. **Related reading:** *Bridal Gown Guide* by Denise and Alan Fields; 1997; Windsor Peak Press. *The Wedding Dress* by Maria McBride-Mellinger; 1993; Random House. **Vintage gowns:** *Bird-n-Hand;* Northport, MI; 616-386-7104.

Chapter 4: A Circle of Friends

Bridesmaid dress designers: *Dessy Creations;* 1385 Broadway, 17th floor, New York, NY 10018; 800-52-DESSY; 212-354-5808. *Watters & Watters Inc.;* 4320 Spring Valley, Dallas, TX 75244; 972-991-6994. **Waistcoat designer**: *Terence Teng;* 212-772-1519.

Chapter 5: The Main Event: The Ceremony

Catholic ceremonies: *Your Catholic Wedding* by Chris Aridas; $8.95; 1997; The Crossroad Publishing Company, 370 Lexington Avenue, New York, NY 10017. **Music:** *The University of Virginia Music Library;* `www.musiclib@virginia.edu`. **Notary publics:** Call 800-USNOTARY. **Humanist and spiritualist resources:** *American Humanist Association;* P.O. Box 1188, Amherst, NY 14226-7188; 800-743-6646; fax: 716-839-5079. *Ethical Society;* 20 chapters, most in the New York metropolitan area; headquarters are at Ethical Union, 2 West 64th Street, New York, NY 10023; 212-873-6500. *National Spiritualist Association of Churches;* P.O. Box 217, Lily Dale, NY 14752-0217; 716-595-2000. *Quaker Information Center;* 1501 Cherry Street, Philadelphia, PA 19102; 215-241-7024; `www.afsc.org/qic.htm`. *Unitarian Universalist Association;* 25 Beacon Street, Boston, MA 02108; 617-742-2100. **Jewish weddings:** *The New Jewish Wedding* by Anita Diamant; 1993; Fireside. **Wedding readings:** *Centuries of Writing and Rituals on Love and Marriage* by Eleanor Munro; 1989; Viking.

Chapter 6: Other Aisle Styles

Gay weddings: *The Essential Guide to Lesbian and Gay Weddings* by Tess Ayers and Paul Brown; Harper Collins; 1995. *Same Sex Unions in Premodern Europe* by John Boswell, Villard Books, 1994 provides an excellent history as well as translations of ancient ceremonies for same sex unions. An organization to contact is *Partners Task Force for Gay and Lesbian Couples,* Box 9684, Seattle, WA 98101; 206-935-1206; www.buddybuddy.com. *The United Fellowship of Metropolitan Community Churches* addresses specifically the needs of Christian lesbians and gays; 800-501-HOPE. **Military weddings:** *Service Etiquette*; by Oretha D. Swartz; 1988; Naval Institute Press, Annapolis, MD. **Period theme resources:** *Society for Creative Anachronism;* 800-789-7486. *Victorian Papers;* 888-512-2753. (For calligraphy resources, see Chapter 13.) *Your Victorian Wedding* by Georgene Muller Lockwood; 1992; Prentice Hall General Reference.

Chapter 7: Music, Sweet Music

Music: *OrrHouse Music*; Nashville, TN 37211; 615-833-8018.

Chapter 8: Booking the Cooking

Caterers: *Great Performances;* 212-727-2424; fax: 212-727-2820. *Abigail Kirsch Culinary Productions, Ltd.;* 212-696-4076 or 914-631-3242. *Robbin's Wolfe Catering;* 521 West Street, New York, NY 10014; 212-924-6500; fax: 212-924-6685. **Hotline for leftovers:** *Food Chain, Inc.* can direct you to one of 126 programs around the country; 912 Baltimore, Suite 300, Kansas City, MO 64105; 800-845-300; fax: 816-842-5145. *Second Harvest National Food Bank Network* can provide you with the number of the food bank nearest you so that you can arrange for them to pick up leftovers for redistribution; 312-263-2303. **Featured menus:** *Along Came Mary;* 5265 Pico Blvd., Los Angeles, CA 90019; 213-931-9082; fax: 213-936-8249. *Calihan Gotoff;* 833 West Haines, Chicago, IL 60622; 312-829-4644; fax: 312-829-3885. *Feastivities, Inc.;* 1016 Lancaster Avenue, Berwyn, PA 19312; 610-889-0750; fax: 610-889-3229. *More Than A Mouthful;* 743 S. Lucerne Blvd., Los Angeles, CA 90005; 213-937-6345; fax: 213-937-3145. *Rainbow Room;* 30 Rockefeller Plaza, New York, NY 10012; 212-632-5115; fax: 212-632-5107.

Chapter 9: A Piece of Cake

Cakemakers: *Ana Paz Cakes Unlimited;* 1460/D Northwest 107th Avenue, Miami, FL 33172; 305-471-5850. *Bijoux Doux;* 304 Mulberry Street, New York, NY 10012; 212-226-0948. *Colette's Cakes;* Colette Peters, New York, NY 212-366-6530. *It Figures* (Melanie Wynn); 310-828-9138. *John and Mike's Amazing Cakes;* 14934 NE 31st Street, Redmond, WA 98032; 206-869-2992. *La petite fleur* (Jan Kish); P.O. Box 872, Worthington, OH 43085; 614-848-5855. *Montclair Baking* (Cheryl Lew, owner); 2220 Mountain Blvd., Suite 140, Oakland, CA 94611; 510-530-8052. *Rosemary's Cakes Inc.* (Rosemary Cheris Littman); 299 Rutland Avenue, Teaneck, NJ 07666; 201-833-2417; fax: 201-833 8227. *Sylvia Weinstock;* 273 Church Street, New York, NY 10013; 212-925-6698; fax: 212-941-9862.

Chapter 10: Cheers!

Related reading: *Wine For Dummies* and *Wine Buying Companion For Dummies* by Ed McCarthy and Mary Ewing-Mulligan; 1995; IDG Books Worldwide, Inc. *Hugh Johnson's Pocket Encyclopedia of Wine;* comes out annually; Fireside. *Fear of Wine* by Leslie Brenner, 1995; Bantam Books.

Chapter 11: Setting the Stage

Butterflies: *Insect Lore and the Butterfly Celebration;* P.O. Box 1535, Shafter, CA 93263-9606; 800-548-3284; 805-746-6047; fax: 800-746-0334. **Mechanical candles:** *Paradise Candles;* P.O. Box 338, Paradise, PA 17562; 800-632-4264. **Things to throw:** *Bouchard;* 612 West Fifth Avenue, Naperville, IL 60563; 630-355-2770. *The GreenWorld Project;* sells tree seedlings, tree and wildflower seed packets, potpourri, and birdseed. 800-825-5122; `www.GreenWorld@ worldnet.att.net`. **Decor designers:** *Anthony Ferraz;* 526 West 26th Street, New York, NY 10009; 212-929-2168; fax: 212-929-2265. *Atlas Floral;* main office, 718-457-4900; sales office at Hotel Pierre, 212-751-6430; sales office at the Plaza Hotel, 212-753-3260. *Martha Meier Designs, Inc.;* Southport, CT; 203-259-4179; New York, NY; 212-352-9712. *Preston Bailey;* 88 Lexington Avenue #16C, New York, NY 10016; 212-683-0035; fax: 212-481-3168. *Stonekelly;* (Jen Stone and Don Kelly); 328 Columbus Avenue, New York, NY 10023; 212-875-0500; fax: 212-875-1920. *Renny Design for Entertaining;* 505 Park Avenue, New York, NY; 800-736-6910; 212-288-7000. *Robert Isabell;* 410 West 13th Street, New York, NY 10014; 212-645-7767; fax: 212-645-7765. **Lighting specialists:** *Frost Lighting;* P.O. Box 489; FDR Station; New York, NY 10150; 212-751-0223; fax: 718-426-6098. *Stortz Lighting;* 70 Laight Street; New York, NY 10013; 212-219-2330; fax: 212-219-2409.

Chapter 12: For Posterity: Photos and Videos

Photo storage: *The Sentry Storage Chest* protects 150 negatives from fires or other disasters; 800-251-0095. **Photographers and studios:**, *Maureen Edwards DeFries;* P.O. Box 0090, Hawleyville, CT 06440; 203-740-9343. *Gruber Photographers, Inc.* (Terry deRoy Gruber); 315 West 57th Street #18C, New York, NY 10019; 212-262-9777. *Harold Hechler Associates* (David Hechler); 654 Madison, Suite 1509, New York, NY 10021; 212-654-8199; 914-633-3331. *Lambert Photographs;* 6809 Dublin Road, Dublin OH 43017; 614-717-9822. *Alex Kirkbride;* 21 East 9th Street #2D, New York, NY 10003; 212-533-7570. *Laurie Klein Gallery;* 290 Federal Road, Brookfield, CT 06804; 203-740-1110; fax: 203-740-1114. *Sarah Merians Photography, Inc.;* 212-633-0502. *Andy Marcus of Fred Marcus Photography;* 245 West 72nd Street, New York, NY 10023; 212-873-5588. **Videographers:** *A Magic Moment;* an affiliate of Fred Marcus Photography; 7733 Sugar Bend Drive, Orlando, FL 32819; 800-345-VIDEO; 407-370-9243. *HQ Productions* (Nate Weil); 377 Park Avenue South, New York, NY 10016; 212-725-7260; fax: 212 679-6108. *Supreme Video* (Tony Arzt); 230 Lonetown, Redding, CT 06896; 203-938-9161.

Chapter 13: Getting the Word Out

Calligraphy: *The Calligraphy Company;* 201-866-1985. **Engraved stationery:** *Cartier;* 800-CARTIER. *Dempsey & Carroll;* 6405 Beckley Street, Baltimore, MD 21224; 800-444-4019; 410-631-7701; fax: 410-631-7705. *Stationers Engraving* (Ted Harrington); 212-242-4600. **Invitations:** *Alpine Creative Group;* New York, NY; 212-989-4198, fax: 212-989-4182. *Creative Intelligence;* 4988 Venice Blvd., Los Angeles, CA 90019; 213-936-9009. *Pendragon Ink. Ltd.;* 508-234-6843; fax: 508-234-5446. *William Arthur Stationery and Invitations;* 800-985-6581 (for nearest retailer).

Chapter 14: Gimme, Gimme

Finding old patterns: *Replacements, Ltd.;* 1089 Knox Road, Greensboro, NC 27420; 800-REPLACE (800-737-5223). *Wedgwood China;* Dept. FBC-EC, 41 Madison Avenue, New York, NY 10010.

Chapter 15: Left Hand, Fourth Finger

Jewelers: *Michael Eigen;* 1198 Madison Avenue, New York, NY 10017; 212-996-0281. *Wedding Ring Hotline;* 800-985-7464; 908-972-7777. *Mish;* 22 East 72nd Street, New York, NY 10021; 212-734-3500. **Related reading:** *Engagement & Wedding Rings: The Definitive Guide for People in Love* by Antoinette L. Matlins, Antonio C. Bonanno, and Jane Crystal; 1990; Gemstone Press; 802-457-4000. For a consumer kit on diamond and colored gemstone jewelry, write to *American Gem Society;* Department MB Special, 1050 East Flamingo Road, Suite 130, Las Vegas, NV 89119. For a free booklet, *Your Guide to Diamond Quality and Value,* write to *Diamond Information Center;* c/o J. Walter Thompson, 466 Lexington Avenue, New York, NY 10017. For *What You Need to Know about Platinum,* write to the Platinum Guild International USA; 620 Newport Center Drive, Suite 910, Newport, CA 92660.

Chapter 16: Nuts and Bolts and Loose Screws

Wedding insurance: *Weddingsurance*, underwritten by Fireman's Fund Insurance Company and administered by R.V. Nuccio & Associates, Inc.; P.O. Box 307, Fawnskin, CA 92333; (800)-ENGAGED (364-2433).

Chapter 19: Let's Get Out of Here

Destinations: *Sandals* and *Beaches;* 800-SANDALS; 800-BEACHES. *HONEYMOON The Romantic Travel Magazine;* 800-513-7112. *Disney's Fairy Tale Weddings and Honeymoons;* 407-828-3400. **Adventure trips:** *Special Expeditions;* an 18-year-old company, recreates the trips that America's first explorers took as well as offers cruises in "uncharted" Alaskan waters and other dramatic journeys; 800-EXPEDITION (397-3348). **Conservation trips:** Call *One World Workforce* for a free newsletter; 800-451-9564. **Spas:** *Miraval Spa and Resort;* Catalina, AZ; 800-825-4000. *Spa Finders;* 212-924-6800. **Marrying abroad:** Contact the embassy or tourist information bureau of the country in which you are getting married. For general information, contact Office of Citizens Consular Services, Room 4817, U.S. Department of State, Washington, DC 20520; 202-514-2000. **Inns and Bed & Breakfasts:** *Country Inns*

Magazine; 800-877-5491. *The Recommended Country Inns Guidebook Series;* 203-395-0440. *The Independent Innkeeper's Association* (see Chapter 2). **Cruises:** *Porthole Magazine*; 800-776-PORT. **Discount air travel:** *Global Travel;* 800-497-6678. *1-800-FLY-ASAP* (the name says it all). *Best Fares* magazine, a monthly publication of insider travel secrets and discounts; $59.95/year, which includes membership in several travel clubs; 1301 South Bowen Road, Suite 405, Arlington, TX 76013; 800-880-1234; 817-860-5761; www.bestfares.com. **Travel agents:** *Institute of Certified Travel Agents;* 800-542-4282.

Chapter 21: Ten Gadgets, Gizmos, and Gimmicks to Make Weddings a Whiz

General Information: *The Knot;* 480 Broadway, New York, NY 10013; www.the knot.com. **Massage:** *Tapper/Vibe* by HWE; 800-742-5493; available at Brookstone, 1655 Bassford Drive, Mexico, MO 65265-1382; 800-846-3000; 573-581-7113. *Shiatsu Foot Massager* #HW508; $229.95; and *Ten-Motor Body Masseur with Heat* #HF708; $198, available from The Sharper Image, 650 Davis Street, San Francisco, CA 94111; 800-344-4444; www.sharperimage.com. **Photography:** *First Hand Images;* 716-882-4120. **Portable voice recorder:** *IQ Voice Organizer,* model 621; by Voice Powered Technology International, Inc.; 15250 Ventura Blvd., Suite 2200, Sherman Oaks, CA 91403; 818-905-0950. **Software:** *Wedding Workshop;* by MicroPrecision Software Inc., 835 Blossom Hill Road, Suite 204, San Jose, CA 95123; www.microprecisionsoft.com. *Wedding Planner;* by Expert Software, 800 Douglas Road, Coral Gables, FL 33134; 305-567-9990; fax: 305-443-0786; www.expertsoftware.com. **Toll-free RSVPs:** *Communications Design Group, Inc.;* 59 Broad Street, Stamford, CT 06901; 203-353-8881; 800-363-7852; fax: 203-328-7176. *R.S.V.P. Services;* P.O. Box 75307, Ft. Thomas, KY 41075; 800-514-9686; 606-572-0060; fax: 606-781-5638.

Related Reading

African-American traditions: *Jumping the Broom; The African-American Wedding Planner* by Harriette Cole; 1993; Henry Holt. *The Nubian Wedding Book* by Ingrid Sturgis; 1997; Crown. **Asian-American traditions:** *Wild Geese and Tea: An Asian-American Wedding Planner* by Shu Shu Costa; 1997; Riverhead Books. **Miscellaneous traditions:** *Weddings Southern Style* by Beverly Reese Church; text by Lisa Rufflin Harrison; 1993; Abbeville Press. *The Perfect Wedding* by Maria McBride-Mellinger; 1997; Collins San Francisco. *Weddings for Grownups* by Carroll Stoner; 1997; Chronicle Books. *A Bride's Book of Wedding Traditions* by Arlene Hamilton Stewart; 1995; Hearst Books. *The Bride: A Celebration* by Barbara Tober; 1984; Harry N. Abrams, Inc., New York. Saving money: *Bridal Bargains* by Denise and Alan Fields; 1997; Windsor Peak Press.

Index

• D •

• J •

(continued)

• N •

• O •

(continued)

(continued)

• T •

• Z •

YOUR
ONLINE
RESOURCE
WWW.DUMMIES.COM

SURF
THE
NET
WWW.DUMMIES.COM

IDG
BOOKS
WORLDWIDE

IDG BOOKS WORLDWIDE BOOK REGISTRATION

Register This Book and Win!

We want to hear from you!

Visit **http://my2cents.dummies.com** to register this book and tell us how you liked it!

- Get entered in our monthly prize giveaway.
- Give us feedback about this book — tell us what you like best, what you like least, or maybe what you'd like to ask the author and us to change!
- Let us know any other *...For Dummies*® topics that interest you.

Your feedback helps us determine what books to publish, tells us what coverage to add as we revise our books, and lets us know whether we're meeting your needs as a *...For Dummies* reader. You're our most valuable resource, and what you have to say is important to us!

Not on the Web yet? It's easy to get started with *Dummies 101*®*: The Internet For Windows*® *98* or *The Internet For Dummies*®, 5th Edition, at local retailers everywhere.

Or let us know what you think by sending us a letter at the following address:

...For Dummies Book Registration
Dummies Press
7260 Shadeland Station, Suite 100
Indianapolis, IN 46256-3945
Fax 317-596-5498

TM

BESTSELLING BOOK SERIES FROM IDG